Lecture Notes in Artificial Intelligence 5398

Edited by R. Goebel, J. Siekmann, and W. Wahlster

Subseries of Lecture Notes in Computer Science

T0242509

Anna Esposito   Amir Hussain
Maria Marinaro   Raffaele Martone (Eds.)

Multimodal Signals: Cognitive and Algorithmic Issues

COST Action 2102 and euCognition International School
Vietri sul Mare, Italy, April 21-26, 2008
Revised Selected and Invited Papers

 Springer

Series Editors

Randy Goebel, University of Alberta, Edmonton, Canada
Jörg Siekmann, University of Saarland, Saarbrücken, Germany
Wolfgang Wahlster, DFKI and University of Saarland, Saarbrücken, Germany

Volume Editors

Anna Esposito
Second University of Naples, Department of Psychology
and IIASS, International Institute for Advanced Scientific Studies
Via G. Pellegrino 19, 84019 Vietri sul Mare (SA), Italy
E-mail: iiass.annaesp@tin.it

Amir Hussain
University of Stirling
Department of Computing Science & Mathematics
Stirling FK9 4LA, Scotland, UK
E-mail: ahu@cs.stir.ac.uk

Maria Marinaro
University of Salerno, Department of Physics
Via S. Allende, 84081 Baronissi (SA), Italy
and IIASS, Italy
E-mail: marinaro@sa.infn.it

Raffaele Martone
Second University of Naples
Computer Engineering & Informatics Department
Via Roma, 29, 81031 Aversa (CE), Italy
E-mail: raffaele.martone@unina2.it

Library of Congress Control Number: 2009921491

CR Subject Classification (1998): I.2.11, I.2.7, I.2, H.5, H.4, K.4, K.3

LNCS Sublibrary: SL 7 – Artificial Intelligence

ISSN   0302-9743

ISBN 978-3-642-00524-4 Springer Berlin Heidelberg New York

Typesetting: Camera-ready by author, data conversion by Scientific Publishing Services, Chennai, India
Printed on acid-free paper   SPIN: 12627752   06/3180   5 4 3 2 1 0

Preface

This volume brings together the peer-reviewed contributions of the participants at the COST 2102 and euCognition International Training School on "Multimodal Signals: Cognitive and Algorithmic Issues" held in Vietri sul Mare, Salerno, Italy, April 22–26, 2008.

The school was sponsored by COST (European Cooperation in the Field of Scientific and Technical Research, www.cost.esf.org) in the domain of Information and Communication Technologies (ICT) for disseminating the advances of the research activities developed within Action 2102: "Cross-Modal Analysis of Verbal and Nonverbal Communication" (www.cost.esf.org/domains_actions/ict/Actions/Verbal_and_Non- verbal _Communication) and by euCognition: The European Network for Advancement of Artificial Cognitive Systems (www.euCognition.org).

COST Action 2102, in its second year of life, brought together about 60 European and 6 overseas scientific laboratories whose aim is to develop interactive dialogue systems and intelligent virtual avatars graphically embodied in a 2D and/or 3D interactive virtual world, able to interact intelligently with the environment, other avatars, and particularly with human users.

The main theme of the school was to investigate the mathematical and psychological tools for modelling human–machine interaction through access to a graded series of tasks for measuring the amount of adjustment (as well as intelligence and achievement) needed for introducing new concepts in the information communication technology domain in order to develop adaptive, socially enabled and human-centered automatic systems able to serve remote applications in medicine, learning, care, rehabilitation, and for accessibility to work, employment, and information.

The field is largely interdisciplinary and complex, involving expertise in human factors and behavioral patterns, verbal and nonverbal communication signals, cross-modal analysis of audio and video in spontaneous face-to-face interaction, advanced processing of acoustical and perceptual signals, audiovisual data encoding, fusion of visual and audio signals for recognition and synthesis, identification of human emotional states, gesture, speech and facial expressions, implementation of intelligent avatars, annotation of extended MPEG7 standard, human behavior and unsupervised interactive interfaces, cultural and socio-cultural variability, computer graphics, animation, artificial intelligence, natural language processing, cognitive and psychological modelling of human–human and human–machine interaction, linguistics, and artificial life.

The book is roughly arranged into two scientific areas according to a thematic classification, even though all the areas are closely connected and all provide fundamental insights for cross-fertilization of different disciplines.

The first area, "Interactive and Unsupervised Multimodal Systems," deals with the theoretical and computational issue of defining algorithms, programming languages, and determinist models to recognize and synthesize multimodal signals, such as facial and vocal expressions of emotions, tones of voice, gestures, eye contact, spatial arrangements, patterns of touch, expressive movements, writing patterns, and cultural differences, in anticipation of the implementation of intelligent avatars and interactive dialogue systems that could be exploited to improve user access to future telecommunication services.

The second area, "Verbal and Nonverbal Communication Signals," presents original studies devoted to the modelling of timing synchronization between speech production, gestures, facial and head movements in human communicative expressions and on their mutual contribution for an effective communication.

The editors would like to thank the COST- ICT Programme for its support in the realization of the school and the publication of this volume, and in particular the COST Science Officers Gian Mario Maggio and Sophie Beaubron for their constant help, guidance, and encouragement and the Chair of euCognition: The European Network for Advancement of Artificial Cognitive Systems (www.euCognition.org), David Vernon, for joining the initiative.

Our special appreciation goes to Tina Marcella Nappi, Michele Donnarumma, and Antonio Natale, of the International Institute for Advanced Scientific Studies, for their invaluable editorial and technical support in the organization of this volume.

The editors are extremely grateful to the International Institute for Advanced Scientific Studies "E.R. Caianiello," the Seconda Università di Napoli, in particular the Dean of the Faculty of Science, Nicola Melone, the Deans of the Department and Faculty of Psychology, Alida Labella and Giovanna Nigro, the Regione Campania, and the Provincia di Salerno for their support in sponsoring, financing, and organizing the school.

In addition, the editors are grateful to the contributors of this volume and the keynote speakers whose work stimulated an extremely interesting interaction with the attendees, who in turn, contributed with their enthusiasm and lively interactions in making this event a scientifically stimulating gathering and a memorable personal experience. Finally, we would like to acknowledge the accurate review work done by the COST 2102 International Scientific Committee and thank them for their dedication and their valuable selection process.

This book is dedicated to our beliefs, expectations, and desires hoping that in pursuing them we will have the chances to enrich ourselves and others.

January 2009

Anna Esposito
Amir Hussain
Maria Marinaro
Raffaele Martone

Organization

International Advisory and Organizing Committee

Anna Esposito	Second University of Naples and IIASS, Italy
Marcos Faundez-Zanuy	Escola Universitaria Politecnica de Mataro, Spain
Amir Hussain	University of Stirling, UK
Eric Keller	University of Lausanne, Switzerland
Maria Marinaro	University of Salerno and IIASS, Italy
Raffaele Martone	Second University of Naples, Italy
Nicola Melone	Second University of Naples, Italy
Anton Nijholt	University of Twente, The Netherlands
Klára Vicsi	Budapest University of Technology and Economics, Hungary

International Scientific Committee

Uwe Altmann	Technische Universität Dresden, Germany
Hicham Atassi	Brno University of Technology, Czech Republic
Nikos Avouris	University of Patras, Greece
Ruth Bahr	University of South Florida, USA
Gérard Bailly	ICP, Grenoble, France
Marian Bartlett	University of California, San Diego,USA
Štefan Beňuš	Constantine the Philosopher University, Nitra, Slovakia
Niels Ole Bernsen	University of Southern Denmark, Denmark
Jonas Beskow	Royal Institute of Technology, Sweden
Horst Bishof	Technical University Graz, Austria
Peter Birkholz	Aachen University, Germany
Jean-Francois Bonastre	Universitè d'Avignon, France
Nikolaos Bourbakis	ITRI, Wright State University, Dayton, USA
Maja Bratanić	University of Zagreb, Croatia
Antonio Calabrese	Istituto di Cibernetica – CNR, Naples, Italy
Paola Campadelli	Università di Milano, Italy
Nick Campbell	ATR Human Information Science Labs, Kyoto, Japan
Antonio Castro Fonseca	Universidade de Coimbra, Portugal
Aleksandra Cerekovic	Faculty of Electrical Engineering, Croatia
Josef Chaloupka	Technical University of Liberec, Czech Republic
Mohamed Chetouani	Universitè Pierre et Marie Curie, France
Gerard Chollet	CNRS-LTCI, Paris, France
Muzeyyen Ciyiltepe	Gulhane Askeri Tip Academisi, Ankara, Turkey
Anton Čižmár	Technical University of Košice, Slovakia
Nicholas Costen	Manchester Metropolitan University, UK

Vlado Delic	University of Novi Sad, Serbia
Marion Dohen	GIPSA-lab, Grenoble, France
Francesca D'Olimpio	Second University of Naples, Italy
Thierry Dutoit	Faculté Polytechnique de Mons, Belgium
Laila Dybkjær	University of Southern Denmark, Denmark
Matthias Eichner	Technische Universität Dresden, Germany
Aly El-Bahrawy	Faculty of Engineering, Cairo, Egypt
Engin Erzin	Koc University, Istanbul, Turkey
Anna Esposito	Second University of Naples, and IIASS, Italy
Joan Fàbregas Peinado	Escola Universitaria de Mataro, Spain
Sascha Fagel	Technische Universität Berlin, Germany
Nikos Fakotakis	University of Patras, Greece
Marcos Faundez-Zanuy	Escola Universitaria de Mataro, Spain
Dilek Fidan	Ankara University, Turkey
Carmen García-Mateo	University of Vigo, Spain
Björn Granström	Royal Institute of Technology, KTH, Sweden
Marco Grassi	Università Politecnica delle Marche, Italy
Maurice Grinberg	New Bulgarian University, Bulgaria
Mohand Said Hacid	Universitè Claude Bernard Lyon 1, France
Jaakko Hakulinen	University of Tampere, Finland
Ioannis Hatzilygeroudis	University of Patras, Greece
Immaculada Hernaez	University of the Basque Country, Spain
Javier Hernando	Technical University of Catalonia, Spain
Wolfgang Hess	Universität Bonn, Germany
Dirk Heylen	University of Twente, The Netherlands
Rüdiger Hoffmann	Technische Universität Dresden, Germany
David House	Royal Institute of Technology (KTH), Sweden
Amir Hussain	University of Stirling, UK
Ewa Jarmolowicz	Adam Mickiewicz University, Poznan, Poland
Jozef Juhár	Technical University Košice, Slovak Republic
Zdravko Kacic	University of Maribor, Slovenia
Maciej Karpinski	Adam Mickiewicz University, Poznan, Poland
Eric Keller	Université de Lausanne, Switzerland
Adam Kendon	University of Pennsylvania, USA
Stefan Kopp	University of Bielefeld, Germany
Jacques Koreman	University of Science and Technology, Norway
Robert Krauss	Columbia University, New York, USA
Maria Koutsombogera	Inst. for Language and Speech Processing, Greece
Bernd Kröger	Aachen University, Germany
Gernot Kubin	Graz University of Technology, Austria
Alida Labella	Second University of Naples, Italy
Yiannis Laouris	Cyprus Neuroscience and Technology Institute, Cyprus
Børge Lindberg	Aalborg University, Denmark
Wojciech Majewski	Wroclaw University of Technology, Poland
Pantelis Makris	Neuroscience and Technology Institute, Cyprus
Maria Marinaro	Salerno University and IIASS, Italy

Raffaele Martone	Second University of Naples, Italy
Dominic Massaro	University of California - Santa Cruz, USA
David McNeill	University of Chicago, USA
Nicola Melone	Second University of Naples, Italy
Katya Mihaylova	University of National and World Economy, Sofia, Bulgaria
Michal Mirilovič	Technical University of Košice, Slovakia
Peter Murphy	University of Limerick, Ireland
Antonio Natale	Salerno University and IIASS, Italy
Eva Navas	Escuela Superior de Ingenieros, Bilbao, Spain
Géza Németh	Budapest University of Technology, Hungary
Friedrich Neubarth	Research Inst. Artificial Intelligence, Austria
Giovanna Nigro	Second University of Naples, Italy
Anton Nijholt	University of Twente, The Netherlands
Jan Nouza	Technical University of Liberec, Czech Republic
Igor Pandzic	Faculty of Electrical Engineering, Croatia
Harris Papageorgiou	Inst. for Language and Speech Processing, Greece
Ana Pavia	Spoken Language Systems Laboratory, Portugal
Catherine Pelachaud	Université de Paris 8, France
Bojan Petek	University of Ljubljana, Slovenia
Harmut R. Pfitzinger	University of Munich, Germany
Francesco Piazza	Università Politecnica delle Marche, Italy
Neda Pintaric	University of Zagreb, Croatia
Isabella Poggi	Università di Roma 3, Italy
Jiří Přibil	Academy of Sciences, Czech Republic
Anna Přibilová	Slovak University of Technology, Slovakia
Michael Pucher	Telecommunications Research Center Vienna, Austria
Jurate Puniene	Kaunas University of Technology, Lithuania
Giuliana Ramella	Istituto di Cibernetica – CNR, Naples, Italy
Kari-Jouko Räihä	University of Tampere, Finland
José Rebelo	Universidade de Coimbra, Portugal
Luigi Maria Ricciardi	Università di Napoli "Federico II", Italy
Matej Rojc	University of Maribor, Slovenia
Algimantas	Rudzionis, Kaunas University of Technology, Lithuania
Vytautas Rudzionis	Kaunas University of Technology, Lithuania
Milan Rusko	Slovak Academy of Sciences, Slovak Republic
Zsófia Ruttkay	Pazmany Peter Catholic University, Hungary
Yoshinori Sagisaka	Waseda University, Tokyo, Japan
Silvia Scarpetta	Salerno University, Italy
Ralph Schnitker	Aachen University, Germany
Jean Schoentgen	Université Libre de Bruxelles, Belgium
Stefanie Shattuck-Hufnagel	MIT, Cambridge, USA
Zdeněk Smékal	Brno University of Technology, Czech Republic
Stefano Squartini	Università Politecnica delle Marche, Italy
Piotr Staroniewicz	Wroclaw University of Technology, Poland

Vojtěch Stejskal	Brno University of Technology, Czech Republic
Marian Stewart-Bartlett	University of California, San Diego,USA
Jianhua Tao	Chinese Academy of Sciences, P. R. China
Jure F.Tasič	University of Ljubljana, Slovenia
Murat Tekalp	Koc University, Istanbul, Turkey
Kristinn Thórisson	Reykjavík University, Iceland
Isabel Trancoso	Spoken Language Systems Laboratory, Portugal
Luigi Trojano	Second University of Naples, Italy
Wolfgang Tschacher	University of Bern, Switzerland
Markku Turunen	University of Tampere, Finland
Henk Van Den Heuvel	Radboud University Nijmegen, The Netherlands
Robert Vích	Academy of Sciences, Czech Republic
Klára Vicsi	Budapest University of Technology, Hungary
Leticia Vicente-Rasoamalala	Alchi Prefectural Univesity, Japan
Hannes Högni Vilhjálmsson	Reykjavík University, Iceland
Carl Vogel	University of Dublin, Ireland
Rosa Volpe	Université De Perpignan Via Domitia, France
Yorick Wilks	University of Sheffield, UK
Matthias Wimmer	Technische Universiät München, Germany
Matthias Wolf	Technische Universität Dresden, Germany
Bencie Woll	University College London, UK
Bayya Yegnanarayana	Institute of Information Technology, India
Jerneja Žganec Gros	Alpineon, Development and Research, Slovenia
Goranka Zoric	Faculty of Electrical Engineering, Croatia

Sponsors

The following organizations sponsored and supported the International Training School:

- European COST Action 2102 *"Cross-Modal Analysis of Verbal and Nonverbal Communication"* (www.cost.esf.org/domains_actions/ict/Actions/ Verbal_and_Non-verbal_Communication)
- euCognition: *The European Network for Advancement of Artificial Cognitive Systems* (www.euCognition.org)
- Second University of Naples, Faculty and Department of Psychology, Faculty of Science, Mathematics, and Physics and Department of Computer Engineering & Informatics, Italy
- International Institute for Advanced Scientific Studies "E.R. Caianiello" (IIASS), Italy
- Regione Campania (Italy)
- Provincia di Salerno (Italy)

Table of Contents

Interactive and Unsupervised Multimodal Systems

Verbal and Nonverbal Communication Signals

Multimodal Human Machine Interactions in Virtual and Augmented Reality

Gérard Chollet[1], Anna Esposito[4], Annie Gentes[1], Patrick Horain[3],
Walid Karam[1], Zhenbo Li[3], Catherine Pelachaud[1,5], Patrick Perrot[1,2],
Dijana Petrovska-Delacrétaz[3], Dianle Zhou[3], and Leila Zouari[1]

[1] CNRS-LTCI TELECOM-ParisTech, 46 rue Barrault, 75634 Paris - France
[2] Institut de Recherche Criminelle de la Gendarmerie Nationale (IRCGN), Rosny
sous Bois - France
[3] TELECOM & Management SudParis, 9 rue Charles Fourier, Evry - France
[4] Second University of Naples, Dept. of Psycology, and IIASS, Italy
[5] LINC, IUT de Montreuil, Université de Paris 8, 140 rue de la Nouvelle France
93100 Montreuil, France
{gerard.chollet, annie.gentes, walid.karam, catherine.pelachaud,
patrick.perrot, leila.zouari}@telecom-paristech.fr
{patrick.horain,dijana.petrovska,dianle.zhou,zhenbo.li}@it-sudparis.eu
{iiass.annaesp}@tin.it

Abstract. Virtual worlds are developing rapidly over the Internet. They
are visited by avatars and staffed with Embodied Conversational Agents
(ECAs). An avatar is a representation of a physical person. Each person
controls one or several avatars and usually receives feedback from the virtual world on an audio-visual display. Ideally, all senses should be used
to feel fully embedded in a virtual world. Sound, vision and sometimes
touch are the available modalities. This paper reviews the technological developments which enable audio-visual interactions in virtual and
augmented reality worlds. Emphasis is placed on speech and gesture interfaces, including talking face analysis and synthesis.

Keywords: Human Machine Interactions (HMI), Multimodality,
Speech, Face, Gesture, Virtual Words.

1 Introduction

Humans communicate through a gestalt of actions which involve much more
than speech. Facial expressions, head, body and arm movements (grouped under the name of gestures) all contribute to the communicative act. They support (through different channels) the speaker's communicative goal, allowing the
speaker to add a variety of other information to his/her messages including (but
not limited to) his/her psychological state, attitude, etc. The complexity of the
communicative act should be taken into account in human-computer interaction research aiming at modeling and improving such interaction by developing
user-friendly applications which should simplify and enrich the end user's ability to interact with automatic systems. Psycholinguistic studies [25,24,42,52,56]

A. Esposito et al. (Eds.): Multimodal Signals, LNAI 5398, pp. 1–23, 2009.

have confirmed the complementary nature of verbal and nonverbal aspects in human expressions, demonstrating how visual information processing integrates and supports the comprehension of messages. In the light of these results, several research works on mutual contribution of speech and gesture in communication and on their characteristics have being carried out also in the field of Human Machine Interaction (HMI). Such studies are mainly devoted to implement synchronization between speech, facial, and body movements in human communicative expressions [29,34,40,44,55,61,73]. Some models include characteristics of emotional expressions [23,32,56] as well as speech and gesture modeling, multimodal recognition and synthesis (virtual agents) of facial expressions, head, hands movements and body postures [1,45,75,31,60,63].

Psycholinguistic studies on human communication have also shown that humans convey meaning by a set of nonlexical expressions carrying specific communicative values such as feedback and regulation of the interaction. Preliminary studies have observed that such nonlexical speech events are highly communicative and show gestural correlates [25,22] stressing the need for their mathematical modeling so as to implement more natural "talking heads" and/or "talking faces".

The above research arguments have led to the development of virtual worlds and virtual realities, where software characters and intelligent devices interact with humans through the plurality of communication modes and/or develop mirror artificial lives in a 3D virtual world created by avatars that perceive, reason and react showing cognitive workloads, consciousness and emerging behaviors. The word "avatar" originates from the Hindu culture, meaning a god's coming to earth in bodily form [46]. Nowadays, it is an embodiment, as of a quality in a person, and it is used in virtual worlds to refer to the graphical representation of a human being in virtual environments. Its appearance, behavior and communication skills are of great importance in virtual worlds.

The present paper is situated in such a context as it reports on the recent research efforts for the development of new models, methods, and communication paradigms to improve information and communication technologies. The rest of the paper is organized as follows. In Sect. 2 issues related to designing 3D applications are presented. Section 3 summarizes the architecture and standards related to Embodied Conversational Agents (ECAs). In Sect. 4 examples of technologies that have been developed to endow systems with acoustic and visual perceptive and generative capabilities are given. They include speech, face and gesture processing. Conclusions and perspectives are given in Sect. 5.

2   Designing 3D Applications: Challenges, Co-design Methodology and Results

3D worlds host a number of activities, organizations, representations and purposes. Today, Second Life[1] is used as a showroom for products or channel of

---

[1] www.secondlife.com

information. People can: visit stores and manipulate virtual objects, organize or join meetings, be interviewed for new jobs by companies such as L'Oreal, or BNP Paribas [28]. The amount of interactions and creations of artefacts testifies to the success of such shared environments [8]. But one may wonder what are the main venues of innovation, apart from increasing the amount of transactions, the number of participants and solving technical issues such as bandwith, persistency of data, etc. To provide an answer, one has to enquire not only into the actual uses and organizations of these 3D environments, but also into other 3D applications and domains of research and to figure what is relevant to the development of new interactions.

Our hypothesis was to associate three axes of research: face and gesture processing, speech recognition, and embodied conversational agents. Our interest is to study their potential in creating significant interactions within 3D environments. The method focuses on combining these technologies to create a situation of interaction. Such creation is based on the analysis of 3D practices, design and tools as well as a sociological study of 3D environments. The purpose is to design a convincing situation and interface so that end-users may actually enjoy an enhanced 3D experience. The design of a demonstrator is to ensure that testers will be able to assess the results and the potential of such a convergence.

3D application research focuses on three main issues. How to: make avatars and contexts more realistic and highly expressive without relying on post production; automate and delegate some behaviors to avatars; and improve interactions in 3D environments. Each area of research is highly challenging as users are expecting very sophisticated representations of characters and settings in relation to our culture of animation movies or videogames. While a certain latitude is acceptable in research circles that allow for basic aesthetics features, it is difficult to design a proper interaction that end-users won't find disappointing. To face this challenge, we followed a co-design methodology which takes into consideration the strong points but also the limits of these technologies as well as some anthropological specificities of virtual worlds.

Virtual worlds are places of creativity where people draw, stage, and invent stories. They offer new modalities to express oneself and communicate with others that can compete or complete traditional media. Primarily, virtual worlds offer a place for people to play with different aspects of their personality. As was analyzed by Sherry Turkle [78] as early as in the 80s, when the first Moos and Muds appeared, the appeal of such systems is in exploring a different self and testing it with other online users. We decided to rely on this sociological and psychological characteristics to design a demonstrator that offers a situation of reflexive learning. The system is a mirror to the user's activity, helping her to analyze and correct her behavior in a situation of recruitment. We also wanted to explore the multidimensional potential of 3D environments including a diversity of information and access: the applicant CV, the online information on the company that is recruiting, the video of the interaction between the avatar and the Embodied Conversational Agent (ECA) that can be replayed. Our hypothesis is that the future of 3D applications is a seamless staging of 2D and 3D elements, texts, images and videos, so that the users can benefit from all ofthem without having to open a new system for each.

The choice of this learning program presents other interesting features. Though the interviews can be varied, they rely on a basic vocabulary centred on expertise, studies, work experience, etc. of the candidate. In terms of acquisition, the database can easily be augmented by the vocabulary of the company—that can be found on its website—and by the CV of the applicant that he can feed the system with. We therefore limit the scope of what the speech recognition system will have to manage, increasing its reliability. The dialog form is also relatively easy to anticipate: greetings, presentation of each other, turns of speech, objectives of the interview, can be defined that will allow for the modeling of the ECA responses to the user. The number of gestures and face expressions is also limited and therefore can be more accurate.

The analysis of the technical characteristics, of the anthropological features of 3D worlds, and of the formal issues (such as access, format, navigation, interface, etc.) provide the theoretical framework for new applications. Here, co-designing means that we are taking into consideration each of these elements, elements that we reformulate and organize in a coherent context. This methodology ties together the inner workings of the technology and its outer workings, including a definition of its original aesthetics.

3   Architecture and Standards

Several multimodal real-time ECA architectures have been implemented, [11,45,13]. MAX (the Multimodal Assembly eXpert) [45] is a real-time system where a 3D agent evolves in a Cave Automatic Virtual Environment (CAVE). The system is composed of three high level modules: *Perceive, Reason* and *Act.* Such an architecture allows the agent to perceive the world it is placed in and to react to any event either cognitively if processing time permits it or reactively. BEAT (the Behavior Expression Animation Toolkit) takes a text as input and provides an animation as output [13]. The architecture is composed of three modules, language tagging, behavior generation and behavior scheduling. The text is sent to an external Text-To-Speech (TTS) system that returns the list of phonemes and their duration. This last information with the behavior description is sent to the animation module. Multi-agent architectures are often used in ECA systems (Open Agent Architecture [14], Adaptive Agent Architecture or even Psyclone [74]). In particular, white board architecture is used to ensure the exchange of messages between the modules (eg. Psyclone [74]). It allows modules and applications to interact together, even if they are running on separate machines connected through TCP/IP.

Situated SAIBA [80] (Situation, Agent, Intention, Behavior, Animation) is a current international effort to define a unified platform for ECAs. SAIBA aims at developing modular and distributable architecture. Its goal is to allow for rapid integration within existing systems. This framework is composed of three main steps: (1) communicative intent planning, (2) multimodal behavior planning, and

Fig. 1. The Situation, Agent, Intention, Behavior, Animation (SAIBA) framework [80]

(3) behavior realization (see Figure 1). The first step outputs what the agent intends to communicate and in which emotional state it potentially is. The second step computes through what verbal and nonverbal means the agent will communicate its intent and emotion. Finally the last steps instantiate these multimodal behaviors in audio and animation files. The interaction between these different steps is done via two markup languages. Between the first two steps, there is the Functional Markup Language (FML) that describes the communicative intent; then the last two steps are connected via the Behavior Markup Language (BML). The animation of the agent is specified through the Facial Animation Parameters (FAPs) and the Body Animation Parameters (BAPs) of the MPEG-4 standard. Lately Thiebaux and colleagues [73] have developed a real-time architecture to implement the *Behavior Realizer* of the SAIBA framework.

4   Multimodal Interaction

Communication is multimodal by essence. It involves not only speech but also nonverbal signals. Voice intonation, facial expressions, arm and hand gestures, gaze, etc, are all communication signals. Moreover communication does not involve separate processes of perception (by the listener) or of generation (by the speaker). Both interactants, speaker and listener, send and perceive signals from the others. Interaction involves a cocontinuous exchange of messages where interactants adapt to each other. Multimodal interaction systems ought to include perception, generation and adaptation capabilities [45,75]. In this section, we present technologies that have been developed to endow systems with acoustic and visual perceptive and generative capabilities.

4.1   Speech Processing

Recognition: In order to make a vocal conversation between an ECA and a human user, the ECA must be able to recognize and understand as much as possible what the human says. Hence, a speech recognition system is needed.

Speech recognition consists in converting the acoustic signal into a set of words (sentences). In the framework of a vocal human machine interaction, these words serve as an input to further linguistic processing in order to achieve speech understanding.

Recent works on speech recognition are based on statistical modeling, [26,57,86,9,36]: given a sequence of observations $O = o_1, o_2, ..o_T$ (the speech samples), the recognition system looks for the most probable set of words $M' = m_1, m_2, .., m_N$ (knowing the observations):

$$M' = argmax \ p(M/O) = argmax \ p(O/M) \times p(M) \qquad (1)$$

where :

- M are the words of the application dictionnary.
- $p(O/M)$, the probability of the observation, given the words, is given by an acoustic model. The Hidden Markov Models (HMMs) are widely used for acoustic modeling and the modeled units are often phonemes, syllables or words.
- $p(M)$, the probability of the words, is given by a linguistic model. A linguistic model aims to restrict the combination of words.

Therefore the global architecture of a speech recognition system is as depicted in the following figure.

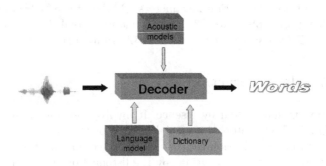

Fig. 2. Architecture of a speech recognition system

Performance of speech recognition systems is often described in terms of Word Error Rate (WER).

$$WER = 100 \times \frac{substitutions \ + \ omissions \ + \ insertions}{number \ of \ correct \ words} \qquad (2)$$

The WER depends on different parameters [57]:

- The speaking mode: isolated words are easier to recognize than continuous speech.
- The speaking style: usually spontaneous speech contains disfluencies and is more difficult to recognize than read speech.
- The size of the vocabulary: when the vocabulary is large, there are more confusions between words.
- The speaker dependency: when the system is speaker dependent, adaptation techniques can be used to improve the modeling.
- Recording conditions: noisy or clean, wide- or telephonic-band speech, etc.

Synthesis: The ECA should be able to talk and interact meaningfully with humans using speech. Most developments in speech synthesis have focused on text to speech systems [20]. A text-to-speech synthesizer is a system that should be able to read any text introduced in the computer. To develop such a system, three main approaches have been proposed:

- Articulatory synthesis: in the early days of synthesis, researchers simulated human speech production mechanisms using articulatory models. Speech is created by simulating the flow of air through the representation of the vocal tract.
- Acoustic synthesis-by-rule: later, text processing was modeled by a set of rules (phonetic theories and acoustic analysis). The resulting technology is referred to as speech synthesis-by-rule. Most of synthesis-by-rule progress has been system dependent due to detailed rules and finely tuned parameters. As a consequence, the expert knowledge can be very hard to reproduce in other systems.
- Concatenative synthesis: speech is produced by combining fragments of pre-recorded speech. Currently, great progress has been made using large-corpus concatenative approaches. Many systems output speech indistinguishable from that of human speakers [17].

The most important characteristics of a speech synthesis system are natural-ness and intelligibility. While work on naturalness continues, the next step in the improvement of intelligibility and conviviality of the text-to-speech systems concern their expressiveness, referred as expressive synthesis.

Voice Transformation: Speaker transformation (also referred to as voice transformation, voice conversion, speaker forgery, or speaker adaptation) is the process of altering an utterance from a speaker (impostor) to make it sound as if it were articulated by a target speaker (client). Such transformation can be effectively used by an avatar to impersonate a real human and converse with an ECA.

Speaker transformation techniques [27,38,85,39,2,7,77,62,16] might involve modifications of different aspects of the speech signal that carries the speaker's identity. We can cite different methods. There are methods based on the coarse spectral structure associated with different phones in the speech signal [38]. Another techniques use the excitation function (the "fine" spectral details, such as [85]). Prosodic features representing aspects of the speech that occur over timescales larger than the individual phonemes can also be used, as well as the "Mannerisms" such as particular word choice or preferred phrases, or all kinds of other high-level behavioral characteristics. The formant structure and the vocal tract are represented by the overall spectral envelope shape of the signal, and thus are major features to be considered in voice transformation [39].

The voice transformation techniques proposed in the literature can be classified as text-dependent or text-independent methods. In text-dependent methods, training procedures are based on parallel corpora, i.e., training data have the source and the target speakers uttering the same text. Such methods include vector quantization [2,7], linear transformation [37,84], formant transformation [77], vocal tract length normalization (VTLN) [71], and prosodic transformation [7]. In text-independent voice conversion techniques, the system is trained with source and target speakers uttering different texts. Text-independent techniques include VTLN [71], maximum likelihood adaptation and statistical techniques, unit selection, and client memory indexing [62,16]. The analysis part of a voice conversion algorithm focuses on the extraction of the speaker's identity. Next, a transformation function is estimated. At last, a synthesis step is achieved to replace the source speaker characteristics by those of the target speaker.

Consider a sequence of a spectral vectors pronounced by the source speaker, $X_s = [x_1, x_2, .. x_n]$, and a sequence pronounced by the target speaker composed of the same words, $Y_s = [y_1, y_2, .. y_n]$. Voice conversion is based on the calculation of a conversion function F that minimizes the mean square error, $E_{mse} = E[||y - F(x)||^2]$, where E is the expectation.

Two steps are needed to build a conversion system: a training step and a conversion step. In the training phase, speech samples from the source and the target speaker are analyzed to extract the main features. Then these features are time aligned and a conversion function is estimated to map the source and the target characteristics (Fig. 3). The aim of the conversion is to apply the estimated transformation rule to an original speech pronounced by the source speaker. The new utterance sounds like the same speech pronounced by the target speaker, i.e. pronounced by replacing the source characteristics by those of the target voice. The last step is the re-synthesis of the signal to reconstruct the source speech voice (Fig. 4). Other approaches have also been proposed in [62].

A way to evaluate the conversion is to measure the displacement of the impostors distribution towards the client distribution. Voice conversion can be effectively used by an avatar to impersonate a real human and hide his identity in a conversation with an ECA. This technique is complementary with face transformation in the creation of an avatar that mimics the voice and face of a real human target.

Speaker Verification: In a virtual word, speaker verification could be used to authenticate an avatar, except if voice conversion is available. It could be

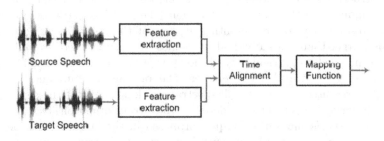

Fig. 3. Training step

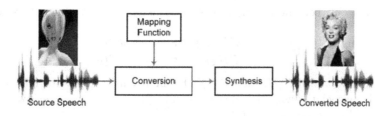

Fig. 4. Conversion step

necessary to authenticate an avatar before starting a dialog, for a bank transfer for instance, but also just to avoid embarrassing confusions in the communication. The speaker verification step could be a preliminary to all kind of communication in a virtual word, where the identity is important. In this paragraph the state of the art of speaker verification is summarized. A more detailed overview is available in [30].

Speaker verification consists in verifying a person claimed identity. Speech actually conveys many characteristics providing discriminative information about the speaker. These characteristics are divided in "high level" and "low level" attributes. The first set of features (high level) includes prosody, phonetic information, pronunciation defaults. The low level features are the ones related to the physical structure of the vocal apparatus. In most cases, automatic speaker recognition system are based on the low level features such as the MFCC (Mel Frequency Cepstral Coefficient) and their derivatives. Some alternative representations are also used, such as the LPC (Linear Predicting Coding) based cepstral features and their derivatives. This step of feature extraction consists in extracting a time sequence of feature vectors representative of the temporal evolution of speech spectral characteristics.

After the parameterization step, generative models including GMMs (Gaussian Mixture Models) and HMMs (Hidden Markov Models) are built to represent the distribution of the speaker's feature vectors. GMMs are defined by a set of parameters. During the training phase these parameters are iteratively estimated using the Expectation Maximization algorithm. Adaptation techniques are usually useful because of the lack of data. The aim of this step is to adapt the parameters of the background model with the speaker's enrollment speech data. Some other techniques can be used based on discriminative algorithms, such as MLP (Multilayer Perceptrons) or SVM (Support Vector Machines).

The principle of a speaker verification task is to take a decision whether the speech data collected during the test phase, belongs to the claimed model or not. Given a speech segment X and a claimed identity S the speaker verification system should choose one of the following hypothesis:

H_S: X is pronounced by S

$H_{\bar{S}}$: X is **not** pronounced by S

The decision between the two hypothesis is usually based on a likelihood ratio given by:

$$\Lambda(X) = \frac{p(X|H_S)}{p(X|H_{\bar{S}})} \begin{cases} > \Theta & accept\ H_S \\ < \Theta & accept\ H_{\bar{S}} \end{cases} \qquad (3)$$

where $p(X|H_S)$ and $p(X|H_{\bar{S}})$ are the probability density functions (called also likelihoods) associated with the speaker S and non-speakers $\bar{S}$, respectively. Θ is the threshold to accept or reject H_S.

Based on this decision, it is possible to claim a probable identity and to verify if the person behind the avatar is the claimed person.

4.2 Face Processing

Face-to-face communication implies visually perceiving the face of engaged people. When interacting in a virtual environment, face perception should be supported through that environment. This requires that the machine will have the capability to see human faces, namely to detect, track and recognize faces, and to render virtual actors with expressive animated faces. In addition, face metamorphosis allows controlling one's virtual appearance.

Face Detection and Tracking: Capturing head pose and facial gesture is a crucial task in computer vision applications such as human-computer interaction, biometrics, etc. It is a challenge because of the variability of facial appearances within a video sequence. This variability is due to changes in head pose (especially out-of-plane rotations), facial expressions, lighting, occlusions, or a combination of all of them.

Face detection: Capturing head pose and facial gesture is a crucial task in computer vision applications such as human-computer interaction, biometrics, etc. It is a challenge because of the above mentioned variabilities of facial appearance within a video sequence.

Feature-based tracking: Face motion and deformation between successive frames of a video sequence can be determined by tracking face features. These are highly discriminative areas with large spatial variations such as eyes, nostrils,

Fig. 5. Face detection using the Adaboost algorithm

or mouth corners to be identified and tracked from frame to frame. Contour of features can be tracked with active contours, or "snakes", that obey internal and external forces. Internal energy terms account for the shape of the feature and smoothness of the contour while the external energy attracts the snake towards feature contours in the image [72]. Face features (eyes, mouth) can be described with sets of wavelet components and linked together in an elastic graph [81].

Appearance-based tracking: An appearance-based tracker matches a model of the entire facial appearance with an input image. The problem of finding the optimal parameters is a high dimensional search problem. Active Appearance Models (AAMs) introduced by Cootes et al. [18] are joint statistical models of the shape and texture of an object (e.g., a face), combined with a gradient descent algorithm for adapting the model to an image. Their ability to vary their shape and appearance to match a person's face relies on an extensive learning of the face variations with respect to identity, expression, pose and/or illumination. Matthews and Baker [51] introduce an inverse compositional algorithm to accelerate image alignment for AAM. Xiao et al. [83] show how to constrain the 2D AAM search with valid 3D model modes. Ahlberg has extended AAM to a 3D face model [4]. Dornaika and Ahlberg [19,5] present a two steps algorithm in which they apply a global RANdom SAmple Consensus (RANSAC) method to estimate the rigid motion of the head in-between video images and a local optimization scheme to estimate the facial animation parameters.

Synthesis: The expressions of the six prototypical emotions are often used in 3D agents technology [58]. The standard MPEG-4 includes them in its specification [58]. These models are based on the categorical representation of emotion, mainly on Ekman's work [21]. In the EmotionDisc model developed by Ruttkay [67], the six prototypical emotions are spread uniformly on a circle. Each quadrant of the circle is further divided. The closest part to the center corresponds to the highest intensity of the emotion represented in this quadrant. The facial expressions associated to any point of the circle are computed as a bi-linear interpolation between the closest known expression of emotion and the neutral

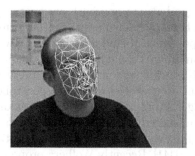

Fig. 6. Real-time face tracking with an Active Appearance Model (video available from http://picoforge.int-evry.fr/projects/myblog3d)

expression. Models of facial expressions based on a dimensional representation of emotions have been proposed [76,6]. In these works, the facial expression associated to an emotion defined by its 3D coordinate in the emotional space is computed as a linear interpolation of the closest prototypical emotions found in the 3D space. A model of complex emotion, ie. emotions arising as a combination of emotions, has been implemented using a fuzzy logic by [10,55]. Duy Bui [10] elaborated a model to blend the expressions of the six prototypical emotion. Niewiadomski et al. [55] extended this model to work on a larger set of complex emotion types and of emotions. In this model, fuzzy rules are defined for each type of complex emotions. Several types are considered: superposition of emotions, masking an emotion by another one, inhibition viewed as masking an emotion by a "neutral" one, etc.

Face Transformation: Different transformations could be considered when a change from one facial appearance to another is requested. They depend on the goal that has to be reached and the available methods that could be used. Facial transformation techniques could be useful for applications, such as customization of an avatar or face transformations methods used for criminalistic purposes.

The variety of representations that an avatar can have are actually limited by the technological possibilities of computer graphics and the imagination of end-users and programmers. End-users should be able to customize their own avatars in order to differentiate them from those of other users. It is important that they have at their disposal the tools necessary for this customization. Currently, systems employ a library of generic bodies, body parts and accessories for avatar creation. The face is one of the most easily recognizable, and expressive features of the human body and it seems natural to attempt to integrate it into the avatar itself. There are some attempts to create personalized avatars, but doing so for 3D facial representations in an automatic way is not a widespread usage. In this paragraph, three examples of face transformation are presented. The first one is related to 2D face morphing. In the second example, a 3D face is reconstructed, using two 2D images (with frontal and profile views) from an individual. In the third example, it is shown how to create a personalized 3D avatar (the face part), using only one 2D face image of that person.

2D face morphing: is a good way to approach progressively one's own face from an avatar for instance. There are many methods to perform face morphing. All of them require the correspondence of landmark points between the source and the target faces. The landmark points could be found manually or automatically. The method presented in [87], does not require human intervention, using a generic model of a face and evolution strategies to find the control (also called landmark) points in both face images. Automatic landmark methods are also used in [41], where a genetic algorithm is used to extract control points. These control points, generally correspond to the eyes and the mouth (like in [47]), and sometimes the nose position is also needed [41]. Recently Wolberg proposed a novel method that is based on the application of a multi-level free-form deformation [82]. The 2D morphing example presented in this paragraph needs a selection of control points

a)   b)

Fig. 7. 2D face morphing: (**a**) control points selection, and (**b**) division of an image

by the user, as well as the number of intermediate images required. morphing is smoother. All operations are made on rectangles rather than on triangles, which decreases the computing times. The morphing process can be defined as follows: make a smooth and fast transformation from a source image to a target one. This process can be divided into three parts: the control points selection, the warping, and the final blending step. The first step of the face morphing is to select the control points such as eyes, the tip of the nose, both extremities of the mouth, and both extremities of the chin (Fig. 7).

After the control point selection step, a warping process is necessary. This process consists in moving the control points of the source image to match the ones in the target image. For two corresponding rectangles, one from the source image and the other one from the target image, this transformation can be performed via the linear transformation method. After this step, the source image control points are matched with the target image control points, thus the application of the next step, blending, will produce a smooth morph, without artifacts.

At this point in the face morphing process, all important elements of the source figure are on the same position as that of the elements of the target figure, that is to say that the source eyes are on the same position as the target eyes, etc. That means that all the elements of the source figure may have been stretched, or shrunk. Then, in order to have the same color for the eyes, the skin, and so on, a color transition has to be performed.

What is interesting in such a case is to morph a face progressively towards another one. Many applications can be imagined, based on this principle like for instance the personalization of an avatar in a virtual world.

3D face reconstruction with two facial images: In addition to the above morphing process, it is interesting to reconstruct a 3D from two photos of an individual [59]. The idea is to reconstruct one's own face for instance in 3D and then to morph the avatar face toward one's face. The aim is to personalize an avatar in order to progressively reveal one's identity. From two photos of the same person (one from a frontal view, the other one from a profile view, as shown in Fig. 8), it is possible to reconstruct a 3D face. The principle is to use a generic model in 3D and to adapt it to the deformation of the photo. After a vertical adjustment between the two photos, depth data are extracted from the profile view and width data

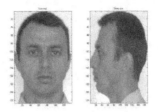

Fig. 8. Example of the two 2D input images, used to reconstruct the 3D model

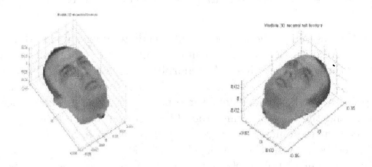

Fig. 9. The reconstructed 3D face, using the two 2D face images, shown in Fig. 8

from the frontal view, by selecting corresponding pairs of points between a photo and the 3D generic model. Thus, a global 3D morphing matrix is computed. This matrix is then applied to the whole generic 3D model to obtain the deformed 3D model (Fig. 9). Geometric and color maps are produced by ray-tracing on the 3D deformed model, with a different grid for each photo. For each coordinate (x, y, z) and the color coordinates, two maps, one for each view, are obtained. They must finally be blended so as to produce a smooth colored 3D model.

Creation of a personalized 3D avatar using one 2D face image: there are some attempts to create personalized 3D face avatars, when only one 2D face image is available. The most important works are those from S. Romdhani et al. [66] related to Morphable Models of Faces. The main idea of morphable faces is to use a statistical (also called generic) 3D face model, in an analysis by synthesis framework in order to synthesize a 3D face model that resembles the face from an unseen input 2D face image. Such a framework is described in Fig. 10. An important issue in this framework is the creation of the generic 3D face model. The idea is to use the 3D a priori knowledge of a set of known 3D human faces in order to reconstruct new 3D models of subjects for whom a 3D face scan is not available.

The example presented in this paragraph is based on the general framework of morphable 3D faces in an analysis by synthesis loop (Fig. 10). There are two main phases in this framework. The first phase is the construction of the generic 3D face model (from an ensemble of 3D scans acquired on real subjects). The second phase is the fitting part, in order to find the fitting parameters of the model that result in a representation as close as possible to the input image.

S. Romdhani et al. [66] use the CyberwareTM laser scanner to acquire full 3D scans of 200 subjects, with shape and texture data in a cylindrical representation. For the example presented in this paragraph, the 3D partial scans from the IV^2 face database (described in [64] and available at [35]) are used. These 3D scans are acquired with the Konica-Minolta Vivid 700 laser sensor. This scanner provides partial 3D information. Three partial face scans (frontal, left and right profile) are employed for the construction of the full IV^2-3D face generic model. Some semi-automatic treatments, such as smoothing, hole filling, hair and ear removal, and noise removal need to be done on the partial scans. The Iterative Closest Point (ICP) algorithm is applied for the registration phase in order to merge the shape partial scans.

The face morphing and 3D reconstruction methods presented above are interesting tools to personalize an avatar in 3D virtual worlds, or to choose different avatars that for instance look like one's favorite actress or actor.

4.3   Gesture Analysis and Synthesis

Gestures are part of human communication, so they should be supported with machine perception and rendering for mediated communication in virtual environments. Two main techniques are used to synthesize gesture: motion capture and key-frame animation. While the first technique produces high quality animation the second one is much more flexible. To animate an ECA procedural animation is often chosen over motion capture technique. The representation of co-verbal gestures in ECAs follows the literature on communicative gesture [42]. A gesture is divided into phases: preparation, pre-hold-stroke, stroke, post-stroke-hold and retraction [42]. Several systems use the approach

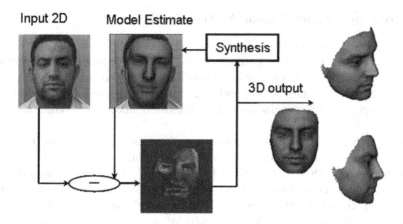

Fig. 10. An example of a personalized 3D face avatar, obtained by the analisis and synthesis framework, using only one input 2D face image of the subject

proposed by Liddell [48] to describe arm position and hand shape for American Sign Language. Each phase of a gesture is defined by the wrist location in the gesture space, palm and finger orientation, finger and thumb shape [45,31]. An interpolation scheme is defined to smoothly join between arm position for each phase. Languages to describe gesture shape for each phase have been elaborated. Examples are MURML [45], Greta formational parameters [31], BML [80]. Cassell and her colleagues developed a representation of gestures that ensure a generation "on the fly" of speech and gesture, depending on the semantic information both modalities convey [12]. The manner of behavior is tackled by Chi et al. [15] who implement the EMOTE model of adapting agent gestures in order to enhance expressivity of behaviors applying transformation at the level of limbs. Hartmann et al. [31] obtained a set of expressivity parameters, tying behavior modificationinto the synthesis stage of gesturing: Mancini and Pelachaud [50] extended this to include facial expressions and head movements. Kipp et al [43] present a gesture animation system based on statistical models of human speakers gestures. Videos of interviewed people have been manually annotated in terms of gestures types (iconic, deictic, etc.) together with their frequency of occurrence and timing (that is the synchronization between the gesture stroke and the most emphasized syllable of the sentence). The statistics on the speaker's gestures are then used to model the agent's set of preferred gestures (the probabilities of their occurrence is computed from the annotated gesture frequency) and synchronization tendency (for example an agent can perform gesture strokes always synchronized with speech emphasis). Mancini and Pelachaud [50] propose a computation model to create ECAs with distinctive behaviors. ECA is defined by a baseline that states the global tendency of the ECA (modality preferences and overall expressivity values for each modality) and a dynamic line that describes how a given communicative intent and/or an emotional state affect the baseline.

Gesture Modeling for Human Motion Tracking

Motion capture by computer vision: Computer vision has become a user-friendly alternative to sensors attached on user limbs [53]. The interest in this research has been motivated by many potential applications (video surveillance, human computer interaction, games, etc.) and their inherent challenges (different human body proportions, different clothes, partial occlusion, uncontrolled environments, etc.) [65].

Recent research can be divided into two main classes. Model-based (or generative) approaches use a model of the human body and a matching cost function to search the pose that best matches input images. Model-free (or discriminative) approaches try to learn a direct relation between image observation and the pose [68]. Different techniques have been proposed using these approaches, as well as using different information sources (color, edge, texture, motion, etc.) [49], sample-based methods [69], and learning methods [3].

We have developed a prototype system for 3D human motion capture by real-time monocular vision without marker. It works by optimizing a color-based

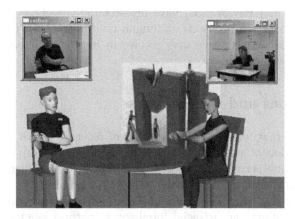

Fig. 11. Real-time motion capture from webcams and virtual rendering (video available from http://picoforge.int-evry.fr/projects/myblog3d)

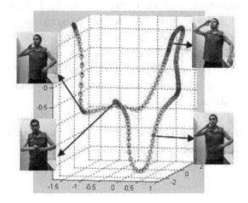

Fig. 12. A GPDM model of drinking. Each point in the 3D latent space corresponds to a human pose.

registration of a 3D articulated model of the human body on video sequences [33]. Model candidate postures are compared with images by computing a non-overlapping ratio between the segmented image and the 3D-color model projection. This evaluation function is minimized to get the best registration. Biomechanical limits constrain the registered postures to be morphologically reachable. Statistical dynamic constraints enforce physically realistic movements. This has been implemented to run at video frame rate [70], allowing virtual rendering of captured motion in real time.

Gesture modeling: Gesture models in low dimensional latent space can be useful as prior knowledge for human motion tracking, especially with monocular vision. Furthermore, tracking in a lower dimensional latent space requires fewer particles for particle filtering. Urtasun [79] used GPLVM and GPDM to learn prior models for tracking 3D human walking, so achieving good results even in case of serious occlusion. Moon and Pavlovic [54] have investigated the effect of dynamics in dimensionality reduction problems on human motion tracking. Gesture models in low dimensional latent space may receive in increasing interest for human motion tracking and animation.

5   Conclusions and Perspectives

In this paper we have presented an overview of recent research efforts towards the implementation of virtual avatars and agents, graphically embodied in a 2D and/or 3D interactive worlds, and able to interact intelligently with the environment, other avatars, and particularly with human users.

The field is largely interdisciplinary and complex, involving expertise in computer graphics, animation, artificial intelligence, natural language processing, cognitive and psychological modeling of human-human and human-machine interaction, linguistics, communication, and artificial life, to name a few. Nevertheless, it provides access to a graded series of tasks for measuring (through realistic, even though virtual, evaluating alternatives) the amount of adjustment (as well as intelligence, and achievement) needed for introducing new concepts in the information and communication technology domain. Adaptive, socially enabled and human centred automatic systems will serve remote applications in medicine, learning, care, rehabilitation, and for the accessibility to work, employments, and information.

In the light of the above perspectives, we will expect that these applications will have a beneficial effect on people's lives and will contribute to facilitate communication within dispersed families and social groups.

Acknowledgments

The authors would like to acknowledge the contributions of Aurélie Barbier, Jean Bernard, David Gomez, Christophe Guilmart and Aude Mamouna Guyot-Mbodji to several aspects of the work reported in this paper.

This work has been partially supported by the COST 2102 action "Cross Modal Analysis of Verbal and Nonverbal Communication (www.cost2102.eu)" and the ANR-MyBlog3D project (https://picoforge.int-evry.fr/cgi-bin/twiki /view/Myblog3d/Web/).

References

1. Abboud, B., Bredin, H., Aversano, G., Chollet, G.: Audio-visual identity verification: an introductory overview. In: Stylianou, Y. (ed.) Progress in Non-Linear Speech Processing, pp. 118–134. Springer, Heidelberg (2007)
2. Abe, M., Nakamura, S., Shikano, K., Kuwabara, H.: Voice conversion through vector quantization. In: International Conference on Acoustics, Speech, and Signal Processing (1988)

3. Agarwal, A., Triggs, B.: Recovering 3D human pose from monocular images. IEEE Transactions on Pattern Analysis and Machine Intelligence, 44–58 (2006)
4. Ahlberg, J.: Candide-3, an updated parameterized face. Technical report, Linköping University, Sweden (2001)
5. Ahlberg, J.: Real-time facial feature tracking using an active model with fast image warping. In: International Workshop on Very Low Bitrates Video (2001)
6. Albrecht, I., Schroeder, M., Haber, J., Seidel, H.-P.: Mixed feelings – expression of non-basic emotions in a muscle-based talking head. In: Virtual Reality (Special Issue Language, Speech and Gesture for VR) (2005)
7. Arslan, L.M.: Speaker transformation algorithm using segmental codebooks (STASC). Speech Communication (1999)
8. Beau, F.: Culture d'Univers - Jeux en réseau, mondes virtuels, le nouvel âge de la société numérique. Limoges (2007)
9. Benesty, J., Sondhi, M., Huang, Y. (eds.): Springer Handbook of Speech Processing. Springer, Heidelberg (2008)
10. Bui, T.D.: Creating Emotions And Facial Expressions For Embodied Agents. PhD thesis, University of Twente, Department of Computer Science, Enschede (2004)
11. Cassell, J., Bickmore, J., Billinghurst, M., Campbell, L., Chang, K., Vilhjálmsson, H., Yan, H.: Embodiment in conversational interfaces: Rea. In: CHI 1999, Pittsburgh, PA, pp. 520–527 (1999)
12. Cassell, J., Kopp, S., Tepper, P., Kim, F.: Trading Spaces: How Humans and Humanoids use Speech and Gesture to Give Directions. John wiley & sons, New york (2007)
13. Cassell, J., Vilhjálmsson, H., Bickmore, T.: BEAT: the Behavior Expression Animation Toolkit. In: Computer Graphics Proceedings, Annual Conference Series. ACM SIGGRAPH (2001)
14. Cheyer, A., Martin, D.: The open agent architecture. Journal of Autonomous Agents and Multi-Agent Systems, 143–148 (March 2001)
15. Chi, D., Costa, M., Zhao, L., Badler, N.: The emote model for effort and shape. In: International Conference on Computer Graphics and Interactive Techniques, SIGGRAPH, pp. 173–182 (2000)
16. Chollet, G., Landais, R., Bredin, H., Hueber, T., Mokbel, C., Perrot, P., Zouari, L.: Some experiments in audio-visual speech processing, in non-linear speech processing. In: Chetnaoui, M. (ed.) Progress in Non-Linear Speech Processing. Springer, Heidelberg (2007)
17. Chollet, G., Petrovska-Delacrétaz, D.: Searching through a speech memory for efficient coding, recognition and synthesis. Franz Steiner Verlag, Stuttgart (2002)
18. Cootes, T., Edwards, G., Taylor, C.: Active appearance models. IEEE Transactions on Pattern Analysis and Machine Intelligence, 681–685 (2001)
19. Dornaika, F., Ahlberg, J.: Fast and reliable active appearance model search for 3D face tracking. IEEE Transactions on Systems, Man, and Cybernetics, 1838–1853 (2004)
20. Dutoit, T.: Corpus-based speech synthesis. In: Jacob, B., Mohan, S.M., Yiteng (Arden), H. (eds.) Springer Handbook of Speech Processing, pp. 437–453. Springer, Heidelberg (2008)
21. Ekman, P., Campos, J., Davidson, R.J., De Waals, F.: Emotions inside out, vol. 1000. Annals of the New York Academy of Sciences, New York (2003)

22. Esposito, A.: Children's organization of discourse structure through pausing means. In: Faundez-Zanuy, M., Janer, L., Esposito, A., Satue-Villar, A., Roure, J., Espinosa-Duro, V. (eds.) NOLISP 2005. LNCS, vol. 3817, pp. 108–115. Springer, Heidelberg (2006)

23. Esposito, A.: The amount of information on emotional states conveyed by the verbal and nonverbal channels: Some perceptual data. In: Stylianou, Y., Faundez-Zanuy, M., Esposito, A. (eds.) COST 277. LNCS, vol. 4391, pp. 249–268. Springer, Heidelberg (2007)

24. Esposito, A., Bourbakis, N.G.: The role of timing in speech perception and speech production processes and its effects on language impaired individuals. In: 6th International IEEE Symposium on BioInformatics and BioEngineering, pp. 348–356 (2006)

25. Esposito, A., Marinaro, M.: What pauses can tell us about speech and gesture partnership. In: Esposito, A., Bratanic, M., Keller, E., Marinaro, M. (eds.) Fundamentals of Verbal and Nonverbal Communication and the Biometrical Issue. NATO Publishing Series, pp. 45–57. IOS press, Amsterdam (2007)

26. Gauvain, J.L., Lamel, L.: Large - Vocabulary Continuous Speech Recognition: Advances and Applications. Proceedings of the IEEE 88, 1181–1200 (2000)

27. Genoud, D., Chollet, G.: Voice transformations: Some tools for the imposture of speaker verification systems. In: Braun, A. (ed.) Advances in Phonetics. Franz Steiner Verlag (1999)

28. Gentes, A.: Second life, une mise en jeu des médias. In: de Cayeux, A., Guibert, C. (eds.) Second life, un monde possible, Les petits matins (2007)

29. Gutierrez-Osuna, R., Kakumanu, P., Esposito, A., Garcia, O.N., Bojorquez, A., Castello, J., Rudomin, I.: Speech-driven facial animation with realistic dynamics. In: IEEE Transactions on Multimedia, pp. 33–42 (2005)

30. El Hannani, A., Petrovska-Delacrétaz, D., Fauve, B., Mayoue, A., Mason, J., Bonastre, J.-F., Chollet, G.: Text-independent speaker verification. In: Petrovska-Delacrétaz, D., Chollet, G., Dorizzi, B. (eds.) Guide to Biometric Reference Systems and Performance Evaluation. Springer, London (2008)

31. Hartmann, B., Mancini, M., Pelachaud, C.: Implementing expressive gesture synthesis for embodied conversational agents. In: Gibet, S., Courty, N., Kamp, J.-F. (eds.) GW 2005. LNCS (LNAI), vol. 3881, pp. 188–199. Springer, Heidelberg (2006)

32. Heylen, D., Ghijsen, M., Nijholt, A., op den Akker, R.: Facial signs of affect during tutoring sessions. In: Tao, J., Tan, T., Picard, R.W. (eds.) ACII 2005. LNCS, vol. 3784, pp. 24–31. Springer, Heidelberg (2005)

33. Horain, P., Bomb, M.: 3D model based gesture acquisition using a single camera. In: IEEE Workshop on Applications of Computer Vision, pp. 158–162 (2002)

34. Horain, P., Marques-Soares, J., Rai, P.K., Bideau, A.: Virtually enhancing the perception of user actions. In: 15th International Conference on Artificial Reality and Telexistence ICAT 2005, pp. 245–246 (2005)

35. IV2: Identification par l'Iris et le Visage via la Vidéo, http://iv2.ibisc.fr/pageweb-iv2.html

36. Jelinek, F.: Continuous Speech Recognition by Statistical Methods. Proceedings of the IEEE 64, 532–556 (1976)

37. Kain, A.: High Resolution Voice Transformation. PhD thesis, Oregon Health and Science University, Portland, USA, october (2001)

38. Kain, A., Macon, M.: Spectral voice conversion for text to speech synthesis. In: International Conference on Acoustics, Speech, and Signal Processing, New York (1998)

39. Kain, A., Macon, M.W.: Design and evaluation of a voice conversion algorithm based on spectral envelope mapping and residual prediction. In: International Conference on Acoustics, Speech, and Signal Processing (2001)
40. Kakumanu, P., Esposito, A., Gutierrez-Osuna, R., Garcia, O.N.: Comparing different acoustic data-encoding for speech driven facial animation. Speech Communication, 598–615 (2006)
41. Karungaru, S., Fukumi, M., Akamatsu, N.: Automatic human faces morphing using genetic algorithms based control points selection. International Journal of Innovative Computing, Information and Control 3(2), 1–6 (2007)
42. Kendon, A.: Gesture: Visible action as utterance. Cambridge Press, Cambridge (2004)
43. Kipp, M., Neff, M., Kipp, K.H., Albrecht, I.: Toward natural gesture synthesis: Evaluating gesture units in a data-driven approach. In: Pelachaud, C., Martin, J.-C., André, E., Chollet, G., Karpouzis, K., Pelé, D. (eds.) IVA 2007. LNCS (LNAI), vol. 4722, pp. 15–28. Springer, Heidelberg (2007)
44. Kopp, S., Jung, B., Lessmann, N., Wachsmuth, I.: Max - a multimodal assistant in virtual reality construction. KI Kunstliche Intelligenz (2003)
45. Kopp, S., Wachsmuth, I.: Synthesizing multimodal utterances for conversational agents. The Journal Computer Animation and Virtual Worlds 15(1), 39–52 (2004)
46. Laird, C.: Webster's New World Dictionary, and Thesaurus. In: Webster dictionary. Macmillan, Basingstoke (1996)
47. Li, Y., Wen, Y.: A study on face morphing algorithms, http://scien.stanford.edu/class/ee368/projects2000/project17
48. Lidell, S.: American Sign Language Syntax. Approaches to semiotics. Mouton, The Hague (1980)
49. Lu, S., Huang, G., Samaras, D., Metaxas, D.: Model-based integration of visual cues for hand tracking. In: IEEE workshop on Motion and Video Computing (2002)
50. Mancini, M., Pelachaud, C.: Distinctiveness in multimodal behaviors. In: Seventh International Joint Conference on Autonomous Agents and Multi-Agent Systems, AAMAS 2008, Estoril Portugal (May 2008)
51. Matthews, I., Baker, S.: Active appearance models revisited. International Journal of Computer Vision, 135–164 (2004)
52. McNeill, D.: Gesture and though. University of Chicago Press (2005)
53. Moeslund, T., Hilton, A., Kruger, V.: A survey of advances in vision-based human motion capture and analysis. Computer vision and image understanding 4, 90–126 (2006)
54. Moon, K., Pavlovic, V.I.: Impact of dynamics on subspace embedding and tracking of sequences. In: Conference on Computer Vision and Pattern Recognition, New York, pp. 198–205 (2006)
55. Niewiadomski, R., Pelachaud, C.: Model of facial expressions management for an embodied conversational agent. In: 2nd International Conference on Affective Computing and Intelligent Interaction ACII, Lisbon (September 2007)
56. Ochs, M., Niewiadomski, R., Pelachaud, C., Sadek, D.: Intelligent expressions of emotions. In: 1st International Conference on Affective Computing and Intelligent Interaction ACII, China (October 2005)
57. Padmanabhan, M., Picheny, M.: Large Vocabulary Speech Recognition Algorithms. Computer Magazine 35 (2002)
58. Pandzic, I.S., Forcheimer, R. (eds.): MPEG4 Facial Animation - The standard, implementations and applications. John Wiley & Sons, Chichester (2002)
59. Park, I.K., Zhang, H., Vezhnevets, V.: Image based 3D face modelling system. EURASIP Journal on Applied Signal Processing, 2072–2090 (January 2005)

60. Pelachaud, C., Martin, J.-C., André, E., Chollet, G., Karpouzis, K., Pelé, D.: Intelligent virtual agents. In: 7th International Working Conference, IVA 2007 (2007)
61. Perrot, P., Aversano, G., Chollet, G.: Voice disguise and automatic detection, review and program. In: Stylianou, Y. (ed.) Progress in Non-Linear Speech Processing. Springer, Heidelberg (2007)
62. Perrot, P., Aversano, G., Blouet, G.R., Charbit, M., Chollet, G.: Voice forgery using alisp: Indexation in a client memory. In: International Conference on Acoustics, Speech, and Signal Processing, Philadelphia, pp. 17–20 (2005)
63. Petrovska-Delacrétaz, D., El Hannani, A., Chollet, G.: Automatic speaker verification, state of the art and current issues. In: Stylianou, Y. (ed.) Progress in Non-Linear Speech Processing. Springer, Heidelberg (2007)
64. Petrovska-Delacrétaz, D., Lelandais, S., Colineau, J., Chen, L., Dorizzi, B., Krichen, E., Mellakh, M.A., Chaari, A., Guerfi, S., D'Hose, J., Ardabilian, M., Ben Amor, B.: The iv^2 multimodal (2D, 3D, stereoscopic face, talking face and iris) biometric database, and the iv^2 2007 evaluation campaign. In: The proceedings of the IEEE Second International Conference on Biometrics: Theory, Applications (BTAS), Washington DC, USA (September 2008)
65. Poppe, R.: Vision-based human motion analysis: an overview. Computer vision and image understanding 108, 4–18 (2007)
66. Romdhani, S., Blanz, V., Basso, C., Vetter, T.: Morphable models of faces. In: Li, S., Jain, A. (eds.) Handbook of Face Recognition, pp. 217–245. Springer, Heidelberg (2005)
67. Ruttkay, Z., Noot, H., ten Hagen, P.: Emotion disc and emotion squares: tools to explore the facial expression space. Computer Graphics Forum, 49–53 (2003)
68. Sminchisescu, C.: 3D Human Motion Analysis in Monocular Video, Techniques and Challenges. In: AVSS 2006: Proceedings of the IEEE International Conference on Video and Signal Based Surveillance, p. 76 (2006)
69. Sminchisescu, C., Triggs, B.: Estimating articulated human motion with covariance scaled sampling. International Journal of Robotic Research, 371–392 (2003)
70. Marques Soares, J., Horain, P., Bideau, A., Nguyen, M.H.: Acquisition 3D du geste par vision monoscopique en temps réel et téléprésence. In: Acquisition du geste humain par vision artificielle et applications, pp. 23–27 (2004)
71. Sündermann, D., Ney, H.: VTLN-Based Cross-Language Voice Conversion. In: IEEE workshop on Automatic Speech Recognition and Understanding, Virgin Islands, pp. 676–681 (2003)
72. Terzopoulos, D., Waters, K.: Analysis and synthesis of facial image sequences using physical and anatomical models. IEEE Transactions on Pattern Analysis and Machine Intelligence, 569–579 (1993)
73. Thiebaux, M., Marshall, A., Marsella, S., Kallmann, M.: SmartBody: Behavior realization for embodied conversational agents. In: Seventh International Joint Conference on Autonomous Agents and Multi-Agent Systems, AAMAS 2008, Portugal (May 2008)
74. Thorisson, K.R., List, T., Pennock, C., DiPirro, J.: Whiteboards: Scheduling blackboards for semantic routing of messages and streams. In: AAAI 2005 Workshop on Modular Construction of Human-Like Intelligence, July 10 (2005)

75. Traum, D.: Talking to virtual humans: Dialogue models and methodologies for embodied conversational agents. In: Wachsmuth, I., Knoblich, G. (eds.) Modeling Communication with Robots and Virtual Humans, pp. 296–309. John Wiley & Sons, Chichester (2008)
76. Tsapatsoulis, N., Raouzaiou, A., Kollias, S., Cowie, R., Douglas-Cowie, E.: Emotion recognition and synthesis based on MPEG-4 FAPs in MPEG-4 facial animation. In: Pandzic, I.S., Forcheimer, R. (eds.) MPEG4 Facial Animation - The standard, implementations and applications. John Wiley & Sons, Chichester (2002)
77. Turajlic, E., Rentzos, D., Vaseghi, S., Ho, C.-H.: Evaluation of methods for parametric formant transformation in voice conversion. In: International Conference on Acoustics, Speech, and Signal Processing (2003)
78. Turkle, S.: Life on the screen, Identity in the age of the internet. Simon and Schuster, New York (1997)
79. Urtasun, R., Fleet, D.J., Fua, P.: 3D people tracking with gaussian process dynamical models. In: Conference on Computer Vision and Pattern Recognition, New York, pp. 238–245 (2006)
80. Vilhjalmsson, H., Cantelmo, N., Cassell, J., Chafai, N.E., Kipp, M., Kopp, S., Mancini, M., Marsella, S., Marshall, A.N., Pelachaud, C., Ruttkay, Z., Thórisson, K.R., van Welbergen, H., van der Werf, R.: The behavior markup language: Recent developments and challenges. In: Pelachaud, C., Martin, J.-C., André, E., Chollet, G., Karpouzis, K., Pelé, D. (eds.) IVA 2007. LNCS, vol. 4722, pp. 99–111. Springer, Heidelberg (2007)
81. Wiskott, L., Fellous, J.M., Krüger, N., von der Malsburg, C.: Analysis and synthesis of facial image sequences using physical and anatomical models. IEEE Transactions on Pattern Analysis and Machine Intelligence, 775–779 (1997)
82. Wolberg, G.: Recent advances in image morphing. Computer Graphics Internat, 64–71 (1996)
83. Xiao, J., Baker, S., Matthews, I., Kanade, T.: Real-time combined 2D+3D active appearance models. In: IEEE Conference on Computer Vision and Pattern Recognition, pp. 25–35 (2004)
84. Ye, H., Young, S.: Perceptually weighted linear transformation for voice conversion. In: Eurospeech (2003)
85. Yegnanarayana, B., Sharat Reddy, K., Kishore, S.P.: Source and system features for speaker recognition using AANN models. In: International Conference on Acoustics, Speech, and Signal Processing (2001)
86. Young, S.: Statistical Modelling in Continuous Speech Recognition. In: Proceedings of the 17th International Conference on Uncertainty in Artificial Intelligence, Seattle, WA (August 2001)
87. Zanella, V., Fuentes, O.: An Approach to Automatic Morphing of Face Images in Frontal View. In: Monroy, R., Arroyo-Figueroa, G., Sucar, L.E., Sossa, H. (eds.) MICAI 2004. LNCS, vol. 2972, pp. 679–687. Springer, Heidelberg (2004)

Speech through the Ear, the Eye, the Mouth and the Hand

Marion Dohen

Speech and Cognition Department, ICP, GIPSA-lab
961 rue de la Houille Blanche – Domaine Universitaire
38402 Saint Martin d'Hères Cedex, France
Marion.Dohen@gipsa-lab.inpg.fr

Abstract. This chapter aims at describing how speech is multimodal not only in its perception but also in its production. It first focuses on multimodal perception of speech segments and speech prosody. It describes how multimodal perception is linked to speech production and explains why we consider speech perception as a sensory-motor process. It then analyses some aspects of hand-mouth coordination in spoken communication. Input from evolutionary perspectives, ontogenesis and behavioral studies on infants and adults are combined to detail how and why this coordination is crucial in speech.

Keywords: multimodal speech, auditory-visual perception, sensori-motor, prosody, hand-mouth coordination, speech and language development, pointing.

1 Introduction

Speech is multimodal and is produced with the mouth, the vocal tract, the hands and the entire body and perceived not only with our ears but also with our eyes (and even our hands in the Tadoma method for example). The aim of this chapter is to draw a general working framework for the analysis of speech in a multimodal perspective.

It will focus on two main points. The first one will be multimodal perception of speech segments and prosody which will be related to their production in order to explain how and why speech perception is a sensory-motor process. The second part of the chapter will explore some aspects of hand-mouth coordination in adult spoken communication. It will describe why this coordination is so important for understanding cognitive communicative processes. A conclusion will then summarize all the ideas developed throughout and describe their implications for studying speech in a multisensory perspective. The framework presented here is based on an analysis and synthesis of previous works which have led to the conception of speech as a multisensory process in nature. It aims at putting forward the importance of conceiving speech as multisensory to analyze and describe the cognitive processes involved.

A. Esposito et al. (Eds.): Multimodal Signals, LNAI 5398, pp. 24–39, 2009.

2 Multimodal Perception of Speech Segments and Speech Prosody in Relationship with Their Production

> "Speech is rather a set of movements made audible than a set of sounds produced by movements."
>
> Raymond H. Stetson [1]

As R.H. Stetson put it, speech is truly multisensory and does not consist of sounds which are produced, somehow, just to be heard.

2.1 Speech Is Also Visual

It is possible to perceive and understand speech with the eyes: 40 to 60% of the phonemes and 10 to 20% of the words (up to 60%) can be recovered through lipreading (data from [2]). This ability is highly inter-speaker dependent: the deaf are often better than the hearing for example. As shown in many studies [3-12], the use of vision for speech perception is obvious when the acoustic modality is degraded by noise. Many other situations however put forward the advantage of seeing a speaker while he/she is speaking. For example, when spelling something over the phone, you often have to disambiguate: M as in 'made', N as in 'nanny'.... Reisberg and colleagues [13] showed that vision also helped for perceiving speech in a foreign language, speech produced by a non-native speaker or semantically complex utterances.

This could lead to think that vision simply provides redundant information: when some of the auditory information is missing, it can be recovered by vision. As shown by Summerfied [14], perceptual confusions between consonants are different and complementary in the visual and the auditory modalities. Another clear and very famous example of the fact that the visual information is not just redundant is the McGurk effect [15]. An audio [ba] dubbed onto a visual [ga] results in a [da] percept. This effect is very robust: it works in many languages and, even when people are aware of it, it can not be suppressed [15]. All these observations suggest that the visual and auditory information are fused rather than the visual information being superimposed on the auditory one.

If the auditory and the visual information are not redundant, it suggests that speaking is producing gestures aiming at being both heard *and* seen. This is further backed by the fact that there is a marked preference for bilabials (consonants articulated with an initial contact of the superior and inferior lips), which are visually salient, at the beginning of babbling [16]. This preference is reinforced in deaf children [17] and unsalient in blind children [18]. Moreover, the [m]/[n] contrast which exists in almost all the languages in the world [19], is not very audible but very visible. Moreover, the fact that we use vision for speech perception does not seem to be a learnt skill. Infants 18 to 20 weeks-old, can indeed identify a speaking face corresponding to a speech signal out of two movies of speaking faces (one congruent to the audio and another incongruent) displayed at the same time [20]. Stetson's statement could therefore be adjusted to:

Speech is (…) a set of movements made audible *and visible*.

2.2 Auditory-Visual Fusion: How and When?

If the auditory and visual information are fused in speech perception, one can wonder which cognitive processes underlie this fusion: how and when does it happen? After analyzing the fusion models proposed in the literature, Robert-Ribes [21], Schwartz and colleagues [22] presented four main potential fusion architectures summarized in Fig. 1:

- **Direct Identification** (DI): the auditory and visual channels are directly compiled.
- **Separate Identification** (SI): the phonetic classification is operated separately on both channels and fusion occurs after this separate identification. Fusion is therefore relatively late and decisional.
- **Recoding in the dominating modality** (RD): the auditory modality is considered to be dominant and the visual channel is recoded under a compatible format to that of the auditory representations. This is an early fusion process.
- **Recoding in the motor modality** (RM): the main articulatory characteristics are estimated using the auditory and visual information. These are then fed to a classification process. This corresponds to an early fusion.

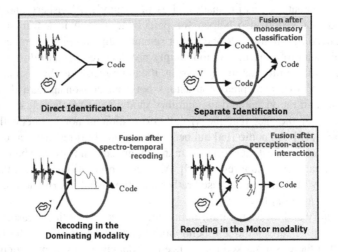

Fig. 1. The four main types of auditory-visual fusion models as presented in [21-22]

As stated in [2], the models which have been mostly tested in speech recognition applications are the DI and SI models because they are easier to implement. Some studies of brain activations however suggest that the interactions between modalities may occur very early (*e.g.* [23]). Moreover, as suggested in [2], a number of behavioral studies provide valuable information on the fusion process. Grant and Seitz [24] suggested the fact that, not only does vision help us better understand speech in noise, it also improves auditory detection of spoken sentences in noise. Actually, when we see a speaker, we perceive him/her as speaking louder. In the line of this observation, Schwartz and colleagues [25] designed an experiment to further test whether there are early interactions between audition and vision. They tested the intelligibility in noise of sequences which are not distinguishable by lip-reading. They found that visual only perception was not significantly better than chance which confirmed that nothing could be recovered from lip-reading. They however found that adding vision significantly improved auditory perception (AV>A). They interpreted this as potentially corresponding to reinforcement of the voicing feature by vision. The beginning of the labial gesture starts about 240ms before the vowel target is reached. In French, voicing is preceded by a prevoicing of about 100ms. Visual perception of the beginning of the labial gesture would therefore announce to the listener that he/she should lend an ear to detect the potential prevoicing. This temporal marker could reduce by a few dBs the detection threshold. The authors also conducted a second experiment in which the visual information of the speaker was replaced with visual information corresponding to a volume bar moving just as the speaker's lips. In this case, they found no improvement of perception when vision was added to audition suggesting that the effect described above is "speech specific". Put together, these behavioral data further suggest that the auditory-visual interactions are early which is incompatible with the DI and SI models.

Another question raised in [2] is that of the control of the fusion process: is there a context bias? For example, as shown by Tiippana and colleagues [26], visual attention can modulate audiovisual speech perception. If visual attention is distracted, the McGurk effect is indeed weaker. There also are strong inter-individual variations (see *e.g.* [27]) as well as inter-linguistic differences (see *e.g.* [28]).

The data presented above suggest that the RD and RM models appear to be more likely to reflect the cognitive processes underlying auditory-visual fusion. The RM model states that the auditory and visual channels would be combined and recoded into motor representations. This suggests that there would be a link between speech perception and speech production.

2.3 Evidence for Perceptuo-Motor Links in the Human Brain

The first thing we should talk about here is mirror neurons: not because it is fashionable but because this system could be important for speech... The mirror-neuron system was found in monkeys (area F5 of the monkey premotor cortex) by Rizzolati and colleagues (for reviews, see: [29,30]). These neurons are neurons which fire during both the production and the perception of goal-directed actions as well as during watching a similar action made by another individual (*e.g.* pick up a peanut on a tray). Kohler, Keysers and colleagues [31,32] suggested the existence of audio-visual mirror-neurons. These particular neurons fire when the monkey hears the sound produced by an action (*e.g.* experimenter breaking a peanut), when it sees the action being produced, when it sees and hears the action being produced and when it produces the action itself. Moreover, these neurons seem to be specialized: each neuron responds to one particular type of action (*e.g.* peanut breaking as opposed to ring grasping). Mirror neurons play a role in orofacial actions [33]: for example, the same neuron fires when the monkey grasps food with the mouth and when the experimenter grasps food with the mouth. This is also the case for "communicative" orofacial actions such as lip-smacking/lip protrusion [33-35]. All these observations were however made for monkeys: is there any evidence for a mirror neuron system in humans? It is not possible to record the activity of a single neuron in humans. A number of neurophysiological (EEG, MEG, TMS) and neuroimaging (fMRI) studies (for reviews see: [29,30,36]) have however showed activations of motor regions involved in performing specific actions in the perception of these actions performed by others. Rizzolatti and colleagues [37,36] have proposed that the mirror neuron system would play a fundamental role in speech processing by providing a neurophysiological mechanism that creates parity between the speaker and the listener and allows for direct comprehension. A number of neurobiological models of speech perception [38-45] actually consider that motor areas linked to speech production (the so-called dorsal stream) intervene in speech perception either always or only under certain circumstances (speech acquisition for example).

Some studies using single-pulse transcranial magnetic stimulation (TMS) have shown a motor resonance in speech perception. This technique consists in exciting a specific motor region (in this case linked to speech production) in order for the hypothesized motor response, which is weak, to go over a threshold and produce a motor evoked potential (MEP) which can be recorded using electromyography (EMG). Using this technique, Fadiga and colleagues [46] showed that, during the perception of a speech sequence, there is an increase in MEPs recorded from the listeners' tongue muscles when the segmental content of speech involves tongue movements compared to when it does not. Another study using this technique [47] showed that there is an increase in MEPs recorded from the listeners' lip muscles during auditory alone perception of speech compared to the perception of nonverbal audio signals and during the visual perception of speaking lips compared to that of moving eyes and brows. Some neuroimaging studies (fMRI: functional Magnetic Resonance Imaging) have shown that the dorsal stream is activated in speech perception [48,49].

All these observations suggest that speech perception is tightly linked to speech production and that it can be considered as a sensori-motor process.

2.4 What about Suprasegmentals?

All the observations described above were made for segmental perception of speech, that is, perception of which phonemes/words are produced by a speaker. Prosody (intonation, rhythm and phrasing) is however crucial in spoken communication as illustrated by a nice example from L. Truss[1]. The two sentences below correspond to exactly the same segmental content, but, pronounced differently, they have completely different meanings (in this example, punctuation is the written equivalent of prosody):

A woman, without her man, is nothing.

A woman: without her, man is nothing.

For a long time, prosody was uniquely considered as acoustic/auditory. However, recent studies conducted in our lab, as well as studies conducted elsewhere (*e.g.* [50-61]) have showed that prosody also has potentially visible correlates (articulatory or other facial correlates). We analyzed contrastive informational focus as described by Di Cristo for French [62]. It is used to put forward a constituent pragmatically and contrastingly to another as in the example below (capital letters signal focus):

---

[1] Truss, L.: Eats, Shoots & Leaves – The Zero Tolerance Approach to Punctuation. Profile Books Ltd, London (2003).

> Did Bob eat the apple?
> No, SARAH ate the apple.

It can be realized using prosody (as in the example). The acoustic (intonational, durational and phrasing) correlates of prosodic focus have been widely studied [63-69]. Several production studies [70-72] in which we measured the articulatory and facial correlates of contrastive prosodic focus in French showed that there are visible correlates to contrastive focus in French. Two main visible articulatory strategies (inter-individual differences) were found:

- Absolute strategy: the speakers hyper-articulate and lengthen the focused constituent;
- Differential strategy: the speakers both slightly hyper-articulate the focused constituent and hypo-articulate the following constituent(s).

Both these strategies result in a visible contrast within the utterance between what is focused and what is not. In the line of other studies ([73-76,59] also see [77-78] for audiovisual perception studies using animated talking heads), we found that prosodic contrastive focus was detectable from the visual modality alone and that the cues used for perception at least partly corresponded to those identified in the production studies [70,71].

In another study [79], we designed an experiment to avoid the ceiling effect: auditory only perception of prosodic focus is close to a 100% and a potential advantage of adding vision cannot be measured. The speech in noise paradigm is not adequate here since voicing is a robust feature to noise [80]. We used whispered speech for which there is no F0. We found that auditory only perception was degraded and that adding vision clearly improved prosodic focus detection for whispered speech (see Fig. 2a). Reaction time (RT) measurements showed that adding vision reduced processing time. A further analysis of the data suggested that audition and vision are actually integrated for the perception of prosodic contrastive focus in French.

These results suggest that, not only is segmental perception of speech multimodal, but supra-segmental perception of speech is as well.

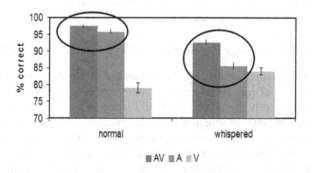

Fig. 2. Percentages of correct answers for each modality (AV, A, V) for loud and whispered speech

3 Some Aspects of Hand-Mouth Coordination in Speech Communication

Speech is vocal and gestural by nature. As shown in the previous section, articulatory gestures are produced aiming at being both heard and seen. Articulatory gestures are however not the only gestures we produce when we speak. We move our entire body and especially our hands [81-84] and this is meaningful as well.

3.1 Gesture and Speech in an Evolutionary Perspective: Towards a Crucial Role of Hand-Mouth Coordination in Language Evolution

From an evolutionary perspective, theories defending vocal origins of language are opposed to those defending gestural origins of language. Vocal origin theories argue that speech and language would derive from animal calls such as alarm calls. In the framework of the Frame then Content theory and deriving phylogenesis (as the study of the evolution of a species) from ontogenesis (as the study of the development of a human being from birth to adulthood), MacNeilage [85,86] argues that the motor control of the articulators used in chewing would have led to speech and language. This suggests an orofacial (related to the face and mouth) basis for language. On the other hand, theories of gestural origins of language argue that the hand was used for communication before the mouth. Corbalis [87] argues that non-human primates (great apes) produce *unvoluntary* vocalizations whereas they *control and understand* manual gestures which are moreover often produced in dyads unlike calls. In his sense, this would have led to a gestural form of communication which would have led to a more complex control of the articulators and to vocal communication. What Arbib [88,89] and Holden [90] argue is that there would have been a co-evolution of manual and speech gestural systems towards language and communication. This is in line with ontogenesis observations by Iversen and Thelen [91] who showed that the motor control of the vocal tract is longer to acquire than that of the hand but that the two systems develop in cooperation. This view underlines the fundamental link there would be between hand gestures and articulation and argues for a hand-mouth gestural basis for language. This suggests that hand-mouth coordination would have played a key role in communication evolution.

3.2 Gestures and Language Development: The Special Role of Pointing

As demonstrated, among others, by the researchers from Goldin-Meadow's team, gestures play a crucial role in language development (*e.g.* [92,93]). A key stage in language development is the combination of a word and a gesture carrying complementary (non redundant) information [94]. An example of such a combination is a baby saying "monster" and producing a gesture miming "big" to mean "big monster". These combinations lead to the production of two-word utterances. [95] underlines the fact that the motor links between the hand and the mouth develop progressively from birth until they reach synchrony (around 16 to 18 months). This association between speech and hand gestures seems to be a motor rather than a perceptive association. Blind children indeed produce gestures as well [96].

As pointed out by Butterworth [97]: "pointing is the royal road toward language for babies". Pointing indeed appears to play a special role at many stages of language development (see *e.g.* [94,98,99]). The first gestures, produced around 9-11 months and predictive of first word onset, are deictic (gestures that show). These are not synchronized to vocal productions. Then babies combine words and pointing gestures carrying the same information as in pointing at a dog and saying "dog" at the same time. Words are then combined to pointing gestures with no information redundancy as in pointing at a dog and saying "eat" to mean "the dog is eating". This leads to the production of two-word utterances at around 18 months. These observations show that pointing plays a special role in speech development in infants.

3.3 Hand-Mouth Coordination in Adult Spoken Communication

Many studies have analyzed hand-mouth coordination in adults' speech. The two main approaches commonly used are "controlled" experiments and analysis of spontaneous productions. "Controlled" experiments make precise quantitative evaluation of the links between gestures and speech possible but involve using controlled material and recordings in an artificial environment such as a lab. Analyzing spontaneous productions enables the evaluation of the "natural" links between gestures and speech but are not replicable and do not allow for quantitative analyses. In this chapter, I will mainly focus on the description of results from "controlled" experiments. For these experiments, two main protocols have been used: dual and single task paradigms and rhythmic tasks. I will describe results from dual and single task studies. In these studies, several conditions are compared to each other: speech alone, speech and gesture and gesture alone.

Hollender [100] conducted several experiments using a dual-task paradigm in which participants were asked to name a letter which appeared on a computer screen and press a key on a keyboard. This showed that, when speech and gesture were combined, the vocal response was delayed compared to the speech alone condition potentially for the two systems to be synchronized. The author concluded that there was an adaptation of the systems due to limitations in processing capacities. Castiello and colleagues [101] also conducted a dual-task study in which the participants uttered the syllable /tah/ while grasping an object. The authors found that "the two-responses were generated independently of each other" (see also [102]). These studies tend to suggest that hand-mouth coordination may not be so strict. However a crucial issue should be addressed: if the hand and mouth are coordinated in adult spoken communication, what could this coordination be like?

McNeill [82] described hand-mouth coordination as a synchronization of the hand gesture to the word which it is related to semantically and co-expressively. This raises a question as for the studies described above: there was no "semantic" relationship between the gestures and the speech. In this sense and as stated in [103,104], it seems particularly interesting to study pointing. For pointing, there should be synchrony between the gesture (which points at something) and the part of speech that shows (determiner, focus...). Levelt and colleagues [105] conducted a dual-task study on pointing and speech in which participants uttered "this lamp" while they pointed at the corresponding lamp. They observed a delay in both the manual and vocal responses in the gesture and speech condition. This delay was greater for the vocal response. These findings were replicated by Feyereisen [106]. These authors concluded that there were different processes which were competing for the same resources. This suggests that the hand and mouth systems would use the same resources and that one system would therefore have to wait for the other to free the resources to be able to use them. This would explain the delay measured for vocal responses. In a slightly different view, this delay could simply be due to coordination requirements: the vocal and gestural responses would have to be synchronized at some point and when a gesture is produced at the same time as speech, speech would wait in order for the synchrony to be achieved. Another important point is that the studies described above analyzed voice onset time. No articulatory measurements were conducted. If the coordination is a hand-mouth motor coordination, it seems unsatisfactory to analyze voice onset as an assessment of the vocal motor response. Finally, in the studies described above, the "part of speech that shows" (mostly a determiner) was always at the beginning of the utterance which probably has an effect on coordination.

Rochet-Capellan and colleagues [104] conducted a study in which they tested the effect of stress on hand-jaw coordination. They used a deictic task in which subjects pointed at a target while naming it. The name of the target was a CVCV bisyllable (2 consonant-vowel syllables) in which stress position was varied (*e.g.* /pápa/ *vs.* /papá/) as well as consonantal context (*e.g.* /pata/ *vs.* /tapa/). The target was always located in the right visual field, either near or far. Twenty native Brazilian Portuguese speakers were tested. The finger and jaw motion were captured using an IRED tracking system (Optotrak). The hypothesis was that, when stress was on the first (resp. second) syllable, the pointing apex would be synchronized with the maximum jaw displacement corresponding to the first (resp. second) syllable. This was actually the case when stress was on the first syllable. When stress was on the second syllable, the pointing apex (furthest position of the index finger corresponding to the extension of the arm in the pointing gesture) was located half way between the two jaw apices and the return of the pointing gesture was synchronized with the maximum jaw displacement corresponding to the second syllable. There was no effect of target position or consonant on the coordinative pattern. A finger adaptation was however observed: a longer plateau (delay between pointing apex and beginning of the return stroke) was measured when stress was on the second syllable. There was also a high subject variability and the authors suggested an adaptation of the jaw from the first to the second stress condition: the jaw response onset was 70ms earlier but the maximum jaw displacements were 100ms earlier. The main conclusion the authors made was that the jaw was synchronized to the finger pointing plateau (the part of the pointing gesture that shows). This study shows that there seems to be a tight coordination of the hand and jaw which serves communication purposes. This study also confirms that the coordination is rather between the hand and the articulatory gestures than between the hand and the sound. However it only analyzed hand-jaw coordination and one can wonder about coordination with other articulators.

3.4 The Co-development of Speech and Sign

Ducey-Kaufman and colleagues [107,108] designed a theoretical framework to analyze the co-development of speech and sign in speech acquisition. This theory mainly puts forward a "developmental rendez-vous" between what the authors call the sign frame (cyclicity of hand gesture in pointing) and the speech frame (jaw oscillations in speech). This meeting point occurs at about 12 months before when the speech and sign frame develop in parallel. This development leads to the possibility of producing two syllables within one pointing gesture and puts forward the potentially crucial role of the foot (phonological unit larger than or equal in size to the syllable and corresponding to the smallest rhythmic group) in speech. They tested this with a longitudinal study on six babies from 6 to 18 months. They found a 400ms mean duration of the syllable and a 800ms mean duration of the pointing gestures. Rochet-Capellan and colleagues tested this on adults [109]. The task they used was to name and show a target at a GO signal twice in a row. The name of the target was either a 1, or a 2, or a 3, or a 4 syllable word (/pá/ vs. /papá/ vs. /papapá/ vs. /papapapá/). They recorded finger motion using an IRED tracking system (Optotrak). The predictions were that the delay between the two pointing apices would remain constant for target names consisting of 1 or 2 syllables. This delay would then increase from 2 to 3 syllables and remain constant from 3 to 4 syllables. This is what they observed. They also analyzed the durations of the jaw gestures (from gesture initiation to the last maximum displacement, corresponding to the last syllable). They found a ratio between the duration of the pointing gesture and that of the jaw gestures of 0.5 whatever the number of syllables. These preliminary observations could confirm the two-syllable for one pointing gesture hypothesis.

4 Conclusion

The aim of this chapter was to draw a general multimodal framework for studying speech. The first aspect presented was the fact that speech is not only auditory. We also perceive speech through the eyes and the role of vision is not only that of a backup channel. Auditory and visual information are actually fused for perceptual decision. A number of potential cognitive fusion architecture models were presented. Some data suggest that audiovisual fusion takes place at very early stages of speech perception. Studies of the cognitive and brain mechanisms show that motor representations are most probably used in speech perception. Speech perception is a sensori-motor process: speech consists of gestures produced to be heard *and* seen. The multisensory aspect of speech is not limited to segmental perception of speech. It appears that there are visible articulatory correlates to the production of prosodic information such as prosodic focus and that these are perceived visually. Moreover, when the acoustic prosodic information is degraded, it is possible to put forward an auditory-visual fusion which enhances speech perception.

The second main aspect of this paper is the fact that we do not communicate only with our mouths. Our entire body, and especially our hands, is involved in this process. An analysis of the evolutionary theories of language development suggests that hand-mouth coordination may have played a crucial role in language evolution. This is at least the case for language development in babies in which the pointing gesture plays a crucial role. In adults, several studies seem to point out that hand and mouth (articulatory gestures) are tightly coordinated for communication purposes (for pointing at least). This still has to be analyzed for "real" speech (not only bisyllables) and for other communicative gestures: is the coordination gesture specific? Is it communication specific? Is it linked to grammar and prosody? Another important point is the fact that it appears that, "naturally" one pointing gesture would embed two syllables (in infants and maybe adults).

Acknowledgments. First of all, I would like to thank Anna Esposito for giving me the opportunity to take part in the International School "E. R. Caianiello" XIII course on Multimodal Signals: Cognitive and Algorithmic Issues. I also thank the two anonymous reviewers who provided insightful comments on a previous version of this chapter. For all the input he provided as well as for his advice and support, I thank Jean-Luc Schwartz. I also thank Amélie Rochet-Capellan for the inspiration I found in her work as well as for some material she provided. I also thank Marc Sato, Hélène Lœvenbruck and Gérard Bailly.

References

1. Stetson, R.H.: Motor Phonetics: A Study of Speech Movements in Action, 2nd edn. North-Holland, Amsterdam (1951)
2. Schwartz, J.-L.: La parole multisensorielle: Plaidoyer, problèmes, perspective. In: Actes des XXVes Journées d'Etude sur la Parole JEP 2004, pp. xi–xviii (2004)
3. Sumby, W.H., Pollack, I.: Visual Contribution to Speech Intelligibility in Noise. J. Acoust. Soc. Am. 26(2), 212–215 (1954)
4. Miller, G.A., Nicely, P.: An Analysis of Perceptual Confusions Among Some English Consonants. J. Acoust. Soc. Am. 27(2), 338–352 (1955)
5. Neely, K.K.: Effects of Visual Factors on the Intelligibility of Speech. J. Acoust. Soc. Am. 28(6), 1275–1277 (1956)
6. Erber, N.P.: Interaction of Audition and Vision in the Recognition of Oral Speech Stimuli. J. Speech Hear. Res. 12(2), 423–425 (1969)
7. Binnie, C.A., Montgomery, A.A., Jackson, P.L.: Auditory and Visual Contributions to the Perception of Consonants. J. Speech Hear. Res. 17(4), 619–630 (1974)
8. Erber, N.P.: Auditory-Visual Perception of Speech. J. Speech Hear. Dis. 40(4), 481–492 (1975)
9. Summerfield, A.Q.: Use of Visual Information for Phonetic Perception. Phonetica 36, 314–331 (1979)
10. MacLeod, A., Summerfield, A.Q.: Quantifying the Contribution of Vision to Speech Perception in Noise. Brit. J. Audiol. 21, 131–141 (1987)
11. Grant, K.W., Braida, L.D.: Evaluating the Articulation Index for Audiovisual Input. J. Acoust. Soc. Am. 89, 2952–2960 (1991)
12. Benoît, C., Mohamadi, T., Kandel, S.: Effects of Phonetic Context on Audio-Visual Intelligibility of French. J. Speech Hear. Res. 37, 1195–1203 (1994)
13. Reisberg, D., McLean, J., Goldfield, A.: Easy to Hear but Hard to Understand: A Lipreading Advantage with Intact Auditory Stimuli. In: Dodd, B., Campbell, R. (eds.) Hearing by Eye: The Psychology of Lip-reading, pp. 97–114. Lawrence Erlbaum Associates, Hillsdale (1987)
14. Summerfield, Q.: Comprehensive Account of Audio-Visual Speech Perception. In: Dodd, B., Campbell, R. (eds.) Hearing by Eye: The Psychology of Lip-reading, pp. 3–51. Lawrence Erlbaum Associates, Hillsdale (1987)
15. McGurk, H., MacDonald, J.: Hearing Lips and Seeing Voices. Nature 264, 746–748 (1976)
16. Vihman, M.M., Macken, M.A., Miller, R., Simmons, H., Miller, J.: From Babbling to Speech: A Re-Assessment of the Continuity Issue. Language 61, 397–445 (1985)

17. Stoel-Gammon, C.: Prelinguistic Vocalizations of Hearing-Impaired and Normally Hearing Subjects: A Comparison of Consonantal Inventories. J. Speech Hear. Dis. 53, 302–315 (1988)
18. Mulford, R.: First Words of the Blind Child. In: Smith, M.D., Locke, J.L. (eds.) The Emergent Lexicon: The Child's Development of a Linguistic Vocabulary, pp. 293–338. Academic Press, New York (1988)
19. Boë, L.J., Vallée, N., Schwartz, J.L.: Les tendances des structures phonologiques: le poids de la forme sur la substance. In: Escudier, P., Schwartz, J.L. (eds.) La parole, des modèles cognitifs aux machines communicantes - I. Fondements, pp. 283–323. Hermes, Paris (2000)
20. Kuhl, P.K., Meltzoff, A.N.: The Bimodal Perception of Speech in Infancy. Science 218, 1138–1141 (1982)
21. Robert-Ribes, J.: Modèles d'intégration audiovisuelle de signaux linguistiques: de la perception humaine à la reconnaissance automatique des voyelles. PhD Thesis, Institut National Polytechnique de Grenoble, France (1995)
22. Schwartz, J.-L., Robert-Ribes, J., Escudier, P.: Ten Years After Summerfield: A Taxonomy of Models for Audiovisual Fusion in Speech Perception. In: Campbell, R., Dodd, B.J., Burnham, D. (eds.) Hearing by Eye II: Advances in the Psychology of Speechreading and Auditory-Visual Speech, pp. 85–108. Psychology Press, Hove (1998)
23. Calvert, G.A., Bullmore, E.T., Brammer, M.J., Campbell, R., Williams, S.C.R., McGuire, P.K., Woodruff, P.W.R., Iversen, S.D., David, A.S.: Activation of the Auditory Cortex During Silent Lipreading. Science 276, 593–596 (1997)
24. Grant, K.W., Seitz, P.-F.: The Use of Visible Speech Cues for Improving Auditory Detection of Spoken Sentences. J. Acoust. Soc. Am. 108(3), 1197–1208 (2000)
25. Schwartz, J.-L., Berthommier, F., Savariaux, C.: Seeing to Hear Better: Evidence for Early Audio-Visual Interactions in Speech Identification. Cognition 93, B69–B78 (2004)
26. Tiippana, K., Andersen, T.S., Sams, M.: Visual Attention Modulates Audiovisual Speech Perception. Eur. J. Cog. Psychol. 16(3), 457–472 (2004)
27. Schwartz, J.-L., Cathiard, M.: Modeling Audio-Visual Speech Perception: Back on Fusion Architectures and Fusion Control. In: Proceedings of Interspeech 2004, pp. 2017–2020 (2004)
28. Sekiyama, K., Tohkura, Y.: Inter-Language Differences in the Influence of Visual Cues in Speech Perception. Journal of Phonetics 21, 427–444 (1993)
29. Rizzolatti, G., Fogassi, L., Gallese, V.: Neurophysiological Mechanisms Underlying the Understanding and Imitation of Action. Nat. Rev. Neurosci. 2(9), 661–670 (2001)
30. Rizzolatti, G., Craighero, L.: The Mirror-Neuron System. Annu. Rev. Neurosci. 27, 169–192 (2004)
31. Kohler, E., Keysers, C., Umilta, M.A., Fogassi, L., Gallese, V., Rizzolatti, G.: Hearing Sounds, Understanding Actions: Action Representation in Mirror Neurons. Science 5582(297), 846–848 (2002)
32. Keysers, C., Kohler, E., Umilta, M.A., Nanetti, L., Fogassi, L., Gallese, V.: Audiovisual Mirror Neurons and Action Recognition. Exp. Brain Res. 153, 628–636 (2003)
33. Ferrari, P.F., Gallese, V., Rizzolatti, G., Fogassi, L.: Mirror Neurons Responding to the Observation of Ingestive and Communicative Mouth Actions in the Monkey Ventral Premotor Cortex. Eur. J. Neurosci. 17, 1703–1714 (2003)
34. Gil-da-Costa, R., Martin, A., Lopes, M.A., Munoz, M., Fritz, J.B., Braun, A.R.: Species-Specific Calls Activate Homologs of Broca's and Wernicke's Areas in the Macaque. Nature Rev. Neurosci. 9, 1064–1070 (2006)
35. Taglialatela, J.P., Russell, J.L., Schaeffer, J.A., Hopkins, W.D.: Communicative Signaling Activates 'Broca's' Homolog in Chimpanzees. Curr. Biol. 18, 343–348 (2008)
36. Rizzolatti, G., Craighero, L.: Language and Mirror Neurons. In: Gaskell, G. (ed.) Oxford Handbook of Psycholinguistics. Oxford University Press, Oxford (2007)

37. Rizzolatti, G., Buccino, G.: The Mirror-Neuron System and its Role in Imitation and Language. In: Dehaene, S., Duhamel, G.R., Hauser, M., Rizzolatti, G. (eds.) From Monkey Brain to Human Brain, pp. 213–234. MIT Press, Cambridge (2005)
38. Hickok, G., Poeppel, D.: Towards a Functional Neuroanatomy of Speech Perception. Trends Cogn. Sci. 4(4), 132–138 (2000)
39. Scott, S.K., Johnsrude, I.S.: The Neuroanatomical and Functional Organization of Speech Perception. Trends Neurosci 26(2), 100–107 (2003)
40. Callan, D.E., Jones, J.A., Munhall, K., Kroos, C., Callan, A.M., Vatikiotis-Bateson, E.: Multisensory Integration Sites Identified by Perception of Spatial Wavelet Filtered Visual Speech Gesture Information. J. Cogn. Neurosci. 16(5), 805–816 (2004)
41. Hickok, G., Poeppel, D.: Dorsal and Ventral Streams: A Framework for Understanding Aspects of the Functional Anatomy of Language. Cognition 92, 67–99 (2004)
42. Scott, S.K., Wise, R.J.S.: The Functional Neuroanatomy of Prelexical Processing in Speech Perception. Cognition 92(1-2), 13–45 (2004)
43. Wilson, S.M., Iacoboni, M.: Neural Responses to Non-Native Phonemes Varying in Producibility: Evidence for the Sensorimotor Nature of Speech Perception. NeuroImage 33, 316–325 (2006)
44. Hickok, G., Poeppel, D.: The Cortical Organization of Speech Processing. Nat. Rev. Neurosci. 8(5), 393–402 (2007)
45. Skipper, J.L., van Wassenhove, V., Nusbaum, H.C., Small, S.L.: Hearing Lips and Seeing Voices: How Cortical Areas Supporting Speech Production Mediate Audiovisual Speech Perception. Cereb. Cortex 17(10), 2387–2399 (2007)
46. Fadiga, L., Craighero, L., Buccino, G., Rizzolatti, G.: Speech Listening Specifically Modulates the Excitability of Tongue Muscles: A TMS Study. Eur. J. Neurosci. 15, 399–402 (2002)
47. Watkins, K.E., Strafella, A.P., Paus, T.: Seeing and Hearing Speech Excites the Motor System Involved in Speech Production. Neuropsychologia 41, 989–994 (2003)
48. Callan, D.E., Jones, J.A., Munhall, K., Callan, A.M., Kroos, C., Vatikiotis-Bateson, E.: Neural Processes Underlying Perceptual Enhancement by Visual Speech Gestures. NeuroReport 14(17), 2213–2218 (2003)
49. Skipper, J.I., Nusbaum, H.C., Small, S.L.: Lending a Helping Hand to Hearing: Another Motor Theory of Speech Perception. In: Arbib, M.A. (ed.) Action to Language Via the Mirror Neuron System, pp. 250–285. Cambridge University Press, Cambridge (2006)
50. Kelso, J.A.S., Vatikiotis-Bateson, E., Saltzman, E., Kay, B.A.: A Qualitative Dynamic Analysis of Reiterant Speech Production: Phase Portraits, Kinematics, and Dynamic Modeling. J. Acoust. Soc. Am. 77(1), 266–280 (1985)
51. Summers, W.V.: Effects of Stress and Final-Consonant Voicing on Vowel Production: Articulatory and Acoustic Analyses. J. Acout. Soc. Am. 82(3), 847–863 (1987)
52. Vatikiotis-Bateson, E., Kelso, J.A.S.: Rhythm Type and Articulatory Dynamics in English, French and Japanese. J. Phonetics 21, 231–265 (1993)
53. De Jong, K.: The Supraglottal Articulation of Prominence in English: Linguistic Stress as Localized Hyperarticulation. J. Acoust. Soc. Am. 97(1), 491–504 (1995)
54. Harrington, J., Fletcher, J., Roberts, C.: Coarticulation and the Accented/Unaccented Distinction: Evidence from Jaw Movement Data. J. Phonetics 23, 305–322 (1995)
55. Lœvenbruck, H.: An Investigation of Articulatory Correlates of the Accentual Phrase in French. In: Proceedings of the 14th ICPhS, vol. 1, pp. 667–670 (1999)
56. Erickson, D., Maekawa, K., Hashi, M., Dang, J.: Some Articulatory and Acoustic Changes Associated with Emphasis in Spoken English. In: Proceedings of ICSLP 2000, vol. 3, pp. 247–250 (2000)
57. Lœvenbruck, H.: Effets articulatoires de l'emphase contrastive sur la Phrase Accentuelle en français. In: Actes des XXIIIes Journées d'Etude sur la Parole JEP 2000, pp. 165–168 (2000)

58. Erickson, D.: Articulation of Extreme Formant Patterns for Emphasized Vowels. Phonetica 59, 134–149 (2002)
59. Keating, P., Baroni, M., Mattys, S., Scarborough, R., Alwan, A., Auer, E.T., Bernstein, L.E.: Optical Phonetics and Visual Perception of Lexical and Phrasal Stress in English. In: Proceedings of ICPhS 2003, pp. 2071–2074 (2003)
60. Cho, T.: Prosodic Strengthening and Featural Enhancement: Evidence from Acoustic and Articulatory Realizations of /a,i/ in English. J. Acoust. Soc. Am. 117(6), 3867–3878 (2005)
61. Beskow, J., Granström, B., House, D.: Visual Correlates to Prominence in Several Expressive Modes. In: Proceedings of Interspeech 2006 – ICSLP, pp. 1272–1275 (2006)
62. Di Cristo, A.: Vers une modélisation de l'accentuation du français (deuxième partie). J. French Lang. Studies 10, 27–44 (2000)
63. Dahan, D., Bernard, J.-M.: Interspeaker Variability in Emphatic Accent Production in French. Lang. Speech 39(4), 341–374 (1996)
64. Di Cristo, A.: Intonation in French. In: Hirst, D., Di Cristo, A. (eds.) Intonation Systems: A Survey of Twenty Languages, pp. 195–218. Cambridge University Press, Cambridge (1998)
65. Di Cristo, A., Jankowski, L.: Prosodic Organisation and Phrasing after Focus in French. In: Proceedings of ICPhS 1999, pp. 1565–1568 (1999)
66. Rossi, M.: La focalisation. In: L'intonation, le système du français: description et modélisation, Ophrys, Paris, ch. II-6, pp. 116–128 (1999)
67. Jun, S.-A., Fougeron, C.: A Phonological Model of French Intonation. In: Botinis, A. (ed.) Intonation: Analysis, Modelling and Technology, pp. 209–242. Kluwer Academic Publishers, Dordrecht (2000)
68. Delais-Roussarie, E., Rialland, A., Doetjes, J., Marandin, J.-M.: The Prosody of Post Focus Sequences in French. In: Proceedings of Speech Prosody 2002, pp. 239–242 (2002)
69. Dohen, M., Lœvenbruck, H.: Pre-focal Rephrasing, Focal Enhancement and Post-focal Deaccentuation in French. In: Proceedings of the 8th ICSLP, pp. 1313–1316 (2004)
70. Dohen, M., Lœvenbruck, H., Cathiard, M.-A., Schwartz, J.-L.: Visual Perception of Contrastive Focus in Reiterant French Speech. Speech Comm. 44, 155–172 (2004)
71. Dohen, M., Lœvenbruck, H.: Audiovisual Production and Perception of Contrastive Focus in French: A Multispeaker Study. In: Proceedings of Interspeech 2005, pp. 2413–2416 (2005)
72. Dohen, M., Lœvenbruck, H., Hill, H.: Visual Correlates of Prosodic Contrastive Focus in French: Description and Inter-Speaker Variabilities. In: Proceedings of Speech Prosody 2006, pp. 221–224 (2006)
73. Thompson, D.M.: On the Detection of Emphasis in Spoken Sentences by Means of Visual, Tactual, and Visual-Tactual Cues. J. Gen. Psychol. 11, 160–172 (1934)
74. Risberg, A., Agelfors, E.: On the Identification of Intonation Contours by Hearing Impaired Listeners. Speech Transmission Laboratory - Quarterly Progress Report and Status Report 19(2-3), 51–61 (1978)
75. Risberg, A., Lubker, J.: Prosody and Speechreading. Speech Transmission Laboratory Quarterly Progress Report and Status Report 19(4), 1–16 (1978)
76. Bernstein, L.E., Eberhardt, S.P., Demorest, M.E.: Single-Channel Vibrotactile Supplements to Visual Perception of Intonation and Stress. J. Acoust. Soc. Am. 85(1), 397–405 (1989)
77. Krahmer, E., Swerts, M.: Perceiving Focus. In: Lee, C.-M. (ed.) Topic and Focus: A Cross-Linguistic Perspective, pp. 121–137. Kluwer, Dordrecht (2006)
78. Granström, B., House, D.: Audiovisual Representation of Prosody in Expressive Speech Communication. Speech Comm. 46, 473–484 (2005)
79. Dohen, M., Lœvenbruck, H.: Interaction of Audition and Vision for the Perception of Prosodic Contrastive Focus. Lang. Speech (in press)

80. Miller, G.A., Nicely, P.: An Analysis of Perceptual Confusions Among Some English Consonants. J. Acoust. Soc. Am. 27(2), 338–352 (1955)
81. Kendon, A.: Gesticulation and Speech: Two Aspects of the Process of Utterance. In: Key, M.R. (ed.) The Relationship of Verbal and Nonverbal Communication, Mouton, The Hague, pp. 207–227 (1980)
82. McNeill, D.: Hand and Mind. University of Chicago Press, Chicago (1992)
83. Kendon, A.: Gesture. Annu. Rev. Anthropol. 26, 109–128 (1997)
84. Kita, S. (ed.): Pointing: Where Language, Culture, and Cognition Meet. Lawrence Erlbaum Associates, Hillsdale (2003)
85. MacNeilage, P.F.: The Frame/Content Theory of Evolution of Speech Production. Behav. Brain Sci. 21(4), 499–511 (1998)
86. MacNeilage, P.F., Davis, B.: On the Origin of Internal Structure and Word Forms. Science 288, 527–531 (2000)
87. Corballis, M.C.: From Mouth to Hand: Gesture, Speech, and the Evolution of Right-Handedness. Behav. Brain Sci. 26(2), 199–260 (2003)
88. Arbib, M.A.: The Evolving Mirror System: A Neural Basis for Language Readiness. In: Christiansen, M., Kirby, S. (eds.) Language Evolution: The States of the Art, pp. 182–200. Oxford University Press, Oxford (2003)
89. Arbib, M.A.: From Monkey-Like Action Recognition to Human Language: An Evolutionary Framework for Neurolinguistics. Behav. Brain Sci. 28(2), 105–124 (2005)
90. Holden, G.: The Origin of Speech. Science 303, 1316–1319 (2004)
91. Iverson, J., Thelen, E.: The Hand Leads the Mouth in Ontogenesis Too. Behav. Brain Sci. 26(2), 225–226 (2003)
92. Iverson, J., Goldin-Meadow, S.: Gesture Paves the Way for Language Development. Psychol. Sci. 16, 368–371 (2005)
93. Ozcaliskan, S., Goldin-Meadow, S.: Gesture is at the Cutting Edge of Early Language Development. Cognition 96, 101–113 (2005)
94. Goldin-Meadow, S., Butcher, C.: Pointing Toward Two-Word Speech in Young Children. In: Kita, S. (ed.) Pointing: Where Language, Culture, and Cognition Meet, pp. 85–107. Lawrence Erlbaum Associates, Hillsdale (2003)
95. Iverson, J., Thelen, E.: Hand, Mouth, and Brain: The Dynamic Emergence of Speech and Gesture. J. Conscious. Stud. 6, 19–40 (1999)
96. Iverson, J., Goldin-Meadow, S.: Why People Gesture as They Speak. Nature 396, 228 (1998)
97. Butterworth, G.: Pointing is the Royal Road to Language for Babies. In: Kita, S. (ed.) Pointing: Where Language, Culture, and Cognition Meet, pp. 9–33. Lawrence Erlbaum Associates, Hillsdale (2003)
98. Pizzuto, E., Capobianco, M., Devescovi, A.: Gestural-Vocal Deixis and Representational Skills in Early Language Development. Interaction Studies 6(2), 223–252 (2005)
99. Volterra, V., Caselli, M.C., Capirci, O., Pizzuto, E.: Gesture and the Emergence and Development of Language. In: Tomasello, M., Slobin, D. (eds.) Elizabeth Bates: A Festschrift, pp. 3–40. Lawrence Erlbaum Associates, Mahwah (2005)
100. Hollender, D.: Interference Between a Vocal and a Manual Response to the Same Stimulus. In: Stelmach, G., Requin, J. (eds.) Tutorials in Motor Behavior, pp. 421–432. North-Holland, Amsterdam (1980)
101. Castiello, U., Paulignan, Y., Jeannerod, M.: Temporal Dissociation of Motor Responses and Subjective Awareness. Brain 114(6), 2639–2655 (1991)
102. Fagot, C., Pashler, H.: Making Two Responses to a Single Object: Implications for the Central Attentional Bottleneck. J. Exp. Psychol. 18, 1058–1079 (1992)
103. Rochet-Capellan, A.: De la substance à la forme: rôle des contraintes motrices orofaciales et brachiomanuelles de la parole dans l'émergence du langage. PhD Thesis, Cognitive Sciences, Institut National Polytechnique de Grenoble, France (2007)

104. Rochet-Capellan, A., Schwartz, J.-L., Laboissière, R., Galván, A.: The Speech Focus Position Effect on Jaw-Finger Coordination in a Pointing Task. J. Speech Lang. Hear. Res (in Press)
105. Levelt, W.J.M., Richardson, G., Heij, W.L.: Pointing and Voicing in Deictic Expressions. J. Mem. Lang. 24, 133–164 (1985)
106. Feyereisen, P.: The Competition Between Gesture and Speech Production in Dual-Task Paradigms. J. Mem. Lang. 36(1), 13–33 (1997)
107. Ducey-Kaufmann, V.: Le cadre de la parole et le cadre du signe: un rendez-vous développemental. PhD Thesis, Language Sciences, Stendhal University, Grenoble, France (2007)
108. Ducey-Kaufmann, V., Abry, C., Vilain, C.: When the Speech Frame Meets the Sign Frame in a Developmental Framework. In: Emergence of Language Abilities (2007)
109. Rochet-Capellan, A., Schwartz, J.-L., Laboissière, R., Galván, A.: Two CV Syllables for One Pointing Gesture as an Optimal Ratio for Jaw-Arm Coordination in a Deictic Task: A Preliminary Study. In: Proceedings of EuroCogSci 2007, pp. 608–613 (2007)

Multimodality Issues in Conversation Analysis of Greek TV Interviews

Maria Koutsombogera[1,2] and Harris Papageorgiou[1]

[1] Institute for Language & Speech Processing, Artemidos 6&Epidavrou,
15125 Athens, Greece
[2] University of Athens, Department of Linguistics, University Campus,
15784 Athens, Greece
{mkouts,xaris}@ilsp.gr

Abstract. This paper presents a study on multimodal conversation analysis of Greek TV interviews. Specifically, we examine the type of facial, hand and body gestures and their respective communicative functions in terms of feedback and turn management. Taking into account previous work on the analysis of non-verbal interaction, we describe the tools and the coding scheme employed, we discuss the distribution of the features of interest and we investigate the effect of the situational and conversational interview setting on the interactional behavior of the participants. Finally, we conclude with comments on future work and exploitation of the resulting resource.

Keywords: non-verbal/multimodal expressions, feedback, turn management, conversation analysis, interview corpus.

1 Introduction

Relations between distinct modalities in natural interaction have been thoroughly studied [1,2,3] in order to deeper understand research questions related to multimodal communication areas such as emotional behavior [4], human-avatar interaction [5,6] etc. In this paper we present a cross-disciplinary research on the communicative role of multimodal expressions in TV face-to-face interviews occurring in various settings.

In general, TV discussions present a mixture of characteristics oscillating between institutional discourse, semi-institutional discourse and casual conversation [7,8]. This media content spans a variety of discourse types such as information exchange, entertainment and casual talk. The setting in which the interview takes place, as well as the social and discursive roles of the speakers are features that formulate the discourse structure and further influence the interactants' conversational behavior in all its expressive dimensions (speech, hand and facial gestures etc.).

Our motivation is to identify and interpret gestural features that critically contribute to the conversational interaction. Specifically, we describe their interrelations as well as their distribution across different types of TV discussions in an attempt to find evidence about their potential systematic role. In this context, we take a first step towards the description and annotation of a multimodal corpus of Greek TV interviews, available for further development and exploitation.

A. Esposito et al. (Eds.): Multimodal Signals, LNAI 5398, pp. 40–46, 2009.
© Springer-Verlag Berlin Heidelberg 2009

2 Corpus Description

The corpus comprises 66 minutes of interviews extracted from 3 different Greek TV shows. Their structure consists of question-answer sequences performed by an interviewer (the *host*) to an interviewee (the *guest*). Apart from the commonly shared features, each interview is uniquely outlined by its setting, its topic, the roles and personalities of its speakers, their interests and their commitments.

The first interview (I1) takes place in a TV studio between the host and a politician and provides information concerning current political issues. It can be regarded as an institutionalized interaction, as it appears to be more standardized in role distribution and turn management predictability.

The second interview (I2) is a pre-filmed informal discussion in a classroom, where the guest (an entertainer) gives an account of social and personal issues and is subsequently confronted with the host's reactions and suggestions. Due to the spontaneous and intimate character of the interaction as well as a relatively lower degree of predictability, the interview is oriented towards casual conversation.

The third one (I3) is a discussion of intellectual bias between the host and a writer taking place in an office. It displays a semi-institutional character, because it is not strictly information-focused; it also promotes the personal and emotional involvement of both speakers, allowing spontaneous and unpredictable behavior to be expressed.

3 Coding Scheme

Multimodality is annotated by discriminating between the description of the form of non-verbal expressions and their respective communicative functions. The descriptive level comprises features related to hand gestures, facial expressions and body posture for each speaker involved, as well as their semiotic type.

At the functional level there are features encompassing the annotation of multimodal feedback and turn management, as well as multimodal relations between speech and a respective non-verbal expression [9]. The labeling of the elements of interest was based on the MUMIN coding scheme [10].

Table 1. Descriptive and functional attributes

Descriptive attributes				Functional attributes		
Facial display	Hand gesture	Body posture	Semiotic type	Feedback	Turn management	Multimodal relations
Gaze	Handedness	Torso	Deictic	Give	Turn gain	Repetition
Eyes	Trajectory		Non-deictic	Elicit	Turn end	Addition
Eyebrows			Iconic			Substitution
Mouth			Symbolic			Contradiction
Lips						Neutral
Head						

4　Annotation Process

The annotators' tasks involved the gradual annotation of the material in line with the coding scheme. Initially, the audio signal was extracted from the relevant video, orthographically transcribed and further enriched with information about pauses, non-speech sounds, etc. using Transcriber[1]. The output was imported to ELAN[2], the tool that was used for the entire video annotation, and it was ensured that the speech transcript was kept synchronized with the video.

The coders identified facial, hand and body gestures of interest marking their start and end points and assigned the respective tags according to their surface characteristics (e.g. smile, single hand up etc.) and their semiotic type at distinct annotation tracks. Next, they labeled the implied communicative functions based on the interconnection between the gestures and the corresponding utterance.

Finally, the data were revised in order to correct possible errors and to assess the consistency of the annotations throughout the corpus.

5　Annotation Output

The study of the annotated corpus reveals the multiple functions of non-verbal (NV) communication. Its significance lies in that it provides information and sheds light on the interplay between verbal and non-verbal signals. Speakers communicate numerous messages by the way they make use of NV expressions, which may repeat, complement, accent, substitute or contradict the verbal message. Moreover, NV means of communication outline the conversational profile of the speakers as they are a powerful means for self expression.

In order to interpret the NV behavior in an interview setting we have to clarify the subtle dynamics of the situations the speakers find themselves in; the content of the communication is framed by the perception of its context (environmental conditions where the interview takes place, identity/role of the participants, and their behaviors during interaction).

NV cues may also explicitly regulate the interaction, as they convey information about when speakers should take or give the turn. In that sense, they give signs of the effective function of the conversation and the degree of success of the interaction. Finally, through NV communication the speakers project their attitudes and feelings towards either their own statements (e.g. confidence about what they say) or to their interlocutor's statements.

In the interviews examined, we attested 1670 NV expressions. The speakers frequently employ simple or more complex multimodal expressions using their facial characteristics (gaze, eyebrows, nods etc.), hand gestures (single or both hands, fingers, shoulders etc.) and upper part of the body (leaning forward and backward) in order to reinforce their speech and express their emotions towards the uttered messages. However, the types and functions of the expressions may vary, as they depend on the role that the speakers assume, the constraints imposed by the host and the discursive nature of the show from which the interview is taken.

---

[1] http://trans.sourceforge.net/
[2] http://www.lat-mpi.eu/tools/elan/

Table 2. Number of non-verbal expressions attested in each interview and distribution between host and guest

Interview	Non-verbal expressions	Host	Guest
I1	613	40.5%	59.5%
I2	665	22.5%	77.5%
I3	392	35.4%	64.6%

5.1 Descriptive Features

A closer look on the data shows that there are repeated patterns that are independent of the message content. For example, there are standard gestures in opening and closing utterances as well as in the hosts' prefatory statements (the gaze direction and hand orientation are towards the interlocutor). This sort of standardized multimodal behavior is aligned to the succession of turns across time and may lead to the formulation of possible conversational multimodal scenarios.

For example, a common behavior by the interviewees in our data was that, when asked a question, they take some time to contemplate on their answer, remember or find an appropriate word. In this time span, they usually have an unfocused gaze (eyes fixed up/down, sometimes head turn away from the interviewer). When they finally take the turn, they gaze towards the host and move the hands or torso in order to denote that they are ready to answer. If they are willing to hold the turn they reinforce their speech with repeated hand gestures or eyebrows raising, while they are using mostly the eyes to elicit an acknowledgement or ensure that the host keeps up. Finally, they complete their turn either by gazing down, or by staring at the host. This kind of scenario describes a regular flow that is subject to modification in case of interruptions, overlapping talk, or strong objections and reactions that declare the speakers' emotional involvement.

Moreover, the turn extent of each interview has an effect in the production of NV expressions. In case of I1 the shifts are largely monitored, so the guest has to express his views in a restricted time interval, he cannot deviate from the agenda or be spontaneous, instead he is more reserved in his expressivity and makes a closed set of simple, accompanying gestures. Conversely, in I2 and I3 where the shifts and topics are more negotiated, the guests are entitled to elaborate on their views; they feel less restricted and thus more prone to produce a variety of facial and gestural expressions.

Semiotic types of NV expressions seem to be independent of the setting; they are however related to the content and the discursive features of the interview. For example, in I1 the politician builds his argumentation based on concrete facts and supports it mainly by non-deictic expressions. At the same time, in more casual discussions such as I2 and I3 a large part of the guests' talk involves narration, a discourse type that is complemented with iconic multimodal expressions. Deictic and symbolic types are quite equally distributed in the three interviews (cf. Table 3).

5.2 Communicative Functions

The correlations between the distinct modalities are captured through the multimodal relations and the annotation of the NV expressions with regards to feedback exchange and the coordination of turns as well.

Multimodal Relations. The annotation of the multimodal relations gives evidence of the contribution of NV expressions to the speakers' message. There is a relatively high percentage of NV expressions that complement the message by providing additional information that is not overtly expressed by speech only (addition) or by replacing unsaid words (substitution). The majority of substitution labels is related to acknowledgements and is represented mostly by facial displays that usually correspond to head nods or smiles. The repetition type comes next, and it is used to denote that no extra information is provided. Few relations were characterized as neutral, where the annotators believed that the NV expression has no significant contribution to the message. Finally, the contradiction relation is rarely used, namely in cases of irony. It is important to report that the contradiction type was found mainly in I1, possibly as a feature of argumentative speech, while it is rarely used in less institutionalized interviews such as I2 and I3.

Feedback. Multimodal feedback in terms of perception and acceptance[3] of the uttered message is usually expressed through gaze and nods rather than hand gestures. NV expressions of feedback-giving evolve in the course of time, as the speaker denotes that he has perceived the message, he is interested or willing to contribute and, as the turn is elaborated, he shows signs of certainty about the content of his talk, possibly by forming an opinion.

The topic of discussion and the role that the participants assume is related to the expression of their emotional and attitudinal feedback towards the message. Emotions and attitudes (e/a) such as joy and satisfaction are non-verbally expressed more overtly in I2 and I3 where the speakers feel more spontaneous. On the contrary, non-verbal declaration of e/a such as disappointment, anger etc. is manifested in I1 in the context of a strictly framed political discussion. E/a of surprise, certainty/uncertainty and interest are attributed to NV expressions of all participants and they seem to be independent of the interview type; they are rather related to the speaker's attitude towards a specific message content.

Turn Management. I1 is more host-controlled and therefore shows certain predictability in turn management, whereas I2 and I3 are more participant-shaped and present a relatively lower degree of predictability and weaker talk control.

Gestures and expressions that are evoked in turn management are different in type and frequency when they take place in a normal flow rather than overlapping talk. During overlapping speech there is a high density of annotated multimodal expressions; apart from prosodic features (e.g. higher intonation) the speakers engage all their expressive potentials (gestures, facial displays) to maintain their turn. In our annotated data, overlapping speech is usually triggered by a pause, a hold or a repair, which are often accompanied by an unfocused gaze or a head side turn. A common scenario is that the guest wants to hold the turn but sometimes he hesitates to answer or takes his time to focus, think or remember what to say. The host then takes advantage and he takes the turn. In most of the cases, the speaker who manages to gain the turn is the one who is most expressive.

---

[3] The annotation values for Feedback pertain to 3 groups: *perception*, *acceptance* and *emotions/attitudes*.

Table 3. Distribution of semiotic and communicative features over interview types

Attributes	Values	I1	I2	I3
Semiotic types	Deictic	5.2%	6.9%	**7.4%**
	Non Deictic	**88.1%**	73.1%	75.9%
	Iconic	4.6%	**15.9%**	13.8%
	Symbolic	2.1%	**4.1%**	2.9%
Multimodal relations	Repetition	15.6%	**17.8%**	6.8%
	Addition	51.7%	54.6%	**71.4%**
	Contradiction	**1.7%**	0.4%	0.3%
	Substitution	19.8%	19.9%	**20.2%**
	Neutral	**11.2%**	7.3%	1.3%
Turn management	Turn Take	**44.8%**	12.1%	16.4%
	Turn Yield	1.9%	8.2%	**9.2%**
	Turn Accept	2.7%	**8.8%**	7.4%
	Turn Hold	42.1%	**45.2%**	40.3%
	Turn Elicit	5.4%	**15.3%**	14.2%
	Turn Complete	3.1%	10.4%	**12.5%**

Moreover, In I1 we rarely see expressions related to the unbiased completion of the turn and its subsequent yielding to the interlocutor. In most of the times, the speakers take the turn without explicitly being asked to do so by their interlocutors.

6 Further Work and Exploitation

In order to provide more accurate and systematic descriptions of the multimodal features contributing to this kind of interaction we are planning to enrich the corpus with more interviews. The communicative function and role of speech features (disfluencies, prosody elements like pitch, loudness) should also be further explored.

Furthermore, we plan to exploit this multimodal corpus in our multimedia processing framework which allows the fusion of different metadata [11] in accordance with the typology and semantic characteristics of the original audiovisual material. In this respect, conversation analysis metadata can be further exploited in order to accommodate multimedia retrieval & summarization applications [12].

This kind of study may also provide descriptive cues for building believable interactive embodied agents for a variety of applications or friendly interfaces.

References

1. Ekman, P.: Emotional and Conversational Nonverbal Signals. In: Messing, L.S., Campbell, R. (eds.) Gesture, Speech and Sign, pp. 45–55. Oxford University Press, London (1999)
2. Kendon, A.: Gesture: Visible Action as Utterance. Cambridge University Press, Cambridge (2004)
3. MacNeill, D.: Hand and Mind: What Gestures Reveal About Thought. University of Chicago Press, Chicago (1992)

4. Douglas-Cowie, E., Cowie, R., Sneddon, I., Cox, C., Lowry, O., McRorie, M., Martin, J.-C., Devillers, L., Abrilian, S., Batliner, A.: The HUMAINE Database: Addressing the Collection and Annotation of Naturalistic and Induced Emotional Data. In: Paiva, A.C.R., Prada, R., Picard, R.W. (eds.) ACII 2007. LNCS, vol. 4738, pp. 488–500. Springer, Heidelberg (2007)
5. Poggi, I., Pelachaud, C., Magno Caldognetto, E.: Gestural Mind Markers in ECAs. In: Camurri, A., Volpe, G. (eds.) GW 2003. LNCS, vol. 2915, pp. 338–349. Springer, Heidelberg (2004)
6. Vilhjalmsson, H.: Augmenting Online Conversation through Automated Discourse Tagging. In: 6th annual minitrack on Persistent Conversation at the 38th HICSS, Hawaii (2005)
7. Heritage, J.: Conversation Analysis and Institutional Talk. In: Sanders, R., Fitch, K. (eds.) Handbook of Language and Social Interaction, pp. 103–146. Lawrence Erlbaum, New Jersey (2005)
8. Ilie, C.: Semi-institutional Discourse: The Case of Talk Shows. Journal of Pragmatics 33, 209–254 (2001)
9. Poggi, I., Magno Caldognetto, E.: A Score for the Analysis of Gestures in Multimodal Communication. In: Messing, L.S. (ed.) Proceedings of the Workshop on the Integration of Gesture and Language in Speech, Applied Science and Engineering Laboratories, pp. 235–244. Newark and Wilmington, Del (1996)
10. Allwood, J., Cerrato, L., Jokinen, K., Navarretta, C., Paggio, P.: The MUMIN Coding Scheme for the Annotation of Feedback, Turn Management and Sequencing Phenomena. Multimodal Corpora for Modeling Human Multimodal Behaviour. Journal on Language Resources and Evaluation 41(3-4), 273–287 (2007)
11. Papageorgiou, H., Prokopidis, P., Protopapas, A., Carayannis, G.: Multimedia Indexing and Retrieval Using Natural Language, Speech and Image Processing Methods. In: Stamou, G., Kollias, S. (eds.) Multimedia Content and the Semantic Web: Methods, Standards and Tools, pp. 279–297. Wiley, Chichester (2005)
12. Georgantopoulos, B., Goedemé, T., Lounis, S., Papageorgiou, H., Tuytelaars, T., Van Gool, L.: Cross-media summarization in a retrieval setting. In: LREC 2006 Workshop on Crossing media for improved information access, pp. 41–49 (2006)

Representing Communicative Function and Behavior in Multimodal Communication

Hannes Högni Vilhjálmsson

Center for Analysis and Design of Intelligent Agents (CADIA)
School of Computer Science, Reykjavík University
Kringlan 1, 103 Reykjavík, Iceland
hannes@ru.is

Abstract. In this paper I discuss how communicative behavior can be represented at two levels of abstraction, namely the higher level of communicative intent or function, which does not make any claims about the surface form of the behavior, and the lower level of physical behavior description, which in essence instantiates intent as a particular multimodal realization. I briefly outline the proposed SAIBA framework for multimodal generation of communicative behavior, which is an international research platform that fosters the exchange of components between different systems. The SAIBA framework currently contains a first draft of the lower level Behavior Markup Language (BML) and is starting work on the higher level Function Markup Language (FML). I also briefly explain the usefulness of this distinction by using examples of several implemented systems that each draws different strengths from it. These systems range from autonomous conversational agents to computer mediated communication.

Keywords: Communicative behavior, communicative function, multimodal communication, embodied conversational agents, mediated communication.

1 Introduction

There is an international community of researchers working on creating what has been called embodied conversational agents. These are autonomous agents that have a human-like embodiment, either graphical or physical, and possess the skill to engage people in face-to-face conversation [4]. One of the main challenges of this research is the proper coordination of verbal and nonverbal behavior, since face-to-face communication relies on the careful production of a wide range of multimodal cues that serve many important communicative functions. For example we often user our body to indicate that we would like the chance to say something and then while we speak, we often emphasize parts of our sentences with synchronized hand movement.

Research groups that work on embodied conversational agents at a high level, for example dialogue planning, have typically had to build the agent's body and implement an animation system from scratch that is capable of producing the right variety of communicative behavior that dialogue requires. Similarly, those research groups looking into sophisticated animation techniques for virtual humans or robots, have

A. Esposito et al. (Eds.): Multimodal Signals, LNAI 5398, pp. 47–59, 2009.

had a hard time finding high level "brains" that properly fit on top of their expressive bodies. Therefore the best looking embodiments often end up being animated through scripted behavior.

Building a fully functional and beautifully realized embodied conversational agent that is completely autonomous, is in fact a lot more work than a typical research group can handle alone. It may take individual research groups more than a couple of years to put together all the components of a basic system, where many of the components have to be built from scratch without being part of the core research effort.

Recognizing that collaboration and sharing of work between research groups would get full conversational systems up and running much quicker and reduce the reinvention of the wheel, an international group of researchers started laying the lines for a framework that would help make this happen. In particular, the emphasis of the group was on defining common interfaces in the multimodal behavior generation process for embodied conversational agents. While the seeds for this work were planted at the 2002 AAMAS workshop "Embodied conversational agents – let's specify and evaluate them!", the first official working meeting of the steering group took place at Reykjavik University in 2005 under the title "Representations for Multimodal Generation".

At this meeting the members of the group pooled their knowledge of various full agent systems and looked into what processes seemed common to all of them, identifying possible areas of reuse and employment of standard interfaces. The group proposed the so-called SAIBA framework as a result [12], [15]. This framework divides the overall behavior generation process into three sub-processes, each bringing the level of communicative intent closer to actual realization through the agent's embodiment (see Figure 1).

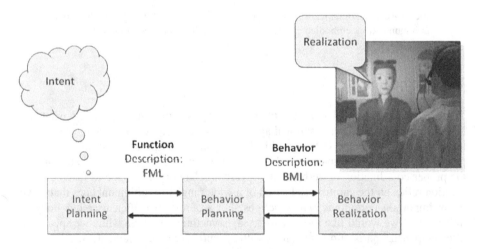

Fig. 1. The SAIBA framework for multimodal behavior generation, showing how the overall process consists of sub-processes at different levels of abstraction, starting with communicative intent and ending in actual realization in the agent's embodiment

In this framework lies an opportunity to define one interface at the high level, between intent planning and behavior planning, and another interface at the lower level, between behavior planning and behavior realization. The group then set out to start defining these interfaces, called Function Markup Language [10] and Behavior Markup Language [12], [14], respectively.

2 Communicative Function vs. Behavior

To appreciate and better understand the difference between communicative function, which is specified with FML, and communicative behavior, specified with BML, let's look at an example. This example is relatively extreme and is constructed solely for illustration, but not to show an actual system implementation.

If you want to tell someone a story about something that happened, you would first shape your communicative intent regarding the story, for example picking a recipient and then organizing major topics and key points in your mind based on who

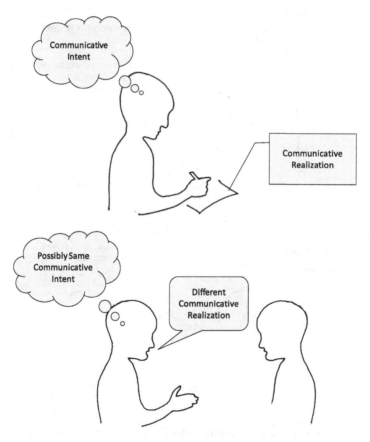

Fig. 2. The same communicative intent could get transformed into written form (top) or oral form (bottom)

the recipient is. If the recipient is not present, you may then decide to realize this communicative intent in writing. The intent is then transformed into concrete form, governed by rules of written discourse (see Figure 2, top). However, if the recipient suddenly shows up in person, you may decide to discard the written realization and instead engage in oral realization of that very same communicative intent. Now the delivery is governed by different rules, essentially creating a different concrete rendering of the original intent (see Figure 2, bottom). The more abstract form of the story stays intact, while the concrete form changes. This seems to indicate that it is useful to distinguish between these two levels of representation.

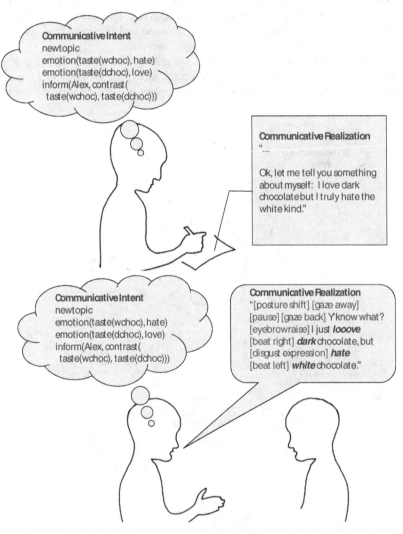

Fig. 3. A story about contrasting tastes gets realized in a letter (top) and face-to-face (bottom). Linguistic devices realize functions in the former, but nonverbal devices also serve functions in the latter.

To further illustrate this distinction, let's imagine that you wish to tell your friend Alex that you love dark chocolate but hate white chocolate, and want to emphasize this difference. Representing this at the level of communicative intent could produce something like the (made up) formal notation shown on the left side in Figure 3. This representation indicates the communicative functions that you wish to perform, starting with a function intended to introduce the new topic of chocolates. You then have a representation of your likes and dislikes, and finally the communicative function of informing Alex of the contrast between your tastes. When you turn this into writing, each function gets realized through some written device, some according to the conventions of letter writing, others through more general rules of grammar and coherent discourse. For example, the introduction of a new topic may manifest itself as the start of a new paragraph and the word "Ok" at the beginning of the first sentence (see top-right side in Figure 3).

If Alex shows up in person and oral delivery is used instead, each of the communicative functions now get realized through a new set of multimodal devices that become available. Of course some of them still involve the production of coherent words, but both the availability of new forms of multimodal expression and the new kind of discourse, call for a surprisingly different realization. For example, the switch to a new topic may now be accompanied by a visible shift in posture, and instead of relying completely on the words to carry the contrast between the likes and the dislikes, hand gestures play an important role (see right side in Figure 3).

This example shows what gets produced is the realization that best serves the original intent in a particular communication environment, given its unique constraints and conventions. In embodied conversational agents, it is helpful to have a way to represent communicative intent before the exact form is chosen, leaving behavior planning to a dedicated process, based on the particular context of delivery.

It is worth noting that dividing the production of human-like behavior into two distinct levels of representation has been attempted across various fields of study, and these levels have received different names. In Figure 4 we see on the left hand side various terms that have been used to describe communicative function at the higher level of abstraction, while on the right we have terms that describe the more concrete realization. The words in the two lists roughly correspond to each other, so that

Fig. 4. Terms used to describe communicative function at higher level of abstraction (left) and a more concrete level of realization (right)

for example the words meaning/sign often occur together. It is important to realize that these different terms exist and that it is quite unlikely that a single pair will become the standard usage. There are always going to be some slight differences in the interpretations of these words, but their purpose is the same: To create meaningful and useful levels of abstraction to better understand or produce discernable acts.

3 The Relationship

There is a large body of work that attempts to describe human behavior in terms of its functions in communication [2], [8], [9], [11]. By thinking about the functions, we start to see the bigger picture and construct whole systems of behavior that somehow seem connected or serve similar purpose. When looking at face-to-face conversation in particular, communicative functions seem to generally fall into one of three broad categories illustrated in Figure 5 [10]. The first category (A) has to do with the establishing, maintaining and closing the communication channel between participants. A communication channel is merely a metaphor for the social contract that binds people together in the common purpose of conversing. This category of functions has received many names, of which *interactional*, *envelope* and *management* functions have been popular [6], [11], [13]. Some examples of functions that fall into this category are given in Table 1A. The second category (B) covers the actual content that gets exchanged across a live communication channel. Given that the functions in category A are doing their job, those in B are made possible. Typically this is the deliberate exchange of information, which gets organized and packaged in chunks that facilitate uptake. The various functions in this category can be divided across the different organizational levels, from the largest organizational structure of discourse down to the specification of each proposition. This is shown in Table 1B. If the second category covers only deliberate exchange of information, then another category is needed that takes care of the various functions contributing to visible behavior giving off information, without deliberate intent. The third category (C) is perhaps a bit of a

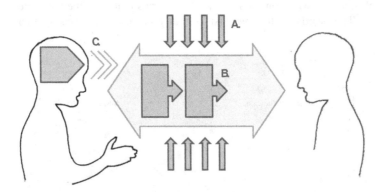

Fig. 5. General categories of communicative functions: Interaction Functions (A), Content Functions (B) and Mental States and Attitudes (C)

Table 1A. INTERACTION FUNCTIONS	
Function Category	**Example Functions**
Initiation / Closing	*react, recognize, initiate, salute-distant, salute-close, break-away, ...*
Turn-taking	*take-turn, want-turn, yield-turn, give-turn, keep-turn, assign-turn, ratify-turn, ...*
Speech-Act	*inform, ask, request, ...*
Grounding	*request-ack, ack, repair, cancel, ...*

Table 1B. CONTENT FUNCTIONS	
Function Category	**Example Functions**
Discourse Structure	*topics and segments*
Rhetorical Structure	*elaborate, summarize, clarify, contrast, ...*
Information Structure	*rheme, theme, given, new, ...*
Propositions	*any formal notation (e.g. "own(A,B)")*

Table 1C. MENTAL STATE AND ATTITUDE FUNCTIONS	
Function Category	**Example Functions**
Emotion	*anger, disgust, fear, joy, sadness, surprise, ...*
Interpersonal Relation	*framing, stance, ...*
Cognitive Processes	*difficulty to plan or remember*

catch-all category, but generally deals with functions describing mental states and attitudes, which in turn may affect the manner in which other functions get realized or give rise to their own independent behavior. Table 1C lists some examples of these.

Now that we have seen that each conversation is governed by a system of communicative functions carried out by participants, we must ask next how they manifest themselves as discernable behavior. What are the rules that map functions to supporting behaviors?

In order to answer this question, scientists generally need to engage in a four step process for each of the communicative functions they wish to map. The first step is the literature search where it is established whether this function has been studied before and existing empirical results provide enough evidence for certain behavior mapping rules. Keep in mind that prior studies may have been performed in situations that are different from those currently being modeled, and therefore it may be necessary to make a few assumptions about how well the data generalizes, or repeat the study in a different setting. If a study is to be repeated or a new study is called for, the second step involves gathering new data. Data is gathered with a good video and audio recording of a communicative event that strikes a balance between being completely naturally occurring and somewhat engineered to ensure a context that matches the one being modeled. But even if the situation is engineered, the subjects being recorded should not be aware of what functions and behaviors are being studied to avoid biased behavior. Once the data has been gathered, the third step is the coding of that data. This is done in at least two distinct passes, preferably with two separate coders. One pass through the data only annotates what is going on at the level of communicative intent or function. For example, one could annotate all places where it is apparent from the transcript that the subjects are changing the topic. On a second separate pass, a particular behavior is annotated, using only the modality of that behavior. For example, looking through the video with the audio turned off and without seeing any previous annotation or transcript, one can annotate the occurrences of head nods. The last step is then to look at these annotations together and understand how well, if at all, the annotated function seems to predict the occurrence of the annotated behavior. Table 4 shows a few examples of communicative functions and how they have been correlated with visible behavior.

Strictly speaking, it is not correct to talk about the mapping from function to behavior as absolute rules. In fact, they are merely regularities that have been

Table 2. Example Mapping Rules	
rheme/new	Gestures are more likely to occur with new material than given material [5]
emphasis	Emphasis commonly involves raising or lowering of the eyebrows [2]
new-topic	People often change posture when they change the topic of conversation [3]
give-turn	Speaker usually selects next speaker with gaze near the end of their own turn (Kendon, 1990)
take-turn	Speakers generally break eye-contact at turn beginning [1]
request-ack/ack	Speaker looks at listeners and raise their eyebrows when they want feedback and listeners raise eyebrows in response [8]

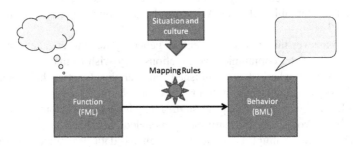

Fig. 6. Rules that map functions to behavior assume a certain context like the social situation and culture

discovered empirically, but there are always going to be some exceptions. We tend to talk about them as rules because that is often how they are implemented in embodied conversational agents. When we apply these rules inside the agents, we are not only assuming they occur without exception, but we are also assuming a certain context that makes the rule applicable, for example a particular culture or social situation (see Figure 6).

4   Applications

To provide an idea of how a SAIBA-like framework with a clear division between function and behavior can contribute to working systems, we'll take a quick look at three different applications where FML and BML play an important role.

The first one is a classic embodied conversational agent where we have a human user interacting with a graphical representation of the agent on a large wall-size display. The agent is capable of receiving multimodal input and produce multimodal output in near real-time, creating the sense of full face-to-face conversation with the human user. In this application, a pipeline architecture is possible where the multimodal input from the user is first described using something like BML (see Figure 7). A special Understanding Module interprets the behavior in the current context (including situation and culture) and produces an abstract description of the user's communicative intent in FML. The agent's decisions about how to respond are then made purely at the abstract level inside a central Decision Module. Decisions are similarly described in FML, and finally a Generation Module maps the agent's intended functions into behavior, visible to the human user, using the current context. Rea, the real-estate agent, was developed with this architecture [6]. BML and FML did not exist at the time, but corresponding representations were used based on the KQML messaging standard.

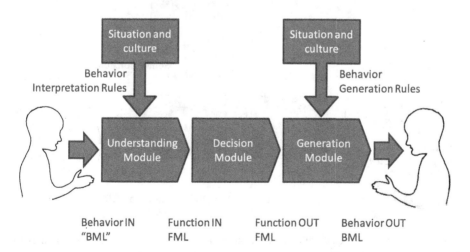

Fig. 7. An embodied conversational agent architecture where the central Decision Module only deals with an abstract representation of intent

One benefit of creating an agent in this fashion, is that the abstract decision making module, which can be quite complex, is isolated from the surface form of behavior, both on the input side and the output side. It may therefore be easier to adapt this agent to interacting in different cultures or even use different means for communication, like calling the user on the phone instead of interacting face-to-face.

Another application is a tool for animators that wish to make a character speak lines from a script and produce appropriate and synchronized nonverbal behavior. The system can then analyze the text to be spoken and look for various linguistic devices (i.e. behavior) that have been shown to be associated with particular communicative functions (see Figure 8). These functions are then annotated in the text using FML. Finally a Generation Module receives the annotated text and applies mapping rules to produce BML that carries out those functions, just like the example with the conversational agent above. Since the functions line up with certain parts of the spoken text, the behaviors that support those functions will coincide with the same parts. The BML can be used to drive animation in real-time or schedule behavior clips in an off-line 3D rendering tool like Maya. It can also be used to simply annotate the script with behavior annotations that a human animator can read and use as suggestions. The BEAT toolkit used this architecture, and did in fact use an early version of BML and FML for annotation purposes [7].

The final application mention here is real-time computer-mediated-communication. In this situation we have people communicating with other people over some kind of a communication channel that is narrower than a typical face-to-face conversation. For example, a person may be sending written messages to a friend over instant messaging. By using the same technique as the animation toolkit described above, the mediating system could analyze the sender's message and annotate communicative

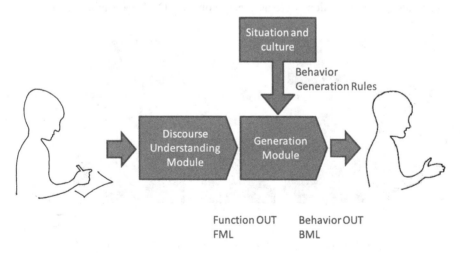

Fig. 8. A script is annotated with communicative functions that a generation module uses to produce appropriate animation

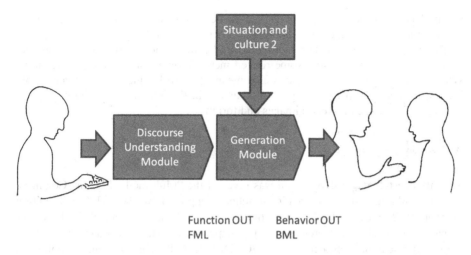

Fig. 9. Communicative functions annotated in a real-time chat message help produce an animated avatar that augments the delivery

functions (see Figure 9). Once the message arrives at the recipient's computer, a Generation Module can look at the message along with the function annotation, and generate a realization of the message that best supports the intended communication. For example, if the sender has an animated avatar, the Generation Module could deliver the message as if it was being spoken by the avatar and produce all the supporting nonverbal behavior according to the FML to BML mapping rules. Interestingly, these mapping rules could be different on different recipient computers, so the same message sent to two different continents could result in two different avatar performances on recipient computers, reflecting the local culture and setting. The Spark system, for group communication and collaboration, is implemented in this manner and uses an early version of BML and FML [16].

5 Conclusions

There is a growing group of researchers that conspires to build a horde of virtual humans capable of mingling socially with humanity. Like in all good conspiracy plots, a plan to make this possible is already underway, namely the construction of a common framework for multimodal behavior generation that allows the researchers to pool their efforts and speed up construction of whole multimodal interaction systems. The overall framework is called SAIBA, and within it, two important interfaces are being defined: FML and BML. FML describes communicative function at the level of intent, regardless of surface behavior, whereas BML describes the surface form which then is realized by an animation engine. This division into two levels of abstraction has helped scientists to make sense of human social and linguistic behavior in the past, but it is also very useful in modern applications that either participate in or support multimodal communication. We are still at an early stage of defining SAIBA and its interfaces, but the growing interest and some promising early tools, are indication that we may be onto something important. Only time will tell.

The purpose of this paper is to clarify the distinction between function and behavior, as well as outlining some related methodologies and system architectures. While providing some answers, it is also meant to provoke questions and get people interested in joining the ongoing discussion within the SAIBA community. A good starting point are the online wiki pages and forums[1].

Acknowledgements

The talk that this paper is based on was given at the "Multimodal Signals: Cognitive and Algorithmic Issues" international school supported by the EU COST Action number 2102. Special thanks go to the COST 2102 management chair, Professor Anna Esposito. The ideas presented in this paper are drawn from collaborations with numerous researchers, especially at RU/CADIA, USC/ISI and MIT, and of course in the SAIBA community. My work is supported by the Icelandic Centre for Research grant number 080027011.

References

1. Argyle, M., Cook, M.: Gaze and mutual gaze. Cambridge University Press, Cambridge (1976)
2. Argyle, M., Ingham, R., Alkema, F., et al.: The Different Functions of Gaze. Semiotica (1973)
3. Cassell, J., Nakano, Y., Bickmore, T., et al.: Non-Verbal Cues for Discourse Structure. In: Proceedings of the 41st Annual Meeting of the Association of Computational Linguistics, pp. 106–115 (2001)
4. Cassell, J., Sullivan, J., Prevost, S., et al. (eds.): Embodied conversational agents. MIT Press, Cambridge (2000)
5. Cassell, J., Steedman, M., Badler, N., et al.: Modeling the Interaction between Speech and Gesture (1994)
6. Cassell, J., Bickmore, T., Campbell, L., et al.: More than just a Pretty Face: Conversational Protocols and the Affordances of Embodiment. In: Knowledge-Based Systems, vol. 14, pp. 55–64. Elsevier, Amsterdam (2001)
7. Cassell, J., Vilhjalmsson, H., Bickmore, T.: BEAT: The Behavior Expression Animation Toolkit. In: SIGGRAPH, pp. 477–486. ACM Press, New York (2001)
8. Chovil, N.: Discourse-Oriented Facial Displays in Conversation. Research on Language and Social Interaction 25, 163–194 (1991)
9. Fehr, B.J., Exline, R.V.: Social visual interaction: A conceptual and literature review. In: Siegman, A.W., Feldstein, S. (eds.) Nonverbal Behavior and Communication, pp. 225–326. Lawrence Erlbaum Associates, Inc., Hillsdale (1987)
10. Heylen, D., Kopp, S., Marsella, S., et al.: The Next Step Towards a Functional Markup Language. In: Proceedings of Intelligent Virtual Agents 2008. Springer, Heidelberg (2008)
11. Kendon, A.: Conducting interaction: Patterns of behavior in focused encounters. Cambridge University Press, New York (1990)

---

[1] http://wiki.mindmakers.org/projects:saiba:main

12. Kopp, S., Krenn, B., Marsella, S.C., Marshall, A.N., Pelachaud, C., Pirker, H., Thórisson, K.R., Vilhjálmsson, H.H.: Towards a Common Framework for Multimodal Generation: The Behavior Markup Language. In: Gratch, J., Young, M., Aylett, R.S., Ballin, D., Olivier, P. (eds.) IVA 2006. LNCS, vol. 4133, pp. 205–217. Springer, Heidelberg (2006)
13. Thorisson, K.: Gandalf: An Embodied Humanoid Capable of Real-Time Multimodal Dialogue with People. In: 1st International Conference on Autonomous Agents, pp. 536–537. ACM, New York (1997)
14. Vilhjálmsson, H.H., Cantelmo, N., Cassell, J., Chafai, N.E., Kipp, M., Kopp, S., Mancini, M., Marsella, S.C., Marshall, A.N., Pelachaud, C., Ruttkay, Z., Thórisson, K.R., van Welbergen, H., van der Werf, R.J.: The Behavior Markup Language: Recent Developments and Challenges. In: Pelachaud, C., Martin, J.-C., André, E., Chollet, G., Karpouzis, K., Pelé, D. (eds.) IVA 2007. LNCS, vol. 4722, pp. 99–111. Springer, Heidelberg (2007)
15. Vilhjalmsson, H., Stacy, M.: Social Performance Framework. In: Workshop on Modular Construction of Human-Like Intelligence at the 20th National AAAI Conference on Artificial Intelligence, AAAI (2005)
16. Vilhjalmsson, H.: Augmenting Online Conversation through Automatice Discourse Tagging. In: HICSS 6th Annual Minitrack on Persistent Conversation. IEEE, Los Alamitos (2005)

Using the iCat as Avatar in Remote Meetings

Dirk Heylen, Mannes Poel, and Anton Nijholt

Human Media Interaction, University of Twente
PO Box 217, 7500 AE Enschede
The Netherlands
{heylen,mpoel,anijholt}@ewi.utwente.nl

Abstract. We compared two ways of remote participation in a meeting. One in which a video-connection existed between the remote participant and the collocated participants and one in which the remote participant was represented by an iCat. We asked the participants to rate the conversations on various dimensions. The remote participants tended to prefer the meetings with the iCat whereas the co-located participants preferred the video connection on most dimensions.

1 Introduction

In this paper we present an analysis of recordings of three-party conversations in which two participants were co-located in the same room and the third participant was in another room. We made recordings of two conditions, which we will refer to as VIDEO and ICAT. In the first condition, we used two cameras in the room of the co-located participants, each directed at one of the participants (see Figure 1). The two video streams were displayed on a computer screen in front of the remote participant. In this condition, the co-located participants could see the image of the remote participants on a computer screen. The image was taken from a webcam placed on top of the computer screen of the remote participant. This set-up more or less resembles a typical video-conferencing situation.

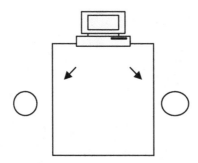

Fig. 1. Schematic view of the co-located participants' room in the VIDEO condition. Circles represent co-located participants sitting at opposite sides of the table (the rectangle), with two cameras pointed at them (the arrows). In the ICAT condition the computer screen is replaced by an iCat and the cameras are removed.

A. Esposito et al. (Eds.): Multimodal Signals, LNAI 5398, pp. 60–66, 2009.

Fig. 2. The ICAT condition

In the ICAT condition, the computer screen in the co-located participants' room was replaced by an iCat[1] that was controlled by the remote participant. The iCat thus functioned as an avatar representing the remote participant. For the remote participant the view on the co-located participants' room now came from the camera positioned in the nose of the iCat.

The remote-participant had several options available to control the iCat. The head of the iCat could be turned in the direction of either of the participants or to the middle of the room. The participant could also have the iCat shake or nod its head and could choose to make the iCat look amazed (raised eyebrows) or smile.

Comparing settings of remote communication in this way allows us to study the effects of manipulating technologies that mediate the communication process comparing the different affordances that each of them offers. The effects we are interested in concern changes in how the conversation proceeds and changes in the appreciation of the communication by the participants. What do participants do differently? What parts of the technological affordances do they use? What do they like or dislike about the opportunities? Our goal is to reach a better understanding of face-to-face conversation and of the need for facial expressions, gaze in processes such as grounding and addressing. This understanding may allows us to improve upon the ways to communicate remotely.

The paper is structured as follows. In the next section, we look at the two conditions in more detail in terms of the affordances offered and present some conjectures about how we expect the participants to behave and appreciate the settings. Next, we present details about the experiment and the measures. This is followed by a section on results and analysis.

2 Remote Presence

Mediated communication far outnumbers face to face conversations in our present lives. It can take the form of exchanges of information through telephone, e-mail, newspapers, television, chat, podcasts, blogs, tele- and videoconferencing, or involve meetings in 3D worlds such as Second Life or in on-line games. It is a common

---

[1] http://www.research.philips.com/technologies/syst_softw/robotics/index.html

observation that these mediated forms of communication offer less rich interactions than face-to-face interactions, mainly because of the inability to convey nuances through nonverbal means of communication and gaze, or because the intimate feedback loop between interlocutors is tampered with in these forms of communication ([2,4,6,7,8]. In studies on Computer Mediated Communication [9] these differences are typically seen as shortcomings and new technologies are introduced to overcome them.

The differences between face-to-face and mediated conversation can be described in terms of the 10 dimensions that characterize direct spontaneous conversation according to [1]: co-presence, visibility, audibility, instantaneity, evanescence, recordlessness, simultaneity, extemporaneity, self-determination and self-expression. In the two conditions that we are studying, one of the participants is remote and thus differs with respect to face-to-face conversations on the dimension of co-presence. In the VIDEO condition, the remote participant can see the others and vice versa through a video connection. However, the view is fixed through the camera-position and the view of the environment is thus severely limited. Eye-contact is also not possible. In the ICAT condition, the co-located participants cannot see the remote participant, but can only see the iCat perform the instructions that are given to it by the remote participant. The view of the remote participant is limited to three options: looking at one participant, the middle of the table or to the other participant. In contrast to the VIDEO condition, the remote participant can thus only look at one co-located participant at the same time [4,8]. On many dimensions one could argue that there are no special differences with respect to face-to-face interactions, but with respect to the two final ones some peculiar aspects can be noted. The iCat can be thought of as a puppet through which the remote participant speaks to the others. As a puppet, the iCat speaks not for itself (as one might consider in the case of an autonomously operating robot) but as a messenger controlled by the remote participant.

The possibilities of nonverbal expressivity of the remote participant are severely limited to the few facial expressions and head movements that can be made. By being able to turn the head of the iCat in the direction of one or the other co-located participant, the remote participant could signal attention or who is being addressed. Agreement and disagreement or affirming or negating could be signaled by nods and shakes. Facial expressions are limited to attitudinal reactions of enjoyment and surprise. One can expect the two conditions to differ in a number of respects, both in the way the communication proceeds and in the way it is perceived and evaluated. In our current analysis of the data we looked at effects on grounding, addressing, turn-taking and feelings of co-presence [10].

With respect to grounding, the question is whether the participants feel that it is easy to acknowledge contributions and whether it is more difficult to receive acknowledgements of contributions. In the ICAT condition the acknowledgements by the remote participant can be given verbally through nodding and shaking the head of the iCat. Also the facial expressions can provide feedback. All of these, however, need to be consciously executed by the remote participant, whereas in the VIDEO condition, the facial expressions can provide a running commentary to what is being discussed.

Gaze plays an important role in addressing. Goodwin [5] observed how at the beginning of a turn, speakers may try to achieve mutual gaze with the interlocutor to make clear who they address and get acknowledgment of this. In the VIDEO condition it is not possible for the remote participant to indicate who is the intended addressee by nonverbal means but in the ICAT condition, manipulating the head orientation of the iCat can be used in this way.

The controls for the iCat that were implemented in this set-up do not allow the remote participant to signal turn-requests with the nonverbal means that people usually use in conversations [3]. In the VIDEO condition, posture shifts and other visual cues for turn-taking, are visible to the co-located participants, however.

The effects on grounding, addressing, turn-taking, and other aspects of the conversation contribute to the general perception of co-presence: the feeling of the interactants that they perceive the others and the others perceive them. The iCat and the video connection differ as media in how they are able to connect people. This feeling will often be different for the co-located and the remote participant, particularly if the affordances of the media are not the same for both parties.

3 Data

We invited four teams of three participants to each conduct two meetings[2]. Two of the teams first conducted a meeting in the VIDEO condition followed by a meeting in the ICAT condition. The order was reversed for the other two teams. Each meeting lasted between 10 to 15 minutes. The teams were given separate tasks for the two meetings. The first task concerned the discussion about the preferred buttons to go on a remote control. Each participant was told to defend a particular favorite. The second task involved a discussion about the shape and colour of the control. The remote participant got instructions on how to use the interface to control the iCat and was shown the effects of the actions.

In the next section we discuss the results of our analysis of the data. We will discuss the use of the controls of the iCat by the remote participant and the various questionnaires that were presented to the participants.

4 Results and Analysis

Table 1 shows the number of times a participant (A-D) used a particular control for the iCat. It appears from the table that of the four participants, B deviated considerably from the others in that the others used the controls more than two (and D even three) times as often.

All participants used the head orientation controls the most. For each of them this constituted more than half of the actions. In total 106 out of the total of 177 actions were head movement actions. Left and Right movements were widely preferred above the movement to the center. With respect to the other two head movements, nods and shakes, the distribution is about equal, except for participant C who lets the iCat nod its head 8 times but lets it shake its head only once. The expressive controls for smile and eye-brow raise are used about as often as those for nod and shake, with about the same amount of smiles and eye-brows occurring for each of the participants.

---

[2] The experiment was carried out by two BSc students Frans van der Veeken and Feitze de Vries (http://referaat.cs.utwente.nl/new/papers.php?confid=9).

Table 1. Each row shows the number of times a particular remote participant used the control for the iCat

Participant	Left	Center	Right	Nod	Shake	Smile	Amazed	Total
A	14	3	14	4	4	6	5	50
B	6	1	4	3	1	3	2	20
C	14	7	11	8	1	3	3	47
D	14	4	14	7	8	6	7	60
Total	48	15	43	22	14	18	17	177

Table 2. Ratings of the quality of the interactions

		ICAT	VIDEO
Influence	C	3.3	**3.9**
(rate your influence in the meeting)	R	**3.8**	3.3
Satisfaction	C	2.7	**3.2**
	R	**3.3**	2.9
Turn-taking	C	3.4	**4.0**
(how well did turn-taking go)	R	2.8	**3.3**
Addressing	C	3.4	**4.1**
(was it easy to address someone)	R	**3.5**	2.3
Getting Addressed	C	3.4	**4.3**
(was it clear you were addressed)	R	**3.5**	3.3
Involved in conversation	C	3.1	**4.4**
(rate your involvement)	R	3.5	**4.0**
Involved in task	C	2.6	**4.0**
	R	**3.5**	3.0
Grounding	C	**6.3**	4.8
(awareness of reactions of others)	R	3.8	**4.3**
Similar F2F	C	**5.4**	4.0
	R	4.3	**6.5**

Our analysis of one of the ICAT meetings showed that the remote participant used the head orientation to direct the camera to the participant that was speaking. One participant was looked at 78% of the time he was speaking and the other was looked at 97% of the time he was speaking.

When asked which controls the remote participants found most useful, they answered *nod*, followed by *shake*, *smile* and *surprise*. They found the interface to control the iCat easy to use and rated it on average 4.25 out of 5.

We asked the participants to fill out questionnaires with various questions. The results are presented in the table below. Participants rated the quality of the meetings in both conditions on a five point scale, except for the last two questions which were rated on a 7 point scale.

The table shows the average ratings for each dimension of the co-located (C) and remote (R) participants separately. For each line the highest figure appears in boldface. From this table it becomes clear that for all questions except the last two, the co-located participants prefer the VIDEO condition. The remote participant, on the other hand prefers the ICAT condition, except when asked about turn-taking, involvement in conversation and for the last two questions on awareness of others and similarity to face-to-face. This can be explained by the fact, that the remote participant has no global view of the co-located participants in the ICAT condition (negative effect on awareness) and needs to communicate through an artificial interface in this condition as well (negative effect on similarity). The co-located participants find talking to an anthropomorphic iCat closer to face-to-face conversations than interacting with the remote participant through a video connection.

5 Conclusion and Future Work

In on-line games and virtual communities, people use avatars as representations of themselves to communicate with each other. There have been a few suggestions in the literature to use avatars in remote meetings as well, instead of using the ordinary means of video conferencing. In our studies, we are looking at the effects of manipulating the communicative expressivity of avatars on the appreciation of the communication and on how the conversations proceed differently. In the case of the iCat, we found that the participants controlling the iCat like it better than the participants that are faced with it. The results reported on in this paper were primarily based on the analysis of the questionnaires that the participants filled out. Currently, we are processing the video's to see in more detail how the conversations proceeded, looking at the timing and placement of the nonverbal controls that were offered.

Acknowledgements

This work is supported by the European IST Programme Project FP6-0033812 (AMIDA). This paper only reflects the authors' views and funding agencies are not liable for any use that may be made of the information contained herein.

References

1. Clark, H.H.: Using Language. Cambridge University Press, Cambridge (1996)
2. Clayes, E.L., Anderson, A.H.: Real faces and robot faces: The effects of representation on computer mediated communication. International Journal of Human-Computer Studies 65(6), 480–496 (2007)
3. Duncan, S.: Some signals and rules for taking speaking turns in conversations. Journal of Personality and Social Psychology 23, 283–292 (1972)
4. Garau, M., Slater, M., Bee, S., Sassa, M.A.: The Impact of eye-gaze on communication using avatars. In: Proceedings of the SIGCHI Conference on Human Factors in Computing Systems, pp. 309–316 (2001)
5. Goodwin, C.: Conversational organisation, Interaction between Speakers and Hearers. Academic Press, New York (1981)
6. Isaacs, E.A., Tang, J.C.: What video can and can't do for collaborations: a case study. In: Proceedings of the first ACM International Conference on Multimedia, pp. 199–206 (1993)

7. Nowak, K., Biocca, F.: The effect of the Agency and Anthropomorphism on Users' sense of Telepresence, Copresence and Social Presence in Virtual Environments. Presence 12(5) (2003)
8. Sellen, A.J.: Remote Conversations: the effects of mediating talk with technology. Human-Computer Interaction 10, 401–444 (1995)
9. Whittaker, S.: Theories and Methods in Mediated Communication. In: Graesser, A., Gernsbacher, M., Goldman, S. (eds.) The Handbook of Discourse Processes, pp. 243–286. Erlbaum, NJ (2002); Richardson, D.C., Dale, R.: Grounding dialogue: eye movments reveal the coordination of attention during conversation and the effects of common ground, COGSCY 2006 (2006)
10. Zhao, S.: Towards a Taxonomy of Copresence. Presence 12(5), 445–455 (2003)

Using Context to Disambiguate Communicative Signals

Mark ter Maat and Dirk Heylen

Human Media Interaction, University of Twente
PO Box 217, 7500 AE Enschede
The Netherlands
{maatm,d.k.j.heylen}@ewi.utwente.nl

Abstract. After perceiving multi-modal behaviour from a user or agent a conversational agent needs to be able to determine what was intended with that behaviour. Contextual variables play an important role in this process. We discuss the concept of context and its role in interpretation, analysing a number of examples. We show how in these cases contextual variables are needed to disambiguate multi-modal behaviours. Finally we present some basic categories in which these contextual variables can be divided.

Keywords: Communicative signals, functions, intentions, context, disambiguation, contextual elements.

1 Disambiguating Signals

In the world of virtual, agents Embodied Conversational Agents (ECA's) take a special place [3]. These agents are capable of detecting and understanding multi-modal behaviour of a user, reason about it, determine what the most appropriate multi-modal response is and act on this.

The SAIBA framework has been proposed as a general reference framework for ECA's in a collaboration of several research groups[1]. In this framework the communicative function, the high-level intention, is separated from the actual multi-modal behaviour (a communicative signal) that is used to express the communicative function. For example, the function 'request turn' is conceptually separated from the act of raising a hand and breathing in to signal that you want to speak. This separation is realized by putting the responsibilities of the functions and signals in different modules. As a result, the modules in the system should be capable of communicating these functions and signals to each other. This communication is performed using specification languages called FML, Function Markup Language, which is used to specify the conversational function, and BML, Behaviour Markup Language, which is the high level specification of the actual multi-modal behaviour. In the current debate about FML an important issue that is being raised is what constitutes a function and how should they be distinguished from contextual elements [8].

---

[1] http://wiki.mindmakers.org/projects:saiba:main/

A. Esposito et al. (Eds.): Multimodal Signals, LNAI 5398, pp. 67–74, 2009.

Contextual elements consist of all the elements that surround the communicative behaviour that is being analyzed. This includes, for example, facial expressions that appear at the same time, the fact that the previous sentence was a question, or the fact that the conversation is taking place in a noisy environment.

Ideally an ECA is capable of perceiving and interpreting the multi-modal behaviours of a human user (or another virtual human): the speech, gestures, facial expressions etc. We call the multi-modal behaviours that an ECA can perceive (detected) "signals". The intelligent agent will try to find out what was meant by the behaviours, which means trying to map the signals on the communicative functions that lie behind them.

As is well-known, determining the intended communicative function from detected signals is not a trivial problem as the same signal may occur in different contexts with widely diverging meanings. For example, if you detect that the other person (who is currently speaking) is suddenly gazing at you, then this might be part of a behaviour complex that signals the intention of a turn offer [12,2] or it may indicate a request for feedback [1,8,10]. In many cases it is immediately clear from the context why the behaviour was performed. But what is context? And what kind of elements does it consists of?

In this article we analyse the notion of context, the influence it has on behaviour selection and behaviour interpretation, and the overlap it has with the definition of signals. Finally, a rough categorisation of the elements that should appear in the context is presented. But first some background information about the use of context is provided.

2   Background

The notion of context in interpretation is an important topic in the literature. In this section we briefly discuss three perspectives on context. The first from the linguistic literature ([9] and [7]). The second from the literature on nonverbal communication ([5]) and the last from the ECA community ([11]).

In [9] the author describes several linguistic situations in which the context should be used, and these situations appear on different levels. For example, on the syntactic level, words can have multiple lexical categories. A word like *phone* can be a noun ('Please pick up the phone') or a verb ('I will phone you tomorrow'). The surrounding words (forming the context of the word *phone*) have to be used to determine the exact lexical class of the word.

On a semantic level the same situation occurs. Also the meaning of a single word also depends on the context. And on an even higher level, the grammatical mood of a sentence also depends on the context. An utterance such as 'I want you to come here' (example taken from [9]) is mostly classified as a declarative sentence, but under the right circumstances (say, a mother that, after a few attempts, tries to call her child with this sentence spoken in a very fierce voice) can also be classified as a command (an imperative sentence).

In [7], consider various aspects of what they call the *context of situation*. This is a reference to the environment in which discourse is situated, and to the extra-linguistic factors that have a relation to the text produced itself. This environment is used to put the text into perspective. For example (taken from [7]) a set of non-cohesive sentences might suddenly become cohesive when it appears in a language textbook as an example set.

According to the authors, the context of situation can be described with three different components: the field, the mode and the tenor. The field is the current topic that is being discussed, the mode is about the communication channel (type of channel, the genre of the interaction), and the tenor is about the participants in the discourse and their relationships to each other. They argue that by describing the context of situation with these three parameters a text can be understood correctly as a coherent passage of discourse.

But not only text needs context. In [5] the authors discuss various aspects concerning the interpretation of non-verbal behaviour. One element of their analysis is the usage of the behaviour, which means looking at the regular and consistent circumstances that surround the non-verbal acts, which basically is the context of the act. These circumstances can be grouped into several categories:

External condition – refers to environmental circumstances, for example the setting (home, work, interview, etc).

Relationship to verbal behaviour – specifies the relationship of the non-verbal with the verbal behaviour, for example if the non-verbal behaviour repeats, augments, accents or contradicts certain words.

Awareness – defines whether the person knows he is performing a particular non-verbal act at the moment he does it.

Intentionality – specifies whether the actor does the act deliberately or not.

External feedback – defines signals that the listener sends back to the speaker to acknowledge the fact that he perceives and evaluates the speaker's actions.

Type of information conveyed – refers to the different types of non-verbal behaviour.

  Informative – an act (which may or may not be intentional) that provides the listener with some information. This means that the act at least bears some meaning for the listener.

  Communicative – a consciously intended act by the sender to transmit a specific message to the listener

  Interactive – an act by one person in an interaction which clearly tries to modify or influence the interactive behaviour of the other person(s).

In [11] the authors analyse the context of multi-modal behaviour of interactive virtual agents. They argue that mapping FML to BML, in other words, choosing the concrete behaviour to perform as an agent when a conversational function is provided, cannot be done without any context. For example, saying hello in the morning ('good morning') is different than in the evening ('good evening'), and this difference can only be made when the local time is known. To add context to the mapping they suggest a new representation, namely CML: Context Markup Language. This language is specifically created to communicate context and consists of three parts: the Dialogue context, the Environmental context and the Cultural context. The dialogue context includes the history of the dialogue, the current topic, the level of tension between characters, etc. The environmental context contains such things as the time of day, the current setting, etc. The cultural context contains "information on the culturally appropriate way to express certain communicative functions".

3   Towards Contextual Elements

In this section the notion of 'context' is discussed, with the intention of finding out what exactly is context and what it consists of. At the end of this section the elements that make up the context (and are used to disambiguate signals) are categorized into three types. To find these elements and categories, this section starts with the question of how to delimitate what constitutes a signal. What elements are part of a signal and which are part of the context? Next the effect that context has in a conversation is discussed and the problem of ambiguity is addressed.

3.1   Context or Part of the Signal

An important distinction to make when talking about signals and their context is what exactly should be defined as context and what should be considered part of a signal.

What constitutes a particular signal is hard to define as this faces two problems: segmentation and classification. The first is the act of determining what elements are part of a particular signal. As we are trying to associate signals with meanings, the question is "What are the meaning-bearing units that we are talking about?" The input of a conversational agent usually is a constant stream of multi-modal behaviours (position and movement of limbs, spoken words, etc). To identify signals in this stream, it has to be cut at certain boundaries. But segmentation not only consists of determining the boundaries of a signal, but also determining which elements within those boundaries are parts of a signal. Is the movement of the eyebrows a single signal? Or should that signal include the complete facial expression? And should the position or the movement of the head be taken into account as well?

The problem of classification arises when a particular signal has been identified. Just as linguistic phonemes may infinitely differ in their phonetic realisation, the realisation of the non-verbal equivalent of a phoneme will each time be realised in a specific ways along various parameters. Examples of such parameters are the placement, duration, extension and the speed with which a behaviour is executed. Head nods, for instance, can differ in the speed, extension and number of repetitions. One nod could be a small nod, performed very slowly while another nod could be very fast and aggressive. This variation might correspond to a systematic difference in meaning.

The classification of a signal based on the settings of the parameters along which it can vary is similar to the disambiguation of a signal in context; just as a head nod can mean different things in different contexts, a nod can also mean different things when the parameters are different. The question may thus arise whether a variation in context should not be seen as a variation within the signal. To clarify this, a short example will be given. Image that a person is saying 'I mean that car.' and he wants to emphasize the word 'that'. He does this by giving a small nod and raising his eyebrows at that moment. The question is what should be seen as a signal and what as context. The head nod could be a single signal, and the eyebrow raise and the word 'that' as the context. But the head nod plus the eyebrow raise could also be seen as a single signal (an accent) with only the utterance as the context. Or in the extreme case the complete setting (head nod plus eyebrow raise plus 'that') could be seen as one single signal with no other signals as context. However, the result for the disambiguation of the signals would be the same. In the first case the intended meaning has to be found of a nod as the eyebrow raise and the utterance as its context. In the second case the signal is more extensive (the head nod and the eyebrow raise) resulting in fewer possible functions, but as the context is also smaller the result is the same. In the last case there is no context to use for disambiguation, but the signal is so specific (head nod plus eyebrow raise plus 'that') that there are probably not a lot of possible intended functions.

What this example shows is that for signal disambiguation it does not really matter where the segmentation line is drawn. What matters for disambiguation is the complete set of data, the information of the signal itself (the parameters) plus the context. It does not matter where the line between these two is drawn because the complete set stays the same. However, a line must be drawn to define what a signal is exactly. As explained, the parameters of that signal are just as important as the context, thus, the first group of contextual elements consists of the *parameters* of the signal itself. The way signals are described determines how they should be mapped to conversational functions.

3.2   What Does the Context Change

Now it is clear that before trying to disambiguate signals they should be concretely defined first. Only then is it possible to look at the context. In a conversation this context influences several things, but what exactly is the effect of the context on the behaviour of people? First of all the context plays an important role in determining the actual multi-modal behaviour that is used to express a conversational function. Maybe several modalities are already occupied (one has just taken a bite of sandwich), or maybe the situation asks for a certain modality rather than another (for example gesturing in a crowded environment).

Going one step higher in the process the context also modifies the function choice. The complete context (previous behaviour, speaker/listener role of the participants, etc) determines what conversational functions the agent or human can or cannot express. The contextual elements that do this are *constraining elements*; they constrain the function choice by defining what is and, mostly, what is not possible in the current context. One type of constraint is an expressive constraint which make it simply impossible to express a certain function. For example, a person cannot decline a turn if this was not offered to him first. And a person that tries to give the turn away when he does not have it will end up showing a continuation signal, signalling to the speaker to continue speaking, instead of a give turn signal. Another type of constraint is an appropriateness constraint, meaning that certain functions just do not fit in the situation. An example would be to give the turn during a sentence while continuing speaking, or greeting a person when you are already talking for quite a while. All these actions are not appropriate or possible in certain contexts and are therefore not expected in those contexts.

When trying to disambiguate a signal, the first kind of modification behaviour of context (influencing the choice of behaviour to express a function) is not relevant. It does not really matter which signal was chosen to express a certain function, the important part is to find the meaning behind the signals. The second modification behaviour however defines the actual problem. One has to know the context to know which functions are appropriate at a certain point and this knowledge can be used to determine what was intended with a detected signal. In this case, the context can act as a filter, making certain interpretations unlikely.

3.3 Ambiguity

The previous paragraph characterized disambiguation of signals as a process of using the context to determine what conversational functions are appropriate at that time. This means that it can happen that the number of possible (appropriate) functions (based on the context) is greater than one. To solve this problem the context has to be used to find *pointer elements*. These elements do not constrain the function choice, but they point in the right direction. They provide the function that was most likely meant. For example, a head nod can mean different things: it can mean yes, it can be a backchannel, it can express an intensification (in the case of beats), etc. If a nod is shown just after a direct yes/no question then the nod is probably meaning yes. But if the nod is expressed at the same time that 'uhuh' was uttered then it was probably a backchannel. Of course there are always exceptions, but these pointer elements from the context can help picking out the most likely function.

Of course it can still happen that there are two or more best guesses, in which case not only the signal is ambiguous (they usually are, which is why disambiguation is needed), but the signal plus the context is ambiguous. So even when taking the complete context into account the signal can still be interpreted as multiple intentions.

This can mean two things. It is possible that only one function is intended by the signal but the signal was 'badly' chosen, meaning that that particular signal was not clear in that context. Thus, for the receiver it is not possible to decide what was intended and an educated guess needs to be made. If the wrong guess is made, the conversation might break down, or a repair action is taken.

It is also possible that the person or agent producing an ambiguous signal intended to communicate all the different meanings. Take for example a backchannel utterance. According to [12] this can be a continuer, an indicator of the listener that he does not want the turn and that the speaker should continue speaking. Another function that uses a backchannel utterance as a signal is an acknowledgement [2,4,6]. In a lot of contexts the difference between these two functions is hardly visible, in a lot of situation both a continuer and an acknowledgement would fit. But it is not unimaginable that a backchannel utterance means both at the same time, which means that the actor really is saying "I'm still following you, please go on".

When disambiguating signals, these types of ambiguities should be kept in mind and it should be realized that sometimes the function of a signal simply is not clear (of course this is not the desired situation but it might happen in certain cases), and sometimes a signal can have multiple meanings at the same time.

3.4   Contextual Elements

An important task in signal disambiguation is to determine what elements from the context are important. For example, it is important to know whether the actor of a signal is the listener or the speaker. Other signals that are sent at the same time are important as well, as is the placement of the signal in the sentence (middle, end). A full list of these contextual elements will not be given here, but based on the previous sections (in which they are already named) they can be divided into three basic categories.

- *Parameters* – The first category of contextual elements contains the parameters of the signals themselves. The way signals are described determines how they should be mapped to conversational functions. When disambiguating signals, the first thing that has to be done is specifying exactly what defines a signal and to what conversational functions these signals (without taking context into account yet) can be mapped. For example, a list has to be created of all possible intentions of an eyebrow raising and an eyebrow lowering.
- *Constraining elements* – The second category contains the elements that constrain the presence of functions in certain contexts. They can be expressive constraints (some functions are impossible to express in certain contexts), or appropriateness constraints (some functions are very inappropriate in certain contexts). For example, a person can not decline a turn he does not have (expressive constraint) and it is very inappropriate to greet a person when you are already talking for a long time (appropriate constraint).
- *Pointer elements* – The last category contains the elements that do not restrict functions, but help to find the most likely one. For example, a nod after a yes/no question probably be interpreted as 'yes', while a nod together with a 'uhuh' probably is a backchannel.

4   Conclusions

In this article the disambiguation problem, mapping detected multi-modal behaviour to intended communicative functions was discussed. To solve this problem the context of the behaviour has to be used and this context also contains the parameters of the signals you are detecting. Using this information the task is to make a list of all communicative functions that are possible in the current context, merge this with the list of functions that the target behaviour can mean and use the resulting as the intended function. Or, if the list of possible functions in the context is too large (maybe even infinite) you can do it the other way around by checking what a signal can mean and then check which meaning fits the current context.

Acknowledgements

The research leading to these results has received funding from the European Community's Seventh Framework Programme (FP7/2007-2013) under grant agreement n° 211486 (SEMAINE).

References

1. Beavin Bavelas, J., Coates, L., Johnson, T.: Listener responses as a collaborative process: The role of gaze. Journal of Communication 52, 566–580 (2002)
2. Cassell, J., Bickmore, T., Billinghurst, M., Campbell, L., Chang, K., Vilhjálmsson, H., Yan, H.: Embodiment in conversational interfaces: Rea. In: Proceedings of the SIGCHI conference on Human factors in computing systems: the CHI is the limit, Pittsburgh, Pennsylvania, United States, pp. 520–527. ACM, New York (1999)
3. Cassell, J., Sullivan, J., Prevost, S., Churchill, E.F. (eds.): Embodied Conversational Agents. MIT Press, Cambridge (2000)
4. Clark, H.H.: Using Language. Cambridge University Press, Cambridge (1996)
5. Ekman, P., Friesen, W.V.: The repertoire of nonverbal behavior: Categories, origins, usage, and coding, semiotical. Semiotica 1, 49–98 (1969)
6. Ekman, P.: About brows: Emotional and conversational signals, pp. 169–202. Cambridge University Press, Cambridge (1979)
7. Halliday, M.A.K., Hasan, R.: Cohesion in English. Longman Pub. Group (May 1976); published: Paperback
8. Heylen, D.: Challenges ahead: Head movements and other social acts in conversations. In: Halle, L., Wallis, P., Woods, S., Marsella, S., Pelachaud, C., Heylen, D. (eds.) AISB 2005 Social Intelligence and Interaction in Animals, Robots and Agents, pp. 45–52. The Society for the Study of Artificial Intelligence and the Simulation of Behaviour, Hatfield (2005)
9. Lyons, J.: Introduction to Theoretical Linguistics. University Press, Cambridge (1968)
10. Nakano, Y.I., Reinstein, G., Stocky, T., Cassell, J.: Towards a model of face-to-face grounding. In: ACL 2003: Proceedings of the 41st Annual Meeting on Association for Computational Linguistics, Morristown, NJ, USA, vol. 1, pp. 553–561. Association for Computational Linguistics (2003)
11. Samtani, P., Valente, A., Johnson, W.L.: Applying the saiba framework to the tactical language and culture training system. In: Padgham, Parkes, Müller, Parsons (eds.) 7th Int. Conf. on Autonomous Agents and Multiagent Systems (AAMAS 2008), Estoril, Portugal (May 2008)
12. ten Bosch, L., Oostdijk, N., de Ruiter, J.P.: Durational aspects of turn-taking in spontaneous face-to-face and telephone dialogues. In: Sojka, P., Kopeček, I., Pala, K. (eds.) TSD 2004. LNCS, vol. 3206, pp. 563–570. Springer, Heidelberg (2004)

Modeling Aspects of Multimodal Lithuanian Human - Machine Interface

Rytis Maskeliunas

Kaunas University of Technology, Speech Research Lab.,
Studentu 65-108, 51367 Kaunas, Lithuania
rytis.maskeliunas@ktu.lt

Abstract. The paper deals with modeling of multimodal human - machine interface. Multimodal access to the information retrieval system (computer) is possible by combining three different approaches: 1) Data input / retrieval by voice; 2) Traditional data input / retrieval systems; 3) Confirmation / rejection by recognizing and displaying human face expressions and emotions. A prototype of multimodal access for web application is presented by combining three modalities. Lithuanian language speech recognition experiment results on transcriptions and outcomes of discriminant analysis are presented.

Keywords: Multimodal interface, Lithuanian speech recognition.

1 Introduction

At the beginning of computer era the only way to interact with the machine was the use of perfect knowledge of programming, database systems and hardware. After developments and advances in microelectronics during 1970 – 1980's more modern computer technologies evolved, enabling new and inexperienced users to access and process the information without the need for special knowledge or the help of specialists. At the same time a human – machine interface began evolving and experiments were started on multimodal ways of interaction. The natural speech input and output allowed greatly enhance traditional communication modes, such as using a keyboard and the manipulation of icons and the text menus on computer display. The inclusion of speech recognition and synthesis greatly improved naturalness and accessibility of the information input and the retrieval, especially for inexperienced and disabled users. The experiments of Chapanis [2] showed the advantages of natural speech vs. the traditional ways: high performance and reliability of task execution and optimized interplay of the modalities make natural and spontaneous communication possible. Later on, the video based systems, such as a gesture, lips recognition, eye tracking, the electroencephalograph, etc. were added as additional mode of the human – machine interaction.

2 Main Human – Machine Interface Modalities

Multimodal systems offer many advantages over the traditional interfaces: the better error correction, improved handling in various situations and tasks and better accessibility [3].

A. Esposito et al. (Eds.): Multimodal Signals, LNAI 5398, pp. 75–82, 2009.

Humans perceive information by the senses known as modes, computers do that by using the artificial alternatives. To facilitate a more fluid human – machine interface it is better to enable machines to acquire the human – like skills, such as recognizing faces, gestures, speech, rather than to demand that humans should acquire the machine – like skills [4].

The best way in developing the most natural multimodal interface is to combine the main input / output types.

The direct manipulation, made popular by Apple and Microsoft graphical operating systems, has been based on the visual display of objects of interest, the selection by pointing, the rapid and reversible actions and a continuous feedback [16]. The virtual representation of information has been created, which can be operated by a user through the physical actions. [5]. It is important, that the traditional user interfaces have not been useful to disabled (blind, paralyzed, etc.) users. In the mobile devices those technologies don't work well either. It is not handy to type a text using a miniature (or simplified) PDA or a smart phone keyboard or a touch screen character recognition. The combining of speech and the traditional input might be a solution. However, there's still no real substitution for a keyboard and a mouse in the traditional computer use scenarios.

The speech plays main role in human communication. The main problem of an application of the speech human – machine interface has been the speech recognition (mostly accuracy in noisy and multi user environments, vocabulary size). Humans usually overestimate the capabilities of a system with the speech interface and try to treat it as another live person [6]. The speech technology has been maturing rapidly and the attention has been switching to the problems of using this technology in real applications, especially applications which allow a human to use the voice to interact directly with the computer-based information or to control the system. The systems therefore involve a dialogue and the discourse management issues in addition to those associated with prompting the user and interpreting the responses [18].

For the many reasons (the visibility, the relationship to a spoken signal, the ease of a graphical representation and the usefulness in speech-reading) the lips have been the most commonly modeled articulatory system [9], [13], [14]. As the speech recognition can degrade in noisy environments, the lip motion modality provides additional performance gains over those which are obtained by the fusion of audio and by the lip texture alone, in both cases of the speaker identification and the isolated word recognition scenarios [1]. Humans naturally use the faces as the organs of expression, reaction and query, which enrich the speech. The facial expression and the head movements are often used, when people express reactive states in conversations with others. The facial information (3D or 2D facial geometry, a skin pattern or a reflection, a facial thermogram, etc.) can also be used for the computer recognition of a personal identity (biometrics) [10], [11], [17].

2.1 Prototype Multimodal Web Access Application - FictionOIL

The multimodal access web application – FictionOIL has been developed to imitate a self service petrol station. A user can input and retrieve data by the voice (human – machine voice dialog), nod his head to confirm or reject a request or use traditional ways, greatly expanding usability and accessibility.

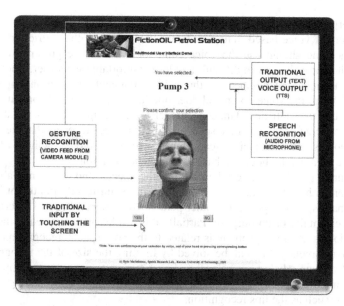

Fig. 1. User can confirm his selection by the voice (saying yes or no), nodding his head (up – down means yes, left – right means no) or pressing the correct button by touching the screen

The multimodal approach is utilized by combining ASP, the Speech Application Language Tags (SALT) or VoiceXML and the human face gesture recognition technologies (Fig. 1).

ASP (or similar markup languages, such as JAVA) can be used to create the traditional user interface. The information is displayed on the terminal monitor, the data are entered by a keyboard (specific actions are mapped to corresponding buttons) or directly manipulating the objects on a screen (using a mouse pointer or a finger with a touch screen display).

SALT or VoiceXML can add the second modality – the voice, which can greatly improve the usability and the accessibility. Therefore a user can input the data by simply saying what he wants and hearing the response. The voice Input can be easily controlled by using the simple syntax SALT elements, such as listen and grammar (W3C standard grammars are supported). The dynamic data (such as fuel prices) can be read by using the Lithuanian text – to – speech engine [7]. Again the prerecorded voice or the simple SALT elements, such as prompt can be used. The Lithuanian speech recognition has been developed on the base of regularized discriminant analysis and by using the transcriptions in the current commercial environments. The human – machine speech dialog has been created based on recommendations by Minker et al. [8].

The third modality can be added by recognizing and displaying a head movement (i.e. nodding to confirm), human face gestures, emotions and lip movements. This also extends the usability and the naturalness of the application. Video data (clusters of speech sounds mapped to the lips) used have been collected and processed by our colleagues at Image processing and analysis lab.

By analyzing the survey of the researchers testing this application, the following observations could be addressed:

The interpretation of the semantic text will be a difficult problem for some time and designers of voice based dialog systems should impose the restrictions on voice user interface and should use the voice commands with some prescribed meanings even if such approach is more difficult and less comfortable for a user. Looking from the speech technologist perspective the voice command recognition imposes own restrictions. Since the voice command does not have a grammatical content it is often difficult to use the statistical language models in such applications. Analyzing the causes of the recent progress in the speech recognition area it seems that the statistical language models have had a significant impact. However, the recognition of the simplified voice commands should be based on acoustic modeling.

The security problems arise when adding the speech and video modalities. The main problem is how to identify a speaking person (significantly important in remote control scenarios) and to prevent another person from intervening and entering incorrect data accidentally or on purpose. Partially this can be solved by using the biometrics technologies. Another problem is related to the poor speech recognition accuracy in noisy environments. This can be solved by limiting the size of the recognition vocabulary (decreasing dialog naturalness as fewer responses are accepted), by using the directional microphones (losing remote control possibility) or by adding the video technologies, such as the lips recognition.

3 Experiments on Lithuanian Speech Recognition

The experiments have been carried out by using the new Lithuanian speech corpus (basic segmentation, large sound units). This corpus has been expanding rapidly (more speakers and phonemic data added) and has been segmentated into small phonetical units. In the near future the experiments are going to be repeated by using the better quality speech data and the transitional parts of the diphones.

3.1 Discriminant Analysis Experiments

The modern automatic speech recognition systems possess the spoken language recognition capabilities that are far below the capabilities of human beings. One of the reasons is the fact that the human speech recognition and the automatic speech recognition have been performed in entirely different manner. This is particularly evident in the adverse environments or in the recognition of semantically meaningless sentences and phrases. These facts advocate that acoustic modeling of a speech signal has been carried out inefficiently in the automatic speech recognition systems.

The state-of-the-art of the speech recognition model which is based on the three state left-to-right continuous density hidden Markov model (CD-HMM) and the Mel – frequency cepstrum coefficients (MFCC) features, supplemented with the delta and delta-delta coefficients, enables to achieve serious progress in the acoustic modeling of the speech signal. However, the CD-HMM has had a lot of drawbacks, such as the relatively weak discrimination abilities. The linear discriminant analysis (LDA) is a method based on the discrimination capabilities with a good stability and a relative simplicity. However, this method needs large amounts of data for training and is sensitive to the data deviations in correlation matrix estimation procedure. To avoid these shortages regularized discriminant analysis (RDA) has been applied [12]. The main idea of RDA is to modify the estimation procedure of correlation matrix and to provide the best recognition accuracy on a given training data set. This is achieved introducing a singular value in the decomposition of the correlation matrix. Then scaling and rotating of its estimates follows:

$$S^{RM} = T^\alpha (D + \lambda I) T^{\alpha'} .$$ (1)

where S^{RM} – the scaled and rotated estimate of a covariance matrix, T and D – are the singular values of the singular value decomposition, α and λ are the scaling and rotation coefficients. The optimal values of α and λ are evaluated empirically from the training data.

Previous experiments [15] showed the effectiveness of RDA approach comparing with other statistical classification methods (such as LDA, k-means, etc.) for the recognition of diphones composed from the nasal consonants or the semivowels and different vowels. These comparisons do not include modeling using CD-HMM for the same tasks. The motivation for it has been to extend phonetic data set and to evaluate the RDA approach efficiency with the results obtained by the Markov model.

A phrase which contains six diphones (ma, na, mi, ni, mu, nu) pronounced in isolation has been used. Each speaker (225 female speakers and 130 male speakers) pronounced these six diphones once. Since some pronunciations were of lower quality than the others, 220 female utterances and 125 male utterances have been used in the experiments. Utterances of 200 female and 110 male speakers were used for training, utterances of 20 female and 15 male speakers were used for testing.

The boundaries of the each diphone in recording and the boundary between a consonant and a vowel were fixed by an expert (human labeler).

An acoustic signal has been described using the MFCC features. They have been compiled using 20 msec analysis frame and 10 msec analysis step. In the recognition experiments with CD-HMM the MFCC feature vectors composed from 12 (cepstrum coefficients only) or 39 (cepstrum coefficients, delta and acceleration coefficients and energy) coefficients have been used. In the RDA discrimination experiments feature vectors composed of 24 coefficients (12 of them describing consonant part of diphone and 12 of them describing vowel part of diphone) have been used. These coefficients were the same MFCC coefficients as in CD-HMM recognition. The consonant part and vowel part descriptions were obtained by averaging MFCC coefficients of 5 consecutive frames from the stationary part of a consonant and a vowel.

For testing CD-HMM based recognition HTK provided tools have been applied. For RDA experiments proprietary software tools have been written in MATLAB.

Table 1 shows six diphones recognition results by applying CD-HMMs.

Table 1. Recognition results by applying the CD-HMM

Experiment type	male		female	
	Correct, %	Accuracy, %	Correct, %	Accuracy, %
12 MFCC, 1 set	78.57	78.57	69.14	68.00
12 MFCC, 2 set	84.29	84.29	68.42	64.66
39 MFCC, 1 set	92.86	92.86	78.57	77.98
39 MFCC, 2 set	90.00	88.57	75.00	74.40

Table 2. Discrimination results by applying the regularized discriminant analysis

Experiment type	Male, correct %	Female, correct %
4 classes, (ma, na, mi, ni)	89	79
4 classes, (ma, na, mu, nu)	92	80.5
6 classes, (ma, na, mi, ni, mu, nu)	83	72

Table 2 shows the results of the recognition experiments by applying the regularized discriminant analysis. Several experiments were performed: with 6 and 4 classes of diphones.

3.2 Deployed Commercial English Recognizers Adapted to the Lithuanian Language

The current commercial products don't support the Lithuanian voice recognition engines. The only way of currently deployed voice server's application for the Lithuanian language is to use the English transcriptions of the Lithuanian words.

The analysis has been carried out for improving the transcription effectiveness. First comparison of single transcriptions (i.e. word KETURI[1] has been changed to K EH T UH R IH) to multiple variations, based on preliminary automatic syllables recognition (i.e. k eh t uh r ih 1 (simple), k eh t uh d iy 1, k eh g ey r ih 1, g ah t uh r ih and so on) has been carried out. Syllables recognition has been conducted by using a set of 6 plosives C= {p, t, k, b, d, g}, a set of 16 vowel like IPA (International Phonetics Association) units V={ao, ah, aa, ih, iy, uh, uw, eh, ae, ey, ay, oy, aw, ow, ax, er}. Thus 96 consonant-vowel (CV) alternatives for the recognition have been processed.

The multiple transcriptions have been created in the following way:

1. A word has been divided into CV syllables (i.e. KETURI = KE + TU + RI);
2. Each syllable has been tested through the syllable recognition engine (100 times);
3. The most frequent answers have been selected (KE was recognized 69 times as g ah, 18 times as t ax);
4. The multiple transcriptions have been combined in most frequent answers (i.e. KETURI(15) = {k eh t uh r ih 1(simple), k eh t uh d iy 1, k eh g ey r ih 1, g ah t uh r ih 1, ...};
5. The best transcriptions have been selected by checking the predefined acceptable utterances against garbage model.

The experiments have been carried out in a noisy environment (street, computer rooms, outside areas, etc.), phoning the test application hosted on Microsoft Speech Server (Microsoft English US Recognition engine) by using a regular GSM mobile phone. Each word (10 Lithuanian digits) was spoken 100 times by 20 speakers.

In the first part of experiment only one transcription of chosen Lithuanian digit has been used. As recognition accuracy was poor for the most speakers (~ 47 %), 15 transcriptions using previously described method have been created. As more transcriptions of a word "keturi" were accessible to a recognizer, the recognition accuracy improved up to 98 %.

---

[1] Word "Keturi" means "four" in Lithuanian.

Table 3. Experiment results (excerpts) of comparison of the recognition accuracy using single and multiple transcriptions

Number of transcriptions	Word „DU"	Word „TRYS"	Word „KETURI"
1	83	77	47
12	84	80	60
13	88	87	84
14	90	91	95
15	97	99	98

The results proved (table 3) that the recognition accuracy depends on a number of transcriptions. The best accuracy is achieved when a larger number of transcriptions is used (allowing a recognizer to choose one from more variations of each word). By decreasing the number of transcriptions (removing the one that was chosen most times) the recognition accuracy decreased (sometimes almost 50% worse). The method of using the transcriptions works well only in limited vocabulary recognition scenarios, as it is impossible to generate qualitative transcriptions in real-time for dictations systems.

4 Conclusions

1. At the moment the Lithuanian speech recognition has been carried out on commercial speech recognition systems. A prototype of multimodal interface for Lithuanian language recognition has its own peculiarities. Because of differences in the English and Lithuanian pronunciations the recognition accuracy has not been satisfactory. To improve the situation the using of the English transcriptions for Lithuanian words have been adapted and recognition accuracy of about 96% for limited vocabulary scenarios has been achieved.
2. To achieve the good recognition accuracy and the performance for large vocabulary scenarios the native Lithuanian language recognition engine has been developed. The experiments based on the discriminant analysis proved an improvement in the recognition accuracy.
3. Another challenge was to introduce biometrical information in situations when identifying a speaking person acting in remote control scenarios. The security of operations can be increased by combining the information on voice recognition and face contours identification technologies.

References

1. Cetingul, H.E., Erzin, E., Yemez, Y., Tekalp, A.M.: Multimodal speaker/speech recognition using lip motion, lip texture and audio. In: Source Signal Processing, vol. 86(12), pp. 3549–3558. Elsevier North-Holland Inc., Amsterdam (2006)
2. Chapanis, A.: Interactive Communication: A few research answers for a technological explosion. In: Neel, D., Lienard, J.S. (eds.) Nouvelles Tendances de la Communication Homme-Machine, pp. 33–67. Inria, Le Chesnay (1980)

3. Cohen, P.R., Oviatt, S.L.: The Role of Voice Input for Human - Machine Communication. Proceedings of the National Academy of Sciences 92(22), 9921–9927 (1995)
4. Dauhman, J.: Face and gesture recognition: Overview. IEEE Transaction on Pattern Analysis and Machine Intelligence 19(7), 675–676 (1997)
5. Grasso, M.A., Ebert, D.S., Finin, T.W.: The integrality of speech in multimodal interfaces. ACM Transactions on Computer-Human Interaction (TOCHI) 5(4), 303–325 (1998)
6. Jones, D.M., Hapeshi, K., Frankish, C.: Design guidelines for speech recognition interfaces. Applied Ergonomics 20(1), 40–52 (1990)
7. Kasparatis, P.: Diphone databases for Lithuanian text – to – speech synthesis. Informatica 16(2), 193–202 (2005)
8. Minker, W., Bannacef, S.: Speech and human machine dialog. Kluwer academic publishers, Boston (2004)
9. Parke, F.I.: Parameterized models for facial animation. IEEE Computer Graphics and Applications 2(9), 61–68 (1982)
10. Pike, G., Kemp, R., Brace, N.: The Psychology of Human Face Recognition. In: IEE Colloquium on Visual Biometrics, Ref. no. 2000/018, pp. 11/1—11/6. IEE Savoy Place, London (2000)
11. Prokoski, F.J., Riedel, R.B., Coffin, J.S.: Identification of Individuals by Means of Facial Thermography. In: Proceedings of the IEEE 1992 International Carnahan Conference on Security Technology, Crime Countermeasures, October 14–16, pp. 120–125. IEEE Press, New York (1992)
12. Raudys, S.: Statistical and neural classifiers: An integrated approach to design. Springer, London (2001)
13. Reveret, L., Bailly, G., Badin, P.: MOTHER: A new generation of talking heads providing a flexible articulatory control for video-realistic speech animation. In: Proceedings of the 6th International Conference of Spoken Language Processing, pp. 16–20. ISCA, Beijing (2000)
14. Reveret, L., Essa, I.: Visual Coding and Tracking of Speech Related Facial Motion. Georgia institute of technology technical report GIT-GVU-TR-01-16. Georgia institute of technology (2001)
15. Rudzionis, A., Rudzionis, V.: Phoneme recognition in fixed context using regularized discriminant analysis. In: Proceedings of EUROSPEECH 1999, vol. 6, pp. 2745–2748. ESCA, Budapest (1999)
16. Shneiderman, B.: Direct manipulation: A step beyond programming languages. In: Human-computer interaction: a multidisciplinary approach, pp. 461–467. Morgan Kaufmann Publishers Inc., San Francisco (1987)
17. Smith, W.A.P., Robles-Kelly, A., Hancock, E.R.: Skin Reflectance Modeling for Face Recognition. In: Proceedings of the Pattern Recognition, 17th International Conference on (ICPR 2004), vol. 3, pp. 210–213. IEEE computer society, Washington (2004)
18. Young, S.: Speech understanding and spoken dialogue systems. In: IEE Colloquium on Speech and Language Engineering – State of the Art (Ref. No. 1998/499), pp. 6/1—6/5. Savoy Place, London (1998)

Using a Signing Avatar as a Sign Language Research Tool

Delroy Nelson

Deafness Cognition and Language Research Centre, UCL,
49 Gordon Square, London WC1H 0PD
delroy.nelson@ucl.ac.uk

Abstract. The first section of this paper introduces the Hamnosys/Visicast sign-ing avatar, which has been designed to produce individual signs and sentences in a number of different sign languages. The operating systems which underlie the avatar are described in detail. The second part of the paper describes a re-search project which aims to use the avatar's properties to develop a toolkit for sign language research.

Keywords: avatar, sign language, SiGML, HamNoSys.

1 Sign Language

It is now universally accepted in the linguistic community that sign languages such as ASL (American Sign Language), BSL (British Sign Language), CSL (Chinese Sign Language), and so on are natural languages with comparable expressive power to that of spoken languages. Indeed, the realisation that signed languages are true languages is one of the great linguistic discoveries of the twentieth century.

In the last 45 years, research on many different languages has revealed profound similarities in the structure, acquisition and processing of signed and spoken lan-guages. There is no suggestion that being a (native) signer rather than a (native) speaker has any negative effect on the ability to communicate or think. To the con-trary, it may be that native signers have better visual and spatial abilities related to the rotation and manipulation of figures than their hearing peers [1].

The difference in modality notwithstanding, it also seems to be the case that the parts of the brain responsible for the acquisition and representation of knowledge of (spoken) language in hearing individuals is essentially the same as the parts of the brain responsible for knowledge of (signed) language in deaf individuals [2] [3].

Although sign languages are often described as manual languages, they use multi-ple channels. The configuration, movement, and arrangement of the hands in space provide most lexical and grammatical information. The mouth provides lexical infor-mation derived from spoken language forms, and is also used to articulate gestures unrelated to spoken language, which perform both specific linguistic functions and reflect motor constraints on action production and planning. The role of the voice in spoken language as a carrier of affect, intonation and prosodic structure is undertaken by the face, head and body. The movements of the eyes, head and body also indicate

A. Esposito et al. (Eds.): Multimodal Signals, LNAI 5398, pp. 83–93, 2009.

lexical, grammatical and discourse features [4]. The visual-gestural modality makes a three-dimensional space available to SLs and appears to allow more frequent iconicity in SL lexicons in comparison to spoken languages. The resources of the visual gestural modality also allow access to a 3-dimensional space for grammatical purposes.

The histories of sign languages do not correspond to those of spoken languages. For example, although hearing people in the USA and the UK use the same spoken language (with some minor differences), BSL and American Sign Language (ASL) are unrelated languages and are not mutually intelligible. In addition to signs, finger-spelling is a way of representing letters of written English. BSL uses a 2-handed alphabet; American Sign Language uses a 1-handed alphabet.

Deaf children, despite normal language learning capacities, often acquire a first language relatively late in comparison to hearing children. For deaf children of deaf parents (about 10% of the congenitally deaf population) sign language can be acquired as a first language, within the normal time-frame for acquisition. For the 90% of deaf children with hearing parents, language acquisition is likely to be delayed: children may only be provided with spoken language input, which they may be unable to fully access because of their hearing loss, or may have late or impoverished exposure to sign language: either because they are raised exclusively with spoken language input for the first years of life, or because their parents are themselves just learning sign language following the diagnosis of their child's deafness. Thus deaf children are the only natural occurrence of a population with delayed learning of a first language. Deaf children are also a unique population with respect to their reliance on visible speech. An additional group of interest is the hearing children of deaf parents (representing about 90% of children born to deaf parents). This group may grow up as bilinguals, with development of both spoken and signed language within the normal timeframe for first language acquisition.

2 The Avatar System

2.1 HamNoSys

Hamnosys [5], (the Hamburg Notation System) (http://www.sign-lang.uni-hamburg.de/software/software.english.html) was created as a computer-based transcription system for sign language. Information about the sign's location relative to the body, configuration and orientation of the hand, and movement can be coded (see [6] for a discussion of its use in coding child sign language). Within the avatar system, Hamnosys interacts with a number of elements. The main component of the system is the eSIGN Editor which is used to compose the sign string for the avatar (Fig. 1).

The editor includes databases with elements for each part of sign language grammar, for example, non-manual elements, different types of verb classes, lexical items, etc. Using the eSIGN Editor the user can choose a sign from the lexicon and modify it with the use of special sub-editing routines. These permit changes to the stock of movements, handshapes, etc. As changes are made, the revisions can be seen immediately on the avatar. An example is given below (Fig. 2) of one part of the Editor.

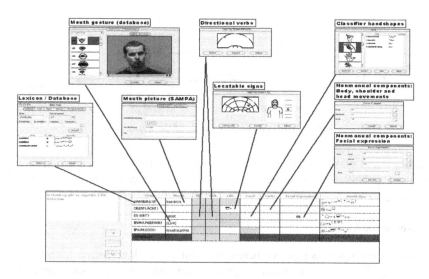

Fig. 1. Components of the eSign Editor [7]

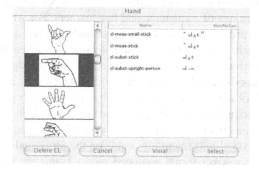

Fig. 2. Section of the Editor concerned with handshapes, orientation and handedness [8]

To drive the avatar, Hamnosys works alongside a system called SiGML (Signing Gesture Mark-up Language) which was developed in two EU-funded projects, ViSi-CAST (http://www.visicast.cmp.uea.ac.uk/Visicast_index.html) and eSIGN (www.sign-lang.uni-hamburg.de/esign/) [9] [10] [11]. ViSiCAST (Signing for the Deaf using Virtual Humans) is a computer system that generates sign language which is then animated by the avatar. XML (Extensible Markup Language) is a simple but flexible format for the exchange of structured and semi-structured data. XML is represented as plain text; which is easy to transfer over the Internet. It resembles the HTML code used for web sites. XML is one of a number of markup languages and is defined as a metalanguage - a language that describes other languages. XML is "optionless", enabling it to remain unchanged, unlike HTML whose many different conventions make it appear very different on different browsers. This means that it is difficult to present data in a uniform fashion using XML. SiGML is a specific form of extensible mark-up language which serves as the encoder for HamNoSys signs. Each sign language is an independent language in its own right, with its own distinctive

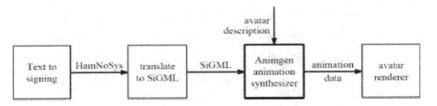

Fig. 3. Diagram of components of the avatar [12]

vocabulary and grammatical characteristics [10] [4]. The SiGML notation incorporates the HamNoSys phonetic model, and hence SiGML can represent any sign language (Fig 3.)

2.2 Research Aims

The avatar developments reported here arose from research on British Sign Language (BSL). Linguistic research on any language often involves asking speakers to make judgements about the grammaticality or acceptability of various forms. The ability to make such judgements and make them rapidly reveals important linguistic differences in between native speakers of a language and late learners. For written language tasks it is easy enough to provide examples of correct and incorrect forms. However, for sign language research – which has no commonly used written form, examples of both correct and incorrect forms must be produced by a human signer. It is difficult to get a human to produce examples of incorrect forms which look as natural as correct forms, and this lack of naturalness can be used by alert research participants to assist them in making their judgements. To get judgements based on linguistic structure, both the correct and incorrect forms must be produced fluently and naturally, in order to ensure that participants' judgements are made on the forms and not on how they are signed. Correct and incorrect forms produced by an avatar are equally natural, and thus enable this sort of study to take place.

2.3 The Tool

The project described here aimed to pilot the development of an avatar research toolkit for use in sign language studies with deaf and hearing subjects who are users of British Sign Language. Although the work is still in its initial stages, the avatar driven by HamNoSys and SigML illustrates a valuable approach to sign language research, and should have applications in a wide range of research studies.

3 The Research Toolkit

The toolkit project aims to create tools for research in four different areas of sign language research: fingerspelling, facial expression, syntax, and semantics. A brief introduction will be provided to these areas before describing the toolkit.

3.1 Fingerspelling of Words

Current experiments are exploring whether signers can recognise errors in finger-spelled words, for example, where all the letters are present but in the incorrect order (contrasting recognition of **shine** (Fig. 4) compared to **sihne** (Fig. 5) or contrasting real words with non-words (pronounceable non-words like **backle** or non-pronounceable non-words like **ybkel**).

3.2 Face Actions

Some signs have obligatory face actions. Current research studies are concerned with the question of whether signs can be understood if the incorrect face action is used.

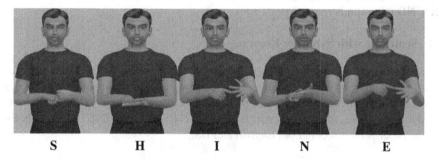

| S | H | I | N | E |

Fig. 4. 'shine' fingerspelled with the British 2-handed manual alphabet

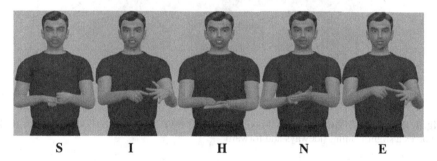

| S | I | H | N | E |

Fig. 5. 'sihne' – incorrectly fingerspelled 'shine'

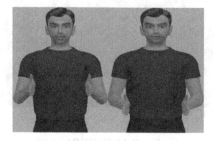

Fig. 6. BSL sign SLIM with correct face action

This is of particular importance in studies of signers who have had strokes, since strokes in certain areas of the brain may impair the ability to recognise the manual component of signs, while strokes in other areas can impair the ability to recognise the facial component (MacSweeney et al, in press). The examples below show signs with incorrect face actions (the manual component of **SLIM** (Fig. 6) combined with the face and body actions accompanying **FAT** (Fig. 7).

3.3 Signs with Semantic Mismatches

In a number of neurolinguistic and psycholinguistic studies, signers are asked to respond when they see a sentence that is grammatically correct but semantically anomalous, for example, **SUN SQUARE** ("the sun is square") (Fig. 8) instead of **SUN ROUND** ("the sun is round") (Fig. 9)

3.4 Sentences with Syntactic Errors

As with other error detection tasks, the ability to make speedy and accurate decisions about whether a sentence is grammatical, is a strong marker of the difference between native and non-native signers. In English, "I always sign wrong(ly)" has the correct word order; in BSL, the correct order is ALWAYS I SIGN WRONG (Fig. 10). In Fig. 11, the order is incorrect in both English and BSL.

Fig. 7. BSL sign SLIM with face and body actions for FAT (note that the body action for FAT involves a slight leaning sideways and forward

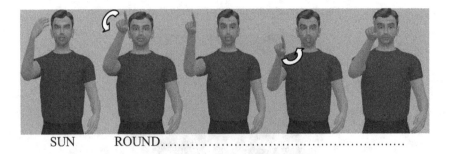

SUN   ROUND..

Fig. 8. SUN ROUND

SUN   SQUARE ....

Fig. 9. SUN SQUARE

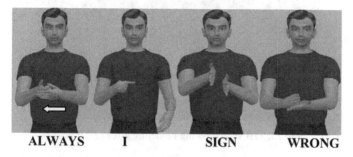

ALWAYS   I   SIGN   WRONG

Fig. 10. Correct version of "I always sign wrong" in BSL

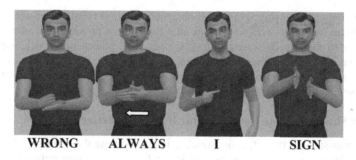

WRONG   ALWAYS   I   SIGN

Fig. 11. Incorrect version of "I always sign wrong" in BSL

4 Issues

In this section, both positive and negative features of the avatar are discussed. Although the avatar has great promise, there are a number of problems which need to be resolved if it is to become a useful research tool.

4.1 Problems with Modelling of Hands

In a number of cases where there is contact between the hands, they appear to go into each other. This can be seen with such signs as HAPPY (Fig. 12) and THINGS (Fig. 13).

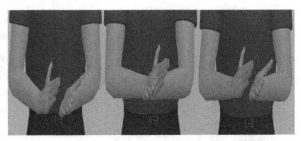

Fig 12. HAPPY showing modelling error (2nd frame)

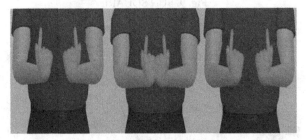

Fig 13. THINGS showing modeling error (2nd frame)

4.2 Advantages: Reliability

One of the biggest advantages of a well-designed avatar is reliability. Both in research and in education, it is essential to ensure that the content provided is correct, relevant and of value to the user. Because avatars don't tire, miss planes, or get sick, users – both children and adults – can interact and maintain interest in experimental tasks using the avatar. Avatar/characters can create interest and also offer some humour, which is a key requirement (according to computer gamers) for bringing an avatar to life.

4.3 Why Should Anyone Use an Avatar If Video Is Better Quality?

In the current state of the art, avatar quality is not yet near the quality of HD or even DV video. However, advantages in how it can be used and manipulated show enormous promise. These include cost, size and the ease of making changes in the content at any point. HD (High Definition) video provides much better quality than standard DV (Digital Video) camcorder tapes. However, moving to HD video increases the cost and person-hours required to get the content right. Not only is an HD camcorder required but also a computer fast enough to run the video. Even if these problems are solved, the size of video files is enormous compared to an avatar clip in HamNoSys.

With research tools, it is often necessary to modify the experimental materials after piloting. The problems associated with changing content in HD video include

- It is necessary to re-record the same person as in the original clips otherwise there is no consistency, which may affect subject responses
- It is sometimes difficult to maintain the same settings used in the initial and subsequent recordings
- If HD clips are compressed sufficiently for most internet speeds, there is too great a loss of quality

5 Conclusions

Hamnosys software and the use of the avatar is still relatively new, even though it has been used since the early 90`s. The latest version at the time of writing this paper is V0 9.5, which has an improved quality of signing, but there are still a number of features that need correction, some of which are currently being worked on by the developers. Although the Hamnosys avatar is still a long way from perfection, it works more easily and quickly than any other avatar software available anywhere else. It can be made to work in any sign language from around the world. The use of the avatar for sign language research applications will mean that for researchers there will be no need for hours of video to be carried around from city to city testing people with different signs and sentences.

This software lets the user create a new sign in less than a minute. Then it is a simple case of adding the body movements and face expressions to the avatar, which takes another two minutes. Within three minutes a new sign can be completed. The best thing about this new sign, compared to filming a human model, is that the face actions and body movements can be changed as often as desired, while still retaining the original sign. So, unlike video, where it would be necessary to spend time setting up the camera, editing the video, converting it to an appropriate format for testing, and then having to transport the materials, HamNoSys fits easily onto a PC or Mac laptop.

5.1 The Avatars

Avatars work well as a research tool, or for piloting versions of materials. The author has successfully used the avatar for piloting a game. Children have greater interest in tests or games using avatars than in conventional video. For them, the avatar transforms the material so that it is not just another "Deaf kids test". They are able to interact with the avatar, rather than losing interest with non-interactive materials. The avatar is fun and straight away not only gets a child's attention but more importantly keeps it.

In spring 2008, an Avatar Debate was held in London and a number of members of the Deaf community expressed concerns about the uses of avatars and their quality. One concern is that avatars might be used as cheap alternatives to interpreters. The current quality of avatars is not adequate for such a purpose and although there have been some pressures to develop automated translation from   subtitling to signing avatars, such systems are unlikely to reach levels of acceptability (the difficulties with automated translation of spoken/written languages is well known, and problems with automated translation of sign languages are substantially greater.

Other concerns include the general quality of the HamNoSys avatar, which is not as natural looking as motion capture systems. The quality of the Hamnosys avatar is still improving, and it offers substantial savings on cost and time. Some uses currently being explored include on-line weather reports and to assist Deaf people to complete on-line forms. Fig. 14 shows an example from the online weather report; The user can click on the hand at the bottom of the page to have the weather signed to them.

Fig. 14. eSign weather forecast [9]

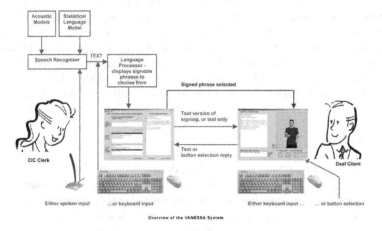

Fig. 15. "Vanessa" [13]

Fig. 15 below shows VANESSA - the Voice Activated Network Enabled Speech to Sign Assistant, designed to facilitate communication between staff and their deaf clients in Information centre's or similar environments.

5.2   Future Research and Developments

There are a great number of research projects that could benefit from the HamNoSys avatar. Hamnosys can be used with any sign language, so once the right language format is built into the software, it can be used in any country. The avatar is also particularly attractive for use in testing children for the reasons described above, by combining fun with an effective research and testing tool.

As well as further work on the Research Toolkit, include the development of teaching avatars for a variety of subjects, such as mathematics, enabling interactive teaching and learning. The avatar can also be fitted with different skins: adult, child, male, female, different ethnic groups. The options are only limited by the imagination of the developer.

Acknowledgements

Bencie Woll from (UCL) University College London for giving me the opportunity to work at DCAL on this and other research projects.

John Glauert from (UEA) University of East Anglia for all the help given to me with the avatar software and having the patience and time for all the questions I kept asking him.

As a result, I have a much greater understanding of the field I am now in and the software used for which I am truly grateful to you both.

References

1. Keehner, M., Gathercole, S.E.: Cognitive adaptations arising from nonnative experience of sign language in hearing adults. Memory & Cognition 35(4), 752–761 (2007)
2. MacSweeney, M., Capek, C., Campbell, R., Woll, B.: The Signing Brain: The Neurobiology of Sign Language. Trends in Cognitive Science (in press, November 2008)
3. Woll, B.: How the Brain processes language in different modalities. In: Esposito, A., Hussain, A., Marinaro, M., Martone, R. (eds.) Multimodal Signals. LNCS (LNAI), vol. 5398, pp. 145–163. Springer, Heidelberg (2008)
4. Sutton-Spence, R.L., Woll, B.: The Linguistics of British Sign Language: an introduction. Cambridge University Press, Cambridge (1999)
5. Prillwitz, S., Leven, R., Zienert, H., Hanke, T., Henning, J.: HamNoSys. Version 2.0. Hamburg Notation System for Sign Languages - An Introductory Guide. Signum Press, Hamburg (1989)
6. Takkinen, R.: Some Observations on the Use of HamNoSys (Hamburg Notation System for Sign Languages) in the Context of the Phonetic Transcription of Children's Signing. Sign Lang Ling 1:8(2), 99–118 (2005)
7. eSIGN annual report (2003), http://www.sign-lang.uni-hamburg.de/ eSIGN/AnnualReport2003/Editor2003/Editor2003.html
8. eSIGN annual report (2003), http://www.sign-lang.uni-hamburg.de/ eSIGN/AnnualReport2003/Editor2003/CLs.html
9. Animating Sign Language: The eSign Approach, http://www.visicast.sys.uea.ac.uk/Papers/eSIGNApproach.pdf
10. Elliott, R., Glauert, J.R.W., Kennaway, J.R., Marshall, I.: Development of language processing support for the ViSiCAST project. In: ASSETS 2000, 4th International ACM SIGCAPH Conference on Assistive Technologies (2000)
11. Elliott, R., Glauert, J.R.W., Kennaway, J.R., Parsons, K.J.: D5-2: SigML Definition ViSiCAST Project Working Document (2001)
12. Glauert, J.R.W.: ViSiCAST Sign Language using Virtual Humans. In: ICAT 2002, International Conference on Assistive Technology, pp. 21–22 (2002)
13. Kennaway, R.: 5th International Workshop on Gesture and Sign Language based Humman-Computer Interaction, Genova, Italy (April 2003)

Data Fusion at Different Levels

Marcos Faundez-Zanuy

Escola Universitària Politècnica de Mataró
Avda. Puig i Cadafalch 101-111, 08303 MATARÓ (BARCELONA)
faundez@eupmt.es

Abstract. This paper summarizes the main characteristics of data fusion at different levels (sensor, features, scores and decisions). Although it is presented in the framework of biometric applications it is general for all the pattern recognition applications because this presentation is focused in the main blocks of a general pattern recognition system. Thus, the application in mind will imply a different sensor, feature extractor, classifier and decision maker but data fusion will be performed in a similar way.

1 Introduction

There has been a paradigm shift in the approach to solving pattern recognition problems [1-2]: Instead of looking for the best set of features and the best classifier, now we look for the best set of classifiers and then the best combination method. To solve really hard problems, we will have to use several different representations. It is time to stop arguing over which type of pattern classification technique is best because that depends on our context and goal. Instead we should work at a higher level of organization and discover how to build managerial systems to exploit the different virtues and evade the different limitations of each of these ways of comparing things.

There are several scientific fields where data fusion is performed. Some examples [3] are the following:

- Weather forecasting: forecasting systems rely on the evidence provided by diverse sources of information such as geostationary meteorological satellites, weather balloons, ground stations, radars, etc.
- Robot navigation: a robot is typically fitted with a variety of sound, light, image, proximity etc. sensors
- Land mine detection: several types of sensor technologies are being used to detect buried land mines: electromagnetic induction, ground penetrating radar, infra-red imaging, chemical detectors, etc.

The general scheme of a pattern recognition system consists of four main blocks, as shown in figure 1. Each block corresponds to one possible data fusion level. Data fusion combines sources of multiple evidences. In the case of biometrics [4], the following sources can be identified:

- Multi-sample (for instance, several snapshots of a face)
- Multi-modal (example: face and speech)

A. Esposito et al. (Eds.): Multimodal Signals, LNAI 5398, pp. 94–103, 2009.

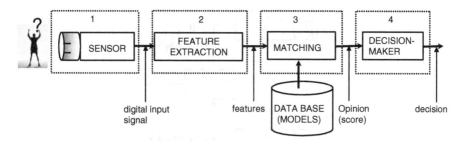

Fig. 1. General scheme of a biometric system

- Multi-sensor (for instance, two microphones for rec. speech)
- Multi-algorithm (for instance, HMM and SVM)
- Multi-instance (for instance, left and right irises)

In all the cases, the system can be classified as:

a)   Unimodal biometric system: it relies on a single biometric characteristic.

b)   Multimodal biometric system: it uses multiple biometric characteristics, like voice plus fingerprint or face plus iris.

Usually the unimodal systems are easier to install, the computational burden is typically smaller, they are easier to use, and cheaper, because just one sensor (or several sensors of the same kind) are needed. On the other hand, a multimodal system can overcome the limitations of a single biometric characteristic.

2 Data Fusion Levels

Considering the main blocks plotted in figure 1, the following levels can be defined:

Sensor Level

In this level, the digital input signal is the result of sensing the same biometric characteristic with two or more sensors. Thus, it is related to unimodal biometrics. Figure 2 shows an example of sensor fusion that consists of sensing a speech signal simultaneously with two different microphones for a speaker recognition application [5]. The combination of the input signals can provide noise cancellation, blind source separation, etc.

Another example is face recognition using multiple cameras that are used to acquire frontal and profile images in order to obtain a three dimensional face model, which is used for feature extraction.

Although this fusion level is useful in several scenarios, it is not the most usual one.

Feature Level

This level can apply to the extraction of different features over a single biometric signal (unimodal system) and the combination of feature levels extracted from different

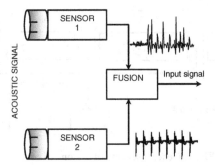

Fig. 2. Example of sensor fusion for speech signals. This block should replace block number 1 in fig. 1.

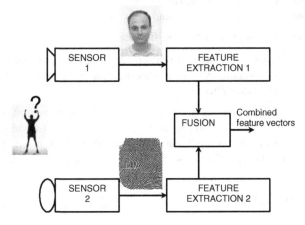

Fig. 3. Example of feature fusion. This block should replace blocks number 1 and 2 in figure 1.

biometric characteristics (multimodal system). An example of a unimodal system is the combination of instantaneous and transitional information for speaker recognition.

Figure 3 shows an example that consists of a combination of face and fingerprint at the feature level.

This combination strategy is usually done by a concatenation of the feature vectors extracted by each feature extractor. This yields an extended size vector set.

Some drawbacks of this fusion approach are:

- There is little control over the contribution of each vector component on the final result, and the augmented feature space can imply a more difficult classifier design, the need for more training and testing data, etc.
- Both feature extractors should provide identical vector rates. This could not be a problem for the combination of face and fingerprint, because one vector per acquisition can be obtained. However, it can be a problem for combining voice with another biometric characteristic, due to the high number of vectors that depend on the test sentence length (if both feature extractors do not provide the same amount of vectors per trial, it is not possible to concatenate the vectors extracted by each feature extractor)

Although it is a common belief that the earlier the combination is done, the better is the result achieved, state-of-the-art data fusion relies mainly on the opinion and decision levels.

Opinion Level

This kind of fusion is also known as confidence level. It consists of the combination of the scores provided by each matcher. The matcher just provides a distance measure or a similarity measure between the input features and the models stored on the database.

It is possible to combine several classifiers working with the same biometric characteristic (unimodal systems) or to combine different ones. Figure 4 shows an example of multimodal combination of face and iris.

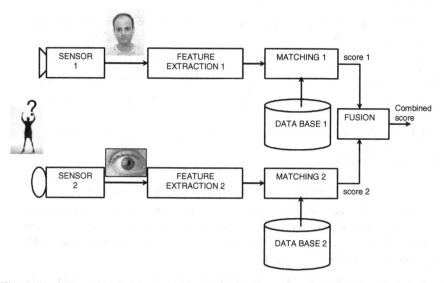

Fig. 4. Example of opinion fusion. This block should replace blocks number 1, 2, and 3 in figure 1.

Before opinion fusion, normalization must be done. For instance, if the measures of the first classifier are similarity measures that lie on the [0, 1] range, and the measures of the second classifier are distance measures that range on [0, 100] two normalizations must be done:

1. The similarity measures must be converted into distance measures (or vice versa).
2. The location and scale parameters of the similarity scores from the individual classifiers must be shifted to a common range. Although several approaches to score normalization exist, this is still an unsolved problem. A given normalization strategy will not be the optimal for all the scenarios. One possible normalization consists of using a sigmoid function: $o_i' = \dfrac{1}{1+e^{-k_i}}$, with $k_i = \dfrac{o_i - (m_i - 2\sigma_i)}{2\sigma_i}$

where:

$o_i' \in [0,1]$, o_i is the initial opinion of the classifier i.

m_i, σ_i are the mean and standard deviation of the classifier i opinions obtained with data belonging to genuine users (scores obtained comparing feature vectors belonging to the same user as the model).

After the normalization procedure, several combination schemes can be applied [6].

Figure 5 shows an example of two speaker recognition system, the first one is based on Covariance matrices and the second one in Vector Quantization.

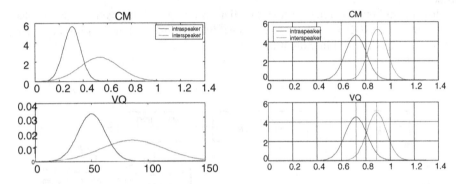

Fig. 5. Example of histograms for intra and interdistances for two speaker recognition systems Covariance matrices (CM) and Vector Quantization (VQ), before (on the left) and after normalization (on the right)

The combination strategies can be classified into three main groups:

1. Fixed rules: All the classifiers have the same relevance. An example is the sum of the outputs of the classifiers. That is: let o_1 and o_2 be the outputs of classifiers number 1 and 2 respectively. For example, a fixed combination rule yields the combined output $O = (o_1 + o_2)/2$

2. Trained rules: Some classifiers should have more relevance on the final result. This is achieved by means of some weighting factors that are computed using a training sequence. That is: $O = \omega_1 o_1 + \omega_2 o_2 = \omega_1 o_1 + (1 - \omega_1) o_2$. Figure 6 shows an example of a trained rule that consists of the combination of two different classifiers for speech recognition. It is interesting to observe that for $\omega_1 = 1$ (83.8% identification rate) just the first classifier is considered, while for $\omega_1 = 0$ (79.2% identification rate) just the second classifier has relevance. For intermediate values, higher identification rates are achieved (84.8%).

3. Adaptive rules: The relevance of each classifier depends on the instant time. This is interesting for variable environments. That is: $O = \omega_1(t) o_1 + (1 - \omega_1(t)) o_2$. For instance, a system that combines speech and face can detect those situations where the background noise increases and then reduce the speech classifier weight. Similarly, the face classifier weight is decreased when the illumination degrades or there is no evidence that a frontal face is present.

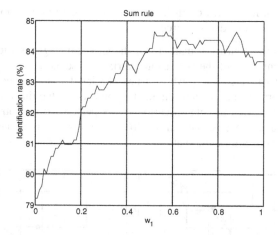

Fig. 6. Example of trained rule for opinion fusion. It combines two different speaker recognition classifiers.

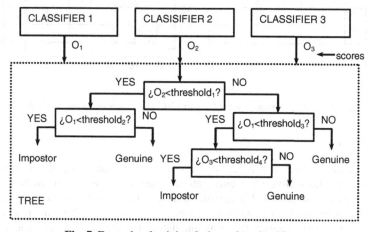

Fig. 7. Example of opinion fusion using classifier trees

The most popular combination schemes are:

1. Weighted sum: $O_j = \sum_{i=1}^{N} \omega_i o_{ij}$. A particular case would be the arithmetic mean.

    for instance, for two classifiers combination assigning equal weight to both of them, $O = (o_1 + o_2)/2$.

2. Weighted product: $O_j = \prod_{i=1}^{N} (o_{ij})^{\omega_i}$. A particular case would be the geometric

    mean. For instance, for a two classifiers combination assigning equal weight to both of them, $O = \sqrt{o_1 \times o_2} = (o_1)^{\frac{1}{2}} \times (o_2)^{\frac{1}{2}}$

3. Decision trees: it is based on if-then-else sentences. Figure 7 shows an example of data fusion using a decision tree.

Figure 8 shows the confusion matrices of the CM and VQ classifiers of figures 5 and 6. Each element (k, r) of the confusion matrix represents the number of instances in the test data set where a pattern whose true class label k is assigned to a class r. If there were no errors all the nonzero elements would be in the diagonal $(k = r)$. It is interesting to observe that the classification errors performed by both classifiers are not exactly the same. That is, they make different errors. This is the key point for obtaining better results after combination.

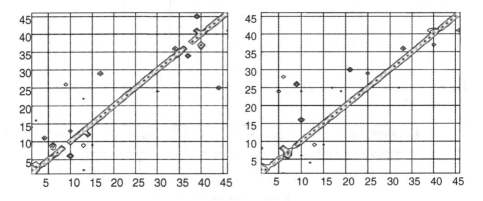

Fig. 8. Confusion matrices for CM and VQ classifiers of figure 5 and 6

Decision Level

At this level, each classifier provides a decision. On verification applications it is an accepted / rejected decision. On identification systems it is the identified person or a ranked list with the most probable person on its top. In this last case, the Borda count method [7] can be used for combining the classifiers' outputs. This approach overcomes the scores normalization that was mandatory for the opinion fusion level. Figure 9 shows an example of the Borda count. The Borda count assigns a score that is equal to the number of classes that are ranked below the given class.

One problem that appears with decision level fusion is the possibility of ties. For verification applications, at least three classifiers are needed (at least two of them will agree and there is no tie), but for identification scenarios the number of classifiers should be higher than the number of classes. This is not a realistic situation, so this combination level is usually applied to verification scenarios.

An important combination scheme at the decision level is the serial and parallel combination, also known as "AND" and "OR" combinations. Figure 10 shows the block diagram. In the first case, a positive verification must be achieved in both systems, while access is achieved in the second one if the user is accepted by one of the systems. If each system is characterized by its False Acceptance Rate (FAR) and False Rejection Rate (FRR) FAR_1 , FRR_1, FAR_2 , FRR_2 ,the combined systems provide:

$FAR_{AND} = FAR_1 \times FAR_2$

$FRR_{AND} = FRR_1 + (1-FRR_1) \times FRR_2$

$FAR_{OR} = FAR_1 + (1-FAR_1) \times FAR_2$

$FRR_{OR} = FRR_1 \times FRR_2$

While serial combination (AND) improves security (FAR is reduced), parallel combination (OR) improves user convenience (FRR is reduced).

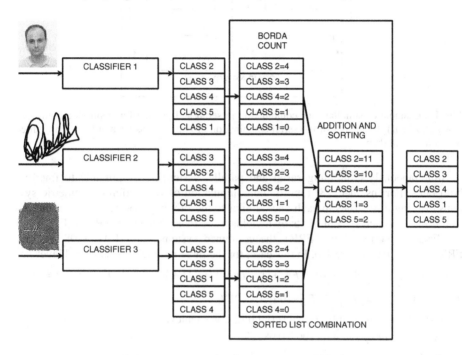

Fig. 9. Example of decision level fusion. It combines face, signature and fingerprint by means of the Borda counts.

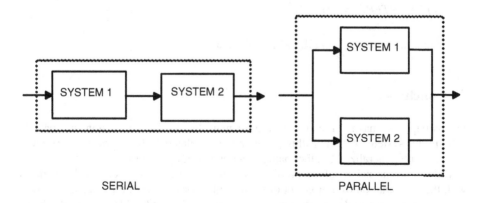

Fig. 10. Serial and parallel decision level combinations

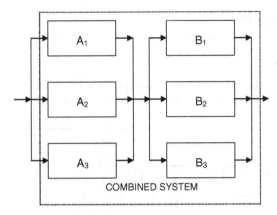

Fig. 11. Example of simultaneous combination in serial and parallel for improving both rates (FAR and FRR). It consists of the serial combination of two systems (A and B) offering three trials on each of them.

Simultaneously combining serial and parallel systems, it is possible to improve both rates. For instance, [8] reports the combination of two different biometric systems offering three trials in each one (similar to the PIN keystroke on ATM cashiers). In this case, if each system on its own yields a 1% False Acceptance Ratio (FAR) and 1% False Rejection Ratio (FRR), the combined system yields FAR=0.0882% and FRR=0.0002. (see figure 11). In this case, for the three parallel blocks we achieve:

$$\begin{cases} TFA(\%) = \left[TFA_1 + (1-TFA_1) \times TFA_2 + \left(1 - \left(TFA_1 + (1-TFA_1) \times TFA_2 \right) \right) \times TFA_3 \right] \times 100 = 2.9\% \\ TFR(\%) = \left[TFR_1 \times TFR_2 \times TFR_3 \right] \times 100 = 0.0001\% \end{cases}$$

And then, for the resulting two serial blocs, we achieve:

$$\begin{cases} TFA_{Eq}(\%) = \left[TFA_A \times TFA_B \right] \times 100 = 0.0882\% \\ TFR_{Eq}(\%) = \left[TFR_A + (1-TFR_A) \times TFR_B \right] \times 100 = 0.0002\% \end{cases}$$

Thus, the improvement is evident because the mean error is:

$$\frac{1}{2} \left(TFA_{Eq} + TFR_{Eq} \right) = 0.0442\%$$

while initially it was $\frac{1}{2} \left(TFA_{Eq} + TFR_{Eq} \right) = 1\%$.

3   Conclusions

In this paper we have summarized the four main blocks for data fusion in a pattern recognition system. Although this presentation is related to biometric recognition it can be easily generalized to other pattern recognition applications.

Data fusion is not a solved problem, and for instance, our recent work [9] deals with the combination of a large set of sources of information. In this scenario a brute force method for weighting computation is not possible and a Maximum likelihood Linear Programming Data Fusion for Speaker Recognition is proposed.

Acknowledgement

This work has been supported by FEDER and the Spanish grant MCYT TIC2003-08382-C05-02.

References

1. Ho, T.K.: Multiple classifier combination: lessons and next steps. In: Bunke, H., Kandel, A. (eds.) Hybrid methods in pattern recognition. Machine perception and artificial intelligence, vol. 47, pp. 171–198. World Scientific, Singapore (2002)
2. Minsky, M.: logical versus analogical or symbolic versus connectionist or neat versus scruffy. AI magazine 12, 34–51 (1991)
3. Ross, A.A., Nandakumar, K., Jain, A.K.: Handbook of multibiometrics. Springer, Heidelberg (2006)
4. Faundez-Zanuy, M.: Biometric security technology. IEEE Aerospace and Electronic Systems Magazine 21(6), 15–26 (2006)
5. Faundez-Zanuy, M., Monte-Moreno, E.: State-of-the-art in speaker recognition. IEEE Aerospace and Electronic Systems Magazine 20(5), 7–12 (2005)
6. Faundez-Zanuy, M.: Data fusion in biometrics. IEEE Aerospace and Electronic Systems Magazine 20(1), 34–38 (2005)
7. Ho, T.K., Hull, J.J., Srihari, S.N.: Decision combination in multiple classifier systems. IEEE Trans. On Pattern analysis and machine intelligence 16(1), 66–75 (1994)
8. Willems, M., Forret, P.: Layered Biometric Verification. White paper, Keyware Technologies (December 1997)
9. Monte-Moreno, E., Chetouani, M., Faundez-Zanuy, M., Sole-Casals, J.: Maximum likelihood Linear Programming Data Fusion for Speaker Recognition. Speech Communication. Elsevier, Amsterdam (in press), doi:10.1016/j.specom.2008.05.009

Voice Technology Applied for Building a Prototype Smart Room

Josef Chaloupka, Jan Nouza, Jindrich Zdansky, Petr Cerva,
Jan Silovsky, and Martin Kroul

Institute of Information Technology, Technical University of Liberec,
Studentska 2, 461 17 Liberec, Czech Republic
{josef.chaloupka,jan.nouza,jindrich.zdansky,petr.cerva,
jan.silovsky,martin.kroul}@tul.cz
http://itakura.kes.tul.cz

Abstract. This contribution is about a system called VoiCenter that allows motor-handicapped people to control PC and standard electric and electronics devices (lights, heating, climate control, electric blinds, TV, radio, DVD, HI-FI etc.) in their homes. The PC and the devices are possible to be controlled with the help of simple voice commands. The wireless connection between PC and the devices was used in this system. This is good for fast installation of this complex system in homes. We have used our own speech recognition and control computer system that is described in this paper too.

Keywords: SmartRoom, Intelligent Home for a Motor-Handicapped Person, Voice Control of PC, Electronic and Electric Devices.

1 Introduction

The real results of many-years research in the area of speech processing and recognition are programs which allow to convert a spoken language to either text or to PC commands in the real time. These applications depend on a particular national language for which the system is developed. The commercial systems especially for voice dictation exist for some world languages - English, French, German or Japanese. We are focused on Czech language because similar commercial systems don't exist till today (2007). The reason is that the Czech language is relatively complicated and it belongs to the inflected languages, therefore the word vocabulary is multiple larger than for example the English vocabulary. We have developed and created several systems with our own speech recognition toolkit in our laboratory SpeechLab in the Technical University of Liberec. The first useful Czech system was the automatic information phone system InfoCity [1] for human - computer dialog via phone (1999). The prototype of Czech dictation system with a vocabulary of 800 000 Czech words was the second system [2] and we have been creating the system for automatic broadcast news transcription (since 2004). The next system was the program MyVoice

A. Esposito et al. (Eds.): Multimodal Signals, LNAI 5398, pp. 104–111, 2009.

(2005) for voice control of a PC [3]. Program MyVoice is developed for motor-handicapped people for whom it isn't possible to use mouse or keyboard and voice is the only possibility how to control any programs in PC. Several tens of handicapped people are using this program at present. We have modified the program MyVoice according to wishes of handicapped people but these people are telling us very often that they have different standard electronic and electric devices in their homes and these motor-handicapped people can not use and control these devices. Therefore the goal of this work was to develop and create some complex system for voice control of PC together with home electric and electronic devices. The modified program MyVoice is the "heart" of this system - we call it VoiCenter.

2 The Voice Control System VoiCenter

This system VoiCenter was developed mainly for motor-handicapped people for controlling of PC and electric and electronics devices in their homes. Several different ways exist at present how to control PC without hands [7], but the voice is the most natural way of them. But the premise is that they can speak. The system VoiCenter consists of several subsystems (modules). They are the following: automatic speaker identification and verification module (ASI/V), automatic speech recognition (ASR) module together with control PC unit - modified program MyVoice, unit for controlling outside devices, and text to speech (TTS) synthesis module, see fig. 1. Single modules and their utilization are described in the following chapter.

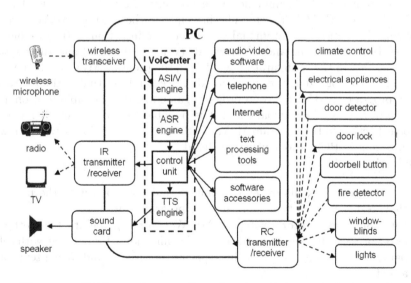

Fig. 1. The system VoiCenter for controlling electric and electronic devices in home of a handicapped person

2.1   Voice Control for PC - Program MyVoice

The core of this program is the unit for automatic speech recognition that was created in our laboratory [3]. This unit works with vocabularies that contain hundreds to thousands of words. It is possible to change a content of that vocabulary according to the settings of the program MyVoice for controlling of single programs in the PC. The recognition system is based on HMM's of single Czech phonemes. The HMM's were trained on several tens of hours of Czech utterances of hundreds of human speakers. Therefore speech recognition is speaker independent (but it is language dependent) and it is relatively easy to add a new word to the vocabulary. Because it is necessary to have a phonetic transcription of this word (or word connection), the phonetic transcription subsystem is a part of the program MyVoice. It is necessary to manually improve phonetic transcription (mainly for foreign and special words) sometimes but it happens only in special cases. Several tens of word groups are for different actions in the program MyVoice and it is possible to switch between single groups by voice commands, for example: One group is for movement in operation system desktop. The voice commands in this group are the following: "Left", "Right", "Down", "Up" and "Take it" - these are equivalent to keyboard keys. It is very easy to select some icon of a program in the desktop and to run the selected program.

If the computer user wants to write text and some text editor was run, then the next group is used for working with text. It is possible to write the text with the help of letters. Where single letters are dictated like: "A" or "Alpha", "B" or "Bravo", etc. or we use for dictation some words (as much as several thousands) that are included in this group. Another group is used for mouse arrow movements. The commands here are like: "Left 10", "Right 50", "Up 200", "To middle", "Click", etc. The principle of the program MyVoice is the following: It connects some virtual computer system action(s) (from mouse or keyboard) to voice commands. New words (voice commands) and their system actions are set in the configuration window in the program MyVoice. If the voice command is recognized, the program MyVoice sends virtual action(s) to the active program (text editor, web browser, game ...). It is possible to pronounce a name of any key in keyboard and it is possible to simulate every mouse or keyboard action in the program MyVoice, therefore we can do every action with any program in PC without using our hands.

What is possible?

1. Run program Calculator, enter numbers and operation with the numbers, show result and use it in some another program if we want it.
2. Run some text editor (Notepad, MS Word or ...), dictate text letter by letter or with the help of words or word connections, format text with select parameters (size of text, font, line spacing, etc.), load and save a text, print a text.
3. Work with Internet, browse any web-pages, look for some information in web-pages, chat with other people and write or read emails.

4. Paint some pictures in different image programs, browse images, photos and videos, play games if we know witch keys or mouse actions are used for playing, play music, etc.
5. If we have in our computer TV or radio card, it is possible to watch TV programs or hear to the radio broadcasting, read a teletext, choose TV and radio stations. If we have a phone card in the PC too, then it is possible to dial phone numbers, talk with friends or with doctors, policemen or firemen (if we need it). These actions are all without using hands, only by simple voice commands.
6. Control electric and electronics devices in the home with the help of some special software and interface that allows communication between PC and the device.

2.2   Speaker Adaptation

We have used speaker independent (SI) HMM's in our speech recognition system but sometimes it is good to use speaker adapted (SA) HMM's if the speaker has some speech defect or if we want to have better speech recognition result. The speaker adaptation module is employed to improve the speech recognition accuracy for individual users of the software. It is very useful to incorporate such a module to the recognition system for handicapped persons because their physical handicap is often connected with a various speech defect (like for people with dysarthria for example).For adaptation, we use the combination of MAP [4] and MLLR [5] methods and gender dependent (GD) models as prior sources: the given GD model (male or female) is adapted by the MLLR method at first and then the created model is used for the MAP based adaptation. The advantage of this approach consists in the fact that also the models not seen in the adaptation data can be adapted (by MLLR) while the parameters of the models with a lot of adaptation data can converge to the values of the theoretically best speaker dependent model (due to the MAP method). The results of performed experiments (see [3] for details) have shown us that the recognition accuracy in the program MyVoice for a quadriplegic girl with a moderate speech defect can be improved by adaptation from the level of 83% on the level of 93% which is not so far from the accuracy for persons with standard pronunciation (97%).

2.3   Practical Experience with Program MyVoice

Practical tests show that it is possible to do any action in PC which is possible to be done with a classical input PC devices - keyboard and mouse with the help of the program MyVoice. The voice command recognition is relatively reliable because it is based on well-tried and many years developed technologies. A user of this program can not narrate any word because all program is based on speaker independent HMM's of single phonemes but a necessary condition is that a human speaker pronounces the voice commands clearly and correctly. It is possible to modify the vocabulary very easily in the configuration program window. The actual group of words is shown in the main program window, therefore it isn't necessary to remember all voice commands. The program is running in the background of active programs and it occupies only a small place on the screen. The vocabulary and recognized words are shown only in this place. The program MyVoice can run well on a PC that has more than 500MHz and the memory larger than 128MB. Then we need a standard sound card and microphone with headphones, and the program is useful only in PC with operation system Windows 2000 and higher. It is possible to order the most frequently used words or sentences by one simple voice command if we dictate some text in the text editor, email client etc. The user can create and use the collection of voice commands for the most frequently used programs like MS Word or for some web browser. It markedly makes working with these programs easy because we can connect several system actions with a single voice command, for example: a single voice command runs some program, opens a new document, sets-up size and fonts, and switches a new word group with the voice commands for this program to the main window of the program MyVoice. The control of the computer mouse is somewhat more difficult with the voice commands then if the user uses the hands but it is possible with a batch of voice commands to move mouse arrow to the exact position in the screen and to simulate a mouse click or double click. More than 50 people use the program MyVoice at present and most of them are motor-handicapped people which told us about their experience with this program and we are improving the program according to their requirements.

2.4   Speaker Verification and Identification Module in VoiCenter

The speaker verification (ASI/V) module is used to secure authorized access to the system VoiCenter only to certain persons or to constrain a command set depending on the speaker identity. This module can be disabled if a handicapped person is alone at home but if not it is reasonable to incorporate such a mechanism since for example children should not have the possibility to tell as much commands as their parents (e.g. cancel the fire alarm). Based on the role assigned to the identified user, a voiced command is accepted and executed or rejected. As the most of state-of-the-art speaker verification systems, our SV module is based on modeling short-time cepstral features by Gaussian mixture models (GMM) and uses a GMM-UBM approach [6]. As well as for speech recognition, MFCC features were used with the difference that c_0, delta and delta-delta features were excluded. Thus feature vector was formed from 12 MFCCs. Speaker verification decision about the claimant identity is based on the log-likelihood ratio test. Claimed identity is accepted if the following condition holds.

$$\frac{1}{T}\left(P\left(X|\lambda^s\right) - P\left(X|\lambda^{UBM}\right)\right) > \Theta \tag{1}$$

where λ^s represents a GMM of a speaker s, λ^{UBM} represents a universal background model, $P\left(X|\lambda\right)$ is the log-likelihood function for a GMM λ, T is the

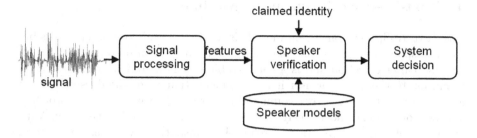

Fig. 2. Principle of speaker verification and identification module in VoiCenter

number of observation used for likelihood evaluation, and finally Θ is a verification threshold.

3   Modules and Interfaces for Controlling of Electric and Electronics Devices in the Homes

At present, a lot of different modules, system and interfaces from some companies for controlling of electric and electronics devices in the homes exist. We wanted to have wireless connections between computers and these devices because the technical installation of such a system is more easier. We have chosen the wireless modules from the Czech company Jablotron. The reason for this choice was that this company is very near to our University therefore the communication with this company was easier for us. We have used wireless (radio) receivers that have two relays which can be controlled. These modules were used for controlling the lights, window-blinds, electric heating and ventilator.

Control of some other electric devices like electric cooker or electric tea-kettle doesn't have sense for motor-handicapped people because they don't have chance to manipulate with these devices. We have got some information how it is possible to use their receiver and transmitter from company Jablotron therefore we have created our own universal transmitter-receiver interface that communicates between PC and wireless modules. This interface can control 20 electric devices in home and it can receive signal from 4 wireless sensors - we have wireless doorbell button, fire detector, door detector and motion detector. The state change of these sensors are shown in the system VoiCenter and the information mesage (audio signal) is sent over sound card to an electronic speaker if the flag output sound is set in the VoiCenter configuration window.

The Text-To-Speech (TTS) synthesis module is used for conversion of information message (sentence) to audio signal. A lot of home electronic devices (TV, radio, HI-FI) have infrared remote controller. Therefore we have used universal infrared remote controller that is connected with PC so that it is possible to control these devices by voice commands. We have a special word group for each infrared controlled electronic device in our system therefore all actions (turns the device on and off, volume increase/decrease, menu, teletext...) in these devices are controlled from PC.

4 Text-To-Speech Synthesis Module

The Text-To-Speech conversion module is used to provide computer a possibility to respond to user's commands. It enables a backward communication in computer-user direction and is a comfortable way how to deliver requested information to the user. For user it is convenient, that he or she doesn't have to look onto monitor after every command to verify if it was recognized properly. Thus he or she can move freely and is not forced to stay in one place. Various kinds of information can be preferably transmitted by voice, e.g. state of the system, command confirmation or alerts. With properly composed dialogue system, monitor becomes unnecessary. Our TTS conversion module is based on concatenation of triphone speech units, with intonation contour modification using TD-PSOLA method. This is today's very common approach. Scheme of the module is in fig.3. Input text is preprocessed first.

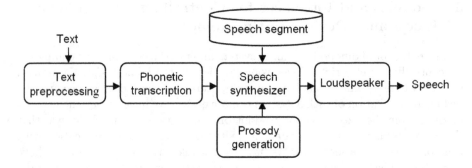

Fig. 3. Scheme of Text-To-Speech (TTS) module

Abbreviations, numbers, web and e-mail addresses are translated to their spoken form (sequence of words), non-printable and unwanted symbols (like *, $ or #) are filtered. Phonetic transcription is performed then - the text is transcribed to sequence of phonemes and sent to a synthesizer. The synthesizer searches for appropriate triphones in a database, concatenates them and applies prosody (intonation, accent and rhythm). Finally, speech signal of the created utterance is sent to a loudspeaker.

5 Conclusion

The system VoiCenter can help motor-handicapped people in many ways. Above all they can work with PC, write and read texts and emails. It is a new element in their lives because they can communicate with some other people from the world or they can start to study.

The work with web browser is relatively easy if they have internet connection, therefore handicapped people have a new possibility how to obtain new information from different web-pages, news, etc. But the novelty in this system compared to the program MyVoice is that it is possible to control a lot of standard home electronics and electric devices from the PC by simple voice commands, therefore they don't need some special cards in PC and they can control such things like heating, climate control, lights etc. so that they are more free in their decisions.

The system VoiCenter is possible to be used in the homes of not-handicapped people too mainly for controlling of electric and electronics devices, but it is better to use computer mouse and keyboard for controlling the PC programs for them. The system VoiCenter is installed in our laboratory at present, but we would like to install this system in the home of some handicapped person in the near future.

Acknowledgments

The research was supported partly by the Grant Agency of the Czech Academy of Sciences (grant no.1QS108040569) and partly by the internal grant provided by the Faculty of Mechatronics at the Technical University of Liberec (grant no. FM-IG/2008/ITE-01).

References

1. Nouza, J., Holada, M.: A City Information System Operating over the Telephone. In: Proc. of IVTTA 1998 Workshop, Torino, Italy, vol. 1, pp. 141–144 (September 1998)
2. Nouza, J., Nouza, T.: A Voice Dictation System for a Million-Word Czech Vocabulary. In: Proc. of ICCCT 2004, Austin, USA, pp. 149–152 (August 2004) ISBN 980-6560-17-5
3. Nouza, J., Nouza, T., Éerva, P.: A Multi-Functional Voice-Control Aid for Disabled Persons. In: Specom 2005, Patras, Greece, pp. 715–718 (2005) ISBN 5-7452-0110-x
4. Gauvain, J.C., Lee, L.H.: Maximum A Posteriori Estimation for Multivariate Gaussian Mixture Observations of Markov Chains. IEEE Trans. SAP 2, 291–298 (1994)
5. Gales, M.J.F., Woodland, P.C.: Mean and Variance Adaptation Within the MLLR Framework. Computer Speech and Language 10, 249–264 (1996)
6. Reynolds, D.A., Quatieri, T.F., Dunn, R.B.: Speaker Verification Using Adapted Gaussian Mixture Models. Digital Signal Processing 10, 19–41 (2000)
7. Evans, D.G., Drew, R.: Blenkhorn. P.: Controlling Mouse Pointer Position Using a Infrared Head-Operated Joystick. IEEE Transaction on Rehabilitation Engineering 8(1) (2000)

Towards Facial Gestures Generation by Speech Signal Analysis Using HUGE Architecture

Goranka Zoric[1], Karlo Smid[2], and Igor S. Pandzic[1]

[1] Department of Telecommunications, Faculty of Electrical Engineering and Computing,
University of Zagreb, Unska 3, HR-10 000 Zagreb
{Igor.Pandzic,Goranka.Zoric}@fer.hr
[2] Ericsson Nikola Tesla, Krapinska 45, p.p. 93, HR-10 002 Zagreb
karlo.smid@ericsson.com

Abstract. In our current work we concentrate on finding correlation between speech signal and occurrence of facial gestures. Motivation behind this work is computer-generated human correspondent, ECA. In order to have a believable human representative it is important for an ECA to implement facial gestures in addition to verbal and emotional displays. Information needed for generation of facial gestures is extracted from speech prosody by analyzing natural speech in real-time. This work is based on the previously developed HUGE architecture for statistically-based facial gesturing and extends our previous work on automatic real-time lip sync.

Keywords: speech prosody, facial gestures, ECA, facial animation.

1 Introduction

Embodied conversational agent (ECA) assumes a human in a computational environment. In human-computer interaction it represents a multimodal interface where modalities are the natural modalities of human conversation: speech, facial displays, hand gestures, body stance [1]. When building believable ECAs, the rules of human behavior must be taken into account.

In face-to-face conversation among humans, both verbal and nonverbal communication takes part. As stated in [2] considerable research is being done on the topic of facial displays with focus on the relationship between facial displays and emotional states. But according to experiments in [3] only one third of nearly 6000 facial displays of psychiatric patients were classified as emotional. In our work we are interested in those facial displays that are not explicit emotional displays (i.e. an expression such as smile). Also, we are not interested in those facial displays that are explicit verbal displays (i.e. visemes) or have an explicit verbal message (i.e. an observation about the size of a massive object may be accompanied by widening of the eyes). In our work we concentrate on the facial gestures. A facial gesture is a form of non-verbal communication made with the face or head, used continuously instead of or in combination with verbal communication. There are a number of different facial gestures that humans use in everyday life, such as different head and eyebrow movements, blinking, eye gaze, frowning etc [4].

A. Esposito et al. (Eds.): Multimodal Signals, LNAI 5398, pp. 112–120, 2009.

In everyday communication humans use facial gestures consciously or unconsciously to regulate flow of speech, accentuate words or segments, or punctuate speech pauses [5]. Work in [6] differentiates several roles of facial gestures in this context:

- Conversational signals – correspond to facial gestures occurring on accented items clarifying and supporting what is being said; facial gestures in this category are eyebrow movements, rapid head movements, gaze directions and eye blinks.
- Punctuators – correspond to facial gestures that support pauses by grouping or separating sequences of words; the examples are specific head motions, blinks or eyebrow actions.
- Manipulators – correspond to the biological needs of a face, such as blinking to wet the eyes or random head nods and have nothing to do with the linguistic utterance
- Regulators - control the flow of conversation. A speaker breaks or looks for an eye contact with a listener. He turns his head towards or away from a listener during a conversation.

ECAs that we deal with in this work act only as presenters and are not involved in conversation so only the first three roles are applicable for them.

Further on, we want to animate our ECAs using only natural speech as input. Speech related facial gestures are connected with prosody and paralanguage. Prosody refers to characteristics of speech which cannot be extracted from the characteristics of phoneme segments, where pauses in speech are also included. Its acoustical correlates are pitch, intensity (amplitude), syllable length, spectral slope and the formant frequencies of speech sounds. Paralanguage refers to the non-verbal elements of communication used to modify meaning and convey emotion and includes pitch, volume and, in some cases, intonation of speech.

In this paper our statistically-based method for automatic facial gesturing in real-time is described. Current version of our system includes the following features:

- head and eyebrow movements and blinking during speech pauses
- eye blinking as manipulators
- amplitude of facial gestures dependent on speech intensity

The rest of the paper is organized as follows. After a description of related work in chapter 2, we describe our system and give discussion on obtained results in chapter 3. At the end, future work and further directions are given.

2 Related Work

In this chapter we summarize work that is related to ours. The first part is more connected to psychological and paralinguistic research relevant to synthesizing natural behavior of ECA with accent on facial gestures which are not directly connected with emotional and verbal signals. In the second part we give an overview of existing systems based on non-verbal speech-related full facial animation where we are specifically interested in systems that are driven by the natural speech. We will mention only several relevant works that give information which helps us correlate characteristics of speech with facial gestures.

Ekman investigated systematically the relation of speech and eyebrow movement in [7]. According to his findings, eyebrow movements occur during word searching pauses, as punctuators or to emphasize certain words or parts of the sentence. Chovil in [2] concentrated on the role of facial displays in conversation. His research results showed that syntactic displays (emphasized words, punctuators) are the most frequent facial gestures accompanying speech and among those facial gestures, raising or lowering eyebrows are the most relevant. Cavé et al. in [8] investigated links between rapid eyebrow movement and fundamental frequency changes suggesting that these are not automatically linked but are consequence of linguistic and communicational choices. Honda in [9] connects pitch and head movement and Yehia et al. in [10] linearly map head motion and F0. Granström et al. investigated in [11] contribution of eyebrow movement to the perception of prominence and later added head movements emphasizing the importance of timing [12].

Existing ECA systems mainly use text or natural speech to drive full facial animation. There is considerable literature on the systems based on text input. To mention a few: [13][6][14][15][16][17]. These systems incorporate facial and head movements in addition to lip movements (voice). Many existing systems are capable of automatic lip synchronization from speech signal [18][19][20][21][22] producing rather correct lip movements but missing natural experience of the whole face because the rest of the face has a marble look. To add facial gestures to such systems, we need more information. As previously noted, knowledge needed for correlating facial gestures and features extracted from the speech signal is based on the results of psychological and paralinguistic research. However, state of the art literature lacks method which would be able to automatically generate a complete set of facial gestures, including head movements, by only analyzing speech signal. Existing systems in this field mainly concentrate on a particular gesture (i.e. head movement), or general dynamics of the face.

Works in [23][24][25][26][27][28][29] generate head movements based on recent evidence which shows that an audio feature, pitch contour (F0), is correlated with head motions [9][10]. In [23] preliminary evidence is given for the correlation between head motion and fundamental frequency. They measured and estimated face and head motion data to animate parametric talking heads. An extension of this work is given in [24], where authors used estimated head and face motion to animate a talking head. Later on, in [25], in addition to F0, they computed a root mean square (RMS) amplitude and concluded that both F0 and RMS amplitude were highly correlated with the kinematics of head motion during the speech. Fully automatic system for head motion synthesis is developed in [26], taking pitch, the lowest five formants, MFCC and LPC as audio features. Work in [27] generates expressive facial animation from speech and similarly as in previously mentioned systems adds head motion, while [28] additionally considers speech intensity as an audio feature. Recent work on automatic head motion prediction from speech data [29] is based on the thesis that temporal properties should be taken into account and therefore the data has to be segmented into longer parts.

Some systems use speech features to drive general facial animation. Work in [30] learns the dynamics of real human faces during speech using two-dimensional image processing techniques. Lip movements and coarticulation is incorporated as well as additional speech-related facial animation. Similarly, the system in [31] learns speech-based orofacial dynamics from video, generating facial animation with realistic dynamics.

While in [32] a method to map audio features (F0, mean power) to video analyzing only eyebrow movements is proposed, Albrecht et al. in [33] introduce a method for automatic generation of several non-verbal facial expressions from speech: head and eyebrow raising and lowering dependent on the pitch; gaze direction, movement of eyelids and eyebrows, and frowning during thinking and word search pauses; eye blinks and lip moistening as punctuators and manipulators; random eye movement during normal speech. The intensity of facial expressions is additionally controlled by the power spectrum of the speech signal, which corresponds to the loudness and intensity of the utterance.

The systems described so far need a preprocessing step. Real-time speech driven facial animation is addressed in [34]. Speech energy is calculated and used as a variable parameter to control the facial modifications such as eyebrows frowning or forehead wrinkling. In our work we include a wider set of speech-driven facial gestures generated in real-time with on-the-fly rendering.

3 Speech-Driven Facial Gestures Based on HUGE Architecture

In speech-driven gestures the idea is to find a correlation between speech signal and occurrence of gestures in order to produce speech-driven facial animation. We are taking into consideration speech prosody features since prosody may reflect turn-taking in conversational interactions, types of utterance such as questions and statements, people's attitudes and feelings etc. – content that cannot be said with words, but shown with non-verbal signals. Prosody is derived from the acoustic characteristics of speech including pitch or frequency, length or duration, loudness or intensity, and pause. While relation between speech and lip movements is obvious, the relation between facial gestures (also gestures in general) and speech isn't so strong. Moreover, variations from person to person are bigger. Research on non-verbal communication of the face [35] [36] gave rules for generating facial gestures during thinking or word-search pauses (i.e. avoidance of gaze, eyebrows raise, frowning), also rules for the use of blinking as a manipulator [6] and rules considering gaze in the function of turn-taking [36]. Many of these rules may be applied when generating speech-driven facial gestures.

In the previous work an automatic lip-sync system was implemented [18]. It takes speech signal as input and performs audio to visual mapping in order to produce visemes. Our current work aims to develop an automatic system for full facial animation driven by speech in real-time. We currently distinguish between several facial animation components:

- head and eyebrow movements and blinking as punctuators
- head and eyebrow movements during thinking and word-search pauses
- blinking as a manipulator

Generation of speech-related facial gestures is based on our HUGE architecture.

3.1 HUGE Architecture

HUGE architecture [37] is a universal architecture for statistically-based human gesturing. It is capable of producing and using statistical models for facial gestures based on any kind of inducement (any signal that occurs in parallel to production of gestures in human behavior and may have a statistical correlation with the occurrence of gestures). The system works in two phases: the statistical model generation phase and the runtime phase.

In the statistical model generation phase, the raw training data is annotated and classified into a timed sequence of gestures and timed sequence of inducement states. An inducement state can be any state determined from the inducement that is expected to correlate well with production of gestures. Next, the statistical model is produced by correlating the gesture sequence with the inducement sequence. Facial gesture parameters that are incorporated in the statistical model are gesture type, duration and amplitude value.

The runtime phase runs in real time and is fully automatic. This phase takes a new sequence of inducement data and uses it to trigger the statistical model and to produce real time animation corresponding to the inducement.

A system based on the speech signal is a special case of HUGE architecture. Its components can be seen on Fig. 1.

Adaption of HUGE architecture to speech signal as inducement included the following crucial issues:

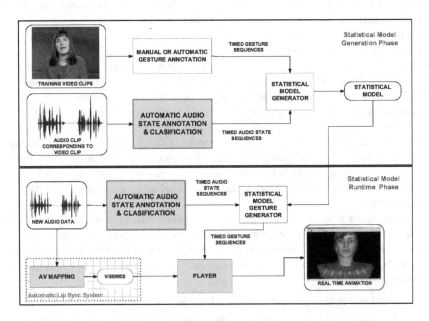

Fig. 1. Universal architecture of HUGE system adapted to audio data as inducement

- Definition of audio states correlated with specific speech signal features
- Implementation of the *Automatic Audio State Annotation & Classification* module, which assumes:
  - o Speech signal analysis and feature set extraction
  - o Speech signal classification into defined audio states
- Integration of the existing Lip Sync system

As a first step we have decided to use a pause in the speech as a base for the definition of audio states. Such decision is motivated by the existing connection between pauses in the speech and occurrence of certain facial gestures shown in the literature. The input speech signal is divided into silence and speech segments. Silence detection algorithm is based on the RMS amplitude value [38]. Speech segments will be used in further work for calculating speech prosody features such as pitch. Silences identified as pauses in speech are used for definition of two audio states – long and short pause. RMS amplitude is calculated for each frame of the speech signal, which is every 16ms just as in the existing Lip Sync system. Lip Sync system calculates visemes for every frame of audio. The results for four consecutive frames are summed and the viseme with the best score is modeled. We follow this idea when classifying speech into audio states. Using the obtained RMS amplitude value and thresholds set in the initial frames, each frame can be potentially marked as pause in the speech. If pause is identified in four consecutive frames, speech signal is classified into the audio state called short pause. When pause in speech is longer than 32 frames, speech signal is classified into the audio state called long pause. Such distinction is motivated by different kinds of pauses that occur during speech. A short pause stands for a punctuator, meaning that its role is to separate or group sequences of words, while a long pause corresponds to a thinking and word-search pause.

3.2 Facial Gesture Generation

Based on the identified audio states, statistical model gives a sequence of facial gestures that might occur on the specific audio state. However, we additionally add certain rules which correspond to the rules that facial gestures have as a communications channel as stated in Introduction. It means that we might add or remove certain gestures depending e.g. on the indentified audio state.

When we consider pause in speech as a punctuator, eyebrow movements, head movements and eye blinks might happen, while during thinking and word-search pauses, eyebrow and head movements are supported. In addition to voluntary eye blinks, we have implemented periodic eye blinks (i.e. manipulators) based on the values given in [6]. If an eye blink does not happen as a punctuator within 5s it will be generated serving as a manipulator.

By using these rules we fine-tune the output from the statistical model. Once we know a gesture type, we know amplitude and duration of the specific gesture since they are also obtained from the statistical model. However, there is a possibility to additionally control amplitude of the facial gesture by calculating speech volume variations.

Having timed gesture sequences and also correct lip movements, we are able to create facial animation (visage|SDK is used). Figure. 2 shows snapshots from a facial animation generated from speech signal and incorporating non-verbal behavior.

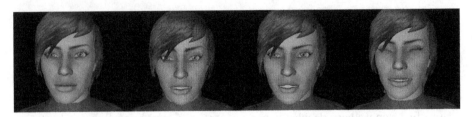

Fig. 2. From left to right: neutral pose, eyebrow movement, head movement, eye blink

4 Future Work

In this paper we have presented a system for creating facial gestures in real-time from a speech signal which incorporates non-verbal behavior. Even by incorporating a small number of prosodic and paralanguage features as well as communication rules, facial animation achieved a lot on naturalness.

However, the system is still in an early stage and there are many things left to do. Next we are planning to add head and eyebrow movements correlated with pitch changes. Adding gaze is an important issue since gaze contributes a lot to naturalness of the face. We will try to integrate as many of the rules found in literature on facial gestures as possible. Fine tuning and evaluation of our system remain an important step in building a believable virtual human.

Acknowledgments. The work was partly carried out within the research project "Embodied Conversational Agents as interface for networked and mobile services" supported by the Ministry of Science, Education and Sports of the Republic of Croatia.

References

1. Cassell, J., Sullivan, J., Prevost, S., Churchill, E. (eds.): Embodied Conversational Agents, p. 430. MIT press, Cambridge (2000)
2. Chovil, N.: Discourse-oriented facial displays in conversation, Research on Language and Social Interaction (1991)
3. Fridlund, A., Ekman, P., Oster, H.: Facial expressions of emotion. In: Siegman, A., Feldstein, S. (eds.) Nonverbal Behavior and Communication. Lawrence Erlbaum, Hillsdale (1987)
4. Zoric, G., Smid, K., Pandzic, I.: Facial Gestures: Taxonomy and Application of Nonverbal, Nonemotional Facial Displays for Emodied Conversational Agents. In: Nishida, T. (ed.) Conversational Informatics - An Engineering Approach, pp. 161–182. John Wiley & Sons, Chichester (2007)
5. Ekman, P., Friesen, W.V.: The repertoire of nonverbal behavior: Categories, origins, usage, and coding, Semiotica (1969)
6. Pelachaud, C., Badler, N., Steedman, M.: Generating Facial Expressions for Speech. Cognitive Science 20(1), 1–46 (1996)
7. Ekman, P.: About brows: Emotional and conversational signals. In: von Cranach, M., Foppa, K., Lepenies, W., Ploog, D. (eds.) Human ethology: Claims and limits of a new discipline (1979)

8. Cavé, C., Guaïtella, I., Bertrand, R., Santi, S., Harlay, F., Espesser, R.: About the relationship between eyebrow movements and F0 variations. In: Proceedings of Int'l Conf. Spoken Language Processing (1996)
9. Honda, K.: Interactions between vowel articulation and F0 control. In: Fujimura, B.D.J.O., Palek, B. (eds.) Proceedings of Linguistics and Phonetics: Item Order in Language and Speech (LP 1998) (2000)
10. Yehia, H., Kuratate, T., Vatikiotis-Bateson, E.: Facial animation and head motion driven by speech acoustics. In: Hoole, P. (ed.) 5th Seminar on Speech Production: Models and Data, Kloster Seeon (2000)
11. Granström, B., House, D., Lundeberg, M.: Eyebrow movements as a cue to prominence. In: The Third Swedish Symposium on Multimodal Communication (1999)
12. House, D., Beskow, J., Granström, B.: Timing and interaction of visual cues for prominence in audiovisual speech perception. In: Proceedings of Eurospeech 2001 (2001)
13. Graf, H.P., Cosatto, E., Strom, V., Huang, F.J.: Visual Prosody: Facial Movements Accompanying Speech. In: Proceedings of AFGR 2002, pp. 381–386 (2002)
14. Granström, B., House, D.: Audiovisual representation of prosody in expressive speech communication. Speech Communication 46, 473–484 (2005)
15. Cassell, J.: Embodied Conversation: Integrating Face and Gesture into Automatic Spoken Dialogue Systems. In: Luperfoy, S. (ed.) Spoken Dialogue Systems. MIT Press, Cambridge (1989)
16. Bui, T.D., Heylen, D., Nijholt, A.: Combination of facial movements on a 3D talking head. In: Proceedings of Computer Graphics International (2004)
17. Smid, K., Pandzic, I.S., Radman, V.: Autonomous Speaker Agent. In: Computer Animation and Social Agents Conference CASA 2004, Geneva, Switzerland (2004)
18. Zoric, G.: Automatic Lip Synchronization by Speech Signal Analysis, Master Thesis (03-Ac-17/2002-z) on Faculty of Electrical Engineering and Computing, University of Zagreb (2005)
19. Kshirsagar, S., Magnenat-Thalmann, N.: Lip synchronization using linear predictive analysis. In: Proceedings of IEE International Conference on Multimedia and Expo., New York (2000)
20. Lewis, J.: Automated Lip-Sync: Background and Techniques. Proceedings of J. Visualization and Computer Animation 2 (1991)
21. Huang, F.J., Chen, T.: Real-time lip-synch face animation driven by human voice. In: IEEE Workshop on Multimedia Signal Processing, Los Angeles, California (December 1998)
22. McAllister, D.F., Rodman, R.D., Bitzer, D.L., Freeman, A.S.: Lip synchronization of speech. In: Proceedings of AVSP 1997 (1997)
23. Kuratate, T., Munhall, K.G., Rubin, P.E., Vatikiotis-Bateson, E., Yehia, H.: Audio-visual synthesis of talking faces from speech production correlates. In: Proceedings of EuroSpeech 1999 (1999)
24. Yehia, H.C., Kuratate, T., Vatikiotis-Bateson, E.: Linking facial animation, head motion and speech acoustics. Journal of Phonetics (2002)
25. Munhall, K.G., Jones, J., Callan, D., Kuratate, T., Vatikiotis-Bateson, E.: Visual Prosody and Speech Intelligibility. Psychological Science 15(2), 133–137 (2003)
26. Deng, Z., Busso, C., Narayanan, S., Neumann, U.: Audio-based Head Motion Synthesis for Avatar-based Telepresence Systems. In: Proc. of ACM SIGMM Workshop on Effective Telepresence (ETP), NY, pp. 24–30 (October 2004)
27. Chuang, E., Bregler, C.: Mood swings: expressive speech animation. ACM Transactions on Graphics (TOG) 24(2), 331–347 (2005)
28. Sargin, M.E., Erzin, E., Yemez, Y., Tekalp, A.M., Erdem, A.T., Erdem, C., Ozkan, M.: Prosody-Driven Head-Gesture Animation. In: ICASSP 2007, Honolulu, USA (2007)

29. Hofer, G., Shimodaira, H.: Automatic Head Motion Prediction from Speech Data. In: Proceedings Interspeech 2007 (2007)
30. Brand, M.: Voice Puppetry. In: Proceedings of Siggraph 1999 (1999)
31. Gutierrez-Osuna, R., Kakumanu, P.K., Esposito, A., Garcia, O.N., Bojorquez, A., Castillo, J.L., Rudomin, I.: Speech-driven facial animation with realistic dynamics. IEEE Transactions on Multimedia (2005)
32. Costa, M., Lavagetto, F., Chen, T.: Visual Prosody Analysis for Realistic Motion Synthesis of 3D Head Models. In: Proceedings of International Conference on Augmented, Virtual Environments and 3D Imaging (2001)
33. Albrecht, I., Haber, J., Seidel, H.: Automatic Generation of Non-Verbal Facial Expressions from Speech. In: Proceedings of Computer Graphics International 2002 (CGI 2002), pp. 283–293 (2002)
34. Malcangi, M., de Tintis, R.: Audio Based Real-Time Speech Animation of Embodied Conversational Agents. LNCS (2004)
35. Cassell, J., Pelachaud, C., Badler, N., Steedman, M., Achorn, B., Becket, T., Douville, B., Prevost, S., Stone, M.: Animated Conversation: Rule-based Generation of Facial Expressions, Jesture & Spoken Intonation for Multiple Conversational Agents. In: Proceedings of SIGGAPH 1994 (1994)
36. Lee, S.P., Badler, J.B., Badler, N.I.: Eyes Alive. In: Proceedings of the 29th annual conference on Computer graphics and interactive techniques 2002, San Antonio, Texas, USA, pp. 637–644. ACM Press, New York (2002)
37. Smid, K., Zoric, G., Pandzic, I.P.: [HUGE]: Universal Architecture for Statistically Based HUman GEsturing. In: Gratch, J., Young, M., Aylett, R.S., Ballin, D., Olivier, P. (eds.) IVA 2006. LNCS (LNAI), vol. 4133, pp. 256–269. Springer, Heidelberg (2006)
38. Rabiner, L.R., Schafer, R.W.: Digital Processing of Speech signals. Prentice-Hall Inc., Englewood Cliffs (1978)
39. http://www.visagetechnologies.com/

Multi-modal Speech Processing Methods: An Overview and Future Research Directions Using a MATLAB Based Audio-Visual Toolbox

Andrew Abel and Amir Hussain

Dept. of Computing Science, University of Stirling, Scotland, UK
aka@cs.stir.ac.uk, ahu@cs.stir.ac.uk

Abstract. This paper presents an overview of the main multi-modal speech enhancement methods reported to date. In particular, a new MATLAB based Toolbox developed by Barbosa et al (2007) for processing audio-visual data is reviewed and its performance potential evaluated. It is shown that the tool does not represent a complete and comprehensive speech processing solution, but rather serves as a standardised, yet versatile base to build upon with further research. To demonstrate this versatility, preliminary examples that make use of these computational procedures with an audiovisual corpus are demonstrated. Finally, some future research directions in the area of multi-modal speech processing are outlined, including future research that the authors aim to carry out with the aid of this newly developed audio-visual MATLAB toolbox, including toolbox customisation, and processing noisy speech in real world environments.

1 Introduction

Speech processing is a diverse field with a range of disciplines, such as speech recognition and speech enhancement. The goal of speech recognition is to have a machine recognise and respond to the speech of a user, whereas speech enhancement is focused on cleaning up a noisy speech signal, with developments such as audio blind source separation (BSS), which aims to solve the "Cocktail Party Problem" [1] by separating a mixture of speech signals. Recently, more research has been focused on multimodal speech processing. It is established that human speech is multimodal [2] [3], with complementarity and coherence between audio and visual signals. For example, it has been found that visual data can help to discriminate between similar sounds such as "f" and "s" [4] [5].

This paper is organized as follows: Section 2 presents an overview of several state of the art multimodal speech enhancement techniques, including kernel based separation, speech fragment decoding and Weiner filtering systems. A recently developed MATLAB Audiovisual Toolbox [6] will be reviewed in section three, which aims to ease and standardise the process of measuring, organising, and analysing speech. Section four will outline some preliminary results and future research directions.

A. Esposito et al. (Eds.): Multimodal Signals, LNAI 5398, pp. 121–129, 2009.

2   State of the Art

2.1   Kernel Based Separation System

Rivet et al [7] have developed a multimodal BSS speech enhancement system, with the aim of removing a speech source from a noisy background mixture. This expands upon previous related work, and is an extension of audio only based BSS solutions. Rivet et al propose to use visual information to complement the audio when BSS is unable to be carried out solely with the audio signal. To provide the convolutive speech mixture, two French speakers are combined. The target speaker utters a mixture of consonants and vowels, and the secondary speaker provides the background noise with well balanced sentences. The two speakers are combined to provide a more realistic convolutive speech mixture.

The speech is extracted by splitting the noisy audio signal into a number of kernels. At a given point in time, the visual vector is made up of the height and width of the mouth opening, and the audio signal is converted to the frequency domain with a Fourier Transform. These parameters are then used to find the permutation of the information that produces the best audio and visual data match, and subsequently the best demixing matrix to be applied to the input signal.

2.2   Speech Fragment Decoding System

Barker and Shao [4] have developed a multimodal speech fragment decoding technique. This is primarily a speech recognition system, but it also covers speech enhancement, and deals with both additive and convolutive mixtures. This system expands on audio only fragment-based BSS. The audio signal is broken up into fragments and grouped by frequency. Fragments dominated by the target speaker are selected, while fragments dominated by background noise are discarded. To provide more information than available in audio only approaches, visual information is used to aid with fragment selection.

The audio signal is passed through a filterbank to split into frequencies, and the visual signal is extracted by carrying out a Discrete Cosine Transform (DCT). Hidden Markov Models (HMMs) are trained to construct a limited word vocabulary, based on a corpus containing a number of small sentences. When attempting to recognise speech, this system works under the assumption that the speaker exists within the trained HMMs, and compares the fragments with a relevant HMM set. The recognition and enhancement stages are intertwined, due to the use of the same HMMs for both.

2.3   Wiener Filtering System

An audiovisual Wiener filtering system has been created by Almajai et al. [8], which attempts to provide an estimation of the noiseless speech signal in order to perform speech enhancement. This research makes use of sentences spoken by a single male speaker, which is then combined with white noise to create a noisy speech mixture. The input audio signal makes use of filterbank vectors, and the visual information is extracted using Active Appearance Models (AAMs) [16]. Two different estimation methods are discussed, global, and phoneme dependent.

The global technique divides the input into frequency domain clusters, and visual information is used to select a single Gaussian Mixture Model (GMM) to apply to the speech mixture. The phoneme dependent method selects a different GMM for each phoneme uttered by the speaker. These are identified with trained HMMs, and the resulting GMM sequence is then applied to the utterance to create an estimation of the noiseless signal. This is compared to the input, and the resulting cleaned up speech is output.

This technique takes a nuanced approach to the content of speech when using visual data. It currently only deals with additive speech mixtures, rather than convolutive mixtures, but preliminary results described by Almajai et al [8] have shown that a lot of the added noise has been removed, with informal listening tests also reporting an improvement in quality.

2.4   Overview of other Multi-modal Speech Processing Approaches

There are many other multi-modal speech approaches that have not been discussed here, including prominent works by Scanlon and Reilly [9], and segment-based recognition research by Hazen el al [10]. Potamianos et al [11] summarise a wide range of speech recognition techniques, with particular concentration on the various visual feature extraction techniques. Another briefer summary is provided by Goecke [12], who review some audio-visual corpora with a focus on multimodal biometric authentication.

3   Audio-Visual MATLAB Toolbox

3.1   Overview

The Audiovisual Toolbox for MATLAB is a collection of functions developed by Barbosa et al [6] for measuring, organising, and analysing multimodal speech data. It makes use of the existing Signal Processing and Image Processing Tool-boxes, and for optical flow analysis, OpenCv is required. Experiments are prepared by converting the data into the appropriate format, and then setting the parameters in an experiment file, inputting information such as the file location and appropriate time windows.

When the data is processed, the raw audio and visual data is converted into more useful values with the aid of a number of functions. These are returned as a matrix, grouping all information about a particular take in one location for ease of analysis. The audio signal is converted into Root Mean Square (RMS), Line Spectral Pairs (LSP), and fundamental frequency (F0) values. If optical flow analysis is carried out, a matrix of pixel movement is returned, along with a greyscale visualisation of movement. Tracked marker data is returned by tracking the movement of pre-defined markers, and performing Principal Component Analysis (PCA). There are also a number of data analysis functions available.

These include functions to resample the data, analyse correlation, window, and enframe signals.

3.2   Limitations

One useful refinement of this toolbox would be to increase the range of visual feature extraction techniques supported. The toolbox can only presently carry out PCA on tracked marker data, and also supports optical flow, has relatively little support for analysis of clean face corpora. It would be useful to update it in order to support some of the more sophisticated clean face techniques such as AAMs or DCT [13]. A suggested outline of additional toolbox functions is shown in Fig.1, showing the current visual techniques supported (3D and 2D Marker Trajectories, and Optical Flow), with proposed AAM modifications.

Active Appearance models were originally developed by Cootes et al. [16], and create models of visual features by making use of shape and texture information. This makes them very suitable for tasks such as the creation of face models, and the generation of appearance parameters for speech processing.

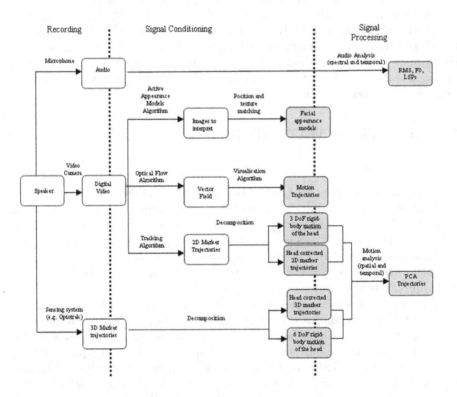

Fig. 1. Modified diagram showing recording, conditioning and processing of speech data, with suggested AAM enhancements. All shaded boxes represent signals that are stored and available to the analysis functions of the toolbox.

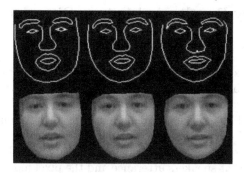

Fig. 2. Example of an AAM trained using selected images from the VidTIMIT corpus. Top row represents shape model only, bottom row shows reconstruction using both texture and shape information.

Existing AAM software can be adapted in a similar manner to the way optical flow is currently utilised. This means that the image modelling and parameter generation are carried out externally, but accessed via MATLAB. The parameters can be read in and converted to the same format as existing audio and visual features, making them compatible with the data structures of the toolbox. This means that the AAM can take advantage of the functions that the toolbox offers such as resampling and correlation analysis. Figure 2 shows an example of a shape and appearance model, trained using images from the VidTIMIT corpus.

There are some advantages to extending the toolbox in this manner. Firstly, although the toolbox is non corpus specific, it is limited to an extent in that if no tracking markers are present in a corpus, only optical flow can currently be used with it. As many corpora do not contain these markers, this reduces the usability of the toolbox. Adding support for AAMs and DCT means that precise visual features can be analysed with more detail than using optical flow, and that the toolbox can be used with a greater range of audiovisual corpora.

Additionally, as the toolbox is still under development, documentation is currently relatively sparse. Functions are inconsistently documented, with no comprehensive guides or tutorials available at this stage in development.

3.3   Benefits

The Audiovisual Toolbox provides a standardised and verifiable set of functions. This saves time as speech analysis functions no longer need to be custom written from scratch, and they provide a degree of automation to ease audiovisual speech analysis. It is also non corpus specific; it can work with a range of different corpora, and can provide a useful starting point to inexperienced researchers.

4   Preliminary Results and Future Directions

4.1   Preliminary Results

Although detailed experiments are at a very early stage, initial experiments have proven the compatibility and feasibility of VidTIMIT with the toolbox.

Fig.3 shows an example of the instantaneous correlation coefficient between the audio signal and lip movement. In this example a single sentence of a speaker from the VidTIMIT corpus is used to demonstrate correlation. The audio and visual signals are processed by functions available in the toolbox to produce the RMS amplitude of that speakers utterance and the pixel movement (attained by performing optical flow analysis, shown in Fig.4) of the image sequence. These

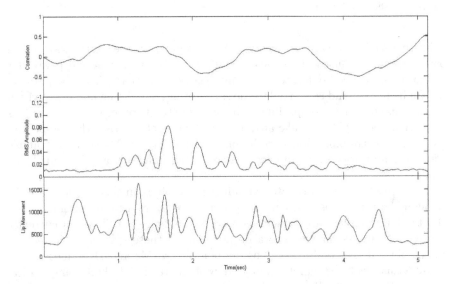

Fig. 3. Instantaneous correlation coefficient between lip movement and RMS amplitude of speech. (Lower plot above shows Lip movement, middle-plot shows RMS amplitude, and the top plot shows the Correlation)

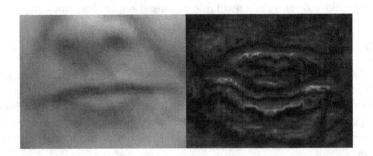

Fig. 4. Example of a cropped VidTIMIT lip image, and optical flow results

are resampled to allow for frame by frame instantaneous correlation analysis, as shown in Fig.3.

It can be seen that the correlation coefficient is usually significantly above or below zero, suggesting that parts of the utterance demonstrate a strong degree of audiovisual correlation. This shows the suitability of VidTIMIT for further audiovisual research. In addition, these initial results also demonstrate the flexibility of the Audiovisual Toolbox. The authors are not aware of any existing examples of this toolbox being used with VidTIMIT, and this work shows the compatibility of the toolbox with untested corpora.

4.2   Immediate Future Developments

For future development, the Audiovisual Toolbox will be used for in depth analysis of the VidTIMIT Corpus [14]. A number of experiments will be carried out, with the goal of deriving a suitable division of speech for HMM or Artificial Neural Network (ANN) allocation. Firstly, the effect of different speakers speaking the same utterance will be carried out, in order to identify speaker independent common visual information. The most suitable division of speech will also be investigated, with the merits considered of dividing speech by single phonemes, multiple phoneme groupings, or whole words.

A comparison of different corpora may be carried out, with VidTIMIT compared to the AviCar [15] corpus. This is to analyse the difference in speech between the quiet VidTIMIT environment, and the noisier automobile background noise provided by AviCar. Speakers talk differently in different environments, and these experiments will attempt to see if there is a significant difference in audiovisual correlation.

4.3   Long Term Future Developments

The completed speech analysis experiments will produce a set of speech utterance divisions that will serve as the basis for construction of an initial wiener filtering system, initially closely related to the one outlined in section 2.3. Once an initial system has been built and tested, it can be refined and improved, for example, by being extended to cover both additive and convolutive mixtures.

The existing audiovisual Wiener filtering system makes use of trained Hidden Markov Models to identify the suitable GMM to use. There is scope for experimenting with other methods of model selection such as Artificial Neural Networks or Genetic Algorithms, and the merits of alternative feature extraction methods could be considered. Finally, this is intended to be a people centred system. Therefore, detailed intelligibility testing on human volunteers will be carried out.

5   Summary

This paper has presented an overview of three state of the art multimodal speech enhancement methods, along with a review of a new MATLAB based Toolbox developed by Barbosa et al (2007) for processing audio-visual data. It is shown that this is not a fully featured speech processing solution, but rather a versatile base for research. Preliminary results have been presented which demonstrate the utility of the Toolbox, along with a summary of immediate and long-term future research developments.

Acknowledgements

This work was funded with the aid of an euCognition travel grant and a research studentship from the University of Stirling. Thanks are also due to Prof. Leslie Smith (University of Stirling) and Dr. Mohamed Chetouani (University Pierre Marie Curie, France) for their invaluable help and input.

References

1. Haykin, S., Chen, Z.: The Cocktail Party Problem. Neural Computation 17(9), 1875–1902 (2005)
2. Sumby, W.H., Pollack, I.: Visual Contribution to Speech Intelligibility in Noise. J. Acc. Soc. America 26(2), 212–215 (1954)
3. Schwartz, J.L., Berthommier, F., Savariaux, C.: Audio-visual scene analysis: evidence for a "very-early" integration process in audio-visual speech perception. In: ICSLP 2002, pp. 1937–1940 (2002)
4. Barker, J., Shao, X.: Audio-Visual Speech Fragment Decoding. In: AVSP 2007, paper L5-2 (accepted, 2007)
5. Almajai, I., Milner, B.: Maximising Audio-Visual Speech Correlation. In: AVSP 2007, paper P16 (accepted, 2007)
6. Barbosa, A.V., Yehia, H.C., Vatikiotis-Bateson, E.: MATLAB toolbox for audio-visual speech processing. In: AVSP 2007, paper P38 (accepted, 2007)
7. Rivet, B., Girin, L., Jutten, C.: Mixing Audiovisual Speech Processing and Blind Source Separation for the Extraction of Speech Signals From Convolutive Mixtures. IEEE Trans. on Audio, Speech, and Lang. Processing 15(1), 96–108 (2007)
8. Almajai, I., Milner, B., Darch, J., Vaseghi, S.: Visually-Derived Wiener Filters for Speech Enhancement. In: ICASSP 2007, vol. 4, p. IV-585–IV-588 (2007)
9. Scanlon, P., Reilly, R.: Feature analysis for automatic speechreading. Mult. Sig. Processing. In: 2001 IEEE Fourth Workshop on, pp. 625–630 (2001)
10. Hazen, J.T., Saenko, K., La, C.H., Glass, J.R.: A Segment Based Audio-Visual Speech Recognizer: Data Collection, Development, and Initial Experiments. In: ICMI 2004: Proceedings of the 6th international conference on Multimodal interfaces, pp. 235–242 (2004)
11. Potamianos, G., Neti, C., Gravier, G., Garg, A., Senior, A.W.: Recent Advances in the Automatic Recognition of Audiovisual Speech. Proceedings - IEEE, part. 9, 91, 1306–1326 (2003)
12. Goecke, R.: Current Trends In Joint Audio-Video Signal Processing: A Review. In: Proceedings of the Eighth Int. Symposium on Signal Processing and Its Applications, pp. 70–73 (2005)
13. Potamianos, G., Neti, C., Deligne, S.: Joint Audio-Visual Speech Processing for Recognition and Enhancement. In: AVSP 2003, pp. 95–104 (2003)

14. Sanderson, C.: Biometric Person Recognition: Face, Speech and Fusion. VDM-Verlag (2008)
15. Lee, B., Hasegawa-Johnson, M., Goudeseune, C., Kamdar, S., Borys, S., Liu, M., Huang, T.: AVICAR: audio-visual speech corpus in a car environment. In: Interspeech 2004, pp. 2489–2492 (2004)
16. Cootes, T.F., Edwards, G.J., Taylor, C.J.: Active Appearance Models. IEEE Trans. On Pattern Analysis and Machine Intelligence 23(6), 681–685 (2001)

From Extensity to Protensity in CAS: Adding Sounds to Icons

Alina E. Lascu and Alexandru V. Georgescu

"LUCIAN BLAGA" University of Sibiu, Romania
Faculty of Political Sciences, International Relations and Security Studies
"POLITEHNICA" University of Timişoara, Romania
Faculty of Automation and Computers
{alina.lascu,alexandrugeorgescu}@gmail.com

Abstract. Being aware of the gap between technological offers and user expectations, the paper aims to illustrate the necessity of anthropocentric designs ("user-pulled") and to reveal the dangers of current ICT designs ("technology-pushed"). Since the gap is deepened because of insufficient innovative use of new agent-oriented technology potential, an affordable manner to "invent new Computer-Aided x" application domains is proposed. To substantiate the approach, the domain must be challenging, easy to implement and "as humanist as possible": Computer-Aided Semiosis (CAS). On this background, the paper also presents a new and challenging concept in IT applied research, borrowed from psychology and meant to assist the process of semiosis: protensity. If the prior researches focused on images and implicitly on extensity (i.e. extensity versus image-based messages; protensity versus sound-based messages), the idea is to extend CAS through innovative attributes, in line with music-oriented user expectations. Thus, the paper refers a newcomer in agent-oriented technology: the Protensional Agents (i.e. interface agents represented on the screen as pseudo-avatars). The paper concludes that CAS is a pathfinder for other researches in this field and the concept of CAS could be used for immediate applied research. Moreover Smart DJ is a good example also for the applicability of CAS in the field of protensity-based messages.

Keywords: Computer-Aided Semiosis (CAS); Anthropocentric trans-cultural interface (ATCI); Protensity; Virtual Disc Jockey (VDJ).

1 Introduction

A relevant indicator of the relationship between users and agent technology is that even very educated people don't realise the peculiarity of the frequent question (with a lot of variants): "What agent is better?" Strange is not the question itself (for instance, the price-performance ratio can be critical for anyone) but from the weird prioritisation: very few users ask such questions after having answers to more burning ones such as: "What could I expect from agents?" or, at least, "If I need something, how could agents help?". Scared by esoteric acronyms, "technology-pushed" users are sure that some of these unknown beasts will invade their lives (the only palliative: choose a palatable

A. Esposito et al. (Eds.): Multimodal Signals, LNAI 5398, pp. 130–136, 2009.
© Springer-Verlag Berlin Heidelberg 2009

one). Such "technological determinism" is not distinctive for agents but here the impact is paramount. In this regard, Protensional Agents (PA) could indulge user's demand by introducing protensity-based semiosis [7], [11] in communication. As Dunlap depicts in [9] "extensity is related to space as protensity is to time"; therefore one can assume that if protensity is more likely to be related to sound-based messages due to its progress in time [7], extensity subsequently can be considered an important characteristic of image-based messages (see Section 3). Hereby, extensity can be associated to images taking into consideration the mechanism through which the human body can easily be aware of being burned, to give just an example, in a blink of an eye, owing to the nervous system. In the same manner an image-based message would transmit an idea in a split second helping this way the user to understand the transmitted message; accordingly, "a picture is worth a thousand words and an interface is worth a thousand pictures" [12] as Ben Shneiderman inferred.

User impact of agent technology. Oddly, some of the user impact of ICTs (Information and Communication Technologies) stems from reversing three questions: "What for?" (the aim: the needs to be addressed); "What?" (the architecture: prospective application portfolio, features, pros and cons, etc.); "How?" (the structure: technological basis best suited to the applications). Thus, the paper tries to redress the balance from an end-user stance, proposing a user-centred one: "What for?" (to get help easy, fast and almost for free); "What?" (the new application domains become affordable); "How?" (a rather different stance: users should impose their needs instead of surrendering to ICTs). Hence, the negative impact of ICTs is partially rooted in the uncertainty caused by the inability to assimilate the magnitude, complexity, diversity, and pace of new ICTs (above all, agents [1]). On the other hand, increased possibilities to interact with other humans or agents have a definitely positive impact. Clearly, such features widen substantially the field of existing application domains and ease the emergence of new ones (as shown below). Thus, the impact (positive or negative) is wrongly attributed to agent technology per se, since it is due rather to its applications.

Motivation. The myth of "inexorable technological determinism" (never truly dead but revived by each powerful technology, such as agents) can be expressed as "modern technology is dangerous for human values; hence, it should be avoided or at least denounced". As "Zeitgeist"-component, such myths, widening the gap, impair trans-disciplinarity [10]. A possible solution: an anthropocentric perspective.

To be relevant the endeavour should address a noteworthy real-world problem: Trans-cultural interfaces, i.e. interfaces able to merge the two complementary premises of a communication between humans belonging to different cultures within the EU: preserve cultural identity; create a common denominator between national identity and the European one. The threads (connotation: train of thoughts) try to explain the need as well as the principles of user-centred design, considering the macro-features promoted by agent technologies. The trends take into account the near future, extrapolating current developments. Finally, describing the threats is the very means to give a warning that the ground is treacherous. To be credible the caveat shall refer to well known and blatant situations; hence, the approach must be based on (counter)examples from a challenging, easy to implement and "as humanistic as possible" domain. Unable to find an appropriate domain, the paper proposes an original, non-existing one: Computer-Aided Semiosis (CAS).

History. The history (before 2004) of this undertaking includes three distinct but inter-related fields: anthropocentric systems; affective interface agents; threats related to the deepening divergence between ICTs and their end users. (Twelve related papers are referred to in [2].) The history (2004-2007) includes some papers in Romanian and calls to more political will to confront the threats regarding e-democracy and trans-disciplinarity [3], [6], [10]).

After the WSEAS Conference in Crete (July 2007), where non-algorithmic e-Learning [16] and CAS were rather loosely related – through their similar approach to visual ontologies – the research attempts now to bring the two fields closer, via a long-range, agent-oriented undertaking: protensity-based semiosis (a main target of [8], described in [7], having e-Learning as application sub-domain [4][5].

2 Approach: Examples Not Models

Why "examples"? Why can the ideas not be exemplified, as usually, by a functional application and why is it necessary to resort to small pieces of virtual applications as examples? Because of:

- "e-Zeitgeist" repercussions: any application shall be a) "just in time", b) extend-able for global use, and c) responding to a socially significant, genuine, and rele-vant user request/need.
- Commercial inefficiency of "solutions in search of problems": before any request, applications must be designed and eventually implemented as fractions with a lim-ited scope, having just enough functionality to become suitable examples. Any pol-ished design is counterproductive.
- The previous reasons are even more pertinent for an innovative domain yet in em-bryo where the request itself is fuzzy.

Why Computer-Aided Intellectual Activities (CAx)? There is always a "new fron-tier" (new research horizons at hand): as regards anthropocentrism in IT an old battle-field exists from the early 70's. Thus, the role of algorithmic reasoning transcended the borders of narrow data processing, penetrating "Computer-Aided x", where x stays for almost any intellectual activity. As a result, "algorithmic reasoning", instead of being perceived as a side effect of "analogue humans loosing the battle with digital computers", became a deeply rooted reasoning paradigm. (Thus, an innovative ap-proach is welcomed [6].)

Why Trans-Cultural Interfaces? The reasons are linked and somehow embedded. The essential one is that ICTs (mainly broad-band) allows an easy implementation of multimodal interfaces. Besides, the broader "Perceptual Bandwidth" (name for the palette of sensorial experiences accessible to humans) obtained as a consequence al-lows the use of also other languages than the spoken/written ones (for instance, body language) [1].

Because users could be assisted by agents in many intellectual activities a sine-qua-non step is to develop affordable and purely software agents able to interpret, evaluate and process protensional and extensional information contained in multimodal mes-sages – in both image-based and sound-based messages.

Such agents must have a "human-like" temporal dimension, action-oriented and highly personalized.

3 Architecture

In the intention to narrow the existing gap between the two stances – the technocetric perspective and the anthropocentric one – tools must be created to make the most of AOSE. Main macro-architectural feature: translation will progress from textual, semantically correct, to multimodal, culturally adequate, based on common concepts and "grammar" (rules to combine them into meaningful sentences).

The ATCI should be able to "translate" the terms using tools designed by a transdisciplinary team. The example in Figure 1 illustrates a correspondence depending on the conversation context (for instance the moneybag put at the right of the apple symbolises a stock exchange context for Apple Computer Inc., Figure 1.a, whereas the same moneybag at left symbolises the market price, Figure 1.b).

The apple is chosen as (counter)example since:

- As an item per se (fruit) it is known all over Europe (apple = pomme, Apfel, mela, manzana ...).
- Being known from prehistoric times it generated a lot of metaphors, symbols, sayings and even traditions (apple alone = fruit, associated with snake = temptation, associated with arrow = struggle for freedom or even the image of Wilhelm Tell).
- Linguistic and/or cultural differences are imprinting a particular style in speaking (connotations, subtlety of language) and, moreover, the use of such metaphors stemming from different cultural environments and heritages. Some of them are common to almost all European peoples (e.g. the apple symbolising or suggesting: temptation, computer logo, and so on, see Figure 1 and 2).
- Nevertheless, some of those metaphors are rooted only in some regions or, if they are widespread, they are relevant only for subpopulation with a higher degree of education; thus trans-cultural interfaces help against distorting the "intentions" (according to Eco: "intentio auctoris", "operis" and "lectoris"). Otherwise, the 'intentio lectoris' could be so altered that the communication process is a failure [2] (see Figure 2).

a) Apple® quotation is rising   b) The price for apples is rising

Fig. 1. Two ways to 'translate' the item apple as 'common denominator' metaphor

- Figure 2 is meant as a counterexample, revealing the necessity of anthropocentric interface design. Thus, if the conversation context is "struggle for freedom" the cultural differences between the continental German cultural tradition and the English one cannot be neglected: the apple (suggesting Wilhelm Tell) had to be put in correspondence with a bow (suggesting Robin Hood); otherwise, treacherous equivalence can destroy the communication process.

a) Wilhelm Tell   b) Robin Hood

Fig. 2. A third way to 'translate' the word apple. The apple and arrow icons usage taking into account cultural differences.

Considering the fact that people from different countries tend to accept diverse kind of icons depending on the nature of their design (from realistic to abstract), the images in Figures 1 and 2 are only partially abstract. Special attention must be paid when designing such an interface, first of all to the icon sets used. As shown in [13] icons are straight-forward when they represent nouns or objects but rather hard to understand when representing actions or verb forms. Also, designing new icons can be a threat because they can lead to a potentially confusing situation where different symbols have the same meaning or, vice-versa, have different meanings in different cultures; thus, existing icons should be used whenever possible. That is why transcultural interfaces are difficult to conceptualize albeit they are easy to implement.

Figure 1 is somehow inspired also from ancient Maya communication techniques, where more subtle differences can be expressed: semantic value is assigned to the iconic space itself. The icon relative position has *syntactic* role (in line with ontology rules) and *semantic* role for CAS (to reduce the differences between 'intentio auctoris' and 'intentio lectoris') as depicted in the Figure where the icon pairs 'moneybag + apple' and 'apple + moneybag' have different meanings. This kind of multimedia ontology based on visual rules can be further enhanced by using animations instead of images.

Recent Modelling. The last developed model is a VDJ (Virtual Disc Jockey) [7] as a response to the modern tendency in music devices to be designed for a larger audience.

Smart DJ should show that *music* and *agents* are linked through their intrinsic *process* nature and as a result, both *semiosis* and *protensity* become vital in agent-oriented research. *Smart DJ* can automatically choose the songs that are going to be played by "hearing" and interpreting the audience's reaction to the type of music previously played.

It uses a microphone to listen to the sounds emitted by the audience/listeners and tries to determine if they mean acceptance (applauses) or rejection (hoots) of the most recently played song.

When a song is accepted or rejected, Smart DJ analyses its attributes to find out the cause (pace, rhythm, etc.). This real time adaptability can be done for example, by playing another song that has one or more similar attributes and observing the audience's reaction it must be interpreted accordingly. Of course, the lack of any reaction (considering in this context, total or partial silence) must be interpreted [7] [8].

Another model illustrating – albeit implicitly – protensity based semiosis is VISON (*VIrtual SOcratic Nurse*) [4] [5].

Both VDJ and VISON are modelled with user-friendly interfaces and agent-oriented software.

4 Conclusions and Intentions

The modular nature of the experimental model at this stage does not allow drawing clear cut conclusions as regards end user evaluations. Thus, the conclusions refer to the approach and the architecture.

- Agent technology, as both stage and trends, is in line with user information and communication requirements. It increases substantially the effectiveness of existing CAx domains and facilitates the emergence of new ones.
- The new domain of CAS responds to actual trans-cultural communication needs for both wide-ranging EU targets and confined bilateral translation. Research in this area must be trans-disciplinary (if not yet in content, at least in spirit and profile) and anthropocentric (in perspective).
- Users should press for a brand certificate ensuring "User-Need inside" (instead of "Intel inside"), to be awarded only when the interface is designed involving them from the beginning (applying the Scandinavian method or the ethnographical one).
- Protensity as message attribute is a motivating research topic both per se (in particular, for music-related activities) and as test bench for agent-oriented software. In this context, the VDJ toy-model presented shows that the approach is both workable and affordable with scarce resources because – albeit quite simple – the VDJ reacts in a relevant manner to audience stimuli.

The following intentions are strongly dependent on possible collaborative work:

- Refining the "apple" example and proposing other relevant pairs of (counter) examples, based on "visual ontologies" shared by agents and humans.
- Founding a framework for CAS as CAx research sub-domain and in particular for: a) helping simultaneous translations in EU meetings; b) improving current e-Learning interface agents (i.e. considering eMaieutics to be more than a starting point in this trial).
- Developing more advanced models of Protensional Agents for different music-related user activities like a *virtual guitar teacher* or a *virtual musicologist* [7], [8].

Acknowledgements

This work was supported by the Ministry of Education and Research through Contract No. 73-CEEX-II-03/31.07.2006.

We thank Professor Ioana Moisil and Boldur Bărbat for their valuable ideas (especially regarding the threats) and Mr. Cătălin Boaru from Apple IMC Romania for kindly granting us the permission to use the Apple® logo.

References

1. Bărbat, B.E.: The Impact of Broad-Band Communication upon HMI Languages (ch. 7). In: Fortunati, L. (ed.) COST Action 269, E-Citizens in the Arena of Social and Political Communication (ch. 8), Communicating in the world of humans and ICTs, EUR21803, Office for Official Publications of the European Communities, Luxembourg (2005)
2. Bărbat, B.E.: Provocative Questions. Session C: Information & communication technologies and the development of democracy. In: Growing up in Europe between Diversity and Equality (seminary), COST Technical Committee for social sciences and humanities, Croatia (2005)
3. Bărbat, B.E.: From e-Learning to e-Nursing, Applying Non-Algorithmic Paths. In: Medinf 2007 Workshop: E-Learning aspects in medicine and nursing. 29th International Conference of the Romanian Medical Informatics Society, Medinf, Sibiu (2007) (to appear on CD)
4. Bărbat, B.E.: E-Maieutics. Rationale and Approach. In: Dzitac, I., Filip, F.G., Manolescu, M.-J. (eds.) International Journal of Computers, Communications & Control (IJCCC). Agora University Editing House - CCC Publications, Baile Felix Spa, Oradea (submitted to ICCCC 2008) (2008)
5. Bărbat, B.E., Bulz, N.: E-World and Real World. From Analysing Concepts towards Integrating Approaches. In: Mulej, M., et al. (eds.) Proc. of the WOSC 13th Internat. Congress of Cybernetics and Systems, pp. 47–57. University of Maribor in cooperation with Encyclopaedia of Life Support Systems, Slovenia (2005)
6. Bărbat, B.E., Negulescu, S.C.: From Algorithms to (Sub-)Symbolic Inferences in Multi-Agent Systems. In: Dzitac, I., Filip, F.G., Manolescu, M.J. (eds.) International Journal of Computers, Communications & Control, ICCCC, vol. 1(suppl.), pp. 68–73. Agora University of Baile Felix Spa, Oradea (2006)
7. Georgescu, A.V.: Agent-Oriented Software for Protensity Messages. Applicattion in Musicology, PhD Thesis: Politehnica University, Timişoara (in preparation)
8. Georgescu, A.V., Lascu, A.E., Barbat, B.E.: Protensity in Agent-Oriented Software. Role, Paths, Example. In: Dzitac, I., Filip, F.G., Manolescu, M.-J. (eds.) International Journal of Computers, Communications & Control (IJCCC), ICCCC. Agora University Editing House - CCC Publications, Baile Felix Spa, Oradea (2008)
9. Knight, D.: A System of psychology. New York, Chicago, Charles Scribner's Sons, Boston (1912)
10. Lascu, A.E., Fabian, R.: eSemiotics for Romanian-German Transcultural Interfaces. In: Sapio, B., et al. (eds.) Conference Proceedings: The Good, the Bad and the Unexpected: The User and the Future of Information and Communication Technologies (on CD). COST Action 298 Participation in the Broadband Society Moscow, Russian Federation (2007)
11. Prudurel, A., Negulescu, S.C., Lascu, A.E.: Mini-Ontology for Trans-Cultural Interfaces. In: Sapio, B., et al. (eds.) Conference Proceedings: The Good, the Bad and the Unexpected: The User and the Future of Information and Communication Technologies, COST Action 298 Participation in the Broadband Society (on CD), Moscow, Russian Federation (2007)
12. Classic Quotes, http://www.quotationspage.com/quote/38372.html
13. ICONS: Much Ado about Something, http://www.humanfactors.com/library/icons.asp

Statistical Modeling of Interpersonal Distance with Range Imaging Data

René Hempel[1] and Patrick Westfeld[2]

[1]Technische Universität Dresden, Faculty of Education,
D-01062 Dresden, Germany
renehempel@hotmail.de
http://tu-dresden.de/die_tu_dresden/fakultaeten/erzw/
[2]Technische Universität Dresden, Institute of Photogrammetry and Remote Sensing,
D-01062 Dresden, Germany
patrick.westfeld@tu-dresden.de
http://www.tu-dresden.de/ipf/photo/

Abstract. The presented work combines automated highly resolved spatio-temporal photogrammetric data acquisition and analysis with statistical approaches for the determination of the interpersonal distance between interacting persons. This topic forms an interesting bridge between engineering and educational research, delivering a new efficient measurement technique to educational research and opening new application fields to photogrammetry.

Keywords: Interpersonal Distance, Range Imaging Data, Image Sequence Analysis, Body Models, Time Series Models.

1 Introduction

Interpersonal distance (IPD) is one dimension of involvement in social interaction and is vital for a broad range of concepts in psychology. Many scientific papers in psychological and educational research focus on this variable in addition to body orientation and mutual gaze (e.g. [3], [4], [5], [16], [24], [25], [26] and [28]). Quantitative data on IPD is usually obtained through questionnaires and/or ratings based on video recordings. In these cases, the evaluation is based on the interpretation of an operator. Besides the significant time effort of interactively processing long videography sequences, unfavorable effects such as unobjectivity as well as a spatial and temporal generalization of the recorded behavioral data are introduced by this procedure. Automatic image sequence processing methods can be used to improve both efficiency and objectivity of videography data processing. These methods have the potential to increase the spatial and temporal resolution at a reduced observational inference. In our research work, we use a novel 3-D camera which simultaneously provides intensity and range images at up to 50 Hz. We adapt existing 2-D image analysis methods to range image (RIM) sequence processing, and we develop new approaches for RIM sequence analysis which allow 3-D tracking of body points over time. This

A. Esposito et al. (Eds.): Multimodal Signals, LNAI 5398, pp. 137–144, 2009.

procedure makes the construction of an abstract body model and the statistical analysis of resulting IPD time series feasible.

2   Photogrammetric Motion Analysis

2.1   Aspects of Photogrammetry

Photogrammetry is a well-established and flexible 3-D object measuring and modeling tool for the determination of the 3-D position, shape and motion of an object (or a person) from one or more images. It uses image analysis methods for the automation of measurement and interpretation tasks and statistical methods to improve accuracy and reliability. The primary results are coordinates of the required object points (over time). Photogrammetric 3-D measurement techniques are characterized by the following features: (i) The objects are measured without being touched. (ii) The spatial and temporal resolution is very high. (iii) The measurement setup is highly flexible. (iv) The data acquisition and analysis is automatically performed with high accuracy and reliability. The applications are widely spread. Up to now, the most important are mainly in the fields of geo-data acquisition as well as in engineering and industrial tasks. This research has the potential to open new application fields to photogrammetry.

2.2   Sensor and Data

At first, photogrammetric motion analysis techniques are restricted to 2-D projections. Capturing real 3-D motion data is possible if (i) additional object information are available (e.g. the proband moves in one plane only) or (ii) one or more additional cameras are used (stereo or multi image).

Fig. 1. Near-infrared intensity image (middle) and color coded range image (right) captured by the 3-D camera *SwissRanger SR-3000* (left, [22])

RIM cameras (3-D cameras, Figure 1) offer an interesting monocular alternative for photogrammetric 3-D data acquisition. RIM sensors allow the simultaneous acquisition of intensity and range images of – in principal – any scene. Additional to the gray value information, the distances to the corresponding object points are measured for every pixel. As a result, a spatiotemporal resolved representation of the object space is given in the form of intensity images and range maps (Figure 1). In the field of RIM sensor technology, 3-D cameras are currently available with a sensor size of up to 25,000 pixels and a frame rate of up to 50 Hz. Advantages of this new 3-D mapping technology are the generation of 3-D data on a discrete raster without stereo compilation, the recording of motion sequences and the marginal dimension. Drawbacks are the limited range, the small spatial resolution and the absolute accuracy in the range of a few centimeters. Possible applications for RIM sensors could be in the field of human-computer-interaction [10], robot vision [15], automotive engineering [31] or human motion analysis [29].

2.3   Range Image Sequence Analysis

Automatic motion analysis in image sequences is a common task in close range photogrammetry. Area-based approaches like cross correlation, optical flow [6] or least squares matching (LSM, [2]) are utilized. The intent of every matching task is the locating of equal features in two or more images and the measuring of the corresponding coordinates. Assuming two images, one image $\mathcal{I}_1$ resp. one image patch $\mathbf{gv_1}$, which is situated around the point of interest, is used as template and the other as search image $\mathcal{I}_2$ resp. search patch $\mathbf{gv_2}$. The best match between template and search patch can be estimated by the maximization of a correlation metric or the minimization of an end function.

2-D LSM formulates the gray value relations between two or more corresponding image patches as non-linear observation equations. The goal is to determine the parameters of a geometric and radiometric transformation by an iterative least squares adjustment. Minimizing the following Equation 1 for each pair of pixels within the image patches at (x, y) resp. (x', y') yields the best guess for the unknown set of parameters.

$$\mathbf{gv_1}(x,y) - \mathbf{v_{gv}}(x,y) = r_0 + r_1 \cdot \mathbf{gv_2}(x',y') \tag{1}$$

whereas r_0, r_1 model changes in brightness and contrast, and $\mathbf{v_{gv}}$ considers a small noise fraction. The geometric affine transformation model in Equation 1 is given by

$$x' = a_0 + a_1 x + a_2 y \quad \text{and} \quad y' = b_0 + b_1 x + b_2 y \tag{2}$$

with two shifts a_0, b_0 and two scales a_1, b_2 in row and column direction as well as two parameters a_2, b_1 for rotation and shear.

With respect to RIM sensors it appears desirable to adapt the primal original LSM algorithm to the RIM data structure. Firstly proposed by [29] and extended and verified by [30], a novel RIM sequence tracking approach (2.5-D least squares tracking; LST) combines RIM intensity and range observations in an integrated geometric transformation model. The intensity observations are used in the same manner as in conventional LSM: Template patch and search patch provide gray value observations for the adjustment. The geometric and radiometric relations between those patches are in accordance with Equation 1.

Based on the same considerations and taken from range value images $\mathcal{R}_1$ and $\mathcal{R}_2$, the relation between two patches $\mathbf{rv_1}$ and $\mathbf{rv_2}$ become

$$\mathbf{rv_1}(x, y) - \mathbf{v_{rv}}(x, y) = d_0 + d_1 \cdot \mathbf{rv_2}(x', y') \qquad (3)$$

at which the 1-D depth shift factor is expressed as $d_0 = \mathbf{rv_1}(x, y) - \mathbf{rv_2}(x', y') = \mathbf{rv_2}(x'^c, y'^c) \cdot (\lambda - 1)$ with a consistent scale in row and column direction $\lambda := \frac{1}{2}(a_1 + b_2)$. (x'^c, y'^c) denotes the position of the center pixel within $\mathbf{rv_2}$. If no scale variations in range patches are assumed, the depth scale parameter d_1 is set to 1. Using Equation 1 and 3 as one integrated model, all transformation parameters can be determined based on intensity and range observations with a standard deviation for shift parameters $\sigma_{a0,b0}$ of up to $1/50$ pixel and a relative accuracy for d_0 of up to 0.25% of the whole distance.

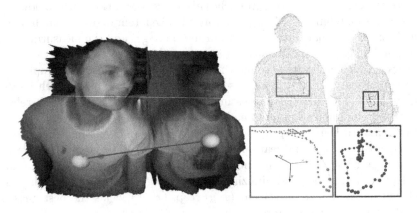

Fig. 2. Visualization of 2.5-D LST results taking probands' centroids as an example. Left: 3-D intensity image with IPD illustration. Right: 3-D point cloud with trajectories.

Applying 2.5-D LST on RIM data, 3-D trajectories of the required body points can be computed automatically (Figure 2). This allows the construction of an abstract body model, which is introduced in the following Section 3.

3   Modeling Interpersonal Distance

The starting point for every statistical analysis is given by a close inspection of data. The data analyzed here is given as a sequence of the RIM vectors $\mathbf{x}_{nit} \in \mathbb{R}^3$ mentioned above, where $n \in N \subseteq \mathbb{N}$, $i \in \{1, 2\}$ and $t \in T \subseteq \mathbb{N}$ is the index of the tracked points, the individual index and time index respectively. For given RIM vectors a simple body model can be formulated. Certain requirements are needed to formulate IPD well. The vital requirement is that the mathematical model allows to define a metric on the underlying space. One is free to choose any metric space at disposal. A natural choice would be $Mat_{3,n}(\mathbb{R}^3)$, the vector space of all $3 \times n$ matrices. In order to collect the given RIM vectors and $\mathbf{x}_{nit}$

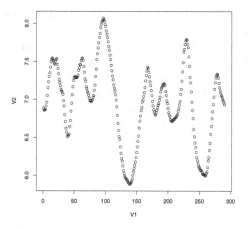

Fig. 3. Time series plot of d_t, $t = 1, ..., 290$

into a matrix $\mathbf{X}_{it} \in Mat_{3,n}(\mathbb{R}^3)$. This vector space is a metric space as is a well known result [1]. Now one is able to define IPD as metric on $Mat_{3,n}(\mathbb{R}^3)$. For the purposes of this article the metric

$$d(\mathbf{X}_{1t}, \mathbf{X}_{2t}) := d_t := [tr(\mathbf{X}_{1t} - \mathbf{X}_{2t})' \Omega (\mathbf{X}_{1t} - \mathbf{X}_{2t})]^{0.5} \tag{4}$$

is chosen. One can also use the vectorized [23] form of d_t for computational reasons. For simplicity reasons Ω is set to the identity matrix and therefore the same weight is given to every RIM vector. Since d_t gives the distance between $\mathbf{X}_{1t}$ and $\mathbf{X}_{2t}$ one can analyze this time series with the available time series tools. A short look at the time series plot may guide the choice of appropriate tools. The plot of the d_t series shown in Figure 3 suggests that modeling IPD by the usual linear filter processes like ARIMA(p, d, q) or even ARFIMA(p, d, q) models [8], [9], [17], [11], [13], [21] is not recommended since the pattern of the trajectory is too smooth for this kind of processes. Although the time series shows an irregular variance with respect to its time average it is also not recommended to use bilinear processes like ARCH(p) or GARCH(p, q) processes [7], [12], [14]. Instead of using the classical time series models we refer to functional data analytic techniques [27]. This techniques assume that there is a true (smooth) curve within in the population. The whole curve is treated as a (function) valued random variable with curves as realizations. Of course one is not able to observe curves. Therefore a main aim of functional data analysis is to derive functional data from discrete observed samples. This is carried out by solving a curve fitting problem by a penalized estimation, given that the true function of the population is an element of a separable function space. In somewhat more rigorous terms one has to solve

$$\min_{\mathbf{c} \in \mathbb{R}^k} \left\{ \|\mathbf{d} - \Phi(t)\mathbf{c}\|_2^2 + \lambda \int_T \left(\frac{d^2}{dt^2} \Phi(t)\mathbf{c} \right)' \left(\frac{d^2}{dt^2} \Phi(t)\mathbf{c} \right) dt \right\} \tag{5}$$

whereas $\mathbf{d} := (d_1, ..., d_T)'$ and $\Phi(t)$ is a matrix valued function of appropriately chosen basis functions. The coefficients $\mathbf{c} \in \mathbb{R}^k$ have to be estimated from the given dataset of $T = 290$ observations and a fixed smoothing parameter λ. It is shown easily that the just mentioned minimization problem has a closed form solution and the estimator $\hat{\mathbf{c}}$ coincides with a ridge type estimator. Hence $\hat{\mathbf{c}}$ shares the mean square efficiency of this estimator [18], [19], [20]. Figure 4 shows the solution of the optimization problem with a spline basis, containing 50 basis functions and a fixed smoothing parameter $\lambda = 1e - 8$.

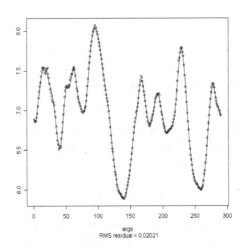

Fig. 4. Time series plot of d_t, $t = 1, ..., 290$ and the estimated IDP curve

The root mean square error (RMS) of 0.02021 indicates a good fit of the given data, which means that the estimated function can describe the behavior of the IPD well. Reducing the amount of basis functions to 40 still yields a good fit of the data by an increase of the RMS from 0.02021 to 0.02733 and a gain of 10 degrees of freedom.

4   Conclusion and Outlook

The presented work shows that data collection of nonverbal interaction data like IPD in dyadic interaction by photogrammetric methods will be a forward-looking tool to model parameters of primary interest in educational research. The data gain compared to the usual questionnaire techniques is outstanding. This huge amount of data makes more sophisticated techniques like functional data analysis feasible since one can rely on the asymptotic behavior of the underlying estimation procedure. The economic effect should not be underestimated as well, since measuring semi-automatically also means that by far not as much human resources (questioners, etc.) are bound in research.

Future work can focus on many generalizations. One can implement a more specific weighting scheme on the tracked RIM vectors. For example one can weight the special parts like hands or even fingers by taking $\Omega \neq \mathbf{I}$; d_t will still be a metric as long Ω belongs to the set of positive definite matrices. The implementation of more general penalty terms like linear differential operators in more than one derivatives could be used to show some sensitivity of IPD, e.g. using indicator forcing functions representing a experimental conflict induced by the researcher. Implementing theory driven lower and upper bounds on the IPD time series which indicates that something might be moving out of normal behavioral baselines is one of the leading problems in educational research that has to be solved appropriately. It will also be important from a photogrammetric point of view to improve the 2.5-D LST. This includes especially handling outlier phenomena and additional geometric parameters. Finally, the proposed approach for modeling IPD needs to be verified in comparison to traditional methods like questionnaires and ratings.

References

1. Amann, H., Escher, J.: Analysis I. Birkhäuser, Basel (2002)
2. Ackermann, F.: High Precision Digital Image Correlation. In: Proceedings of the 39th Photogrammetric Week, vol. 9, pp. 231–243 (1984)
3. Aiello, J.R.: A further look at equilibrium theory: Visual interaction as a function of interpersonal distance. Environmental Psychology and Nonverbal Behavior 1(2), 122–140 (1977)
4. Aiello, J.R., De Carlo Aiello, T.: The development of personal space: proxemic behavior of children 6 through 16. Human Ecology 2(3), 177–189 (1974)
5. Argyle, M., Dean, J.: Eye-contact, distance and affiliation. Sociometry 28(3), 289–304 (1965)
6. Ballard, D.H., Brown, C.M.: Computer Vision. Prentice-Hall, Englewood Cliffs (1982)
7. Bollerslev, T.P.: Generalized autoregressive conditional heteroscedasticity. Journal of Econometrics 31, 143–327 (1986)
8. Box, G.E.P., Jenkins, G.M.: Time Series Analysis - Forecasting and Control. Holden Day (1970)
9. Brockwell, J.P., Davis, R.A.: Time Series: Theory and Methods, 2nd edn. Springer, Heidelberg (1991)
10. Du, H., Oggier, T., Lustenberger, F., Charbon, E.: A Virtual Keyboard Based on True-3D Optical Ranging. In: British Machine Vision Conference 2005, pp. 220–229 (2005)
11. Durbin, J., Koopman, S.: Time Series Analysis by State Space Methods. Clarendon Press (2001)
12. Engle, R.F.: Autoregressive heterscedasticity with estimates of the variance of U.K. inflation. Econometrica 50, 987–1008 (1982)
13. Granger, C.W.J., Joyeux, R.: An introduction to Long-Memory Time Series Models and fractional differencing. Journal of Time Series Analysis 1, 1–15 (1980)
14. Gouriéroux, C.: ARCH Models and Financial Applications. Springer, Heidelberg (1997)

15. Gudmundsson, S.A.: Robot Vision Applications using the CSEM SwissRanger Camera. Informatics and Mathematical Modelling, Technical University of Denmark, Master's thesis (2006)
16. Hall, E.T.: Die Sprache des Raumes. Pädagogischer Verlag Schwann (1976)
17. Hamilton, J.D.: Time Series Analysis. Princeton University Press, Princeton (1994)
18. Hoerl, A., Kennard, R.: Ridge Regression: Biased Estimation for Nonorthogonal Problems. Technometrics 12, 55–67 (1970a)
19. Hoerl, A., Kennard, R.: Ridge Regression: Applications to Nonorthogonal Problems. Technometrics 12, 69–82 (1970b)
20. Hoerl, A., Kennard, R.: Ridge Regression: Iterative Estimation of the Biasing Parameter. Communications in Statistics A 5, 77–88 (1970b)
21. Hosking, J.R.M.: Fractional differencing. Biometrica 68, 165–176 (1981)
22. Mesa Imaging, A.G.: Zurich, Switzerland
23. Magnus, J.R., Neudecker, H.: Matrix Differential Calculus with Applications in Statistics and Econometrics. Wiley & Sons, Chichester (1999)
24. Patterson, M.L.: A sequential functional model of nonverbal exchange. Psychological Review 89(3), 231–249 (1982)
25. Patterson, M.L.: Nonverbal behavior. A functional perspective. Springer, Heidelberg (1983)
26. Patterson, M.L.: Intimacy, social control, and nonverbal involvement: A functional approach. In: Derlega, V. (ed.) Communication, intimacy, and close relationships, pp. 105–132. Academic Press, Inc., New York (1984)
27. Ramsay, J.O., Silverman, B.W.: Functional data analysis, 2nd edn. Springer, Heidelberg (2005)
28. Sommer, R.: Personal space. The behavioral basis of design. Prentice-Hall, Englewood Cliffs (1969)
29. Westfeld, P.: Development of Approaches for 3-D Human Motion Behaviour Analysis Based on Range Imaging Data. Optical 3-D Measurement Techniques VIII, II, pp. 393–402 (2007)
30. Westfeld, P., Hempel, R.: Range Image Sequence Analysis by 2.5-D Least Squares Tracking with Variance Component Estimation and Robust Variance Covariance Matrix Estimation. In: International Archives of Photogrammetry, Remote Sensing and Spatial Information Sciences, Part B5, vol. XXXVII, pp. 457–462 (2008)
31. Zywitza, F., Massen, J., Brunn, M., Lang, C., Görnig, T.: One-to-Three-dimensional Ranging for Future Automotive Safety Systems. In: Proceedings of the 1st Range Imaging Research Day at ETH Zurich in Switzerland (2005)

How the Brain Processes Language in Different Modalities

Bencie Woll

Deafness Cognition and Language Research Centre, UCL, 49 Gordon Square,
London WC1H 0PD
b.woll@ucl.ac.uk

Abstract. Establishing which neural systems support processing of sign languages informs a number of important neuroscience and linguistic questions. In this chapter, the linguistic structure of sign languages is introduced with a discussion of common myths about sign languages. This is followed by a more detailed discussion of the linguistics of British Sign Language, with special reference to features which resemble or contrast with spoken languages. The final section describes language and the brain by describing a number of neuroimaging studies with signers and research on signers who have aphasia or other language deficits following strokes. The neuroimaging and aphasia data are used to explore the 'core language system' – the regions of the brains used for language regardless of modality.

Keywords: sign language, neuroimaging, language and brain, modality.

1 Introduction

1.1 What Are Sign Languages?

Sign languages are the languages of the various Deaf[1] communities of the world; (for example, BSL (British Sign Language) is the language of the approximately 50,000 members of the British Deaf community. There are records of deaf people in different countries using sign language going back several thousand years (in Britain, the first records go back to the 1570s). Sign languages arise naturally wherever there are Deaf communities – they have not been invented by hearing people to 'help' deaf people.

1.2 Isn't Sign Language Universal?

It's exciting to think that there might be a universal language that would unite all people in the world, and many people think that sign language is an example of a universal language. But in fact there are many different sign languages in the world (over 100 have already been recorded (www.ethnologue.com)). Some sign languages are related to each other, like British Sign Language (BSL) and Auslan (Australian

---

[1] The upper case D is used to refer to membership of a sign language-using community. Lower case d refers to hearing impairment.

A. Esposito et al. (Eds.): Multimodal Signals, LNAI 5398, pp. 145–163, 2009.

Sign Language), and users of one can understand the other. But other sign languages – like American Sign Language (ASL) and BSL – are not related, and a Deaf Briton cannot understand a conversation between two American signers. Sometimes people are very disappointed to find this out, but sign languages differ from each other for the same reasons spoken languages differ from each other. Some of these reasons will be discussed below.

1.3 Aren't Signs Just Gestures?

To a person unfamiliar with BSL, signs may appear to consist of random hand and body movements accompanied by facial expressions. Sign languages are of course different from spoken languages because they use the visual, instead of auditory channel. But both spoken and signed languages has a unique set of rules that specifies how words/signs are formed, combined, and understood. All languages have similar grammatical categories, such as nouns and verbs. Every language has the means for indicating time, for forming questions, or negating statements, and so on. All languages are equally complex and capable of expressing any idea.

In spite of the difference in communication channel, linguists find striking similarities between the structure of spoken and sign languages. Additional evidence from functional imaging studies of the brain are described below.

1.4   Are Signs Just Like Pictures in the Air?

Many signs do resemble the concepts they represent (they are 'iconic'), but each sign language uses different icons. People learning a sign language need to learn the signs used in that language. Learning a sign language takes as much time and effort as learning a foreign spoken language. We also know from research that iconicity seems to play very little role in how fluent signers learn and use a sign language.

Sometimes people think that sign languages are like Chinese writing. But the symbols in Chinese writing are representations of spoken Chinese words. Signs are visible representations of concepts. They do not represent either spoken or written words.

1.5   Can Abstract Concepts Be Expressed in a Sign Language?

One of the most common beliefs is that although sign languages can express concrete concepts, they are restricted in their ability to deal with abstract ideas. But all languages are able to meet the communication needs of the communities that use them, and all languages have the flexibility and creativity to meet new needs – the vocabulary of the language expands as new concepts arise. Sign languages are no exception. For example, in recent years, new signs have appeared in BSL for 'fax', 'mobile phone', 'wi-fi', etc. New signs can be borrowed from spoken and written languages, from other sign languages, or new signs can be created. Thus there are no intrinsic limitations on what can be expressed in a sign language. The assumption that sign languages have inherent deficiencies in vocabulary or that they have a simple structure is without basis.

1.6 Are Sign Languages Grammatical?

Word-for-word translations from one language to another often result in ungrammatical or meaningless sentences because each language has its own vocabulary and grammar. The belief that sign languages are ungrammatical, or that they have no grammar, is based on the assumption that a sign language must have a structure identical to that of the spoken language of the community in which the sign language is used. But sign languages are independent languages, not derived from spoken languages and have their own vocabularies and grammar.

2 Sign Language

Following groundbreaking work by linguists and cognitive scientists over the last thirty years, it is now generally recognized that sign languages of the Deaf, such as ASL or BSL are structured and processed in a similar manner to spoken languages. The one striking difference is that they operate in a wholly non-auditory, visual-spatial medium. How does the medium impact on language itself? For some linguistic features there appear to be no effects of modality ([1] p. 2):

- Conventional vocabularies: learned pairing of form and meaning.
- Duality of patterning: Meaningful units built of meaningless sub-lexical units, whether orally or manually produced units
- Productivity: new vocabulary may be added to signed and spoken languages:
- Syntactic structure:
  - o Same word classes: nouns, verbs and adjectives
  - o Embedding to form relative and complement clauses
  - o Trade-offs between word order and verb agreement in how grammatical relations are marked
- Acquisition: similar timetables for acquisition of signed and spoken language.

Despite these similarities, signed and spoken languages may differ because of the characteristics of the modalities in which they are produced and perceived, in particular the differing properties of the sensory and perceptual systems utilized. Pinker and Bloom ([2] p. 713) have noted that the properties of the speech apparatus require that "[…] grammar for spoken language must map propositional structures onto a serial channel […]" (i.e. the sound stream produced by the vocal apparatus where one word follows another over time). In contrast, sign languages are conveyed through a multi-dimensional medium (two hands + face + body) with the articulators moving in both space and time.

Detailed, empirical linguistic research into sign languages is recent, with modern sign linguistics usually traced back to Stokoe's seminal work on the phonological structure of American Sign Language [3]. Since that time, over 100 sign languages used by Deaf[2] people have been identified and described). The sign languages of Deaf communities have not been invented by hearing people and are independent of - although frequently influenced by - spoken languages. These languages operate

---

[2] The term Deaf (upper case 'D') is a cultural term, referring to membership of the Deaf community; lower case 'd' is an audiological term, used when referring to hearing loss.

Table 1. Breakdown of impact of modality differences between signed and spoken language

Spoken language	Sign language
Production	
Articulatory rhythm coupled to respiration and oscillating mandible	Articulatory rhythm not coupled to respiration; no oscillator
Articulators largely hidden	Articulators fully visible
Small articulators	Large articulators
Single articulatory system	Paired and multiple articulators
Perception	
Addressee doesn't need to see speaker	Signer must be visible
High temporal resolution: low spatial resolution	High spatial resolution: low temporal resolution
Acoustic events are the object of perception	Visual events are object of perception
Potential for iconic representation	
Auditory representations usually rely on arbitrary symbol-referent links	Visual representations have greater access to iconicity
Co-speech gesture used for pointing	Indexical signs used for pointing
Suitable for segmented, combinatorial, categorical encoding	Possibilities for mimetic, analogue encoding

entirely within the visual modality (with modified forms employing tactile or proprioceptive reception used by deaf blind signers) and reflect the grammatical options available to visual spatial languages. The vocabulary is frequently highly visually motivated and the grammar exploits the possibility of locating and moving signs through space. Unlike spoken languages, in which there is only one major articulator set, signed languages have multiple articulators, allowing two or even more signs to be articulated simultaneously [4].

These articulatory options are available to all sign languages, but unrelated sign languages of different Deaf communities are mutually unintelligible, although it is a common folk belief that the visual gestural nature of sign languages might make them universal. However, even visually motivated signs can focus upon different features of a referent. For example, a sign referring to "tea" might either reflect the way the tea is brewed or how it is drunk. Further, cultural differences between language users will lead to different signs. For example, the form of signs referring to doors may depend upon whether doors in that language community slide open or open on hinges.

2.1 Iconicity in the Sign Lexicon

In spoken language, an arbitrary link between an object and the word that represents it is the norm. In sign languages, while some signs exhibit an arbitrary mapping between their form and meaning (e.g. NOT-YET), many signs exhibit iconicity: a visual relationship to a real world object or concept they express. The majority of signs in BSL, for example, (estimated at 75% of core vocabulary) are iconic (e.g. TELEPHONE).

NOT-YET   TELEPHONE

.As mentioned above, iconicity is often culturally determined [5]. Iconic links often make reference to only part of an object's visual appearance, so some abstraction may be required to see a link. Children who acquire a sign language as their first language seem unaware of the 'etymology' of a sign such as BSL MILK (it imitates the action of milking a cow by hand) and iconicity plays a minimal role in the first stages of sign acquisition in child learners [6] [7]. It is likely that only later, once the core grammar has been mastered, that young children return to the language forms they have learned previously and carry out a metalinguistic analysis akin to what happens when children discover overtly the segmentation properties of their language during the development of literacy. The link between a sign and its iconic root enters the child's encyclopedic knowledge after the sign's phonological and grammatical properties have been acquired.

On the other hand, iconicity probably plays a major role in second language-learning: it is plausible that adult learners will use their world knowledge in learning the meaning of a sign or in guessing the meaning for a novel sign, and adult learners may be highly motivated to create such links between form and meaning as BSL has no written script, and forming an imagistic representation may be a useful learning strategy. For example the sign for PARIS in BSL refers to the shape of the Eiffel tower [8]. In other words, iconicity is often apparent only with hindsight.

2.2 A Grammar of the Face

When language is not restricted to manipulations of the vocal tract and to auditory perception, it is free to recruit any parts of the body capable of rapid, variegated articulations that can be readily perceived and processed visually. All established sign languages that have been investigated use non-manual signals – facial expressions and head and body postures - grammatically. These expressions are fully conventionalized and their distribution is systematic.

Early research on ASL showed that certain facial articulations, typically of the mouth and lower face, function as adjectivals and as manner adverbials [9]. Other sign languages have been reported to use lower face articulations in similar ways, although the specific facial expressions and their associated meanings vary from sign language to sign language.

A different class of facial articulations, particularly of the upper face and head, predictably co-occur with specific constructions, such as yes/no questions, WH- questions (questions with words such as 'what', 'when', which'), and relative clauses in ASL and in many other sign languages as well. Some of these facial articulations may be common across sign languages (especially those accompanying yes/no and WH-questions) [10] and some researchers have proposed that they evolved from more general affective facial expressions associated with emotions.

2.3 Space and Vision

Representations of events and ideas by humans can involve either a conceptual structure, coding linguistic representations; and an image structure, coding spatial representations [11]. Spoken languages do not encode spatial distinctions directly, but have developed a range of lexical and pragmatic devices for doing so [12] [13] . By contrast, in signed languages, space can be used directly for linguistic expression [14]. While the syntax of spoken language is primarily organized in a linear fashion, reflecting the temporal organization of the speech articulators and of hearing, syntax in signed languages exploits visuospatial organization.

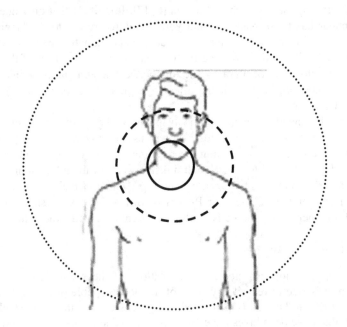

Visual acuity

1.00 ‒‒‒‒
0.05 ‒ ‒ ‒
0.25 ....

Fig. 1. Sign space and visual acuity

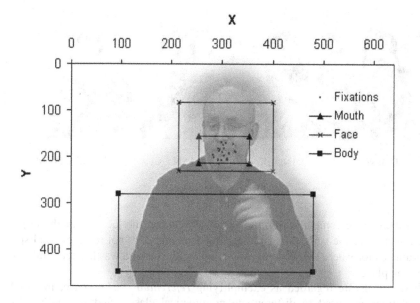

Fig. 2. Eye fixations while observing BSL © [15]

All signing occurs in the "sign space", an area in front of the signer extending from the hips to just above the head, and the width of the extended elbows. Figure 1 shows sign space, with concentric circles indicating relative visual acuity. This decreases rapidly towards the periphery of the visual field.

This decrease in visual acuity towards the periphery is mirrored in BSL by the form of signs. Those signs located towards the periphery of sign space tend to have fewer contrastive handshapes, larger movements, and are more often 2-handed. Signs located in the central visual area have smaller movements, many more contrastive handshapes and are most often 1-handed. In receiving sign language, attention and eye fixations are directed only at the area of central vision (Figure 2).

2.4 Space and Grammar

The use of sign space may be regarded as a continuum. At one extreme, sign space can be employed simply as a region for execution of signs in which the movement or location of signs is purely phonological. Further along this continuum, entirely abstract entities can be represented as spatially related. In the BSL translation of the sentence "Knowledge influences belief", one location in the space in front of the signer is assigned to "knowledge", a second location to "belief", and the verb "influence" moves from the location of "knowledge" to that of "belief". A similar use of space can be applied to more concrete sentences, such as "The man filmed the wedding (see Figure 3 below). In this sentence, he index finger in Frame 2 points to a location associated for referencing purposes to the previous sign, WEDDING; in the 4th frame, the sign BEEN-FILM is directed to the location to which the index pointed.

1. WEDDING   2. INDEX   3. MAN   4. BEEN-FILM

Fig. 3. Referential Space

Although there is agreement within the sentence between the location of the object and the direction of the verb, this is purely linguistic and does not represent real spatial coordinates for where the wedding was or where the camera was located while the filming took place.

Such sentences are regarded as exemplifying *referential* use of space, in which spatial relations are used to differentiate grammatical classes and semantic roles. Space can also be used metaphorically in translations of sentences such as "The professor criticized the students," where a higher location may be assigned to the higher status role of "professor," with the verb moving downwards towards "students." However, the locations of these events in sign space do not represent and are not constrained by "real-life" spatial relations. As concepts move to more concrete meanings, the extent to which real-world spatial features are represented can increase. Thus, at the far end of the continuum, signed languages can convey spatial relations directly: Sentences can be constructed *topographically*. In this case, the space within which signs are articulated is used to describe the position and orientation of objects or people. The spatial relations among signs correspond in a topographic manner to actual relations among objects described. The linguistic conventions used in this spatial mapping specify the position of objects in a highly geometric and non-arbitrary fashion by situating certain sign forms (e.g., classifiers) in space such that they maintain the topographic relations of the world-space being described. [16] (see Figure 4 below).

Signed language grammar requires that the handshapes in verbs of motion and location in topographic sentences agree with real object features or classes (how objects are handled, their size and shape, or their function): These are signed language *classifiers* [17] [18] [19]. In producing the verb in Fig. 4, the sentence translated as "The pen is next to the book on the table" illustrates topographic space. In the third frame the signer establishes a flat-object classifier representing BOOK at the same height as that used for the sign TABLE (Frame 1) and simultaneously produces the lexical sign PEN. In the final frame the thin-object classifier representing PEN is located next to the flat-object classifier and at the same height. Thus the hands form a 'map' of the real world relationships between these referents.

Signed languages thus appear to differ from spoken languages, not only because space is obligatorily recruited for language, but additionally in that certain linguistic

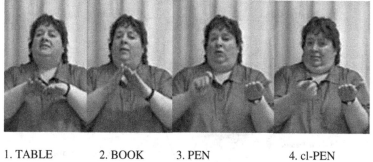

1. TABLE   2. BOOK   3. PEN   4. cl-PEN
                                   cl-BOOK.........................

Fig. 4. Topographic Space

structures use spatial characteristics of semantic roles (classifiers) and spatial locations topographically. Such sentences map a number of spatial and image characteristics, both globally in terms of the relative locations of referents and the action paths
that link them, and at a relatively fine grain, capturing local relationships [4].

At least one study in American Sign Language (ASL) suggests that this continuum
between topographic and non-topographic sign representations has psychological
reality. Emmorey et al. [16] showed fluent signers ASL sentences followed by a probe
item which could appear at a locus in the sign space that was congruent with the noun
phrase in the test sentence or at an incongruent locus. Viewers made a speeded response indicating whether or not they had seen the probe before. Probes that had been
indexed incorrectly were slower to process and more error prone, but the effect of
probe incongruity was much greater for topographic than for non-topographic material. This study suggests that spatial information is processed and represented differently when space serves a topographic function than when it does not.

3   Sign Language and the Brain

Such differences as those relating to the use of space for grammatical purposes open
up new research opportunities. Of particular interest is whether sign languages are
processed by the same neural regions as spoken languages. Differences might suggest
that processing is sensitive to modality. For example, we might hypothesize that the
right hemisphere plays a major role in processing sign language, because this hemisphere specializes for visual-spatial information.

3.1   Brain Structure and Function

Figure 5 below shows a diagrammatic lateral view of the left hemisphere of the human brain. The four different lobes of the brain and some cortical landmarks for language processing are indicated. The primary auditory cortex lies within Heschl's
gyrus. This is hidden from view within the Sylvian fissure on the upper surface of the
temporal lobe. The secondary auditory cortex includes surrounding superior temporal

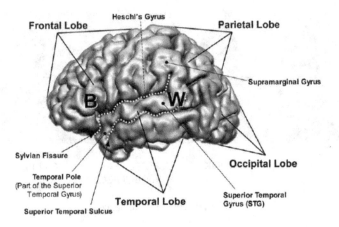

Fig. 5. The left hemisphere of the human brain [20] (©

areas. The area marked with a B is Broca's area, named after the 19th century neurologist who first linked aphasia with a specific area of the brain. Broca's area is located in the anterior region of the left frontal lobe of the cortex, and its function is related to speech and language. When this area is damaged in hearing people, Broca's aphasia, characterized by slow, halting, telegraphic and ungrammatical speech is evident. Conversely, in Wernicke's aphasia, damage is found in the posterior region of the left temporal lobe. Damage to this region does not impair the processing of speech and grammar; instead, it affects the semantic core of language: a hearing patient may speak fluently but often in semantically disorganized sentences ('word salad'). This region also serves auditory processing, so damage to the region is often associated with impaired auditory comprehension.

In the past 10 years, a variety of neuro-imaging methods have been employed to explore the neural systems underlying sign language processing. Campbell et al. [20] provide an excellent description and review of brain imaging techniques and recent functional imaging studies. These studies reveal patterns of activation for sign language processing which are for the most part closely similar to those observed for processing spoken languages, but with some interesting exceptions. In the following section these will be reviewed in some detail.

3.2 Similarities and Differences between Sign Language and Spoken Language Processing

MacSweeney et al. [21] compared hearing non-signers' processing of audio-visually presented English with Deaf native signers' processing of BSL. They found remarkably similar patterns of activation for BSL and English (see Figure 6).

For both BSL and English, although there is involvement of the right hemisphere, language processing is left-lateralized. Also, for both BSL and English there is activation in the inferior prefrontal region, including Broca's area, and in the middle/superior temporal region, including Wernicke's area. There are some differences,

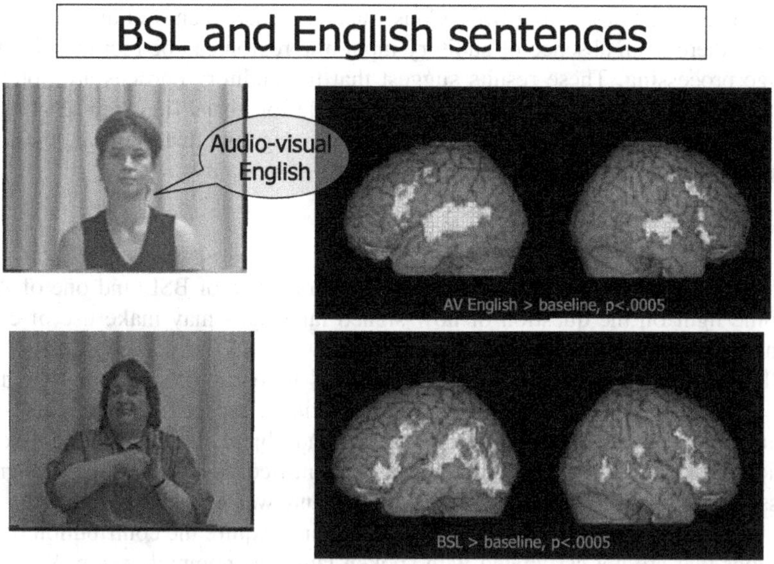

Fig. 6. Processing of BSL and English

however. Although both BSL and English involve processing in auditory cortices, there is greater activation in the primary and secondary auditory cortices for audio-visual English in hearing subjects than for BSL in deaf signers. Conversely, deaf signers show enhanced activation in the posterior occipito-temporal regions responsible for processing of visually perceived movement. In sum, the results of Mac-Sweeney et al. [21] provide evidence both for the modality independent processing of language (whether spoken or signed) but also for some influence of the perceptual channels (visual or auditory). This influence is only partial, since both BSL and English processing involve auditory and visual areas of the brain.

The primary and secondary auditory cortices which process speech in hearing people have often considered to be unimodal; in other words, responding to auditory input only. However, the study above and other recent research suggests that these areas can be responsive to non-auditory stimuli. For example, the primary auditory cortex is activated during silent speech reading by hearing people [22] [23] [24] and during reading of written words [25]. Other studies with deaf participants indicate that the auditory cortices can be involved in processing non-auditory stimuli, such as tactile input [26] and visual (sign language) input [27] [28]. In general, it is clear that many of the areas of the left hemisphere previously considered to be involved in processing of audible speech are also activated in sign language processing.

MacSweeney et al. [21] argue that the region's polymodal potentiality is evident *only* in the absence of auditory input. In their study they looked at deaf and hearing native signers of BSL to ascertain whether hearing status affects sign language processing. Their results indicate that processing of BSL by deaf native signers activated areas in the left superior temporal gyrus; this region includes primary and secondary auditory cortex. Hearing native signers showed much less, and inconsistent, activation in these areas when processing BSL. Consequently, MacSweeney et al. [21] conclude that when there is an absence of auditory input, the region can be recruited for visual language processing. These results suggest that the auditory cortices are potentially plastic, with these left hemisphere areas recruitable for visual (i.e. sign language and speechreading) as well as auditory language processing, and that therefore these areas are specialized for language processing regardless of modality.

3.3   Modality-Specificity

Two recent studies of two groups of native signers – one of BSL and one of ASL – cast some light on the question of how signed languages may make use of cortical systems specialized for spatial processing. MacSweeney et al. [29], in a fMRI study of BSL users, contrasted the comprehension of topographic and non-topographic space, exploring the extent to which precise locational aspects of space, captured by specific language forms (topographic sentences and object classifiers), might activate specific cortical systems. The critical region identified specifically for topographic processing was within superior parietal cortex and was left-lateralized. This study shows that some aspects of sign language processing require the contribution of cortical regions that are not associated with spoken language comprehension. When English translations of the topographic sentences were presented audio-visually to hearing participants in the scanner, they showed no condition-dependent activation, and none in superior parietal regions. Since the visual medium affords the identification of objects and their spatial locations as a function of their forms and locations on the retina and sensory cortex, it is not surprising that cortical systems specialized for such mappings are utilized when sign languages capture these relationships.

4   Aphasia Studies

The first understanding that specific areas of the brain might be involved in language processing came from the pioneering 19th century aphasia studies of Broca and Wernicke. Initially, most research on aphasia concentrated on looking at those areas of the brain which are responsible for auditory perception, speech production and language processing. These early studies often equated speech processing with language processing. However, if sign language processing is left hemisphere dominant, this should be reflected in patterns of impairment following brain damage. In other words, sign language aphasia, like spoken language aphasia, should follow left but not right hemisphere damage. There is now overwhelming evidence that this is the case (e.g. [30] [31] [32] [33] [34] [35] [36] [37] [38]). Furthermore, symptoms are broadly consistent with those found in spoken language impairments. Thus, some individuals have fluent aphasias resulting from damage to Wernicke's area, while others have non-fluent, agrammatic signing, resulting from damage to Broca's area.

Other studies have explored specific features of sign aphasias. Since sign language differs from gesture, in that signs exhibit phonological structure and are combined into grammatically governed sentences, dissociations between sign and gesture should be observed following brain damage. Two individuals, WL (an ASL signer) [39] and Charles (a BSL signer) [35] have shown just such a dissociation. Although WL had a fluent aphasia and Charles had non-fluent aphasia, both produced and understood gestures well, and often substituted gestures for the signs they could not access. Thus, difficulties with signing could not be attributed to poor motor skills. Rather, it seemed that their lesions had impaired the linguistic system, which controls sign, while leaving non linguistic gesture skills intact. Research with Charles and other BSL signers with aphasia also addressed the question of whether iconicity affects the processing of sign. For example the BSL sign CIGARETTE is very similar to a typical gesture for smoking a cigarette. As this example suggests, iconic signs have a degree of transparency, in that people who are unfamiliar with sign language might be able to guess their meaning (e.g. see [40] or detect a connection between the sign and its referent [41]). It is possible, therefore, that these signs are processed differently from non iconic signs, i.e. with greater involvement of gestural systems. However, the available evidence argues against this. Deaf children acquiring sign language appear to show no advantage for iconic signs [7]. Similarly, in tests of sign recall with adults, iconic signs show no advantage over non iconic signs [41]. Emmorey et al. [42] demonstrate that areas activated in the brain when processing signs or words for tools and their associated actions are the same although the signs are heavily iconic while the words are abstract. The dissociation between signs and gestures in Charles' signing pertained regardless of sign iconicity or any similarity between the forms of gestures and signs.

Charles was asked to sign the names of 40 iconic and non-iconic items in response to simple line drawings. Five deaf BSL signers without any sign language disabilities were also asked to sign the names of the stimuli. Overall the control subjects made just 3 errors (mean score 39.4). All errors were due to picture recognition problems. In contrast, Charles was impaired in naming both iconic and non iconic items (see table 1). The small numerical difference between the iconic and non-iconic signs was not significant (chi square=0.92, p>0.5).

Charles made a variety of errors. Many were semantically related to the target, e.g.:

Target	Error
tunnel	TRAIN ... BRIDGE
factory	WORK

Charles also made several phonological errors. All but one of these involved handshape errors, e.g. when SHEEP was produced with a flat hand (an unmarked handshape), rather than a fist with the little finger extended (a marked handshape). There

Table 2. Errors in naming pictures

	Iconic items	Non-iconic items	Total
Correct	13	10	23
Semantic errors	2	3	5
Phonological errors	4	3	7
Fingerspelling only	1	2	3
Gesture		2	2
Total	20	20	40

were 3 occasions when Charles only attempted a finger spelling of the target instead of a sign. One of these was correct (g-a-r-d-e-n); while the others entailed further errors, such as b-o-s for 'bus'. Twice he produced a non-linguistic gesture in response to a request to produce a sign, for example, when he gestured washing for 'soap'.

To compare Charles' ability to sign and gesture, he was presented with a task in which he was asked either to give the name or gesture the use of 50 items. For half the items, the signs were similar to a gesture for the item, such as 'toothbrush'. These were termed SLG items (Sign Like Gesture). For the other half, the signs were different from the gesture, such as 'knife'. These were termed SDG items (Sign Different from Gesture). Items were represented by pictures, with the same pictures used to elicit both gestures and signs. Table 3 below shows the results for this task.

Table 3. Sign vs. Gesture

	SLG Items	SDG Items	Total
sign score	16/25	9/25	25/50
gesture score	23/35	18/25	41/50

Charles was significantly better at gesturing than signing these items (McNemar chi square = 10.22, $p<0.01$). This was true, even when the sign was very similar to the gesture (16/25 vs. 23/25, McNemar chi square = 4, $p<0.05$). Charles's signing errors consisted of semantic and phonological errors, fingerspelling attempts and substitutions of gesture for sign.

Thus despite the superficial similarities between iconic gestures and sign language, they appear to be represented differently in the brain and gesture may remain intact following left hemisphere stroke even when sign language is impaired.

5 Lateralization: Sign Language and the Right Hemisphere

Neville and her colleagues, who pioneered brain imaging studies of ASL, have consistently reported relatively greater contributions of right hemisphere processing to sign language than might occur for processing English (e.g. [43] [44]). These findings have generated a good deal of debate: Although they demonstrated that ASL processing makes use of right hemisphere systems, there are three possible explanations: 1) this reflects linguistic processes lateralized to the right hemisphere; 2) represents a right hemisphere contribution to a left hemisphere linguistic processing system [32] [45]; 3) these findings are an artifact of the experimental design.

The study of signers with right hemisphere strokes can contribute to evaluating the various explanations suggested above for the involvement of the right hemisphere in sign language processing. As already mentioned, in contrast to the effects of left hemisphere stroke, most features of sign language are still intact after right hemisphere damage, even when there are substantial visual-spatial impairments (e.g. [31]). Studies exploring impairments in processing of spatial grammatical structures and of facial information will be discussed here.

Although space is the medium in which sign language is expressed, in general, spatial processing disabilities following right hemisphere impairment have a minor impact on linguistic processing. There are exceptions: right hemisphere strokes cause some impairments in the processing of sentences involving the description of spatial relationships [36]. However, in line with the fMRI studies described above [29] [46] , Atkinson et al. [36] found that signers with right hemisphere strokes are equally impaired on topographic and non-topographic constructions, suggesting that the problems of this group with spatial relationships is a result of non-linguistic cognitive impairments which feed into language, rather than specific linguistic impairments. The second exception to the observation that right hemisphere strokes do not cause sign language impairments is discourse [47] [48] [49]. However, discourse is also vulnerable to right brain damage in hearing people, suggesting that this is one area of language which is not strongly lateralized to the left [50] [51]. It should be noted that while the left hemisphere's role is central in the processing of core elements of language: phonology, morphology and syntax, it has always been recognized that the right hemisphere is involved in discourse and prosody. This is true for both signed and spoken language [52].

This issue was explored in a study investigating the linguistic function of negation in six BSL signers with unilateral brain damage [35]. We have already noted that syntactic processing in signed languages appears to engage the same left perisylvian regions as syntactic processing in spoken languages. In BSL, headshake, a furrowed brow, and a frowning facial gesture are the nonmanual actions constituting the unmarked way of expressing negation. Because negation is considered syntactic, the investigators predicted that processing nonmanual negation ought to be difficult for left hemisphere lesioned patients who had language impairments. Contrary to prediction, however, all three patients with left-sided lesions, who were aphasic for signed language, understood negation perfectly when it was expressed nonmanually.

Negation can also be expressed in BSL by a manual negation marker such as the sign NOT. The patients with right-sided lesions had no difficulty in recognizing negation when the manual sign NOT was present, but failed to understand nonmanual (facial) negation. This unexpected finding alerts us to the possibility that non-manual negation is not syntactic at the surface level, but instead is prosodic.

6   Associated Language Issues

British Sign Language is fully independent of English, both lexically and grammatically. There is no doubt however that English has influenced BSL. This influence is to be expected when any powerful majority language surrounds a minority language. Given that BSL and English have been in such close proximity for many generations, signers have come to use certain forms derived from English.

We would expect BSL to borrow from English for new terminology, and we see this occurring, especially through the use of fingerspelling [4]. Signers can also borrow from any written language using fingerspelling. BSL also reflects the influence of English in its use of mouth patterns derived from spoken English (*mouthings*). BSL uses mouthings in a wide variety of ways [53] and in conjunction with other mouth patterns unrelated to English (*mouth gestures*). The use of mouthings varies with the age and social and linguistic background of the signer, as well as with the situational variety. Comparative research on a range of European sign languages, as well as other sign languages including ASL and Indo-Pakistani Sign Language shows that mouthings feature in all languages, and function in similar ways [54]. However, the amount of use and the exact functions of these components vary.

Recent imaging studies have explored both fingerspelling and the role of the mouth. Waters et al. [55] used fMRI to compare cortical networks supporting the perception of fingerspelled, signed, written, and pictorial stimuli in deaf native signers of BSL. All input forms activated a left fronto-temporal network, including portions of left inferior temporal and mid-fusiform gyri. To examine the extent to which activation in this region was influenced by orthographic structure, orthographic and non-orthographic stimuli were contrasted: fingerspelling vs. signed language. In the fingerspelling vs. signed language contrast, there was greater activation for fingerspelling than signed language in an area of the brain known to be activated when processing orthography – the visual word form area – indicating that fingerspelling, despite existing in the visual-manual modality, is still processed as orthographic, reflecting its role in representing written language.

Capek et al. [56] investigated mouthings and mouth actions. In an fMRI study they established that differential activation from superior temporal to inferior/posterior temporal regions reflected the relative presence or absence of speech-like mouth gestures. While a common perisylvian network is activated by sign language and by seen speech in native deaf signers, differentiation of activation can be sensitive to the type of articulation seen in the stimulus: speechlike orofacial patterns (whether within speech or sign language) consistently activate more superior temporal regions; manual actions more posterior temporal regions. McCullough et al. (57 2005) have studied facial actions in ASL, using fMRI to investigate the neural systems underlying recognition of linguistic and affective facial expressions, and comparing deaf ASL signers and hearing non-signers. Within the superior temporal sulcus, activation for emotional expressions was right lateralized for the non-signing group and bilateral for the deaf group. In contrast, activation within STS for linguistic facial expressions was left lateralized only for signers, and only when linguistic facial expressions co-occurred with verbs. The results indicate that function (i.e. linguistic or non-linguistic) in part drives the lateralization of neural systems that process human facial expression.

7 Summary and Conclusions

The research which has taken place over the past 20 years has confirmed that sign language for the most part uses the classic language processing areas associated with spoken language. Differences are found, and these for the most part relate to the different modalities in which signed and spoken language exist. As Campbell et al. [20: p. 15] state:

> The specialization of cortical networks for language processing does not appear to be driven either by the acoustic requirements for hearing a spoken language or by the articulatory requirements of speaking. It seems likely therefore, that it is the specialized requirements of language processing itself including for instance, compositionality syntax, and the requirements of mapping coherent concepts onto a communicable form, that determine the final form of the specialized language circuits in the brain.

References

1. Meier, R.P.: Why Different, Why the Same? Explaining Effects and Non-effects of Modality upon Linguistic Structure in Sign and Speech. In: Meier, R.P., Cormier, K., Quinto-Pozos, D. (eds.) Modality and Structure in Signed and Spoken Languages, pp. 1–25. Cambridge University Press, Cambridge (2002)
2. Pinker, S., Bloom, P.: Natural Language and Natural Selection. Behav. Br Sci. 13/4, 707–784 (1990)
3. Stokoe, W.C.: Sign language structure. An Outline of the visual communication system of the American deaf. Studies in Linguistics. Occasional Papers 8. University of Buffalo, Buffalo, NY (1960); revised edition. Linstok Press, Silver Spring (1978)
4. Sutton-Spence, R.L., Woll, B.: The linguistics of BSL: An introduction. Cambridge University Press, Cambridge (1999)
5. Pizzuto, E., Ardito, B., Caselli, M.C., Volterra, V.: Cognition and Language in Italian Deaf Preschoolers of Deaf and Hearing Families. In: Clark, M.D., Marschark, M., Karchmer, M.A. (eds.) Context, Cognition, and Deafness: An Introduction, pp. 49–70. Gallaudet University Press, Washington (2001)
6. Morgan, G., Herman, R., Woll, B.: The Development of Complex Verb Constructions in BSL. J. Ch. Lang 29, 655–675 (2002)
7. Tolar, T.D., Lederberg, A.R., Gokhale, S., Tomasello, M.: The Development of the Ability to Recognize the Meaning of Iconic Signs. J. Deaf. Stud. Deaf Ed. 13(2), 225–240 (2008)
8. Campbell, R., Martin, P., White, T.: Forced Choice Recognition of Sign in Novice Learners of British Sign Language. App. Ling 13(2), 185–201 (1992)
9. Liddell, S.K.: American Sign Language Syntax. The Hague, Mouton (1980)
10. Zeshan, U.: Interrogative constructions in signed languages: crosslinguistic perspectives. Language 80(1), 7–39 (2004)
11. Jackendoff, R.: The Architecture of the Linguistic– Spatial Interface. In: Bloom, P., Peterson, M.A., Nadal, L., Garrett, M.F. (eds.) Language and Space, pp. 1–30. MIT Press, Cambridge (1996)
12. De Vega, M., Cocude, M., Denis, M., Rodrigo, M.J., Zimmer, H.D.: The interface between language and visuo-spatial representations. In: Denis, M., Logie, R.H., Cornoldi, C., De Vega, M., Engelkamp, J. (eds.) Imagery, Language, and Visuo-Spatial Thinking, pp. 109–136. Psychology Press, Hove (2001)
13. Kemmerer, D.: 'Near' and 'Far' in Language and Perception. Cognition 73, 35–63 (1999)
14. Emmorey, K.: The Effects of Modality on Spatial Language: How Signers and Speakers Talk about Space. In: Meier, R.P., Cormier, K., Quinto-Pozos, D. (eds.) Modality and Structure in Signed and Spoken Language, pp. 405–421. Cambridge University Press, Cambridge (2002)
15. Agrafiotis, D., Canagarajah, N., Bull, D.R., Dye, M.: Perceptually optimised sign language video coding based on eye tracking analysis. Electron. Lett. 39(24), 1703–1705 (2003)
16. Emmorey, K., Corina, D., Bellugi, U.: Differential processing of topographic and referential functions of space. In: Emmorey, K., Reilly, J. (eds.) Language, Gesture and Space, pp. 43–62. Lawrence Erlbaum Associates, Hillsdale (1995)
17. Emmorey, K.: Language, cognition, and the brain: Insights from sign language research. Lawrence Erlbaum Associates, Hillsdale (2001)
18. Engberg-Pedersen, E.: Space in Danish Sign Language: the Semantics and Morphosyntax of the Use of Space in a Visual Language. Signum Press, Hamburg (1993)
19. Supalla, T.: The Classifier System in ASL. In: Craig, C. (ed.) Noun Classification and Categorization, pp. 181–214. John Benjamins, Amsterdam (1986)
20. Campbell, R., MacSweeney, M., Waters, D.: Sign Language and the Brain: a Review. J. Deaf. Stud. Deaf Ed. 13(1), 3–20 (2008)

21. MacSweeney, M., Woll, B., Campbell, R., McGuire, P.K., David, A.S., Williams, S.C.R., Suckling, J., Calvert, G.A., Brammer, M.J.: Neural Systems Underlying British Sign Language and Audiovisual English Processing in Native Users. Brain 125, 1583–1593 (2002)
22. Calvert, G.A., Bullmore, E.T., Brammer, M.J., Campbell, R., Williams, S.C., McGuire, P.K., Woodruff, P.W., Iversen, S.D., David, A.S.: Activation of Auditory Cortex During Silent Lipreading. Science 25:276 (5312), 593–596 (1997)
23. MacSweeney, M., Amaro, E., Calvert, G., Campbell, R., David, A.S., McGuire, P.K., Williams, S.C., Woll, B., Brammer, M.J.: Silent Speechreading in the Absence of Scanner Noise: An Event-related fMRI Study. Neurorep. 11(8), 1729–1733 (2000)
24. MacSweeney, M., Campbell, R., Calvert, G.A., McGuire, P.K., David, A.S., Suckling, J., Andrew, C., Woll, B., Brammer, M.J.: Dispersed Activation in the Left Temporal Cortex for Speech-reading in Congenitally Deaf People. Proc. Roy. Soc. B 268, 451–457 (2001)
25. Haist, F., Song, A.W., Wild, K., Faber, T.L., Popp, C.A., Morris, R.D.: Linking Sight and Sound: fMRI Evidence of Primary Auditory Cortex Activation during Visual Word Recognition. Br Lang. 763, 340–350 (2001)
26. Levänen, S., Jousmäki, V., Hari, R.: Vibration-induced Auditory-Cortex Activation in a Congenitally Deaf Adult. Curr. Biol. 8, 869–872 (1998)
27. Nishimura, H., Hashikawa, K., Doi, K., Iwaki, T., Watanabe, Y., Kusuoka, H., Nishimura, T., Kubo, T.: Sign Language 'Heard' in The Auditory Cortex. Nature 3976715, 116 (1999)
28. Petitto, L.A., Zatorre, R.J., Gauna, K., Nikelski, E.J., Dostie, D., Evans, A.C.: Speech-like Cerebral Activity in Profoundly Deaf People Processing Signed Languages: Implications for the Neural Basis of Human Language. Proc. Nat. Acad. Sci. USA 97, 13961–13966 (2000)
29. MacSweeney, M., Woll, B., Campbell, R., Calvert, G.A., McGuire, P.K., David, A.S., Simmons, A., Brammer, M.J.: Neural Correlates of British Sign Language Comprehension: Spatial Processing Demands of Topographic Language. J. Cog. Neurosci. 14, 1064–1075 (2002)
30. Poizner, H., Klima, E., Bellugi, U.: What the Hands Reveal about the Brain. MIT Press, Cambridge (1987)
31. Hickok, G., Say, K., Bellugi, U., Klima, E.: The Basis of Hemispheric Asymmetries for Language and Spatial Cognition: Clues from Focal Brain Damage in 2 Deaf Native Signers. Aphasiol. 10, 577–591 (1996)
32. Hickok, G., Bellugi, U., Klima, E.: The Neural Organization of Sign Language: Evidence from Sign Language Aphasia. Trans. Cog. Sci. 2, 129–136 (1998)
33. Corina, D.P.: Aphasia in Users of Signed Languages. In: Coppens, P., Lebrun, Y., Basso, A. (eds.) Aphasia in Atypical Populations, pp. 261–309. Lawrence Erlbaum Associates, Mahwah (1998)
34. Corina, D.P.: The Processing of Sign Language: Evidence from Aphasia. In: Stemmer, B., Whitaker, H.A. (eds.) Handbook of Neurolinguistics, pp. 313–329. Academic Press, NY (1998)
35. Atkinson, J.R., Campbell, R., Marshall, J., Thacker, A., Woll, B.: Understanding 'not': Neuropsychological Dissociations between Hand and Head Markers of Negation in BSL. Neuropsychologia 42, 214–229 (2004)
36. Atkinson, J.R., Marshall, J., Woll, B., Thacker, A.: Testing Comprehension Abilities in Users of British Sign Language following CVA. Br Lang. 94(2), 233–248 (2005)
37. Marshall, J., Atkinson, J.R., Smulovitch, E., Thacker, A., Woll, B.: Aphasia in a user of British Sign Language: Dissociation between sign and gesture. Cog. Neuropsychol. 21(5), 537–554 (2004)
38. Marshall, J., Atkinson, J.R., Woll, B., Thacker, A.: Aphasia in a Bilingual User of British Sign Language and English: Effects of Cross Linguistic Cues. J. Cog. Neuropsychol. 22(6), 719–736 (2005)

39. Corina, D.P., Poizner, H., Bellugi, U., Feinberg, T., Dowd, D., O'Grady-Batch, L.: Dissociation between Linguistic and Nonlinguistic Gestural Systems: a Case for Compositionality. Br Lang. 43, 414–447 (1992)

40. Pizzuto, E., Volterra, V.: Iconicity and Transparency in Sign Languages: A Crosslinguistic Cross-cultural view. In: Emmorey, K., Harlan, L. (eds.) The Signs of Language Revisited: An Anthology in Honor of Ursula Bellugi and Edward Klima, pp. 261–286. Lawrence Erlbaum Associates, Hillsdale (2000)

41. Klima, E.S., Bellugi, U.: The Signs of Language. MIT Press, Cambridge (1979)

42. Emmorey, K., Grabowski, T., McCullough, S., Damasio, H., Ponto, L., Hichwa, R., Bellugi, U.: Motor-iconicity of Sign Language Does Not Alter the Neural Systems Underlying Tool and Action Naming. Br Lang. 89, 27–37 (2004)

43. Neville, H., Bavelier, D., Corina, D., Rauschecker, J., Karni, A., Lalwani, A., Braun, A., Clark, V., Jezzard, P., Turner, R.: Cerebral Organization for Language in Deaf and Hearing Subjects: Biological Constraints and Effects of Experience. Proc. Nat. Acad. Sci. USA 95, 922–929 (1998)

44. Newman, A.J., Bavelier, D., Corina, D., Jezzard, P., Neville, H.J.: A Critical Period for Right Hemisphere Recruitment in American Sign Language Processing. Nat. Neurosci. 5, 76–80 (2002)

45. Paulesu, E., Mehler, J.: Right on in Sign Language. Nature 392, 233–234 (1998)

46. Emmorey, K., Damasio, H., McCullough, S., Grabowski, T., Ponto, L., Hichwa, R., et al.: Neural Systems Underlying Spatial Language in American Sign Language. Neuroimage 17, 812–824 (2002)

47. Kegl, J., Poizner, H.: Crosslinguistic/crossmodal Syntactic Consequences of Left-Hemisphere Damage: Evidence from an Aphasic Signer and his Identical Twin. Aphasiol. 11, 1–37 (1997)

48. Loew, R.C., Kegl, J.A., Poizner, H.: Fractionation of the Components of Role Play in a Right-Hemisphere Lesioned Signer. Aphasiol. 11, 263–281 (1997)

49. Hickok, G., Wilson, M., Clark, K., Klima, E.S., Kritchevsky, M., Bellugi, U.: Discourse Deficits Following Right Hemisphere Damage in Deaf Signers. Br Lang. 66, 233–248 (1999)

50. Wapner, W., Hamby, S., Gardner, H.: The Role of the Right Hemisphere in the Apprehension of Complex Linguistic Materials. Br Lang. 14, 15–33 (1981)

51. Kaplan, J.A., Brownell, H.R., Jacobs, J.R., Gardner, H.: The Effects of Right Hemisphere Damage on the Pragmatic Interpretation of Conversational Remarks. Br Lang. 38(2), 315–333 (1990)

52. Rönnberg, J., Söderfeldt, B., Risberg, J.: The Cognitive Neuroscience of Signed Language. Acta. Psychol. 105(2-3), 237–254 (2000)

53. Sutton-Spence, R., Day, L.: Mouthings and Mouth Gestures in British Sign Language. In: Boyes-Braem, P., Sutton-Spence, R. (eds.) The Hands are the Head of the Mouth, pp. 69–86. Signum Press, Hamburg (2001)

54. Boyes-Braem, P., Sutton-Spence, R. (eds.): The Hands are the Head of the Mouth. Signum Press, Hamburg (2002)

55. Waters, D., Campbell, R., Capek, C.M., Woll, B., David, A.S., McGuire, P.K., Brammer, M.J., MacSweeney, M.: Fingerspelling, Signed Language, Text and Picture Processing in Deaf Native Signers: The Role of the Mid-fusiform Gyrus. Neuroimage 35(3), 1287–1302 (2007)

56. Capek, C., Woll, B., MacSweeney, M., Waters, D., David, A.S., McGuire, P.K., Brammer, M.J., Campbell, R.: Hand and Mouth: Cortical Correlates of Lexical Processing in BSL and Speechreading. J. Cog. Neurosci. 20, 1220–1234 (2008)

57. McCullough, S., Emmorey, K., Sereno, M.: Neural Organization for Recognition of Grammatical Facial Expressions in Deaf ASL Signers and Hearing Nonsigners. Cog. Br. Res. 22, 192–203 (2005)

From Speech and Gestures to Dialogue Acts

Maciej Karpinski

Institute of Linguistics & Center for Speech and Language Processing,
Adam Mickiewicz University, Al. Niepodleglosci 4, 61-874 Poznan, Poland
maciej.karpinski@amu.edu.pl

Abstract. In the present paper, selected problems related to the annotation of
the DiaGest corpus are discussed. A system of dialogue acts is proposed along
with a conceptual framework that allows for independent labelling of the contributions provided by various modalities and channels. Both auditory and visual modalities are considered. Four channels are defined as major ways of
providing quasi-independent modal contributions. A four-dimensional categorisation of dialogue acts is proposed. It includes a separate dimension for atti-
tude-related tags. Dialogue acts are conceptualised as multidimensional entities
built on the basis of modal contributions provided by respective channels.

Keywords: dialogue act, multidimensionality, multimodality, annotation.

1 Introduction

Dialogue acts belong to the most popular units of dialogue annotation and analysis.
However, both their definitions and their taxonomies vary in a number of meaningful
ways as they are designed for various corpora and applications. This is also related to
some conceptual and methodological problems discussed, for example, by Traum [1].
The majority of recent approaches to defining and classifying dialogue acts account
for the fact that each utterance may have a number of functions [2]. Accordingly, dialogue act taxonomies offer the possibility of labelling each utterance with more than
one tag. Technically, a number of annotation tiers is employed or multi-tags are used.
The way the idea of multidimensionality is implemented also vary. For example, in
DAMSL [3], it was proposed to group functions in the backward- and forward-
looking dimensions. Popescu-Belis [4] discusses the question of dimensionality and
gives a detailed review of four popular dialogue act tagging schemes. As Bunt [2]
points out, the definitions of the very fundamental notion of "dimension" not only
differ from one system to another, but they are frequently hazy. To ensure better
communication among researchers and to facilitate data exchange, some standardisation efforts have been undertaken. A relatively flexible approach was suggested in the
influential MATE project [5]. More recently, on the basis of the Dynamic Interpretation Theory (DIT) [6], a new standard of dialogue act labelling was proposed (referred to as DIT++; see [7] and http://dit.uvt.nl/). In this system, special attention was
paid not only to the logical coherence of the system, but also to its accuracy and to its
relation to the conceptual status of the dimensions proposed. Nevertheless, Popescu-
Belis [8] suggests that the standardisation should be limited only to the ways of

A. Esposito et al. (Eds.): Multimodal Signals, LNAI 5398, pp. 164–169, 2009.

building new systems. Much flexibility should be retained in order to build systems that would be appropriate for various aims and applications. Moreover, one may suspect that an inflexible and obligatory standard would pose the danger of slowing down the progress in dialogue studies.

2 DiaGest Project: Motivation for a New Dialogue Act System

Presently, the DiaGest Corpus [9] includes audio and video recordings of 12 pairs of subjects, each participating in four session with different tasks. Two of the tasks ("origami" and "objects") are typical task-oriented dialogues. They involve the reconstruction of three-dimensional structures. In the case of "origami", it is a figure made of paper, and in the case of "objects", it is a spatial structure build with items of everyday use (e.g., a cup, a battery, a pen). Only the instruction giver can see the structure. The instruction giver and follower can see each other, and he instruction-giver can see the reconstruction by the instruction follower who, in turn, is equipped with all items needed for the reconstruction.

The DiaGest project involves the study of the communicational relevance of selected lexical, syntactic, prosodic and gestural phenomena. Consequently, a detailed annotation of these components is necessary. Besides phonemic transcriptions and "low-level" annotations, the corpus is being tagged on the level of dialogue acts. In the attempts of adopting existing systems and during the design of a new one, some major obstacles and problems were faced. Along with some working solutions, they are described in the following sections of this paper.

3 DiaGest Dialogue Act System

3.1 Dimensions

The DiaGest system provides four tiers, referred to as "dimensions", for describing the functions of dialogue units:

1) *Task Action Control (TAC)*
2) *Dialogue Flow Control (DFC)*
3) *Information Transfer Management (ITM)*
4) *Approach Expression Marker (AEM)*

The *dimension* is defined as a subfield of communicational activity. Although it would be more comfortable to have dimensions which are completely independent, it seems to be impossible in practice. This results from the properties of the communicational environment as well as from fact that the fields of communicational activity influence each other.

The two first tiers are shared by some labelling systems, although they may be named in different ways, differ in details of their definitions or form parts of wider dimensions. *Task Action Control* is here confessed to the aspects of utterances that directly influence task-related activities. This includes, first of all, *instructions, suggestions, explanations* as well as the acts of *accepting* or *rejecting* them by the other dialogue party. *Dialogue Flow Control* tier is meant to provide space for tags that refers to the control of the process of conversation and it includes mostly turn-taking mechanisms (e.g., *keeping turns, handing turns over, releasing turns*). *Information Transfer Management* is intended to reflect the direction of the information flow. While in certain contexts it may seem to be redundant (with most of "instructing" or "ordering" actions in the *TAC* dimension, the *ITM* would be *provide information*), it proves to be especially useful in the case of the utterances which are not directly related to task actions nor to dialogue flow control. They convey certain amounts of information or express emotional or attitudinal meaning. They frequently occur in grounding ([10]; for more recent approaches, see [11]), providing contextual information, clarifying as well as expressing attitudes.

The fourth dimension, *Approach Expression Marker*, is intended to reflect a bunch of socio-psychological factors. The meaning of the term *approach* as it is used here slightly remains the psychological concept of *attitude* (for a comprehensive review, see, e.g., [12]), but it still differs from it in a number of ways. Firstly, the *AEM*, as a component of a dialogue act, should be related to the *intentionally controlled* aspects of attitude. Secondly, it can be only described when it occurs externally, somehow influences the behaviour of a speaker and, accordingly, it counts as an intentional attempt to change the informational state of the listener. Thirdly, the *AEM* may change its values relatively quickly while the psychological attitude is normally quite stable or changes very slowly. It also seems reasonable to distinguish the *approaches* towards (a) the conversational partner; (b) towards oneself; (c) towards the topic of conversation as well as (d) towards the audience witnessing the conversation. In this relatively flexible framework, certain aspects of emotions and feelings may also be tagged as long as they contribute to *AEM*. In the DiaGest system, the resolution of the *AEM* dimension is low: It offers only three basic values: *positive, neutral, negative*. Still, with its four (as listed above) subdimensions, the *AEM* may offer a substantial amount of valuable information.

For each dimension, a predefined set of available values (dialogue functions) is provided. For example, in the case of the *ITM*, it includes the following ones: *provide_information* (e.g., "The tree is on the left") *request_information, confirm_information* (e.g., "Okay, that's right"), *reject_information* (e.g.,"That's not what I wanted to know.", "Bullshit!", "No, it's impossible"), *accept_information* (e.g., "Okay, thanks!"), *clarify_information* (e.g., "Yes, but slightly further than the tree."), *request_clarification* (e.g., "Are you saying it is it exactly in front of me?"). (Please note that these examples work only with appropriate context.) All the sets for the respective dimensions share two additional values: *irrelevant* and *other*. The former is used when a given utterance does not seem to act on the the presently considered dimension; the latter is used when the utterance seemingly has a certain function in a given dimension, but this function is not listed in the available inventory. It is generally recommended to avoid these values. However, the analysis of their occurrences in the labelled corpus may provide valuable information on the performance of the labelling system and the work of labellers.

3.2 Modalities

In the DiaGest system, *modality* is defined as a set of communication channels using one sense and a relevant class of signals (e.g., *auditory modality* and *sounds*, respectively). Two modalities are taken into account here: *AUDITORY* and *VISUAL*. Each of them may provide many *communication channels*. Their number is restricted for the purpose of the present system:

AUDITORY:	*textual channel (words and syntactic structures),*
	prosodic channel (rhythm and intonation)
VISUAL:	*gesture*
	facial expression

The channels are defined here not only by the choice of the medium but also in terms of how they use a given medium. The auditory modality can be used not only for speech, but also for other sounds. And even within the speech signal, one can convey a number of parallel communicates. As dialogue acts are intentional units, certain communication channels which are frequently used in an unintentional way are excluded from further considerations (e.g., small subconsciously or unconsciously produced gestures). Nevertheless, they should be taken into consideration in a holistic dialogue model that goes besides dialogue acts and intentionality.

It is difficult to separate the contributions to the meaning provided through various modalities or channels and the final message is not their simple "sum." The information conveyed through one modality or channel may be contrary to what is conveyed through the other; it may modify it or extend it in many ways. Accordingly, the meaning of a multimodal utterance should be, in principle, always regarded and analysed as a whole, and not decomposed into the meaning of speech, gestures, facial expressions and other possible components. For example, a smile and words of appraisal or admiration may produce the impression of being ironic in a certain context. On the other hand, each modality may provide information on its own that can be somehow interpreted in the absence of other modalities, and that can influence the process of communication as well as the informational state of the addressee. Is it then justified to annotate both separate modalities and the meaning of entire utterances in terms of dialogue acts? To relieve this problem, the concept of *modal contribution* is introduced. *Modal contribution* is defined as the information provided through a given modality within the boundaries of a given dialogue act. A dialogue act realised in a multimodal utterance can be conceptualised as composed on the basis of modal contributions. The realisation of each dialogue act is built on the basis of at least one modal contribution. A single modal contribution may become the realisation of a dialogue act once it is put in the dialogue context.

Each modality and each channel has its particular properties and they vary in the range of "meanings" they may convey and in the way they are typically employed. For example, the modality of gestural expression is frequently sufficient for answering propositional questions, ordering simple actions or expressing certain attitudes. The facial expression is especially frequently used for feedback (backchannelling) or emotional reactions. Speech is normally the most precise tool for expressing complex intentions. Prosody may act on different levels, facilitating (or impeding) lexical and syntactic processing, expressing feelings and attitudes, organising higher levels of discourse. It contributes to topic identification processes and turn taking mechanisms. The abundance of its functions makes it difficult to describe in a consistent way and is a source of endless controversies [13].

Presently, the distinction of two annotation levels (*modal contributions* and *dialogue acts*) should be regarded as a purely technical solution, but further research may show that it somehow reflects the process of realizing dialogue acts as multimodal utterances. Moreover, the *modal contribution* level is currently regarded as optional and used mostly when the "total meaning" of an utterance is not clear enough or the utterance is composed of the modal contribution in an atypical way.

3.3 Dimensions, Modalities and the Problem of Complexity

As noted above, the modalities taken into consideration in the present system differ in their "space" for the expression of various types of meaning. Accordingly, their contribution to various dimensions of dialogue acts also differ and the inventories of possible modal contributions should also be adjusted for each modality. The inventory of values designed for various modal contribution is still being designed for the DiaGest system. It should be also stressed that, independently on the form and number of the modal contributions, each utterance is also tagged as a whole with the dialogue acts labels in the four dimensions. According to the experience gained so far, it is useful to employ different labellers for tagging modal contribution and dialogue acts.

The system presented here is relatively complex and still it reflects the complexity of the real communicational events in a very limited way. In an extreme case, the full multi-label for one utterance may contain as many as sixteen modal contribution tags (four channels by four dimensions) and four dialogue act tags referring to the multimodal utterance as a whole (and including one complex multi-tag for *AEM*). In practise, however, the number of modal contribution labels is much lower and frequently they take "neutral" values. The labels for the dialogue act as well as for the modal contributions are built according to a system which make them easy to memorize. Consequently, the system seems to be manageable and relatively easy to use in spite of its apparent complexity.

4 Conclusion

The dialogue act system sketched in the present text is currently in the stage of fine-tuning and evaluation. It is not limited to the taxonomy of the dialogue acts. It provides a conceptual framework for multi-layered annotation of a range of multimodal dialogues. Due to the fact that two major modalities and four channels are labelled across four dimensions of dialogue functions, it is difficult to avoid complexity. Nevertheless, a number of attempts has been made to solve this problem.

Multidimensional dialogue act labelling with quasi-independent dimensions provides the possibility of expressing more subtle shades of behaviour, which may be quite important in real life situations. Independent labelling of the modalities in question allows for more a more realistic and convincing reconstruction of dialogue behaviour. While dialogue acts in their present form may be an efficient tool of dialogue analysis, it is still necessary to investigate the status and communicational relevance of a number of unintentional, uncontrolled signals produced during the process of communication and influencing the mental (informational) state of the observer.

References

[1] Traum, D.R.: 20 Questions for Dialogue Act Taxonomies. Journal of Semantics 17(1), 7–30 (2000)

[2] Bunt, H.: Dimensions in dialogue act annotation. In: Proceedings of the Fifth International Conference on Language Resources and Evaluation LREC 2006 (2006)

[3] Core, M.G., Allen, J.F.: Coding Dialogues with the DAMSL Annotation Scheme. In: Traum, D. (ed.) Working Notes of the Fall Symposium in Communicative Action in Humans and Machines, pp. 28–35. AAAI, Menlo Park (1997)

[4] Popescu-Belis, A.: Dimensionality of Dialogue Act Tagsets: An Empirical Analysis of Large Corpora. Language Resources and Evaluation 42(1), 99–107 (2008)

[5] Klein, M.: Standardisation Efforts on the Level of Dialogue Act in the MATE Project. In: Towards Standards and Tools for Discourse Tagging: Proceedings of the Workshop (1999)

[6] Bunt, H.: Dialogue pragmatics and context specifcation. In: Bunt, H., Black, W. (eds.) Abduction, Belief and Context in Dialogue. Studies in Computational Pragmatics, pp. 81–150. John Benjamins, Amsterdam (2000)

[7] Bunt, H., Girard, Y.: Designing an Open, Multidimensional Dialogue Act Taxonomy. In: The Proceedings of DIALOR 2005 Workshop, Nancy (2005)

[8] Popescu-Belis, A.: Normalizing dialogue act tagsets: how to keep ISO standards general. 6th ACL-SIGSEM & ISO TC37/SC4/TDG3 Meeting on Multimodal Semantic Representation, Tilburg, The Netherlands (invited talk) (2007)

[9] Jarmolowicz, E., Karpinski, M., Malisz, Z., Szczyszek, M.: Gesture, Prosody and Lexicon in Task-oriented Dialogues: Multimedia Corpus Recording and Labelling. In: Esposito, A., Faundez-Zanuy, M., Keller, E., Marinaro, M. (eds.) COST Action 2102. LNCS (LNAI), vol. 4775, pp. 99–110. Springer, Heidelberg (2007)

[10] Clark, H.H., Schaefer, E.F.: Contributing to discourse. Cognitive Science 13, 259–294 (1989)

[11] Bunt, H., Morante, R., Keizer, S.: An empirically based computational model of grounding in dialogue. In: Proceedings of the 8th SIGdial Workshop on Discourse and Dialogue, Antwerp, Association for Computational Linguistics, pp. 283–290 (2007)

[12] Pratkanis, A.R., Breckler, S.J., Greenwald, A.G. (eds.): Attitude Structure and Function. Lawrence Erlbaum, Mahwah (1989)

[13] Fox, A.: Prosodic Features and Prosodic Structures: The Phonology of Suprasegmentals. OUP, Oxford (2000)

The Language of Interjections

Isabella Poggi

Dipartimento di Scienze dell'Educazione, Università Roma Tre
Via D.Manin 53
00185 Roma, Italy
poggi@uniroma3.it

Abstract. The paper presents a theoretical view of interjections. It defines them as holophrastic codified signals, whose meaning corresponds to complete speech acts including a specific performative and propositional content. Interjections are then distinguished from exclamations and onomatopoeias, and some devices are analyzed that characterize them. An overview of the syntactic, lexical and semantic features of interjections is provided, and a typology of Italian interjections is presented.

Keywords: interjections, onomatopoeia, exclamation, holophrastic language, emotional language.

1 Introduction

A quite distinctive feature of speech as opposed to written language is the presence in it of interjections: a kind of utterances with a peculiar acoustic structure, generally considered a typical case of emotional language.

In the last decade, research on speech has allowed us to widen and deepen our knowledge concerning the vocal expression of emotions and the prosodic, intonational and acoustic features of face to face interaction. Many of these findings will be certainly of use in gaining new knowledge about interjections. But to make sense of possible findings about their phonetic and acoustic structure, a general view of their communicative structure and function may help. In this work I present a theoretical perspective about interjections, their nature and status as a communicative system, and a taxonomy of the meanings they convey.

2 A Neglected Part of Speech

Interjection in Traditional Grammar is classified as the ninth part of discourse. Its name, from latin *inter iecto*, (= I throw in the middle) means that it is inserted in the middle of a sentence or discourse. Examples of interjections are *oh, wow, my God!*. In modern Linguistics, interjections have been studied by [1], [2], [3], [4], [5], [6], [7], [8], [9]. While in Traditional Grammar they are often put together with onomatopoeia and exclamation, in recent Pragmatics they are generally dealt with in connection with hesitations, particles and backchannel signals. Yet, not all interjections are onomatopoeic,

A. Esposito et al. (Eds.): Multimodal Signals, LNAI 5398, pp. 170–186, 2009.

while as to exclamations, also entire sentences can be called so; moreover, not all interjections are hesitations, nor are they all used as such; again, many other kinds of particles exist beside interjections proper; and finally, interjections are not used only for backchannel, nor does backchannel necessarily exploit interjections. A clear definition of the category of interjections is thus lacking.

3 Interjections: A Definition

As acknowledged by various scholars [7], [8], an interjection constitutes an utterance by itself. This means that, in terms of [6], [10], [11], an interjection can be defined as a *holophrastic signal*, in that it conveys the information of a whole sentence (*holos phrasis* = entire sentence). In fact, if we want to provide a synonym of it, what is equivalent to an interjection is not a single word, but a whole speech act, that is, a communicative act including the meaning of both a performative and a propositional content. Indeed, more than a synonym, a paraphrase.

For example, *"Ouch!"* can be paraphrased as "I am feeling pain". This speech act has a performative of information, and the information provided concerns the Speaker feeling some unpleasant physical sensation. *"Hey!"* can be paraphrased as "I ask you to pay attention": it is a requestive speech act, and the action requested is for the Hearer to pay attention to the Speaker and / or the context.

Thus, my definition of interjection is the following: an interjection is a **codified signal** [11], that is, a perceivable signal – a sound sequence in the speech modality, and a sequence of graphemes in the written modality – which is linked in a stable way, in the minds of the speakers of a language, to the meaning of a speech act, that is, to information including both a performative and a propositional content.

In this **speech act**, the propositional content concerns either some mental state that is presently occurring in the Speaker's mind, or an action requested from the Hearer or a third entity; and the performative is the type of communicative action the Speaker is performing towards the Hearer, his/her goal of informing, asking about, requesting or wishing what is mentioned by the propositional content.

An interjection is a codified signal in that the signal – meaning link is stored in a permanent way in the long term memory of Speakers [11]: not only is so for the propositional content, but also for the specific performative, which is then "incorporated" in the interjection, that is, it makes an integral part of the interjection's meaning.

4 Interjections and Elliptical Sentences

The definition provided allows us to distinguish an interjection from an elliptical sentence. Both convey a whole speech act, but while an elliptical sentence conveys a different speech act in every different context, an interjection always conveys one and the same speech act, just because it is a codified signal – meaning pair permanently represented in the Speaker's lexicon.

Very often, in everyday conversation, speakers use a single word to convey the meaning of a whole sentence. Take this case:

(1) A gets into a pub and the barman asks him: *"What do you want?"*
   B answers: *"Beer."*

In this case B's single word works as a complete sentence like

(2) *"I ask you to pour me beer"*:

A speech act with a performative of request and a propositional content concerning the Addressee pouring beer to the Speaker.
   But suppose the following:

(3) B is walking with his friend A, and while passing along the walls of a big old factory, A asks B: *"What did they produce in this factory?"*
   B answers: *"Beer."*.

In this case B's single word still conveys the meaning of a whole sentence, but one that can be paraphrased as

(4) *"In this factory they used to produce beer"*;

This speech act conveys a performative of information and a propositional content concerning people that produce beer.
   Here is, therefore, the difference between a single word used as an elliptical sentence and an interjection. In the interjection, the meaning of the whole speech act is codified – permanently stored in memory – while in the elliptical sentence the word uttered only conveys a part of a speech act, either a predicate or an argument of the logical structure of the propositional content, or in some cases only the performative, but not the whole speech act; and the remaining parts of the speech act are to be retrieved from context. For instance, in (3) the non-mentioned parts of the speech act – that beer is what was produced by the factory, and that B's performative is one of information and not one of request – can only be understood from context: A must fill in the gaps of B's elliptical speech act, while only a part of it – what was produced – is explicitly meant by B's word. In this way, however, the complete speech act conveyed is different from time to time.
   This is also the case in the so-called "holophrastic" stage in a child's language development. As a child says *"Ball"* to mean "Give me the ball", he is using a single word to mean a whole sentence. But the sentence meant is not always the same: in a different context he may simply mean "Look at the ball". Strictly speaking, this is an elliptical sentence too. But take this case instead:

(5) Student A is talking to student C during class, and Teacher B summons him by *"Hey!"*.

Here, that B is asking A to pay attention is all conveyed by B's single "word" *"Hey!"*; and it is so on a codified basis.
   To sum up, an interjection is a particular type of "word": a **holophrastic** word, a "sentence-word". It is the only case, within a verbal language, in which a single sound sequence conveys, as its meaning codified in the lexicon, a whole speech act all by

itself. In all other cases – for all other grammatical categories: nouns, verbs, adjectives, prepositions… – a single sound sequence only bears a part of the whole speech act, either a predicate or an argument of the logical structure of the propositional content or of the performative, but not all of it. So we can say that all those types of signals – nouns, verbs and so on – are "articulated" signals, in that they convey only a part of a sentence (an *"articulum"*, a "little limb" of it, as Saussure [12] would have put it), while the interjection conveys the whole sentence.

Actually, we can distinguish between holophrastic and articulated signals in various communication systems: for example, among gestures. The gesture *with palm down and fingers bending down* that means "come here" is holophrastic in that it conveys not only the propositional content of the Addressee coming to the Sender, but also a performative of request [11]. On the other side, an articulated gesture is *the hand with palm to Sender and index and middle finger in V shape moving back and forth in front of the mouth*, which can mean "smoke", or "cigarette", or "do you have a cigarette?" or "he is a smoker"; it conveys either a question or an information depending on the context and on the facial expression performed along with the gesture. So, this gesture just works as the word *"beer"* in the example above since, different from the gesture for "come here", it does not convey a whole propositional content nor does it incorporate a specific performative in its codified meaning.

In conclusion, interjections are the only codified holophrastic signals within a verbal language.

5 A Deictic Signal

As pointed by [7], an interjection can be also seen as a *deictic signal*, if we define as deictic every signal that, in order to be thoroughly understood, requires you to take contextual information into account. Actually, if we look at (5) above, also in the interjection a small part of its meaning is not codified but must be retrieved from context. If we say that *"Hey!"* means "I (the Speaker) want you (the Interlocutor) to pay attention to something", to understand who is asked to pay attention, and what he should pay attention to, one has to be present in the same spatial-temporal context in which the interjection is uttered. If we say that *"Wow!"* means "This event causes me (the Speaker) to be pleasantly surprised/amazed", to understand each particular occurrence of *"Wow!"* one should know what is the specific surprising event. In other words, the piece of information to be retrieved from context in an interjection – that we may call its "reference element" – is, for the interjections mentioning a mental state of the Speaker, the event that causes that mental state, while for those requesting some action it can be the point or the object of the action requested.

6 Syntactic Aspects of Interjections

From the definition of an interjection as a single signal that conveys the meaning of a whole communicative act, it follows the syntactic property that gave birth to its name: the fact that it can be "thrown into" the sentence: that it can in principle occur in any of its phrases, even within a phrase, because it is not syntactically linked to any phrase in the sentence [10].

Thus, the interjection is subject to very peculiar syntactic rules. First, different from all other parts of discourse it can stay alone. A greeting, like *"hello!"*, or an acknowledgment of memory retrieval, like *"oh!"*, can occur in the total absence of linguistic context. Second, an interjection does not entertain syntactic relations with other words in a sentence: it can be inserted in various positions in a sentence, even within a phrase, for instance between article and noun in a noun phrase, like in (6).

(6) *I am the... mhm ... girl friend of your cousin.*

Notwithstanding this, we cannot say that interjections are completely out of the scope of syntactic rules. Actually, their position with respect to a sentence is not completely free: their being uttered at the beginning, in the middle or at the end of a sentence, or finally as completely detached from the sentence itself, is determined by their meaning. For example, the Italian interjection *"toh"*, when it means "what I am telling you is trivial" can only be uttered at the end of the sentence

(7) *Chi vuoi che sia al telefono. E' Giovanni, tòh!*
    (Who do you think is calling on the phone? It's Giovanni, *wow!*)

On the contrary, some interjections expressing surprise or acknowledgment of a belief just assumed generally precede the sentence containing their "reference element".

(8) *Wow, you repainted your shutters!*

And finally, those expressing doubt or hesitation are preferably uttered in the middle of the sentence, like in (6), and they are not acceptable at the end of the sentence.

7 The Lexical Structure of Interjections

If every interjection is a codified signal – meaning pair, a whole list of interjections form a lexicon: a subpart of our mental lexicon, differing from other words only because they are holophrastic words. So let us now see how interjections might be represented in our mental lexicon.

Ever since [13], various scholars have distinguished primary vs. secondary interjections. Primary interjections, like *Oh!*, *Uh!*, are close to natural cries, to instinctive vocalization or, in terms of [14], [15], to affect bursts. Secondary interjections, instead, like *"God!"*, or *"well"* are simply words of a language that are used as holophrastic utterances. Primary interjections have a phonological structure that is hardly similar to that of the language they belong to, even if there is always some kind of "normalisation" that makes them homologous to its phonological system. Secondary interjections, instead, by definition maintain the phonological structure of the language they make part of, since they are, in a certain sense, "canonical" non-holophrastic words.

Yet, if you think of interjections as items in a lexicon – possibly to be simulated in an Artificial Agent – it is useful to distinguish them into "univocal" vs. "plurivocal" interjections [6]. An "univocal" interjection is a sound sequence that only has (one or more) holophrastic meanings; while a "plurivocal" interjection is a sound sequence that has two or more different meanings, with at least one of them holophrastic. In this sense, a plurivocal interjection is a case of polysemic word: a word with two or more meanings.

Thus, not only *ouch* but also *caramba* are "univocal" interjections, because they both only have a meaning as an interjection. Instead, *Jesus* is "plurivocal" in that it is both an interjection and a noun.

Often, as for all polysemic items [11], between the two or more meanings of a plurivocal interjection it is possible to find out a semantic connection, because generally the meaning as an interjection derives from the meaning as a non-holophrastic word. Take for example the plurivocal interjection *già* in Italian. *Già* is an adverb (corresponding to "already") in this sentence

(9) B: *Maria si è già svegliata*
    (Maria has *already* waken up)

But in the following case, it is an interjection.

(10) A: *Ricordati che devi chiamare Maria*
     (Remember you have to call Maria).
     B: *Già.*
     (Uh uh)

In this case, *già* in its meaning as an interjection means that I am presently remembering something; I did not have this in mind at the moment, but now you remind me of it, I remember that I did know it. Thus, there is in fact something in common between the meaning of *già* as an adverb and that of *già* as an interjection. The adverb means that a certain event has occurred (also) before the moment in which the Speaker is speaking. But also in the holophrastic *già* a certain event has occurred before a given time: this event is the presence, in the Speaker's mind, of some belief (B's having to call Maria).

(11) *Già*: meaning as an adverb

C0: Speaker B speaks
C1: Maria woke up
C2: C1 **occurred before C0**

(12) *Già*: meaning as an interjection

C0: Speaker B speaks
C1: B believes C2
C2: B has to call Maria
C3: C1 **occurred before C0**

Plausibly, *già* as an interjection might derive from *già* as an adverb, by a mechanism through which a whole sentence that contains the adverb, and occurs often in dialogue, gets condensed into a single word. A sentence like

(13) *Questa cosa la sapevo già (ma al momento non ci pensavo)*
(This is something that I already knew (but I wasn't thinking
of it now)).

This sort of "condensation" might be a general device for the evolution of plurivocal interjections starting from non-holophrastic words.

8 Semantics of Interjections

Let us now see what are the meanings that interjections convey, by leaning on a previous analysis of Italian interjections [6], [10]. Since the meaning of an interjection
contains a performative and a propositional content, it is possible to distinguish them,
according to their performative, into four classes:

- INFORMATIVE, like *ah* (this belief is new to me, and I am coming to believe
  it) and *uffa* (I am tired / bored), whose goal is to let the Hearer know the
  mental state occurring in the Speaker;
- INTERROGATIVE, like *eh?* (what did you say?) or *beh?* (why is this so?), that
  ask the Hearer to provide a belief to the Speaker;
- REQUESTIVE, like *ehi* (please, pay attention to me) or *via!* (go!) to ask the
  Hearer to perform an action; and
- OPTATIVE, like politeness formulas (e.g. *buonanotte = goodnight*) or imprecations (*Dio!*, *mamma!*), that ask a third entity (the fate, a deity) to have
  something happen.

What are the meanings of interjections? Traditional grammar, but also research in
the twentieth century, have always viewed them as a kind of emotional language. But
this is not always so. First, there is a difference between the interjections of the first
class above, those with a performative of information, and those of other classes. In
general, informative interjections make part of the class of "Mind Markers" [11]:
those signals that convey Information on the Speaker's Mind: beliefs, goals and emotions. Actually, also in this class, it is not only emotions that are conveyed by interjections, but more generally mental states. Yet, if we examine the contents conveyed by
the other classes of interjections, mainly requestive but also interrogative and optative
ones, we can see that they often refer to mental states, actions, or events concerning
not so much the Speaker, but the Hearer.

To provide a general view of their meanings, I present a typology of Italian interjections (Tables 1 – 4).

Among informative interjections (Table 1), some inform about the Speaker's cognitive state, namely about the relations between incoming and previously assumed
beliefs, while others inform about the current state of the Speaker's goals, whether
they are fulfilled or thwarted.

Let us start from the interjections about the Speaker's beliefs. *Ah* (= oh) informs
that the incoming belief is new for the Speaker, and she is coming to assume it right
now; *già* (literally, = already) tells that the belief has already been assumed, or at least
it was potentially available (for example, it could have been drawn through inference)
in the Speaker's mind.

Various interjections confirm an incoming belief, by telling that the Speaker already knew it from another source: *davvero* (= indeed), *eh* (= yes, just so), *öh* (= just so, and more than that!), *okay, sì* (= yes), *altro che!* (= definitely yes).

No and *macché* (= definitely not) inform that the Speaker assumes the incoming belief as definitely not true. *Mah* (= I don't know, I'm not sure) tells she is doubtful, *boh* (= I don't know, I am doubtful) and *chissà* (= who knows?), that she does not know, while *bah* (= gee, I don't know), pretends ignorance but in fact leaks perplexity and possibly disapproval. *Che?* (= what?!), *no!* (= I can't believe it!) express incredulity; *bum!* (= boom!), by imitating a shooting gun, alludes to the Italian idiom *"spararla grossa"* (to shoot a hard blow), meaning "You're telling a big lie".

Beh, ehm, dunque (= well) express hesitation, while *oh, tòh, no!, però!* (= wow!) express surprise. Actually, both indecision and surprise are in some sense a lack of assumption: before decision, the Speaker has two alternatives between which she does not know which to choose; and when she is surprised, a new incoming belief disconfirms her expectations, and she cannot find a belief that accounts for the new one.

Among the informative interjections concerning the state of the Speaker's goals, some regard her thwarted goals, by indicating various kinds of physical suffering: pain (*ahi*), cold (*brrr*), disgust (*bleah* = yuk), fatigue (*uffa*); and psychical suffering: boredom (*uffa*), displeasure and desperation (*ahimé!* = alas!, *peccato!* = what a pity!, *no!*), disappointment (the indirect meaning of *bèh?* = but why?), worry (*ńc*), indignation (*ohibò*), contempt (*puah*). Other interjections inform that a goal of the Speaker has been fulfilled: a specific goal, like to succeed in doing something (*là!* = there!), to be introduced to some person (*piacere* = nice to meet you) or to meet someone you have not seen for long (*uée!*), to feel a pleasant taste (*iùm!*), to find out some solution to a problem (*eureka*), to see some rival's goal thwarted (*ha!, tiè!*). Finally, one can tell a goal of one's is fulfilled, without specifying which goal it is (*òoh!, ecco*); while one can sometimes specify that the satisfaction for this fulfilment is particularly intense (*iuhù, evviva, hurrà*).

Also the beliefs requested by interrogative interjections (Table 2) are connected with the Speaker's beliefs and goals. *Eh?, no?, vero?* are requests for confirmation, and in fact they are also frequently used as *tag questions*. *Eh?* and *come?* ask for an information already requested but not heard; *beh?* asks for explanation.

Among requestive interjections (Table 3), some specify the requested action, like *aiuto* (help), *silenzio* (shut up), *sciò* (a rude form of "go away"). Others instead are "pure" incitations, in that they solicit to get active, but they do not tell you what to do: *dài* (come on), *prego* (please), *su* (come on!). Among these, a specific performative may be marked: *dèh* prays, *suvvia* encourages. Others are incitations marked as to the "aspect" of action, since they do not specify the requested action, but they solicit the Addressee to start (*via!, sotto!* = go!), to stop or end (*stop, basta* = that's enough), to do it again (*bis*), to go on (*avanti* = go on). Finally, some are requests for attention (*ehi, ehilà, aho'*).

The ones I call optative interjections (Table 4) include a great part of routine formulas: greetings like *ciao* (hello), *arrivederci* (goodbye) *buongiorno* (goodmorning); politeness formulas, like *grazie* (thanks) *salute!* (gesundheit!), *congratulazioni* (congratulations); wishing formulas, like *auguri* (wishes) and interjective idioms, like *in bocca al lupo* (an apotropaic way of wishing good luck: literally = get into the wolf's mouth). Within these we have a class of interjections I call "ejaculative", that include invocations like *Gesù* (Jesus), *mamma* or *mamma mia* (mummy), *misericordia* (pity on me!) and imprecations, like *accidenti*, *Cristo* (Christ), *dannazione* (damn it), *merda* (shit).

There is also a group of interjections that in part are only informative while in part they can be either informative or optative, but whose semantic origin seems to be always the same. They are derived from three different sources, that I call: **vocatives**, **external force**, and **cacophemism**.

Table 1. Informative interjections

TYPE			SPECIFIC MEANING	EXAMPLE
Beliefs			Understanding	*Ah*
			Acknowledgment	*Già*
			Confirmation	*Caspita, davvero, diamine, eh, mhm, oh, okay.* *Appunto, anzi! Cacchio, cavolo cazzo, certo, diavolo, ostia!* *Proprio, sì, sicuro, vero, altro che!*
			Negation	*Macché, see..., ńc,* *Affatto*
			Ignorance	*Bah, boh, chissà, mah*
			Incredulity	*Bum!, che!* *No!*
			Doubt or hesitation	*Beh, èeh, ehm, mhm, mah* *Allora, cioè, così, dico, dunque...*
			Surprise	*Ah, ih, oh, öh, olla, toh, uh, caspita, caspiterina, cribbio, diamine, ullallà* *Accidenti, boia, cacchio, capperi, cazzo...*
Goals	Thwarted goals	Physical disease	Pain	*Ahi, ahia, ahio, uhi*
			Cold	*Brrr*
			Disgust	*Bleah, puah*
			Fatigue	*Aùff, uffa*
		Psychic suffering	Boredom or annoyance	*Uffa, uh*
			Resignation	*Pazienza*
			Contempt	*Puah, pfui, poh*
			Displeasure or Desperation	*Ahimè, ohimè, no!* *Peccato*
			Worry	*Ńc*
			Shudder	*Aaah! Noo!!*
			Indignation	*Èeh, ohibò, ooh*
			Disappointment	*Acciderba, accipicchia, alé, beh?, caspiterina, cribbio, diamine* *Vacca, la Madonna*
	Achieved goals	Generic	Satisfaction	*Aah, òh, òoh, ecco, meno male*
			Exultance	*Evviva, hurrà, iuhù,* *Alleluia, osanna*
		Specific		*Aah, eureka, ha iùm, maramèo, tiè, uée!, vivaddio, ecco, là, piacere, mi rallegro*

Table 2. Interrogative interjections

TYPE	EXAMPLES
Requests for confirmation	*Eh?, nevvero?* *Davvero?, no?, vero?*
Requests to tell or repeat	*Eh?, beh?,* *che?, come? Cosa?*
Requests for explanation	*Beh?*

Table 3. Requestive interjections

TYPE		SPECIFIC MEANING	EXAMPLES
Generic requests	Attention request		*Aho, ehi, ehilà, ohé, ohilà, èst, uehi, uehilà*
	Pure incitations		*Alé, avanti, coraggio, dài, prego, su*
	Marked as to performative	Pray	*Dèh*
		Encourage	*Orsù, suvvia, coraggio*
		Forbid	*No*
	Marked as to aspect	Start	*Marsch!, sotto!, via!*
		Go on	*Avanti*
		Do again	*Bis*
	Miscellaneous		*Altolà. Arri, pardòn, scc..., sciò, ss..., tè tè, aiuto, allegria, avanti, calma, cuccia, largo, perdono, permesso, prego, pietà, pista, pronto, scusa, silenzio, soccorso, sveglia, vergogna, via, va là*

Table 4. Optative interjections

TYPE		EXAMPLES
Ejaculations	Invocations	*Gesù, Madonna, mamma, Maria, misericordia*
	Imprecations	*Cribbio, perbacco, perbaccolina, perdiana,* *Boia, cacchio, cavolo, Cristo, dannazione, diavolo, Dio,* *maledizione, merda, ostia*
Formulas	Greetings	*Arrivederci, addio, buonanotte, buonasera, buongiorno, ciao*
	Auguri	*Auguri, in bocca al lupo, cento di questi anni*
	Politeness formulas	*Complimenti, congratulazioni, condoglianze, grazie,* *rallegramenti, salute, salve*

Any time a speaker is surprised or disappointed by some event, he can express his surprise or disappointment by informative interjections like *però, tòh!, no!*. In some cases, though, that mental state is felt in such an intense way that he can need a more vivid or enhanced communicative action.

A first possibility – vocatives – is to call someone as a witness of the event at issue, in such a way as to remark how peculiar it is; in this case you can use vocatives like *gente!* (people!), *ragazzi!* (boys!), and you may do so very often and recurrently; so much that in the long run, beyond the performative of requesting attention conveyed by the vocative, an expression of surprise becomes idiomatically part of the meaning.

A second possibility – external force – is to curse or to make an appeal to some force to which you attribute the responsibility for that event, or the power to neutralize it: hence, imprecations and invocations, like *Cristo!* or *mamma!*, which indirectly may imply remarking one's surprise.

A third strategy – cacophemism – is to express the intensity of the felt mental state by resorting to lexical items whose form or meaning is particularly crude or aggressive. This is the reason for using some lexical items that can be defined cacophemistic (the opposite of euphemistic, [16], [11]), like *boia* (executioner), *miseria* (misery), *vacca* (cow) *merda* (shit), that are cacophemistic as to their meaning; or *corbezzoli* (good gracious!, literally, arbutus!), cacophemistic as to the phonic appearance of the signal; or finally *cazzo* (cock), that is on both sides so.

Out of these three types of interjections, those stemming from vocatives can be used only to express surprise or disappointment, while those deriving from external force and cacophemism can be used, not only as informative interjections expressing surprise and disappointment, but also as optative ones, namely as invocations or imprecations. Moreover, among all three types some, like *cazzo!* (cock!), *diavolo!* (devil!) *diamine!*, *perbacco* (by gosh!) can also work as an emphatic confirmation, something like "Of course!" or "Definitely so!".

9 Related Concepts

Once provided a clear definition of interjection, it is easier to distinguish it from other entities studied by Linguistics with which they have been sometimes put together across centuries: exclamations and onomatopoeia. Of course, there definitely is some overlapping between interjections and each of these phenomena. So the confusion is probably due to this partial overlap.

9.1 Interjection and Exclamation

Many interjections, and among them all ejaculations, are typically uttered with an exclamatory intonation. But this does not imply that every interjection is an exclamation or the other way around.

To single out commonalities and differences between interjection and exclamation, I will first propose a definition of the latter.

Exclamation is sometimes considered (see for example [17], [18]) as a type of sentence, and hence – in analogy with declarative sentences typically marked by a declarative intonation, or questions marked by interrogative intonation – as a type of intonation. Moreover, just as within interrogative sentences some are Wh questions, necessarily introduced by interrogative Wh pronouns (*who, how, what, where...*), also some exclamative sentences use Wh pronouns. For example:

(14) *What a pretty girl she is!*

(15) *How many people were there!*

Yet, in particular cases *any* sentence can be uttered in an exclamatory way, and, if written, it can be closed by an exclamation mark. So, what distinguishes an exclamation from a non-exclamatory sentence?

According to [18], an exclamatory sentence connotes all or part of the content of a sentence as unexpected. My hypothesis is that when a sentence is produced as an exclamation, in that either it has an exclamatory syntactic construction, or it is uttered with an exclamatory intonation, the Speaker has the goal to convey that she is feeling some emotion – sometimes just a generic emotional arousal, sometimes more specifically an emotion of surprise – concerning the content of the sentence. Thus a speech act produced in an exclamatory way conveys a generic emotional loading, but one of particular intensity, over the content of the speech act; generic in that the emotion felt is not specified from a qualitative point of view, or at most it is typically loaded with the emotion of surprise: that sentence or part of the sentence is viewed by the Speaker as unexpected, therefore surprising [6], [19], [11], and consequently more important to be conveyed. This is why an exclamation is often defined as a type of emphatic sentence [17].

This account of exclamation can perhaps explain why exclamations and interjections are often confused: the two phenomena have in common their being linked to emotional expression. Exclamation is a way to impress emotional loading to any communicative act, while interjections typically convey emotional states.

9.2 Interjection and Onomatopoeia

Again on the basis of our definition, it is easier to distinguish the notion of interjection from that of onomatopoeia, with which it has often been merged.

Onomatopoeia is in general a case of iconicity in a vocal language. By iconicity we mean [11] the fact that, in a communicative item, between the signal and the meaning there is a relationship of similarity by way of imitation: for example, the above mentioned gesture, *hand palm to Sender with index and middle finger in V shape moving back and forth in front of the mouth*, is iconic in that it imitates (aims at being similar to) some or all of the perceivable aspects that make part of the corresponding meaning, "to smoke". Here the whole gesture, with the shape of the hand, its orientation, location and movement, imitates the action performed in smoking. The gesture is iconic in that it imitates the visual appearance produced by the action which constitutes its meaning. Similarly, a word like *"cock-a-doodle-do"* is iconic – onomatopoeic – in that with its sound it imitates the acoustic appearance of the sound produced by a rooster.

Thus onomatopoeia can be defined as the fact that some vocal signal with its sound imitates the sound produced by some event, action, object, animal or person which is the meaning of that signal.

Actually, if onomatopoeia is as defined, we can well say that some interjections are onomatopoeic. In Italian, for example, an onomatopoeic interjection is *"uffa"*, that expresses one is tired, bored, bothered or fatigued with something. The sound *"uffa"* imitates the air puff, the loud expiration one often emits when fatiguing in some effort. Another onomatopoeic Italian interjection is *"òoh!"*: an expression of satisfaction one utters when he has managed to do something he was striving for; and this too imitates the serene expiration emitted in relief, possibly due to when one finally relaxes after an effort that achieved the result hoped for.

But that some interjections are onomatopoeic does not mean that all of them are. Some interjections are not onomatopoeic – for example, the Italian interjection *"ah"*, and the corresponding English *"oh"*, that mean "I acknowledge I am coming to assume a new belief", do not seem to imitate sounds anyhow linked to their meaning. On the other hand, many onomatopoeic signals are not interjections, since they do not convey complete codified speech acts, comprised of a performative. For example, the signal *"cock-a-doodle-doo"* can be used in a sentence like

(16) *At dawn, today, I heard the rooster's cock-a-doodle-do,*

where it works as a noun, therefore not a whole communicative act. Also in her motherese language a mother can often use an onomatopoeic signal as a noun for an animal:

(17) *Oh, here is the bow-wow!.*

In conclusion, onomatopoeic signals and interjections do not cover the same range of phenomena, since some interjections are not onomatopoeic and some onomatopoeic signals are not interjections.

10 "Primitive" Devices?

In general, what interjection and onomatopoeia have in common, and what accounts for their confusion, is that they are both characterized by some features which can be considered primitive, that is, cognitively simpler, and then probably of earlier emergence, than those typical of modern languages.

That interjections are a way of communicating somehow "primitive" has been acknowledged by ancient and modern scholars [20], and recently reaffirmed by language evolution research [9].

Some of the devices that make interjections more primitive than, for instance, sentences in a language, are the following.

10.1 Holophrastic Versus Articulated

At a high stage of language evolution, for instance in a modern verbal language, the most relevant feature is the device of articulation, due to the capacity for fractionation [21], thanks to which the semantic content of a communicative act comes to be split and distinguished into chunks, and each of them is conveyed through a single communicative unit, so that the whole communicative act is borne by a combination of units. From this point of view, an interjection is more primitive than a sentence, since it conveys a whole chunk of meanings through a single vocal unit.

10.2 Expressive Versus Communicative

As pointed out by [22], [6] and [9], an interjection differs from a sentence due to its, so to speak, "communicative status". If we take an interjection and the corresponding sentence – for instance *"ouch!"* as against *"I am feeling pain"* – both convey the same internal mental state, but the former simply "expresses" it, while the latter " describes" it, it "communicates" it [6]. Let me define the difference between expression and communication in terms of two dimensions.

Presence and awareness of the goal of communicating. According to Poggi [11] we can distinguish three different cases in which meanings pass through from an agent A to an Agent B due to A producing a signal: a) ego-centered, or non-communicative expression; b) communicative expression; c) communication in the strong sense. Non-communicative expression, or more simply **expression**, as defined according to the etymological sense (Latin *ex-premere* = to push out), occurs when an Agent (not yet a Sender, strictly speaking!) feels some mental state and in order to give vent to it, but not in order to share it with someone else, produces a physical perceivable stimulus, which for an external observer can work as a signal in that it provides information, but which is produced by the Agent only to obtain relief from his internal state. If I smash a glass in anger, this is not necessarily aimed to communicate my anger to someone else; I may simply want to give vent to my emotion, to discharge the physiological arousal I feel [23]. This is a case of expression but not communication, in that it is not aimed to have some Addressee know something, it is not even a social action, it may, even, not take another into account.

On the opposite end we have **communication** in the strong sense – communication as defined by [24] and [25] – in which a Sender has a goal of having an Addressee believe some belief, but also has the goal for the Addressee to believe that the Sender has the goal to have him believe that belief. Communication in this strong sense necessarily implies some kind of meta-communication: I not only want you to know, but also want you to know I want you to know. Yet, communication in this sense is only possible with some kind of meta-consciousness or self-awareness of what one is communicating, and thus cannot be afforded by Senders with low levels of cognitive sophistication, like animals or human infants. But since constraining the very definition of communication to only conscious and deliberate human communication would imply too narrow a notion of it, a more basic definition of communication is needed: communication in a weaker sense, not a self-conscious nor a meta-communicative one.

Thus we have a third case in between ego-centered non communicative expression and communication in the strong sense. This is **communicative expression** (or **expressive communication**), which is a case of communication: the perceivable stimulus produced can be called a communicative signal since it is aimed to the goal of having someone else know something. Nonetheless, this is a case of communication in a weak sense, in that the Sender of the signal is not aware of his own goal of communicating.

In terms of this dimension – the presence and self-consciousness of the goal of having others know – all signals in a verbal language are in general cases of communication in this strong sense. On the other side, typical examples of expressive communication are some cases of facial expression, gaze, posture; finally, affect bursts [14] and music [26], [11] may sometimes be cases of expressive communication, but more often they are non communicative expression. Interjections may, very rarely, be non-communicative at all, but more typically they are communicative in the weak sense.

When we utter an interjection, we communicate some mental state, but, different from when we do so through an articulated sentence, we do not necessarily have a high level of awareness of that mental state ourselves, nor do we need, therefore, to have a conscious goal that the other know we are feeling it.

Types of meaning conveyed. According to [11], any meaning of any possible signal belongs to one of three broad types of Information: 1. on the World (concrete and abstract events and entities – objects, persons, animals, times and places); 2. on the *Sender's Identity* (stable characteristics of the Sender: sex, age, culture, personality, image and self-image); 3. on the *Sender's Mind*: his/her mental states (beliefs, goals and emotions). Now, in expression, as opposed to communication in the strong sense, the beliefs conveyed do not concern Information about the World, but only Information on the Sender's Mind or the Sender's Identity.

In conclusion, in terms of the two criteria proposed, communicative status and type of meaning conveyed, we can define **expression** (both communicative and ego-centered) as the act of producing signals 1. about either one's identity or one's mental states (but not about states of the world) and 2. either with a non-meta-conscious communicative goal or without any goal of communicating at all.

And interjections typically belong to the field of **communicative expression**.

10.3 Context-Dependent Versus Context-Independent

Another aspect is peculiar of interjections as opposed to articulated sentences. The interjection, due to its being, as a deictic item, strictly linked to context, does not exhibit the property of displacement, a typical feature, according to [27], of verbal language. In a sentence we can talk about things that happened in the past or will happen in the future. With an interjection, instead, I can only express a mental state that is occurring right here and now. I can say

(18) *I am amazed with this now*;

or

(19) *I was amazed with this then*;

but while I can say

(20) *Wow!*

referring to something that I am coming to know right now, I cannot say

(21) **At that time, wow!*.

unless I am feeling that mental state again, right now.

In other words, an interjection can only be used "in praesentia" of (simultaneously with) the mental state it mentions: that mental state cannot be simply remembered or hypothesized, it must be *lived* at the time the interjection is uttered.

This can be connected with the above mentioned aspect of the interjections: their being deictic items. If the cause of the mental state must necessarily be retrieved through context, this is why an interjection can only be used when the mental state is being felt.

11 Conclusion

Interjection is a holophrastic signal that conveys information about the Speaker's mental states, and requests action and information from the Addressee or a third party, through a communicative device that does not imply meta-consciousness and does not allow displacement in space and time. Nonetheless, this peculiar type of language is rich and deep in the communication of our mental reality.

References

1. Spitzer, L.: Italienische Umgangssprache, Schroeder, Bonn &Leipzig (1922)
2. Karcevski, S.: Introduction à l'étude de l'interjection. Cahiers Ferdinand de Saussure I, 57–75 (1941)
3. Elwert, T.: Interjections, onomatopées et système linguistique, à propos de quelques examples roumains. In: Actes du 10e Congrès internationale de Linguistique et Philologie romanes, Klincksiek, Paris, vol. 3, pp. 1235–1246 (1965)
4. James, D.M.: The Syntax and Semantics of Some English Interjections. Papers in Linguistics, University of Michigan, Ann Arbor (1974)
5. Nencioni, G.: L'interiezione nel dialogo teatrale di Pirandello. In: Atti del Seminario sull'Italiano parlato. Studi di Grammatica italiana, Accademia della Crusca, Firenze (1977)
6. Poggi, I.: Le interiezioni. Studio del linguaggio e analisi della mente. Boringhieri, Torino (1981)
7. Ameka, F.: Interjection: the universal yet neglected part of speech. Journal of Pragmatics 18, 101–118 (1992)
8. Wierzbicka, A.: The semantics of interjections. Journal of Pragmatics 18, 159–192 (1992)
9. Wharton, T.: Interjections, language and the showing/telling continuum. In: 3rd Conference on The evolution of Language, Lyon, April 3-6 (2000)
10. Poggi, I.: L'interiezione. In: Renzi, L., Salvi, G., Cardinaletti, A. (eds.) Grande grammatica italiana di consultazione, Il Mulino, Bologna, vol. III, pp. 403–425 (1995)
11. Poggi, I.: Mind, hands, face and body. A goal and belief view of multimodal communication, Weidler, Berlin (2007)
12. de Saussure, F.: Cours de Linguistique générale, Payot, Paris (1916)
13. Wundt, W.: Völkerpsychologie. I. Die Sprache, Engelmann, Leipzig (1900)
14. Scherer, K.R.: Affect Bursts. In: van Goozen, S.H.M., de Poll, N.E., Sergeant, J.A.S. (eds.) Emotions: Essays on Emotion Theory. Erlbaum, Hillsdale (1994)
15. Schroeder, M., Heylen, D., Poggi, I.: Perception of non-verbal emotional listener feedback. In: Speech Prosody 2006, Dresden, Germany (2006)
16. Castelfranchi, C., Parisi, D.: Linguaggio, conoscenze e scopi, Il Mulino, Bologna (1980)
17. Crystal, D.: Rediscover Grammar with David Crystal. Pearson Longman, London (2000)
18. Benincà, P.: Il tipo esclamativo. In: Renzi, L., Salvi, G., Cardinaletti, A. (eds.) Grande grammatica italiana di consultazione, Il Mulino, Bologna, vol. III, pp. 127–152 (1995)
19. Lorini, E., Castelfranchi, C.: The unexpected aspects of surprise. International Journal of Pattern Recognition and Artificial Intelligence 20(6), 817–835 (2007)
20. O'Connell, D.C., Kowal, S., King, S.P.: Interjections in literary readings and artistic performance. Pragmatics 17(3), 417–438 (2007)
21. Arbib, M. (ed.): Action to language via the mirror neuron system. Cambridge University Press, Cambridge (2006)
22. Goffman, E.: Forms of Talk. Blackwell, Oxford (1981)

23. Poggi, I., Pelachaud, C., De Carolis, B.: To display or not to display? Towards the architecture of a Reflexive Agent. In: Proceedings of the 2nd Workshop on Attitude, Personality and Emotions in User-adapted Interaction. User Modeling 2001, Sonthofen, Germany, July 13-17 (2001)
24. Grice, H.P.: Meaning. The Philosophical Review 66, 377–388 (1957)
25. Strawson, P.F.: Intention and Convention in Speech Acts. The Philosophical Review 73, 439–460 (1964)
26. Checchi, M., Poggi, I.: Bimodality in films: the meaning of music in the sound-track. In: Santi, S., Guaitella, B., Cavé, C., Konopczynski, G. (eds.) Oralite' et gestualite', communication multimodale, interaction, L'Harmattan, Paris (1998)
27. Hockett, C.: The origins of Speech. Scientific American 203, 89–96 (1960)

Gesture and Gaze in Persuasive Political Discourse

Laura Vincze

PhD Student, Department of Linguistics, Via Santa Maria 85,
56126 Pisa, University of Pisa, Italy
l.vincze@ling.unipi.it

Abstract. Persuasion in political discourse is a very popular topic, which raised a lot of debate among researchers. Yet, not so much literature has been devoted to the persuasive impact of facial expression and gaze in persuasion. This paper is an introduction to further research and gives some examples of persuasive gesture and gaze, by trying to prove how important these aspects of communication may be in persuasive political discourse. Also, the focus of the paper is to show how politicians make use of them in order to express positive or negative evaluations about the opponent and thus, raise emotions in the public.

Keywords: Gesture, gaze, persuasion, persuasive strategies.

1 Introduction

In persuasive discourse, as argued by Poggi (2005), locutor A has the goal to convince interlocutor B that the goal proposed by A is the best possible option also for the goals of B, and not just an option among many others. Therefore, to persuade is to convince others about the importance of the goals we propose them to pursue.

In order to do so, politicians use many persuasive strategies. To better exploit the persuasive techniques of *logos* (rational arguments), *ethos* (the Speaker's credibility and reliability) and *pathos* (the appeal to emotion), already illustrated by Aristotle, politicians, along with words, often employ gestures and gaze in a persuasive way.

A resolute gaze may be used for example when one wants to stress that he is being serious and therefore he is a person that people can count on, one who keeps his promises. On the contrary, the speaker may employ a discontent facial expression and an accusing gaze while talking about his opponent, thus implying that the other candidate is not worthy of the audience's trust.

2 Gesture in the Greek and Roman Treatises

The importance of gesture in political discourse has been acknowledged back since the ancient Roman treatises of Rhetorics. While in the Greek treatises, Aristotle didn't consider it essential in the delivery of a discourse, which, he believed, should contain only facts, in the Roman treatises, instead, gesture starts to be seen differently.

A. Esposito et al. (Eds.): Multimodal Signals, LNAI 5398, pp. 187–196, 2009.
© Springer-Verlag Berlin Heidelberg 2009

Cicero thought that gesture is worthy of cultivation and emphasized how gesture and especially the face should be used to express the feelings that lie behind a discourse.

The most complete analysis of gesture is that of Quintilianus in his XI Book of Institutio oratoria. His book is a comprehensive treatise on all aspects of rhetoric (Kendon, 2004).

For Quintilian, *gestus* refers not only to actions of the hands and arms, but also to the posture and carriage of the body, the actions of the head and face, and also to the glance. Glance, to Quintilian, is the most important for the "creation of the overall emotional effect of the discourse" (Kendon, 2004).

According to Quintilian, by gesture and other body movements, "we can demand, promise, summon, dismiss, threaten, supplicate, express aversion or fear, question or deny [...], indicate sorrow, hesitation, confession, penitence, measure, quantity, number and time [...], express approval, wonder or shame." (Quintilian, 2006).

I follow Quintilian's view, who designated by *gestus* not only actions of the hands and arms, but also the posture and carriage of the body, the actions of the head and face, and also the glance.

In fact, in my analysis of gesture, I took into account the facial expression as well (for instance smile, grimaces), and not only the actions of hands.

3 The Absence of Gestures in Absence of Speech

As we saw, both gesture and facial expression are extremely important in the delivery of the political discourse. Many handbooks dedicated to young orators have been written with the purpose of teaching them how to employ gesture and facial expression in order to obtain the desired effect.

Gesture and gaze, though, may have a persuasive impact not only in the accompaniment of speech, but also while one is silently listening to the opponent's speech and cannot interfere verbally (for example, when it's the opponent's turn to speak, the other candidate may express his disapproval by making use of gestures or facial expression).

A very expressive gesture which can be made in absence of speech, and which may be employed by a candidate while his opponent is speaking , is the symbolic gesture of the "tulip hand". According to Poggi (2007), this is an ambiguous gesture, which can be disambiguated by looking at the context, that is, at the non-manual components like facial expression. The audience may easily disambiguate the "tulip hand" gesture, which has more than one interpretation, and see that in that particular case, the meaning of the gesture is one of criticism.

4 Persuasive Gesture and Persuasive Gaze

In order to analyze and classify several persuasive gesture and gaze items in the political discourse, I adopted the annotation scheme built up by Poggi and Pelachaud (2008), where they investigated the impact of gesture in political discourse.

As in the study conducted by these two authors, my hypothesis was that the persuasive import of gaze, just as that of words and gestures, depends on the meanings it conveys. Therefore, to assess how persuasive the gesture or gaze exhibited in a discourse might be, one has to assess its meanings.

The annotation scheme below contains the analysis of gesture and gaze items, and is divided into 12 columns.

The columns contain, respectively:

- In column 1 there is the number of the gesture under analysis and its time in the video;
- Column 2 contains the speech parallel to the gesture under analysis;
- In column 3 there is a description of the gesture in terms of its parameters (Poggi, 2007): handshape, location, orientation and movement.
- Column 4 contains the literal meaning of the gesture. A gesture, as any communicative signal, by definition means something, that is, it corresponds to some meaning; this meaning can be codified, as in a lexicon, or created on the spot but in any case comprehensible by others, and then shared; and it may be paraphrased in words. (For examples of the signal-meaning pairs in gestures, see Poggi, 2007). This verbal paraphrase is written in col. 4;
- In column 5 there is a classification of the meaning written down in col. 4, according to the semantic taxonomy proposed by Poggi (2007), who distinguishes meanings as providing information on the World (events, their actors and objects, and the time and space relations between them), the Sender's Identity (sex, age, socio-cultural roots, personality), or the Sender's Mind (beliefs, goals and emotions);
- Since, according to Poggi (2007), any signal, beside its literal meaning can have one or more indirect meanings, that is, a level of information that can be inferred from the literal meaning, columns 6 and 7 contain, for possible indirect meanings of the gesture, the same analysis of columns 4) ,5). (Poggi & Pelachaud 2008).
- Columns 8), 9), 10), 11) and 12) contain the same analysis as for gesture, but this time for gaze. (Poggi and Vincze 2008)

Also in this case I wrote down the meanings I attributed to the Speaker's uses of gaze, on the basis of the lexicon of gaze hypothesized by Poggi & Roberto (2008). They are the meanings and persuasive functions I think the Speaker has the goal (not necessarily a conscious goal) to convey, and make no assumption as to whether they in fact are persuasive for the real audience.

The political character under analysis is Ségolène Royal, the Socialist Party's candidate for President of France in may 2007.

The one minute fragment is drawn from the political show *"A' vous de juger"*, held in the studios of the French channel France 2, after the first electoral round, when Royal came second after Nicolas Sarkozy. The host, Arlette Chabot, interviews Mrs. Royal about her political vision and projects for France.

In the fragment presented below, Royal mimics Sarkozy's discourse, expressing in this way her disapproval and her rebellion against her opponent's politics. She even compares him to Père Fouettard[1], the evil counterpart of Saint Nicolas.

The French legend says that during the night of 5th December, the two characters go together and visit all the children. The latter brings presents and sweets to those who behaved properly, and the former whips the bad ones.

By comparing her opponent to Père Fouettard, she implies that his program is too punitive against the unemployed people: unless they accept one of the first 2-3 job offers, the unemployment subside will be stopped.

Also, by making appeal to irony in order to criticize her opponent, she evokes a negative emotion in the public. Due to the fact that emotions have got a very strong motivational power, often rhetorical figures are employed in speech to induce an emotion.

The decision who to vote is also based on what the electors think about the speaker and about his opponent. Therefore, in such important moments as pre-electoral encounters, which may change people's opinions (at least as far as the "undecided" segment of population is concerned), there is a high desire of controlling the impressions of the public.

But what are the persuasive means through which politicians try to appear credible or through which we infer our interlocutor's honesty?

5 Persuasion : A Case of Social Influence

In Petty's and Caciopppo's view, persuasion goes through two routes : central and peripheral. The central route consists of attentive examination of the arguments which are present in the message, and occurs only when a receiver possesses both the motivation and ability to think about the message and topic. The peripheral route occurs when the receiver lacks ability and/or motivation to engage in much thought on the issue. Using the peripheral route, the listener decides whether to agree with the message based on other cues besides the strength of the arguments in the message, such as whether the source is credible or attractive, the number (but not the quality) of arguments in the message, or length of the message. (Petty, Cacioppo, 1986).

Petty's and Cacioppo's central route reminds us of Aristotle's *logos*, while the peripheral route could be identified with the persuasive strategies of *ethos* and *pathos*.

The two authors sustain that we use the central route when we have to make important decisions which will affect our future, and on the contrary we let ourselves conduced by the peripheral route when it's about less significant things. In this last circumstance, we may choose for instance a car by taking into account the less significant properties of the vehicle, as let's say colour or model, and don't pay attention to aspects as cylinder capacity or how many miles per litre you may achieve. In this case we would let emotions and aesthetics principles govern us, and not rational arguments.

But is it always the case?

---

[1] Fouet (fr.) – whip.

While in Petty and Cacioppo's theory, one of the routes excludes the other and vice-versa, in Chaiken's view, one and the same individual may elaborate the peripheral and central cues simultaneously. For example, the reliability and credibility of the source of the message may influence the listener in the elaboration of the message, along with the rationality of his arguments.

According to Poggi (2005) as well, people is persuaded more by emotion than by logical arguments, because of the fact that emotion triggers important goals. Emotions are there in order to protect our most important goals. For example, why do we have the emotion of fear? Because it makes us run away when our life is in danger. Therefore fear protects us and monitors our goal of survival.

Due to the fact that emotions protect our most important goals, the goals triggered by emotions are important as well. That's why, in our case, if the Persuader (A) tries to influence the electors (B) to adopt her goals not only by rational arguments, but also by making appeal to emotions, there are more possibilities that the electors pursue A's goal.

Also, if the relation between A's goal and B's goal is made credible not only through arguments but also by emphasizing the reliability of the Persuader, A's goal is more likely to be pursued. Therefore, B must evaluate as positive not only the goal proposed by the Persuader, but also the Persuader himself. (Poggi 2005).

We can see now in what great extent pathos and ethos – that is the peripheral route – are important in persuasion. According to this view, the decision of adopting the Persuader's goals is taken on the basis of the two routes considered altogether, or in other words, on the basis of the three persuasive strategies described by Aristotle : *logos, ethos, pathos.*

Therefore, when judging Ségolène Royal's speech, the electors take into account the logical arguments brought by her (that is her political ideology and projects for France), her credibility and honesty and last but, as we saw not least, the emotions which she induces to the audience.

6 Qualitative Analysis of Gesture and Gaze in Persuasion

The fragment below comes right after the part where Ségolène Royal tells the public that she has met a man at the RMI[2], who leaves home every morning, with a suitcase in his hand, because he doesn't want to let his child understand he is unemployed. He doesn't want his child to be ashamed of the fact that his father doesn't have a job.

This is the fragment under analysis:

Donc quand je vois des misères sociales comme cela et que j'entends une espèce de discours tonitruant euh... ils n'y a qu'à, vous allez voir ce que vous allez voir, de Père Fouettard disant aux uns et aux autres vous vous allez faire ça, ou sinon vous serez sanctionnés, alors qu'il y a tellement d'abus de l'autre côté parmi les amis du pouvoir, je me dis que ça... ça n'est pas bon pour la France, ça n'est pas ma vision des choses.

---

[2] Revenu Moyen d'Insertion (Fr.) – Guaranteed minimum income. System of social welfare provision that guarantees that all citizens or families have an income sufficient to live on, provided they meet certain conditions. The primary goal of a guaranteed minimum income is to combat poverty.

So when I see cases of extreme poverty like this one, and when I hear a sort of thunderous discourse...for all that I care, you can do whatever you like, you just wait and see, a Father Spanker discourse, telling everybody you, you are going to do this, otherwise you'll be sanctioned, when there are so many abuses on the other side among the friends of power, I say to myself that this, this is not my vision of things.

At line 2, she starts to mimic Sarkozy. As far as her nonverbal behaviour is concerned, we notice that she lets the public know that she is about to start mimicking her opponent by the exaggerated rotation of the head, performed while speaking about his *"thunderous discourse"*. In fact, the literal meaning of her gesture is that she is mimicking Sarkozy, and by doing so she raises an emotion in the public. The indirect meaning of her gesture is to make fun of the opponent, and in the same time, she is showing the public what kind of person Sarkozy is.

By making fun of her opponent, she expresses a negative evaluation about him, inducing the public to feel the same. We can interpret her dramatisation as a parody, a way to make fun of Sarkozy's proposal. In this way she conveys a negative evaluation of her opponent through a pathos strategy.

In fact, if the persuader (A) when trying to convince the persuadee (B), makes appeal to emotions and not only to logical arguments, there are more possibilities that B pursues A's goal (GA), because emotions are a very important motivating device. This way Royal pursues a pathos strategy by raising an emotion in the public. (see Poggi 2005).

We understand she is enumerating the things Sarkozy said, because of her intonation, typically employed in enumeration. In fact, she says : " *for all that I care, you can do whatever you like, you just wait and see",* and rapidly gazes in an accusatory way at both interlocutors (Arlette Chabot and Gilles LeClerc), addressing both of them. She employs a discontent facial expression and an accusing gaze while talking about Sarkozy, thus implying that she totally disagrees with his manner of treating the unemployed. The tone of her voice rapidly changes, because now she is imitating Sarkozy directly addressing to the unemployed people: *"you, you are going to do this, otherwise you'll be sanctioned".* While saying this last sentence, she looks down, as if looking at the unemployed, though performing a "deictic in absence" gaze (that is, a gaze that points to someone who is absent) and her right shoulder raises at the same time. We can't see her right hand, but from the movement of her shoulder we understand she did the performative gesture of order, mimicking this way Sarkozy giving orders to the unemployed. During all her mimicking, she keeps her head and chin raised, imitating Sarkozy's superiority posture.

In line 5, while saying: *"when there are so many abuses on the other side among the friends of power",* she makes a grimace of disgust (see Picture 1). The literal meaning of her facial expression is that she is disgusted by Sarkozy's power abuses, and in this case there is an indirect meaning as well, she is trying to transmit to the public that they should be disgusted too. While saying *"so many abuses among the friends of power",* she frowns, squeezes eyes and her right eye winks. This is a complicity look, meaning that Sarkozy and the powerful people who do the abuses are his friends, while as an indirect meanings she aims to transmit that people can trust her, that she is on their side.

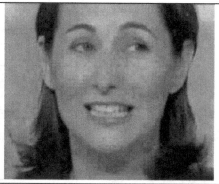

Picture 1. [...] *"when there are so many abuses on the other side of the power* | **Picture 2.** *I say to myself that this, this not my vision of things"*

In line 6, while stating *"I say to myself that this.."*, she shakes her head in sign of denial. The direct meaning of her gesture is one of disagreement with Sarkozy's politics, while at an indirect level aiming to transmit that this is not good for France.

In fact, in line 7, she says it verbally as well: *"this is not good for France, this is not my vision of things"*. While saying this last sentences, she smiles, the literal meaning of her facial expression being that she is happy with her vision of France, which is totally opposite to that of Sarkozy. She thus transmits a positive emotion to the public, and the indirect meaning of this is that she wants to induce courage and hope to people. She has her eyebrows raised and an oblique gaze, looking towards the interlocutor. The literal meaning of her oblique gaze is demanding for approval. She turns her head away, but still keeping eyes on her interlocutor (in this case, Arlette Chabot) in order to see her facial expression and so to understand if she agrees with her. (see Picture 2). The meaning type of her gaze item is a performative. There is also an indirect meaning: even if she is in search of approval from her interlocutor, she is sure of the correctness of her statements. In fact, it seems that she is stating something, and then obliquely looks at her interlocutor, as if asking : "Isn't it?". She doesn't ask the question verbally, but she doesn't has to, her gaze is very expressive by itself.

7 Conclusions

What I presented above only gives some examples of persuasive gaze and gesture used in political discourse.

It's important to specify that while the gestures' meaning is not universal, but culture-specific, the meaning of gaze might be universal. As Poggi emphasizes, only the norms of use of the gaze are certainly different, according to the country from which the Sender of the signal comes from, but as far as the meanings of a specific gaze are concerned, they might be the same everywhere.

Subsequent research will imply analyzing more items of gesture and gaze extracted from political debates and assessing if the meaning of these items are actually persuasive for the audience.

n.	Speech	Gesture Description	Literal. M	Type	Indirect M.	Type	Gaze	Literal. M	Type	Indirect M.	Type
1 51.17	*Donc quand je vois des mi-sères sociales comme cela et que j'entends* So when I see cases of extreme poverty like this one, and when I hear	Open hands on the table. Beat of hands on the table	I emphasise it.	ISM Important PERS Logos			Looks rapidly to both Int.	I address both of you I'm indignant	ISM Performative ISM Emotion	Pay attention, it's important I want you to be indignant	ISM Importance PERS Pathos
2 51.19	*une espèce de discours toni-truant* a sort of thunderous discourse	Rotation of the head Angry and disgusted grimace Raised head and chin	I am mimicking Sarkozy I feel superior to Sarkozy	ISM Emotion	I am ridiculing Sarkozy → I show you what kind of person he is I am less punitive than Sarkozy	ISM Emotion PATHOS ISM Negative evaluation of the opponent LOGOS ISI Ethos benevolence	She looks straight at Int. Looks down at Int.	I accuse Sarkozy I feel comptempt towards Sarkozy	ISM Perf Logos ISM Emotion		ISM PERS Pathos
3 51.23	*euh ils n'y a qu'à, vous allez voir ce que vous allez voir, de Père Fouettard disant aux uns et aux autres* for all that I care, you can do what you like, you wait and see, of "Père Fouettard, telling everybody	Short, rapid movements of the head by looking to both Int. Beat of the head	I am strict. I emphasize my words.	IW ISM Importance Logos	I am miming Sarkozy. I want you to make fun of him. What I say is important	ISM Emotion PERS Pathos ISM Pathos	She rapidly looks at both Int and then keeps gaze fixed on Int. 1.	I address both of you.	Important PERS Logos	I ask you to feel the same I do.	ISM PERS Pathos

#	Speech	Gesture	Intention	Cat.	Rhetorical	Cat.	Gaze	Intention	Cat.	Intention	Cat.
4 51.29	*vous vous allez faire ça, ou sinon vous serez sanctionnés* you, you are going to do this, otherwise you'll be sanctioned	Raised head and chin Left shoulder raises, she raises the left hand to mime Sarkozy who gives an order.	Feel indignant of Sarkozy's judgement. I give you an order	ISM Emotion ISM Performative	I mime the way of speaking of Sarkozy. I make fun of him.	PERS Pathos ISM Negative evaluation of the opponent Logos	Looks down, looking at the people Sarkozy gives orders to. Looks to both Int.	I am miming Sarkozy looking at the people to whom he is giving orders. I address to both Int. I am ridiculing Sarkozy.	IW Deixis in absence ISM Meta discursive	I want to make fun of him.	PERS PATHOS
5 51.32	*alors qu'il y a tellement d'abus de l'autre côté parmi les amis du pouvoir* when there are so many abuses on the other side among the friends of power	Grimace, the angles of the mouth are lowered.	I am disgusted (by the power abuses of Sarkozy and his men.)	ISM Emotion	Be disgusted as well!	ISM PERS Pathos	Frowns brows, Squeezes eyes. Right eye winks. Looks down while saying "on the other side, among the friends of power"	Complicity look Friends in illicit things She looks at the opponent's party.	ISM PERS Pathos IW Deixis in absence	Sarkozy favours his friends.	IW Negative evaluation of the opponent
6 51.36	*je me dis que ça...* I say to myself that this..	Head down Shakes the head in sign of denial. Blank expression of the face.	I don't agree (with Sarkozy's politics.)	ISM Evaluation	This is not good for France.	ISM PERS Logos	Raised brows. She looks down at Int. Eyes wide open, she looks straight into the Int.'s eyes.	Emphasis on this part. Demanding for approval.	ISM Important PERS Logos ISM Performative		
7 51.37	*ça n'est pas bon pour la France, ça n'est pas ma vision des choses.* this is not good for France, this is not my vision of things.	Smiles.	I am happy with my view of France	ISM Emotion	I want to induce you courage, hope.	ISM PERS Pathos	Raised eyebrows Looks obliquely to her interlocutor.	I ask you for your approval	ISM Performative	I am sure of this	ISM Certainty Ethos Competence

References

1. Aristotle: Retorica. Laterza, Bari (1973)
2. Cicero, M.T.: Dell'oratore, Rizzoli, Milano (1994)
3. Chaiken, S.: Heuristic vs. systematic information processing and the use of source vs. message cues in persuasion. Journal of Personality and Social Psychology 39, 752–766 (1980)
4. Kendon, A.: Gesture. Visible Action as Utterance. Cambridge University Press, Cambridge
5. Petty, R.E., Cacioppo, J.T.: Communication and Persuasion. Springer, New York (1986)
6. Poggi, I.: The goals of persuasion. Pragmatics and Cognition, pp. 297–336. John Benjamin Publishing Company (2005)
7. Poggi, I.: Mind, Hands, Face and Body. Weidler Buchverlag, Berlin (2007)
8. Poggi, I., Roberto, E.: The eyes and the eyelids. A compositional view about the meanings of Gaze. In: Ahlsén, E., Henrichsen, P.J., Hirsch, R., Nivre, J., Abelin, A., Stroemqvist, S., Nicholson, S. (eds.) Communicaion – Action – Meaning. A festschrift to Jens Allwood, Dpt. Linguistics, Goteborg University, pp. 333–350 (2008)
9. Poggi, I., Vincze, L.: The persuasive import of gesture and gaze. In: Proceeding on the Workshop on Multimodal Corpora, LREC, Marrakech, pp. 46–51 (2008)
10. Quintilianus, M.F.: Institutio oratoria. Book XI, III. In: Reinhardt, T., Winterbottom, M. (eds.), pp. 85–87. Oxford university press, New York (2006)

Content in Embedded Sentences

A Typology by Context Shift[*]

Uli Sauerland[1,2] and Mathias Schenner[2]

[1] Stanford University
[2] ZAS Berlin

Abstract. In this overview, we look at embedded clauses that report somebody's attitude or speech. Semantic content in the embedded clause can in some such cases be interpreted from either of two perspectives: that of the speaker or that of the attitude holder/speaker being reported on. Other classes of content do not exhibit this ambiguity. Our overview shows which factors determine the interpretation of embedded linguistic and non-linguistic material and develop a partial explanation.

1 Introduction

Humans are able to assign meaning to complex sentences that they have never heard before. For this reason, semanticists assume generally that sentence interpretation is compositional (cf. Heim and Kratzer, 1998 among many others): the procedure interpreting sentences associates stored meanings to certain basic sentence parts and then applies general principles to combine the meanings of the parts to generate the sentence meaning. The compositionality of sentence meaning is one of the characteristic features of human language and perhaps a major contributor to our species's evolutionary success (Spelke, 2003). Compositionality is necessary for the interpretation of recursive structures because recursion leads to an infinite number of structures that can be generated.

In this paper we consider one way in which possibly all languages allow the recursive generation of an infinity of sentences: embedding of one sentence as a subordinate sentence within another.[1] How is the meaning of the embedded sentence joined into the meaning of the whole sentence? As we will see, the content of an embedded sentence is affected by and contributes in several different

---

[*] This work benefited from the comments of the audience at the COST 2102 meeting in Vietri sul Mare. We are also grateful to John Tammena for correction our English. Finally, we would like to acknowledge financial support from the following sources: Project CHLaSC in the NEST initiative of the European Union's Commission for Research and the Emmy-Noether research group 'Interpretation of Quantifiers' funded by the German research foundation DFG.

[1] Sentence embedding is generally thought to be a linguistic universal (Cristofaro, 2003 and others). Everett, 2005 claims that Pirahã lacks embedded sentences altogether, but our evidence at this point does not support this conclusion (Sauerland *et al.*, in preparation).

A. Esposito et al. (Eds.): Multimodal Signals, LNAI 5398, pp. 197–207, 2009.

ways to the interpretation of the entire sentence. We propose one way to classify embedded content – namely, a classification based on the context shift behaviour of the embedded content. This classification can be applied not only to linguistic content, but also to non-linguistic content. We show, however, that non-linguistic content is distinguished from linguistic content by shiftability: While many types of linguistic content can shift when embedded, a shift of non-linguistic material is always impossible.

Context dependence underlies our classification of embedded content by context shift. There are many ways in which the content of an utterance may depend on the context in which it is made (Kaplan, 1978; Zimmermann, 1991). A prototypical context-dependent expression is the first person pronoun *I*, which always refers to the person who utters the expression. Hence the content of a sentence like (1) varies with the identity of the speaker.

(1)   I was born in Italy

Context-dependence is not restricted to pronouns, but is a pervasive phenomenon in natural language and *contextualist* philosophy even espouses the view that context-*in*dependent sentences don't exist (e.g. DeRose, 1999). For example, if we replace the pronoun in (1) with a proper name, as in (2), do we eliminate thereby the context-dependence of the sentence? Not quite, since there is still a temporal component in it that tells us that the described event is located in the past of the context of utterance.

(2)   Umberto Eco was born in Italy

Context-dependent expressions are usually interpreted with respect to the speaker's perspective (or the utterance context). For example, in (3-a), *here* refers to the location of the speaker, *tasty* means tasty to the speaker and *soooo* indicates a high degree from the speaker's perspective. However, there are linguistic devices that introduce additional perspectives, one prominent example being clausal complement taking predicates. If we embed (3-a) under a propositional attitude verb like *think*, as in (3-b), two different perspectives are available in the embedded clause: the perspective of the speaker (the utterance context) and the perspective of Jane (Jane's beliefs).

(3)   a.   The food here is soooo <yawn> tasty
       b.   Jane thinks that the food here is soooo <yawn> tasty

It turns out that not all context-dependent expressions behave alike in embedded clauses. For example, in (3-b), the temporal adverbial *here* still refers to the location of the speaker, not Jane's location, whereas *tasty* is now interpreted with respect to Jane (it's her taste, not the speaker's, that matters).

In the following we want to examine more closely, what kind of expressions tend to shift or tend not to shift under what circumstances. Section 2 sketches the linguistic and philosophical background of the discussion and introduces some basic terminological conventions. In Section 3 we examine the behavior of various types of context-dependent expressions in embedded contexts and identify some important patterns of variation.

2 Context Dependence and Shifting

It is an essential feature of human language (called 'displacement' by Hockett, 1960) that we are able to talk about things beyond the immediate here and now.

(4)   a.   It is raining [here] [now]
      b.   It is raining [in Naples] [now]   place shift
      c.   It was raining [here] [six weeks ago]   time shift
      d.   It was raining [in Naples] [six weeks ago]
      e.   It could be raining [here] [now]   world shift

In (4-a) the context of evaluation is simply the context of utterance: An utterance of (4-a) is true if and only if it is raining at the time and place of that utterance. However, the contexts of utterance and evaluation need not coincide. The examples in (4-b)–(4-e) contain expressions that effectively change the context of evaluation: in (4-b) spatially, in (4-c) temporally, in (4-d) both spatially and temporally, and in (4-e) modally.

We have implicitly distinguished between a context of utterance and a context of evaluation. The assumption that natural language expressions are doubly context dependent goes back to Kaplan, 1978. The standard picture is as follows: The context of utterance determines the content of the utterance and cannot be changed (*shifted*) by linguistic means, whereas the context of evaluation determines the truth of an utterance and can be changed by linguistic means like adverbials or tense and aspect marking (as in (4-b)–(4-e)). In the following, we will call an expression *shifted* if it is not interpreted relative to the utterance context but relative to some other context.

One way to motivate the distinction between the two kinds of contexts is to look at expressions that are semantically similar, but differ in being evaluated with respect to different contexts. For example, the first person pronoun *I* is evaluated with respect to the context of utterance and cannot be shifted by temporal adverbials like *twenty minutes ago*. By contrast, the definite description *the speaker* is evaluated with respect to the context of evaluation and hence is affected by temporal adverbials. That's why (5-a) is perfectly informative (saying that the person who is speaking now is not identical to the person who was speaking twenty minutes ago), whereas (5-b) and (5-c) seem contradictory when understood literally.

(5)   a.   Twenty minutes ago, I was not the speaker
      b.   Twenty minutes ago, the speaker was not the speaker
      c.   Twenty minutes ago, I was not me

In the past decade, the assumption that the utterance context cannot be shifted has been questioned on empirical grounds. It has been noted that in some languages, first person pronouns can be shifted, i.e. refer not to the speaker but to the matrix subject of the embedding clause, as illustrated in the Amharic example in (6) from Schlenker, 2003.

(6)   ǰon ǰəgna nəññ   yɨl-all
       John hero be.PF-1SO 3s.say-AUX3M
       'John says that I'm a hero.' / 'John says that he's a hero.'

We have already observed that something similar is going on in examples like (3-b) with other kinds of expressions. In the next section we will look at examples of this type more systematically.

3 Typology of Context Shift

There are various factors that affect shifting in some way, among them the type of embedding (e.g. direct vs. indirect speech), the type of embedding predicate (e.g. 'say' vs. 'believe'), the type of embedded element (e.g. pronoun vs. definites) and the interaction with other elements in the same clause (e.g. it has been suggested that there is a preference for elements in the same clause to "shift together", cf. Anand and Nevins, 2004).

We concentrate on two factors, the type of embedding and the type of embedded element. The main types of embedding in English are illustrated in (7). Direct Discourse (DD, quotation) is a faithful reproduction of some utterance or thought, as in (7-a). Standard Indirect Discourse (SID) is a description of the content of some utterance or thought, as in (7-b). Finally, Free Indirect Discourse (FID) is a special narrative style to convey what a character says or thinks, as in (7-c), where the parenthetical *John thought* is optional.

(7)   a.   John said "I will go to Boston soon."
       b.   John said that he would go to Boston soon.
       c.   He would go to Boston soon [John thought]

The second factor is the type of embedded element. We will cover descriptions (e.g. *the man with the hat*), directional expressions (e.g. *across the street* or *come* vs. *go*), personal pronouns (e.g. *I, you*), evidentials, epistemic modals, (e.g. *must, might*), taste predicates (e.g. *is tasty, is beautiful*), expressives (e.g. *the damn dog, that jerk*), honorifics and politeness strategies (e.g. German *Du* vs. *Sie*) and qualities of voice (e.g. angry, excited, sad, tired).

Concentrating on Standard Indirect Discourse (SID), we will argue for the following four-way classification of shift of semantic content:

(8)   *always shifted*:   main predicate, epistemic modals, taste predicates
       inter-language variation: pronouns, evidentials
       intra-language variation: descriptions, directionals
       never shifted: expressives, politeness

3.1 Group 1: Always Shifted

This group includes the main predicate of a sentence when there is no adverbial quantifier taking scope over the predicate (Percus, 2000). Percus describes this as obligatory binding of the highest open world variable in a sentence by the world-variable binder of the embedded clause.

Epistemic modals express the necessity or possibility of the embedded proposition in view of what is known (typically by the speaker). Embedded epistemic modals always receive a shifted interpretation (cf. Stephenson, 2008, Hacquard, 2006), i.e. they behave just like main verbs.

(9)   a.   It must be raining
    b.   John thinks it must be raining
    c.   Mary thinks that John thinks it must be raining
    d.   [Every boy]$_i$ thinks he$_i$ must be stupid

Predicates of personal taste are interpreted relative to a judge, in root contexts typically the speaker (autocentric perspective). Embedded taste predicates typically receive a shifted interpretation.

(10)   a.   The chili is tasty
     b.   John says/thinks that the chili is tasty
     c.   Mary says that John thinks that the chili is tasty
     d.   Every boy thinks that the chili is tasty

In addition, the highest sentence adverbial belongs to this category, as Percus, 2000 shows. See also Keshet, 2008 for recent extensions and modifications of Percus's analysis.

3.2   Group 2: Inter-language Variation

The items in this group are fixed in their shiftability in some languages, but possibly not in others or they are fixed too, but in the opposite direction.

Pronouns. First and second person pronouns in English are never shifted in standard indirect discourse. For example, the embedded occurence of *I* in (11-a) cannot refer to the matrix subject, but only to the author of the whole sentence. By contrast, in languages like Amharic, both an English-type (unshifted) and a shifted interpretation of the first person pronoun is possible, as in (11-b) from Schlenker, 2003.

(11)   a.   John says that I'm a hero
     b.   ǰon   ǰəgna nəññ   yɨl-all
        John hero   be.PF-1sO 3s.say-AUX3M

        'John says that I'm a hero.' / 'John says that he's a hero.'

Similarly, in so-called Role Shift (RS) constructions in Sign Languages (cf. Lillo-Martin, 1995) personal pronouns are often shifted. An example from Catalan Sign Language (LSC) is given in (12) (from Quer, 2005). The first person pronoun 'IX-1' does not refer to the person who utters the sentence, but to Joan, whose belief is reported in the embedded clause.

(12)   ───────────────────TOPIC   ──────────────────── RS-i
     IXa MADRID_m MOMENT JOAN_i THINK IX-1_i STUDY FINISH
     HERE_b

     'When he was in Madrid, Joan thought he would finish his study here'

Note that RS in LSC differs from direct discourse in English in that not all context-dependent expressions are obligatorily shifted. Although the spatial adverbial 'HERE' in (12) can receive a shifted interpretation, it is by default interpreted with respect to the utterance context. The fact that 'IX-1' and 'HERE' in (12) can be interpreted with respect to different contexts is evidence against strong versions of the *Shift Together Constraint* of Anand and Nevins, 2004.

As far as we know there are no languages where embedded indexicals must be shifted; either they cannot be shifted or they can be shifted but remain ambiguous. Logophoric pronouns are analyzed by Schlenker, 2008 as obligatorily shifted indexicals, but they cannot usually occur out of embedded clauses.

Evidentials are linguistic markers that indicate the speaker's type of source of information, e.g. whether she witnessed the reported state of affairs herself (direct evidentials), only heard about it (reportative evidentials) or inferred it from other information (inferential evidentials). Evidentials are typically hard to embed, especially in in complement clauses, but there are languages that do allow evidentials in embedded positions.

For example, in Tibetan evidentials can be embedded under verbs of speaking and thinking and always receive shifted interpretations, just like epistemic modals in English (cf. Garrett, 2001). Example (13-a) illustrates an unembedded use of the indirect evidential *red*, where it receives a speaker-oriented interpretation. If this evidential marker occurs in complement clauses of *bsam* 'think', as in (13-b), only a shifted interpretation is available, according to which the person in possession of the indirect evidence is the matrix subject, not the speaker.

(13)   a.   yang.chen dge.rgan red
           Yangchen teacher   [ind cop]
           'Yangchen is a teacher.'
           (Speaker's source: hearsay/inference)

       b.   bkra.shis kho dge.rgan red   bsam-gi-'dug
           Tashi   he teacher [ind cop] think-[dir imp]
           'Tashi$_i$ thinks he$_j$ is a teacher.'
           (Tashi's source: hearsay/inference)

However, evidentials do not behave alike in all languages. Whereas embedded evidentials in Tibetan require a shifted interpretation, evidentials in Bulgarian are typically not shifted (cf. Sauerland and Schenner, 2007).

(14)   a.   Maria kaza če Todor ima červena kosa.
           Maria said that Todor has-DIR red hair

       b.   Maria kaza če Todor ima-l červena kosa.
           Maria said that Todor has-REP red hair

In sum, both personal pronouns and evidentials show inter-language variation: In some languages they may or even must be shifted, in other languages they cannot be shifted at all.

3.3   Group 3: Free Intra-language Variation

Some items are generally ambigous and are ambiguous in the same way across languages. Namely, definite descriptions and directional adverbials belong to this category.

Definite descriptions in embedded contexts can systematically receive both an embedded (*de dicto*) and an unembedded (*de re*) reading. This observation goes back to Quine, 1956. For example consider (15) in a scenario where John thinks I met person 1 yesterday, but I actually met person 2. (15) has an interpretation that requires person 1 to be a spy, but also one that requires that person 2 be a spy.

(15)   John thinks that the man I met yesterday is a spy

Directional adverbials behave similarly. Consider *across the street*. In (16), John could think that the president could live across the street from me or from John.

(16)   John thinks that the president lives across the street

As far as we know there are no known cases of expressions that show free intra-language variation in one language, but not in another. Indexical pronouns come close, but as far as we know their shiftability is always constrained in some way or other as Anand, 2006 and Malamoud, 2006 show.

3.4   Group 4: Never Shifted

Finally, there are aspects of content that can never be shifted. In this category, we find politeness marking on pronouns, expressives, non-voluntary aspects of speech such as accent, and gestural content.

A clear case that is never shifted are formal pronouns of address in German (and presumably in other languages that have similar pronouns too). In German, the second person singular can only be used to address people someone is friends with, otherwise the third person plural pronoun *Sie* is used.[2]

This component of the meaning of the pronoun never shifts in German: use of a polite pronoun in indirect discourse could always indicate the speaker's attitude towards the addressee and never that of the subject of the embedding clause. For example, (17-a) and (17-b) both allow only a speaker oriented interpretation of *Du* and *Sie*.

(17)   a.   John sagte, dass Sie   nach Italien fahren
            John said   that you.formal to   Italy   travel
            'John said that you are going to Italy.'
       b.   John sagte, dass du   nach Italien fährst
            John said   that you.informal to   Italy   travel

---

[2] Sauerland, 2003 shows that it is not necessary to analyze this form as a separate politeness form homophonous with the third person singular, but as a real occurrence of the third person plural form.

Expressives (Cursing) behave similar. Embedded expressives cannot be shifted as illustrated by (18), though there may be a few exceptions discussed by Potts, 2007 and Schlenker, 2007.

(18)   Sue believes that that bastard Kresge should be fired.
         # I think he's a good guy.   Potts, 2007

Non-voluntary aspects of speech like the speaker's accent are not usually considered part of meaning following Grice, 1957. While we do not disagree with this concept of meaning, it is nevertheless instructive to note that non-voluntary aspects are never shifted. Only if they are willfully imitated can they be shifted – for example, the partial quotation 'beea' in (19) can be an indication of John's accent.

(19)   John said he would like a 'beea', meaning a 'beer'.

Gestural elements combined with speech also seem to belong to the category of non-shiftable items even though they are voluntary. Consider the example in (20), where we imagine two gestures indicating the height of a person. For example, the speaker may hold his hand out flat in the air at the height stated with the fingers straightened as if measuring a person's height. (20) can be used even if John does not know Mary's height or believes her to be of a height other than 150cm. But, if I, the speaker, know that Mary is 200cm while John believes that she is only 150cm, it would be odd to use the height-indicating gesture.[3]

(20)   John hopes that he [gesture indicating height = 200cm] is going to dance with Mary [gesture indicating height = 150cm].

Furthermore, gesture can be used in embedded sentences seemingly inconsistent with the verbal content as in (21). The only reading of (21) is that John's internet girlfriend is actually 150cm tall, but John has been led to believe that she is 200cm tall.

(21)   John hopes that he is going to dance with the 200cm tall woman [gesture indicating height = 150cm] he met on the internet.

4   Towards an Analysis

Existing analyses to the shiftability of semantic content under embedding have, for the most part, not considered the full array of data that we have laid out above. The data are summarized in the following table:

(22)   *always shifted*:   main predicates, epistemic modals, taste predicates
         inter-language variation: pronouns, evidentials
         intra-language variation: descriptions, directionals
         never shifted: expressives, politeness, involuntary content, gesture

It will be useful to investigate to what extent this table has cross-linguistic validity. Our investigation to this point has been merely cursory.

---

[3] There is a use of the gesture embedded under a verb of speech which does shift. But this case is parallel to the partial quotation in (19).

Nevertheless we attempt to provide some explanations for the date in the above table. It seems clear that some explanation must be found, since otherwise we would expect more variation. A clear case that can be explained is that of involuntary content. Since involuntary content is produced by the speaker of an utterance without his control, it is necessary that any information the involuntary content carries must be attributed to the speaker. Now first consider the other unshiftable cases.

For the case of expressives, two possible lines of explanation come to mind: on the one hand, their behavior may be related to the fact that expressives also seem to have involuntary uses. For example, I may say 'Shit!' without conscious intent as some unfortunate event happens. If used in this way, 'Shit!' may not be shifted for the same reason that other involuntary content cannot be shifted. However, why this would carry over to voluntary uses of expressives remains unclear – possibly the involuntary uses affect the shiftability of the voluntary. A second explanation has been suggested in Sauerland, 2007: Expressives usually express extreme degrees of some emotion. If expressives were to shift, the resultant meaning would be one where the extreme degree of some emotion is attributed to third persons. This could be perceived as so unlikely or unpolite that hearers usually – perhaps via a kind of habit – do not consider that option.

For politeness the explanation might be different: Polite expression is often related to register choice. If we assume that register choice is similar to the choice of a grammar, it seems reasonable to assume that the register is chosen once per utterance. Christian Huber (p.c.) pointed out to one of us that in the Upper Kinnaur area in India different languages are used depending on the social relationship between the speakers – high caste speakers use one language, low caste speakers a different language, and in inter-caste interaction only one language is used even if both speakers are proficient in the other language as well. In the Kinnaur culture, register choice involves code-switching between two grammars. If we are right, all register amounts to a kind of code-switching though the grammars involved are usually much more similar than in Kinnaur.[4] We speculate based on our personal experience that code-switching is most natural at sentence boundaries, though intra-sentential code-switching does of course exist (cf. Belazi et al., 1994). Politeness understood as register/language choice should then similarly only occur at sentence boundaries.

That leaves only the case of gesture unaccounted for. Though further investigation is necessary, we think it might be amenable to an analysis similar to one of those we gave for expressives above given that gesture occurs involuntarily, and perhaps is involuntary more frequently than voluntary.

The difference between content with complete freedom (descriptions and directions) on the one hand and items that must be shifted (main predicate, epistemic modals, taste predicates) has been successfully analyzed already in recent work by Percus, 2000 and Keshet, 2008. The idea of this work is that independent constraints on world variable indexation predict the differences. That leaves an

---

[4] Yang, 2002 emphasizes the view of several grammars being active in parallel even in monolinguals. This is clearly compatible with our proposal here.

account of the two cases of interlanguage variation (pronouns and evidentials) left to be given. As we mentioned, both cases are subject to some constraint and are completely free in no language that we know of. A detailed study of the general constraints on the shiftability of pronouns and evidentials is beyond the scope of this paper. See though Anand, 2006 for a recent attempt.

5   Conclusion

In this paper, we provided an overview of content in embedded clauses. We restricted our overview to cases of complement clauses embedded under attitude and speech verbs, like (22). In these cases, we looked at what perspective is taken for the interpretation of semantic content that occurs in an embedded clause: that of the speaker or that of the subject of the embedding verb. Both readings are usually imaginable, and they are clearly distinct: We can give paraphrases for any contentful material where it is interpreted relative to the speaker and also where it is interpreted relative to the subject of the embedding verb.

(23)   Jane thinks that the food here is soooo <yawn> tasty (repeated from (3-b))

As we observed, though, many imaginable interpretations are not actually available – natural language is restricted as far as the potential ambiguity of embedded material is concerned. We have seen that there are four categories of content under embedding as classified by their shiftability, and we have suggested an explanation of the shiftability of some of the classes in the last section.

Bibliography

Anand, P.: De de se. PhD thesis, Massachusetts Institute of Technology, Cambridge, Mass (2006)

Anand, P.: Re-expressing judgment. Theoretical Linguistics 33(2) (2007)

Anand, P., Nevins, A.: Shifty operators in changing contexts. Unpublished Ms., MIT (2004)

Belazi, H.M., Rubin, E.J., Toribio, A.J.: Code switching and X-bar theory: the functional head constraint. Linguistic Inquiry 25, 221–237 (1994)

Cristofaro, S.: Subordination (2003)

DeRose, K.: Contextualism: An explanation and defense. In: The Blackwell Guide to Epistemology, pp. 187–205. Blackwell Publisher, Oxford (1999)

Everett, D.: Cultural constraints on grammar and cognition in Piraha: Another look at the Design Features of human language. Current Anthropology 46, 621–646 (2005)

Garrett, E.J.: Evidentiality and Assertion in Tibetan. PhD thesis, UCLA, Los Angeles (2001)

Grice, H.P.: Meaning. Philosophical Review 66, 377–388 (1957); reprinted in Grice, 213–223 (1989)

Grice, P.: Studies in the Way of Words. Harvard University Press, Cambridge (1989)

Hacquard, V.: Aspects of Modality. PhD thesis, Massachusetts Institute of Technology, Cambridge, Mass (2006)

Heim, I., Kratzer, A.: Semantics in Generative Grammar. Blackwell, Oxford (1998)

Hockett, C.F.: The origin of speech. Scientific American 203, 88–96 (1960)

Kaplan, D.: On the logic of demonstratives. Journal of Philosophical Logic 8, 81–98 (1978)

Keshet, E.: Good Intensions: Paving Two Roads to a Theory of the De re /De dicto Distinction. PhD thesis, Massachusetts Institute of Technology, Cambridge, Mass (2008)

Lillo-Martin, D.: The point of view predicate in American Sign Language. In: Emmorey, K., Reilly, J.S. (eds.) Language, Gesture and Space, pp. 155–170. Lawrence Erlbaum Associates, Hillsdale (1995)

Malamoud, S.: Semantics and Pragmatics of Arbitrariness. PhD thesis, University of Pennsylvania, Philadelphia (2006)

Percus, O.: Constraints on some other variables in syntax. Natural Language Semantics 8, 173–229 (2000)

Potts, C.: The expressive dimension. Theoretical Linguistics 33(2) (2007)

Quer, J.: Context shift and indexical variables in sign languages. In: Georgala, E., Howell, J. (eds.) Proceedings from SALT 15, pp. 152–168. CLC Publications, Ithaca, NY (2005)

Quine, W.: v. O. Quantifiers and propositional attitudes. Journal of Philosophy 53, 177–187 (1956)

Sauerland, U.: A new semantics for number. In: The Proceedings of SALT 13, Ithaca, N.Y, pp. 258–275. Cornell University, CLC-Publications (2003)

Sauerland, U.: Beyond unpluggability. Theoretical Linguistics 33(2), 231–236 (2007)

Sauerland, U., Sakel, J., Stapert, E.: Syntactic vs. semantic embedding (in preparation)

Sauerland, U., Schenner, M.: Embedded evidentials in Bulgarian. In: Puig-Waldmüller, E. (ed.) Proceedings of SuB 11, pp. 495–509. Universitat Pompeu Fabra, Barcelona (2007)

Schlenker, P.: A plea for monsters. Linguistics and Philosophy 26, 29–120 (2003)

Schlenker, P.: Expressive presuppositions. Theoretical Linguistics 33(2) (2007)

Schlenker, P.: Indexicality and de se reports (2008)

Spelke, E.: What makes us smart? Core knowledge and natural language. In: Gentner, D., Goldin-Meadow, S. (eds.) Language in Mind, pp. 279–311. MIT-Press, Cambridge (2003)

Stephenson, T.C.: Judge dependence, epistemic modals, and predicates of personal taste. Linguistics and Philosophy (to appear) (2008)

Yang, C.D.: Knowledge and Learning in Natural Language. Oxford University Press, Oxford (2002)

Zimmermann, T.E.: Kontexttheorie (Context Theory). In: Von Stechow, A., Wunderlich, D. (eds.) Semantik: Ein internationales Handbuch der zeitgenössischen Forschung (Semantics: An International Handbook of Contemporary Research), ch. 9, pp. 156–229. De Gruyter, Berlin (1991)

A Distributional Concept for Modeling Dialectal Variation in TTS

Friedrich Neubarth[1] and Christian Kranzler[2,3]

[1] OFAI, Austrian Research Institute for Artificial Intelligence, Vienna, Austria
friedrich.neubarth@ofai.at
[2] ftw., Telecommunications Research Center, Vienna, Austria
[3] SPSC, Signal Processing and Speech Communication Lab, TU Graz, Graz, Austria
kranzler@ftw.at

Abstract. Current TTS systems usually represent a certain standard of a given language, regional or social variation is barely reflected. In this paper, we describe certain strategies for modeling language varieties on the basis of a common language resource, in particular Austrian varieties from German sources. The goal is to find optimal procedures in order to represent these differences with minimal efforts in annotation and processing. We delimit the discussion to the lower levels of the transformation of linguistic information – phonetic encoding. One question is if it is necessary or desirable to aim at maximal accurateness of the phonetic transcriptions. We will show that while certain differences could in principle be captured by the context within the speech data, other differences definitely have to be re-modelled, since they either involve ambiguous correspondences, or the string of phones is different in such a way that automatic procedures such as alignment or unit selection would be negatively affected, hence degrade the overall quality of the synthesized speech.

Keywords: TTS, language varieties, dialects, Austrian German, regionalization.

1 Introduction

With human-computer interfaces regionalization and user adaptation gain increasingly more importance. For TTS systems, this means we have to deal with new challenges since language processing as well as speech synthesis components are available and confined to certain standard varieties of many languages in the world, but regional or socially determined varieties often deviate from these standard varieties to an extent that would suggest treating them as entirely new languages. This would be an uninteresting solution, and it would be (and at present actually is) unattractive to implement these varieties from an economic perspective.

In this paper, we will describe certain strategies one may adopt in order to deal with the problem of modeling different varieties of a given language within a TTS system. We will explicate these strategies based on work done in a project which aims at developing sources and speech-synthesis voices for several Austrian German varieties. The key problem is the trade-off between re-using existing language resources and adaptation of these sources for better accurateness. We will show that while

A. Esposito et al. (Eds.): Multimodal Signals, LNAI 5398, pp. 208–215, 2009.
© Springer-Verlag Berlin Heidelberg 2009

certain differences between varieties and the given standard could be neglected in principle, because these differences are covered systematically by the speech data, other differences do not display unambiguous correlations, which makes a thorough re-modeling indispensable. However, exploiting linguistic knowledge about the source language and its varieties makes this process feasible in terms of automatic and semi-automatic adaptation.

In the mentioned project, we develop four synthetic voices within the Festival platform [1], one representing Austrian German, and three representing different Viennese varieties, which have to be regarded rather as sociolects than as dialects. Only a few adaptations have to be made from the German standard to Austrian German, and most of them can be done automatically. On the other hand, dialects and sociolects pose more severe problems, and it turns out that adaptations have to be implemented on all levels of linguistic representation, from syntactic processes over lexical specifics to the encoding of the sound inventory.

The German standard is generally defined as the (normative) standard for the language varieties in Germany, Austria and Switzerland. Publicly available resources usually refer to such a standard – for example CELEX for phonetic transcriptions of German words. In reality, German, as many other languages, has to be regarded a pluricentric language, with an Austrian and Swiss variety, as well as a large set of locally (and/or socially) determined varieties [2]. Furthermore, one has to take into account that the boundaries between more standard-like varieties such as Austrian German and more specific varieties are not always as clear-cut as one would wish. Neither is it straightforward to assign a speaker's idiom to a specific variety, nor do speakers restrict themselves to just one idiom, but very often, they display a more or less continuous shift between various levels [3]. Therefore, it is important to exact a strict control over these variables, since the material to be recorded as speech data must be both consistent and characteristic for the language variety to be represented.

2 Levels of Representation

In order to deal with potential shifts between standard and dialectal varieties, but also to be able to represent different dialectal varieties exhaustively it is indispensable to establish methods for the transfer of linguistic information. The two constraints guiding such methods are minimization of efforts and full coverage of ambiguities. So, for example, if one variant differs from the other systematically only in vowel qualities, nothing has to be done beyond recording.

However, this is rarely the case. Rather, we expect differences on all levels of representation. In the example at hand, the set of phones[1] cannot be transformed in a one-to-one fashion. Certain phonologically active processes like l-vocalization, while being quite regular, affect neighboring segments and also involve deletion. Certain morphemes are different between standard and varieties, but not always in a systematic

---

[1] We rather use the term 'phone' here, not only because it is not theoretically biased, but also because it is far more precise. The term 'phoneme' has its origin in structuralist phonology and does not refer to sounds of speech. Moreover, one should ask, whether its alleged status as a cognitive unit is not entirely mistaken.

Table 1. Levels of representation encoding differences between Austrian German and Viennese

Linguistic level	Austrian German	Viennese	Coding level
sound	[ə]	[ɛ]	sound
symbol set – phones	[æ̃] [a]	[aː] / [æː] / [œː] [a] / [ɔ/ü]	lexicon setup
phonology	[fiːl] *viel* 'much' [væ̃l] *weil* 'because'	[fyː] *füü* [vœː] *wäu*	rules
morphological	*pass-te* 'would fit' *Gläs-chen* 'glass'diminutive	*pass-ert* *Glas-erl*	lexicon transfer
morpho-syntactic	*lesen können* 'can read' *ertrinken* 'drown'	*derlesen* *dersaufen*	

lexicon
– open class
– functional:
  – articles
  – pronouns
	fett, dick 'fat'
	Kopf 'head'
	der 'the'
	hinaus 'to-out'
	heraus 'from-out'
		blad
		bluzer
		d' / da / der
		ausse
		aussa
			lexicon specific

phrasal	*weil du weggehen sollst!* 'because you should leave' *er ging* 'he went'	*wäusd di iba d'* *heisa haun soisd!* *ea is gangen.*	post-lexical transformation

way. Regarding lexical specificities it is evident that one needs a cascaded structure of lists of lexicon entries for items that occur only in a certain dialectal variety (or a set of related varieties). Since it has to be assumed that these lists are rarely complete certain decisions regarding pronunciation have to be made on the basis of an estimation taking into account also a morphological analysis and the orthography used in the input. And finally, in Austrian dialects certain processes are active at the phrasal level which also affect the pronunciation of neighboring words: unstressed personal pronouns behave phonologically as clitica, complementizers show up with (cliticized) inflected forms etc. This means that post-lexical rules have to be taken into account as well. In addition, the morphological paradigms lack certain forms systematically: there is no genitive, and there is no indicative preterit (except for auxiliary *sein* 'to be'). With idiomatic differences on the phrasal level, there is almost no chance to provide automatic procedures, at best we can list and use them in semi-automatic translations between standard texts and their counterparts in one of the varieties. A summary of all these differences distributed over various levels of linguistic encoding is given in Table 1,

In the following, we will concentrate on those levels, which have the greatest potential for automatization: the set of symbols representing speech sounds and their correspondences between specific varieties and phonological processes that can be formalized in a rule based way.

3 Phone Substitution

The set of speech sounds of a given variety naturally will show differences to other varieties. If only some phones are produced differently, shifted in place of articulation for example, no efforts would have to be spent to adapt the respective transcriptions, even if some of the used symbols would not depict the correct phonetic items. The retrieval of the correct units would be granted anyway. However, this is not the situation we find. There are n-to-n matchings between the sets, deletions and sometimes insertions as well. So-called neutralizations are a very good candidate for the automatic transfer of lexical information, because they can be formalized as n-to-1 transformations. (In many cases, the situation is not as trivial, since neutralizations are often conditioned by the phonological context.)

To give a few examples, Austrian dialectal varieties and most varieties of the Austrian standard lack voiced sibilants (*singen* /zI.N@n/ → /sI.N@n/ '*sing*')[2]. This is a case of total neutralization. Plosive consonants in onset position are neutralized toward a (voiceless) lenis variant (*Tante* /tan.t@/ → /dan.t@/ '*aunt*'), except for the velar /k/ (*Karten* /ka:.t@n/ → /kA6.tn=/ '*cards*'). As can be seen in the first example, post-nasal (and post-/r/, realized as /6/) contexts also block neutralization. This is a case where both, phonological structure and local information about neighboring segments have to be taken into account in order to formalize the context adequately.

To extend this example, between vowels (but also before syllabic nasals and /l/) the lenis stops tend to spirantize (*Leber* /le:.b6/ → /le:.B6/ '*liver*'), whereas geminated or fortis stops are not affected by this kind of lenition (*schnuppern* /SnU.p6n / → /Snu.p6n/ '*snuffle*'). Interesting is the context at the end of the syllable, normally targeted by final devoicing. If for example a clitic pronoun starting with a vowel follows within the same prosodic phrase, this position turns into an intervocalic context, which blocks final devoicing and enhances lenition. So for example the PRES.3P.SG ending /t/ turns out as a /d/ (or /D/) – (*kommt+er* /kOmt ?E6/ → /kUm.d6/ '*comes_he*'). Therefore, we have to assume that in Austrian varieties of German the morpheme representing the inflectional ending is underlyingly a /d/. However, there are certain endings that are /t/, and those are stable. We find them in the (preterit/subjunctive) forms of modals: (*könnte+er* /k9nt@ ?E6/ → /kEn.t6/ '*could he*'). The lesson we should learn from these data is that it is more than just useful to encode also certain aspects of morphological structure [4].

A case where Austrian German differs from the German standard is the palatal velar fricative /C/: orthographically "*ch*", in onset position, and as part of the derivative ending '*–ig*' it is pronounced /C/ in the German standard, but as /k/ in Austrian German. (The ending '*–ig*' is /IC/ again in dialectal varieties.) Here, we have to resort to orthographic information, since other contexts where the string /IC/ occurs (but written as '*–ich*') do not take part in that shift.

Much more problematic are cases where phones are not neutralized, but split up into two (or more) different correspondents. The vowel /a/ from the standard language is realized by default as rounded ([ɔ/ü]) in dialectal varieties. However, most (but not all) foreign and loan words, and some indigenous ones retain the /a/. The diphthong /aI/ shows up as a monophthong in the Viennese variety (3 : [æ:]), but

---

[2] Phonetic transcriptions are given in German-SAMPA notation, slightly adapted for the Austrian varieties. Wherever it deviates from the standard, IPA symbols are given in square brackets.

Table 2. Phone correspondences for /a/ and /aI/

word	gloss	German standard		Viennese	
Pass	passport	a	/pas:/	A	/bAs:/
pass	fit-IMPERATIVE	a	/pas:/.	a	/bas:/
zwei	two	aI	/tsvaI/	a:	/tsva:/
drei	three	aI	/draI/	3:	/dr3:/
weil	because	aI	/vaIl/	&:	/v&:/

sometimes it is pronounced as an /a/, and in the context of l-vocalization the monophthong definitely is a different phone (&: [œ:]) which is not present in the German varieties. Examples are given below in the following table.

It is not possible to deal with such ambiguity in an automatic way, the only thing one can do is to find out which of them constitutes the more marked case (e.g., /aI/ → /a/), or whether there is a correlation between different strata of a language (foreign words). In the latter case an additional problem is whether these strata can be identified automatically, we suggest that in the case discussed it is possible only to a certain extent. At the present stage, we employ a semi-automatic procedure – automatic transformations with manual corrections.

4 Phone String Rules

There are certain rules that do not refer to correspondences between sets of phonesymbols, but reflect phonological processes that are sensitive to local context and/or syllable structure. They are normally easy to capture and we formalize them as regular expressions over strings of phones. There are two rules of that type that capture the differences between the German standard and Austrian German: r-vocalization and syllabic nasals (with assimilation of the nasal to the preceding onset consonant). In Table 3 there are some examples illustrating these rules.

Table 3. /r/-vocalization and syllabic nasals in Austrian German

word	gloss	German standard	Austrian German
Lehrer	teacher	le:.r@r	lE:6.r6
werben	solicit	vEr.b@n	vE6.bm=
mehrere	several	me:.r@.r@	mE:6.r6.r@
beruhigen	calm down	b@.ru:.I.g@n	b@.ru:.I.GN=
Barbar	Barbarian	bar.'ba:r	ba.'ba:

In principle, these differences are already captured by the speech data, and the local context should be precise enough to identify the correct units. However, these rules also involve deletion and insertion within the string of phones, so the results of automatic alignment significantly improve if those rules are reflected in the lexicon that applies to the speech data. Notice that the process of r-vocalization is not solely determined by the local context but also by morphological information that determines the phonological domain where this process may apply. In the case of *'beruhigen'* r-vocalization is blocked although the /r/ follows a vowel (schwa), because that vowel is part of a prefix, hence invisible for the process.

Table 4. /l/-vocalization in Viennese varieties

word	gloss	German standard	Viennese
Wald	forest	vald	vAId
Holz	wood	hOlts	hoIts
voller	full with	fO.1:6	fo.1:6
Walter	Walter	val.t6	val.t6
viel	much	fi:1	fy:
viele	many	fi:.1@	fy:.1@

In Viennese varieties and many other Austrian dialects, another process is at work that has similar effects in terms of structure modification: l-vocalization. If the preceding vowel is a front vowel, /l/ affects the quality of this vowel (+round) and deletes if it is not in an onset position of a syllable with a phonetically realized vowel (pace syllabic nasals). This is how the phones +round/+front (i.e., /y/ and /2,9/) emerge again in the phone inventory, since the corresponding phones of the standard varieties are unrounded in the dialectal varieties (e.g., *Füße* /fy:.s:@/ → /fI6s:/ 'feet', but *fühlt* /fy:1/ → /fy:/ 'feel'). After non-front vowels and in non-onset position /l/ reduces to a front glide, phonetically speaking it forms a diphthong (e.g., /oI/) with the preceding vowel. Just in the case of /a/ (which is the non-default correspondent to /a/ in the standard variety) it remains unaffected.

The implementation of this rule is rather straightforward, and, as indicated above, it improves the quality of automatic segmentation as well as the accuracy of unit selection.

It has been mentioned already that if certain processes also affect the phonological structure of lexical items (deletions and insertions) then a thorough remodeling of the whole phonetic lexicon is advisable, at least in order to guarantee the desired quality of automatic alignment of the speech database for speech synthesis. We have shown that many transformations can be formalized easily – provided the resources of the standard variety are rich enough in information (morphological information, word stress assignment etc.) a new version of the pronunciation dictionary can be generated automatically and only ambiguous cases have to be checked manually. One way to tackle the problem of ambiguous transformations would be to employ decision-making methods in the stage of automatic alignment. This, however, would only resolve items that are present in the recorded speech data.

What is striking is the amount of linguistic expert knowledge that is incorporated in the establishment of such a transformation component as opposed to machine learning techniques, such as existing letter-to-sound conversion methods. At present, it was easier to follow this path, but we suspect that in the future it will be possible to establish methods that incorporate both, some (much more abstract) linguistic knowledge about phonological systems and processes, and a statistically based component that automatically extracts the rule module. This would be a great achievement towards the applicability of such methods·independently of specific languages or varieties.

We have deliberately shied away from commenting on a severe problem that immediately arises if we proceed higher in the hierarchy of linguistic modules (morphology, lexicon, phrases): orthographic encoding of dialectal variants. The problem arises in the moment when words have to enter the lexicon that do not exist at all in the standard variety. Dialectal varieties in most cases have no conventionalized system of orthographic transcription, if there exist some, there exist many of them which oscillate between phonetic accuracy and similarity to the standard orthography, and in many cases, the available resources suffer from low consistency. In order to permit dialectal input for a TTS system, this problem has to be dealt with by some means or other. At present, we cannot report any results yet, but only give an outline of the strategy we want to adopt: Provided we know the processes at work that transform phonetic encodings of one language variant to the other – a either by linguistic analysis or by application of machine learning techniques – we can generate a list of potential candidates both in the standard lexicon and the dialect lexicon by applying the rule module in both directions, which potentially has multiple outputs. The selection of the hopefully right candidate must be triggered by factors such as which rules have applied in which order, word frequency, but perhaps also statistic language modeling can help to improve this task.

5   Conclusion

In this paper, we have described certain strategies one may adopt in order to establish linguistic resources for (dialectal/sociolectal) language varieties from available sources representing a given standard, in our case Austrian varieties from common resources for the German language. We concentrated on the adaptation and (re-) modeling on the level of phone strings, leading to the question how accurate the phonetic encoding of a given variety must be. Certain differences between the standard language and its varieties either involve ambiguous or non-predictable variants or, if they are regular, they alter the phone string in a way that would negatively affect the quality of automatic procedures such as segmentation or unit selection. The conclusion was to re-model the variety as a whole, exploiting the regularities as much as possible. Future research will have to focus on the question, whether non-regular or ambiguous derivations can also be resolved by statistically based methods, such as decision making during alignment, or with the help of machine-learning techniques.

Acknowledgements

This paper reflects work done within the project "Vienna Sociolect and Dialect Synthesis" (VSDS), supported by the Vienna Science and Technology Fund (WWTF). The Telecommunications Research Center Vienna (ftw.) is supported by the Austrian Government and by the City of Vienna within the competence center program COMET. OFAI is supported by the Austrian Federal Ministry for Transport, Innovation and Technology and by the Austrian Federal Ministry for Science and Research.

References

1. Black, A.W., Lenzo, K.A.: Building synthetic voices,
   `http://festvox.org/festvox/festvox_toc.html`
2. Muhr, R., Schrott, R.: Österreichisches Deutsch und andere nationale Varietäten plurizentrischer Sprachen in Europa. öbv&hpt, Wien (1997)
3. Moosmüller, S.: Die österreichische Variante der Standardaussprache. In: Morgan, E.M., Püschel, U. (eds.) Beiträge zur deutschen Standardaussprache, Werner Dausien, Hanau, Halle, pp. 204–214 (1996)
4. Fitt, S., Richmond, K.: Redundancy and productivity in the speech technology lexicon – can we do better? In: Proceedings of Interspeech (2006)

Regionalized Text-to-Speech Systems: Persona Design and Application Scenarios

Michael Pucher, Gudrun Schuchmann, and Peter Fröhlich

ftw., Telecommunications Research Center, Donau-City-Strasse 1,
1220 Vienna, Austria
pucher@ftw.at, schuchmann@ftw.at, froehlich@ftw.at

Abstract. This paper presents results on the selection of application scenarios and persona design for sociolect and dialect speech synthesis. These results are derived from a listening experiment and a user study. Most speech synthesis applications focus on major languages that are spoken by many people. We think that the localization of speech synthesis applications by using sociolects and dialects can be beneficial for the user since these language variants entail specific personas and background knowledge.

Keywords: speech synthesis, dialect, sociolect, persona design.

1 Introduction

When we hear a speaker with a certain dialect we are familiar with we think that this speaker has a certain regional knowledge of the region that is associated with this dialect. This is demonstrated through the case of a taxi reservation system, which was launched in Austria. Users could order taxis for Vienna while the actual call center was located in the region of Salzburg. Since some of the call center agents spoke like people from Salzburg, users did not think that they were competent enough to know the streets of Vienna.

This example is another manifestation of the similarity attraction effect. [1] found the similarity attraction effect for language accents, where users preferred voices with a similar accent to their own. [1] could show that synthetic voices were more attractive, when they had the same gender and personality as the speaker. Previous studies did not entail dialects and sociolects [1]. Some work has been performed on cultural dimensions in user interface design were it is assumed that the language part of a user interface can be translated from one language to the other [2]. Such an assumption must necessarily neglect information that is encoded in a specific voice.

Spoken dialog systems that are using text-to-speech (TTS) technology are successfully deployed in a number of application domains like voice-web portals, online banking, and taxi service [3]. State-of-the-art data driven speech synthesis methods can achieve natural sounding speech output. The data-driven unit selection method can be used with small [5] and large speech corpora [5]. We think that these methods can be used to adapt speech synthesis to dialects and sociolects.

In our project on sociolect and dialect speech synthesis we aim at exploiting the effects of localization or regionalization [2] of voice user interfaces also for TTS

A. Esposito et al. (Eds.): Multimodal Signals, LNAI 5398, pp. 216–222, 2009.

systems. We are developing synthetic voices for different sociolects, first contextualizing it in the region of Vienna. This is the first attempt to develop multiple synthetic voices that represent the space of sociolects for a certain language. To achieve this goal we will develop 3 synthetic sociolect voices with speakers from Vienna. The adaptation methods and application scenarios that we develop are applicable to synthetic voices for dialects and sociolects of other languages.

The TTS paradigm of producing spoken output from written text is of course problematic for synthesizing dialects and sociolects. These language variants do not have a standardized written form, which means that it is not possible to apply standard TTS methods directly. In our work on building such voices we develop methods that allow us to use resources from standard German and apply those for Viennese variants. This is also a reason why the development of synthetic dialect voices has not been investigated intensively. Another reason is of course that some dialects are only spoken by relatively small groups of people. This is however not generally true if one thinks of Bengal or Arabic dialects. In speech recognition there has been work on the dialectal adaptation of speech recognizers [6].

Persona design is used to enhance the user experience of spoken dialog systems [8]. With this design method system prompts, dialogs, and system behavior can be designed in a way such that a consistent persona is perceived by the user. The choice of a synthetic voice constrains the type of persona that can be realized with this voice. The synthetic voices have a certain gender, age, dialect, sociolect, and voice characteristic. An application for electronic banking for example excludes voices with a certian age and sociolect. The persona underlying such an application has to be mature and earnest. For an entertainment application on the other hand these excluded voices may produce a more realistic persona. The question when to use and when not to use dialect and sociolect synthetic voices is addressed in this paper. Furthermore these voices allow for the extension of the standard user models, which represent the well-educated, adult, middle-aged, computer-literate, male user. A persona that is often implicit in synthetic voices of standard language.

We performed listening experiments to find salient features in voices of Viennese speakers that define the sociolect space for persona design. Furthermore a user study was conducted to find application scenarios appropriate for dialect/sociolect TTS.

2 What's in a Voice: Salient Voice Features for Persona Design

The method of unit selection speech synthesis uses a large corpus of recorded speech of a specific speaker. It achieves a high degree of naturalness, but it is difficult to change speaker and voice characteristics, such that the range of realizable personas is constrained. For this reason the selection of the right speaker is crucial. To represent the sociolect space for synthetic voices it is necessary to determine the dimensions of this space. [8] shows age and education as fundamental sociolect dimensions for Viennese German. [8] found acoustic correlates for these dimensions. We investigated the validity of these dimensions through a listening experiment.

In our listening experiments we evaluated what kind of information might be retrieved from user utterances of Viennese speakers. We carried out a perception test

Table 1. Accuracy of speaker/dimension association (in percent) and correlation between estimated and "real" values

Accuracy	Mean	Min	Max	Correlation
Age	0.55	0.88	0.12	0.85, p<0.01
Gender	0.94	1.0	0.88	0.82, p<0.01
Education	0.57	0.81	0.31	0.61, p<0.01
District	0.08	0.19	0	Not significant
Std. German	0.54	0.96	0.12	Not significant
Coll. Language	0.58	0.96	0.04	Not significant
Dialect	0.61	0.92	0.15	0.21, p<0.01

with 9 voices perceived by 26 listeners to see whether the parameters in [8] are also perceivable. And in order to rank these aspects in importance to our speaker selection process. Tokens of 5 – 10 sec were played twice and listeners had to put down their judgment of *age*, *gender*, *district*, and the speaker's claimed competence in *standard German* ("Hochdeutsch"), *colloquial language* ("Umgangssprache") and *dialect*. The group of speakers consisted of 6 females and 3 males, aged from 17 to 80 (average 42,0), they were distributed with respect to educational level (3 university degree holders, 4 A-levels, and 2 below A-levels) and district (8 districts in 9 subjects). The group of listeners consisted of 15 males an 11 females, average age 31 (min: 16, max: 59) , who were rather highly educated (20 university degree holders, 2 A-levels, 4 below A-levels). At large there is a wide-spread though not representative coverage of the dimensions under investigation.

The listeners were asked to guess the age, gender, educational level, and district where the speaker comes from. This was compared to the reality. For the dimensions associated with language we did use a subjective measure because we are mainly interested in the stereotypes of language perception. So we decided to differentiate between self-perception and perception-by-others. The listeners were asked which type of language the speakers stated they were able to speak: Standard German (*Hochdeutsch*), colloquial language (*Umgangssprache*), and dialect (*Dialekt*). This was compared to the self-perception of the speaker.

Table 1 shows the accuracy for the different dimensions. The *min / max* values are the percentages of the best/worst estimated speakers for this dimension. For the *age* dimension we accepted judgments within an interval of 15%(+/-) as correct. There are significant correlations for real and estimated *age*, *gender*, *education*, and *dialect*, while there are no correlations for *district*, *Standard German* and *colloquial language*.

2.1 Implications for Persona Design

The correlations within *age* and *educational level* are in accordance with [8]. This shows a tendency towards these dimensions as basic dimensions of Viennese sociolects. The lack of correlation within the *district* dimension contrasts with the cliché of regional differences in Vienna.

Taking into account the correlations within the *gender* dimension we decided to realize 3 personas/voices that represent this 3-dimensional (*age, gender, education*) sociolect space.

Concerning the language dimension there is only a weak but significant correlation within the dialect dimension. These results show that self-perception and perception-by-others concerning language competence do not match and that these features are not reliable cues for speaker and persona selection.

3 Application Scenarios for Regionalized Voice Interfaces with Sociolect and Dialect Speech Synthesis

The user study aims to select appropriate application scenarios for a dialect speech synthesis system. We conducted 26 interviews with experts and non-experts regarding our research objective. Participants were aged between 17 and 80 (mean 39,6), 12 male 14 female. The 11 experts were from various fields: media art, usability, computer science, sociolinguistics, dialect phonetics.

Five application scenarios were presented to the users who had to decide if a sociolect/dialect voice is appropriate. Then they were encouraged to comment on the decision and to suggest further application scenarios. The user comments were merged into 9 negative and 7 positive classes (Figure 3 and 4). The application scenarios were a *district information system*, a *talking clock*, a *computer game*, an *application for administrative information*, and a *health information system*. As can be seen from

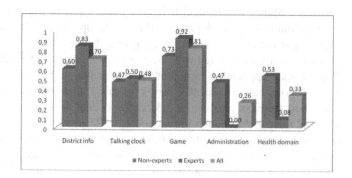

Fig. 1. Application scenarios for dialect voices

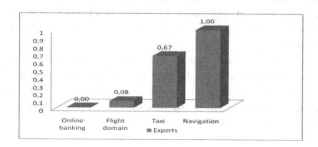

Fig. 2. More application scenarios for dialect voices

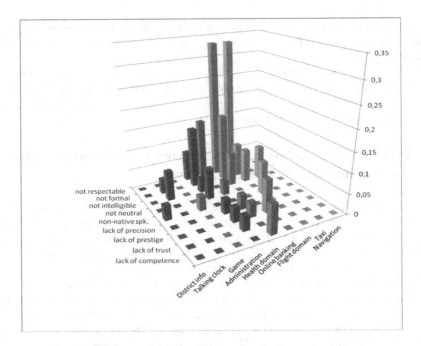

Fig. 3. Reasons to reject dialect voices in these scenarios

Fig. 1 there was a tendency to distinguish between two types of applications with *game*, *district info*, and *talking clock* being in the one group and *administration* and *health domain* being in the other group. A grouping can also be found with four more application scenarios that we evaluated with the expert users (Fig. 2). The *online banking* and the *flight domain* application were found unacceptable by the expert users.

Fig. 3 and Fig. 4 show the attributes that were chosen for applying or rejecting dialect voices. The most frequent reasons for rejecting a dialect persona were that it is *not respectable* and *not formal* enough in that situation. The reasons to apply dialect voices are *fun* (*game*, *navigation*), optional (*district info*, *talking clock*, *navigation*), *personal* (*navigation*), *regional* (*district info*, *taxi*, *navigation*), and that they are able to represent the adequate persona as in the *taxi* reservation system, where the dialect voice may represent the taxi driver.

Application scenarios for sociolect and dialect speech synthesis that were suggested by the users were an application for a site of Vienna's local government, for reserving barbecue places, for audio books of Viennese songs and stories, and for Second Life avatars.

The main difference between experts and non-experts is that the latter are not as consistent in their judgments as the former. For the dialect voices in the *health domain* for example there was only one expert who voted for it. The positive attribute for this expert was *democratic* (*BürgerInnennähe*) which means that a dialect persona creates familiarity between patient and doctor.

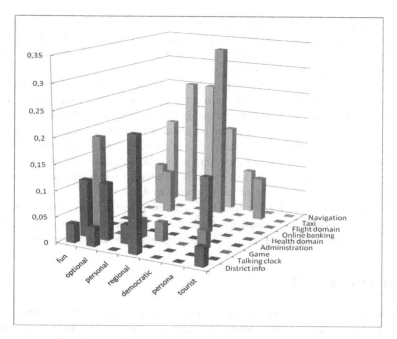

Fig. 4. Reasons to apply dialect voices in these scenarios

3.1 Implications for Application Scenarios

For the *district info*, *talking clock*, *game*, *taxi*, and *navigation* applications we got positive feedback. This shows that there is a range of scenarios where the dialect voices can be deployed. The *optional* attribute shows that an adaptive voice user interface that allows for switching between a dialect and a standard persona is valued.

We also saw that there is a class of applications where a *respectable* and *formal* persona is required. A dialect voice is not considered appropriate for this persona.

4 Conclusions

Our listening experiments showed that age, gender, and educational level are the appropriate dimensions for defining the sociolects in Vienna. Considering these dimensions speakers can be selected to representatively cover the space of sociolects.

Users consider dialect TTS applications *fun*, *regional*, and *personal*. But they reject them when a *respectable* persona is expected. Additional application scenarios can incorporate dialect personas if they are *optional* to a standard persona.

The above results support us in developing multiple synthetic voices, which realize different personas representing the Viennese sociolect space. Therefore the target personas are going to cover both genders, three different age groups, and three sociolects namely Viennese dialect, Viennese youth language (slang), and Viennese standard German.

In our future work we will evaluate our released synthetic voices in a similar study such that a comparison between natural and synthetic dialect speech is possible. Since we will release these voices under an open source license we encourage other researchers to perform further studies.

One open problem for unit selection speech synthesis is the synthesis of emotional speech. We think that dialect and sociolect speech synthesis evokes emotions in the listener because only a specific social group is associated with the persona, and each other social group has specific perception patterns for this persona. For these reasons one has to be considerate when realizing a sociolect speech synthesizer. One expert suggested to choose personas based on sociolects that are stereotyped and known through mass media. This area of research is open to sociolinguistic investigations concerning the perceptual judgments between sociolects.

Our approach is transferable to other fields of research where considering social and regional aspects can increase the naturalness of human computer interaction. We advocate the development of socially enabled agents with realistic personas.

Acknowledgements

This work has been supported in by the Vienna Science and Technology Fund (WWTF). The Telecommunications Research Center Vienna (ftw.) is supported by the Austrian Government and by the City of Vienna within the competence center program COMET.

References

1. Dahlbäck, N., Wang, Q., Nass, C., Alwin, J.: Similarity is more important than expertise: Accent effects in speech interfaces. In: Proc. SIGCHI conference on human factors in computing systems 2007, pp. 1553–1556 (2007)
2. Nass, C., Lee, K.M.: Does computer-generated speech manifest personality? Experimental tests of recognition, similarity-attraction, and consistency-attraction. Journal of Experimental Psychology 7(3), 171–181 (2001)
3. Marcus, A., Gould, E.W.: Crosscurrents – Cultural dimensions and global web user-interface design. Interactions 7(4), 32–46 (2000)
4. Voice Award (2007), http://www.voiceaward.de/
5. Pucher, M., Neubarth, F., Rank, E., Niklfeld, G., Guan, Q.: Combining non-uniform unit selection with diphone based synthesis. In: Proc. Eurospeech 2003, pp. 1329–1332 (2003)
6. Hunt, A., Black, A.: Unit selection in a concatenative speech synthesis system using a large speech database. In: Proc. ICASSP 1996, pp. 373–376 (1996)
7. Baum, M., Erbach, G., Kubin, G.: SpeechDat-AT: A telephone speech database for Austrian German. In: Proc. LREC workshop very large telephone databases (XL-DB) (2000)
8. Cohen, M.H., Giangola, J.P., Balogh, J.: Voice user interface design. Addison-Wesley, Reading (2004)
9. Moosmüller, S.: Soziophonologische Variation im gegenwärtigen Wiener Deutsch. Franz Steiner Verlag, Stuttgart (1987)

Vocal Gestures in Slovak: Emotions and Prosody

Štefan Beňuš[1,2] and Milan Rusko[2]

[1] Constantine the Philosopher University, Stefanikova 67, 94974 Nitra, Slovakia
[2] Institute of Informatics of the Slovak Academy of Sciences, Dubravska cesta 9, 845 07
Bratislava, Slovakia
sbenus@ukf.sk, milan.rusko@savba.sk

Abstract. Hot-spot words are indicators of high emotional invovement of
speakers in the conversation and contain cues to the emotional state of the
speaker. Understanding and modeling of these cues may improve the effectiveness and naturalness of automated cross-modal dialogue systems. In this paper
we investigate the relationship between prosody and emotions in a subgroup of
hot-spot words: non-verbal vocal gestures with a problematic textual representation. We extracted these gestures from a recording of a puppet play and argue that
this corpus is well suited for investigating emotional speech. We identify the expressive load of non-verbal vocal gestures in Slovak and report on multiple ambiguities in their emotional and discourse functions. The relationship between
prosody and emotions in non-verbal hot-spot words is very complex and a ToBI-
based framework of discrete representation of prosody is useful but not sufficient
for modeling this relationship.

Keywords: Nonverbal vocal gestures, emotional speech, prosody, ToBI.

1 Introduction

Signals about the internal state of the speaker are both visual and auditory. For example deception could be cued by gestures such as putting a hand over the mouth [1] but
it may also correlate with the use of filled pauses [2] or higher pitch [3]. Similar examples of cross-modal characteristics could be found for many types of emotions.
Hence, a comprehensive model of human communication relies on both visual and
auditory characteristics.

Efforts in understanding and modeling the visual and auditory aspects of the internal
state of a speaker are essential in improving applications relying on human-machine
communication. For example, in automated call-center applications, detecting a frustrated
or angry customer is important so that s/he can be switched to a human operator. Or, the
efficiency of tutoring systems is increased if they can reliably detect uncertainty. Generation of good quality emotional dialogues is usable in gaming and other industries.

One of the promising approaches in utilizing emotions in speech is related to so-
called hot-spot words. The presence and acoustic characteristic of these words may
facilitate the detection of high involvement in meetings and thus point to important
information for automatic retrieval [4]. Additionally, prosody of these ambiguous
hot-spot words can signal emotional valence of the speaker, that is if the speaker's

A. Esposito et al. (Eds.): Multimodal Signals, LNAI 5398, pp. 223–231, 2009.

emotions are positive or negative (e.g. [5] on 'whatever'). Therefore, as a long-term goal, the presence and the acoustic and prosodic characteristics of a hot-spot word may be used for measuring the expressiveness of larger units of analysis such as utterances, speaker turns, or whole conversations.

In this paper we concentrate on the auditory expressions of emotion of special type of hot-spot words that we call non-verbal vocal gestures. (see [6] for the taxonomy of gestures in the visual mode). Following [6] we consider non-verbal speech gestures those "speech sounds that have their own phonetic content, phonological function, and prosody, but [they] do not have an adequate linguistic (or text) representation". In this view, non-verbal gestures belong among hot-spot words with significant expressive power and information about the speaker's internal state. The major question is how to describe the information they contain so that it could be utilized to improve the effectiveness of systems based on the recognition and generation of emotional speech. In the following, we discuss a scheme for labeling the prosody of these gestures and report on an experiment testing the perception of emotions signaled by these gestures.

2   Prosody Description of Emotional Speech

The best way of studying how prosody conveys emotions and attitudes is when prosodic features are represented in a theoretical framework of a prosodic model [7]. Previous research has shown that both discrete and continuous features that capture acoustic and prosodic information and the voice quality features are useful in characterizing emotional speech. For example, [8] supported the view that automatically extracted pitch and energy features correlate with the activation of emotions; that is to what degree the speaker is emotionally involved. Interestingly, discrete features that capture the intonational contour were useful in characterizing the valence of emotions, that is, if the emotion is positive or negative. More specifically, [8] used the ToBI system of intonation description [9] and in their corpus, utterances with plateau contours (H-L%) were positively correlated with negative emotions while utterances with falling contours (L-L%) correlated with positive emotions.

The use of ToBI for describing the prosodic characteristics of emotional speech was also supported by proponents of the British school of intonation (e.g. [10]). Hence, given the usefulness of the ToBI framework for capturing important information in emotional speech, we decided to continue our efforts at building a ToBI version suitable for describing Slovak intonation (henceforth SK-ToBI, [11]) and test its usefulness for describing non-vocal gestures.

2.1   ToBI System

ToBI [9] is a model that captures phonologically and pragmatically meaningful aspects of intonation with the use of a finite set of discrete symbols. Primarily, ToBI is concerned with identifying intonationally prominent events as pitch targets (=Tones) and the degree of disjuncture between pairs of words (=Break Indexes). ToBI labeling scheme was developed by linguists and speech scientists in order to study the functional differences conveyed by intonation and to enable sharing speech corpora labeled in a uniform scheme due to the fact that labeling intonation is very time and effort consuming.

The original ToBI developed for Mainstream American English (MAE) recognizes three tonal targets: H(igh), L(ow), and !H that represents a down stepped high target after another high target within a single intonational phrase. There are three types of tonal targets: pitch accents that signal intonational prominence on a given word, marked with '*', and boundary tones that signal the right edge of the intermediate and intonational units marked with '-' and '%' respectively. This system then gives the following inventory:

- Pitch accents: H*, !H*, L*, L+H*, L+!H*, L*+H, L*+!H, H+!H*
- Phrase accents: H-, !H-, L-
- Boundary tones: H%, L%

Every intonational boundary is assumed to contain both phrase accent and boundary tone while intonational phrase is only marked with a phrase accent. The ToBI framework has been adapted for the description of intonation of many unrelated languages (see [12] for a review).

2.2 SK-ToBI

Slovak is a west-Slavic language spoken by roughly 5 million people in Slovakia. Our current ToBI framework for description of Slovak intonation is based on a corpus of 246 utterances that could be divided into two groups. The first group is a set of 74 sentences balanced for syntactic and pragmatic meaning, and read by a single speaker. The second part of the corpus comes from a recording of a play acted by a single puppet-player [14]. We selected the utterances of 2 characters (Faust and Jester) with similar lengths of the speech material (79 and 93 utterances respectively).

All material was transcribed, manually aligned with the speech signal, and labeled following the annotation conventions developed for MAE ToBI. Using PRAAT [13], three annotators participated in labeling; one is an expert annotator of MAE ToBI, the other two are beginners. Inter-labeler agreement was measured by Fleiss' κ [15]. The agreement for presence vs. absence of pitch accent and boundary tones was measured at 0.74 and 0.76 respectively, where values between 0.6 and 0.8 correspond to substantial agreement. The agreements for the type of the pitch accent and the boundary tone were worse (below 0.5).

The analyses of our labeled corpus showed that ToBI is a suitable system for capturing the range of differences cued by intonation in Slovak. We identified three areas where SK-ToBI might differ from MAE ToBI but more research is needed to see if the changes of the inventory of tones are warranted or just the alignment of tonal targets with the segmental material is different.

First, H-L% boundary tone in MAE ToBI describes so called plateau intonation, especially after a preceding H* pitch accent. In Slovak, a similar plateau intonation is possible and H-L% was used to label it. However, yes/no questions in Slovak tend to rise toward and during the final pitch accented syllable but then the pitch stays flat on the following non-stressed syllables. Current MAE ToBI does not give other option but to use H-L% for this type of contour. Hence H-L% in Slovak is ambiguous between a question rise and a plateau, both of which occur frequently, and some utterances with identical H-L% labeling in the two languages sound significantly different.

The second, issue is the presence of trailing tones that seem to mark the right edge of a prosodic word in Slovak. A similar proposal for tones that mark the edges of words has been made for Catalan [16] but no generally accepted addition to the ToBI framework has been made.

Finally, Slovak may require the addition of H*+L tone, already suggested for German [17] and other languages while contrastive function of some rare tones such as L*+!H or !H-H% is questionable in Slovak.

3 Corpus of Non-verbal Vocal Gestures

Designing a corpus suitable for experimental investigation of emotional speech represents significant obstacles. Spontaneous unscripted speech of good sound quality rarely contains a rich variety of emotions. Hence, the primary method of data acquisition in the past was to ask professional actors to act emotions on semantically neutral utterances such as series of numbers. This approach allows for a rich source of emotions and control of other variables such as linguistic context. However, elicited acted emotions are not realized identically to the ones occurring in spontaneous speech. More specifically, the elicited emotions are more exaggerated than the real ones and many times may sound artificial and stilted. On the other hand, [18] showed that although acted emotions are more exaggerated than real-life ones, the relationship of these two types of emotions to acoustic correlates is not contradictory.

In our approach, we use the corpus of a play acted by a single puppet-player [13]. The corpus is rich with emotional speech since the visual cues to emotions are significantly limited for characters in a puppet play. Hence, the speech of the puppet player must be expressive. On the other hand, despite the existence of a script, the emotions are not really elicited, but they are expressed semi-spontaneously as it is required by the plot and the development of the play. Our corpus of puppet plays thus represents an intermediate level between elicited acted speech of actors and spontaneous everyday communication. Therefore, we believe that our corpus has potential to improve our understanding of the system that underlies the production and perception of features linked to the emotional state of the speaker.

Table 1. Frequency distribution of non-verbal vocal gestures in the corpus. The transcriptions in the square brackets are approximated broad IPA transcriptions.

NVG	N	%	NVG	N	%
[joj]	15	16.9	[ejha]	3	3.4
[he]	12	13.5	[jej]	3	3.4
[aha]	10	11.2	cry	2	2.2
[e]	8	9	[heja]	2	2.2
[jaj]	8	9	[hm]	2	2.2
laugh	8	9	[mmhm]	2	2.2
inhale	4	4.5	[e-e]	1	1.1
[juj]	4	4.5	exhale	1	1.1
[a]	3	3.4	[mm]	1	1.1

In order to study the form and function of non-verbal gestures we extracted 89 instances of non-verbal vocal gestures from the transcribed and aligned recording of the puppet play. We extracted the instances of both true non-verbal gestures such as laughs, cries, inhale and exhale sounds, or filled pauses, as well as semi-verbal gestures that represent particles such as [joj], [juj], [he], [a], [e], or [aha], and could convey a range of emotions. The distribution of the non-verbal gestures is summarized in Table 1.

The prosody of these gestures was transcribed using SK-ToBI. It should be noted that the labeling of true non-verbal gestures such as inhales, laughs or grunts was very problematic in SK-ToBI due to the fact that the activity of the vocal folds (and consequently the F0 contour) is often very limited. The labeling of semi-verbal gestures was much more straightforward. Here we concentrate on the Tones labeling since each non-verbal gesture constituted a prosodic phrase on its own and thus the juncture following each gesture was identical in terms of ToBI.

In terms of the number of pitch accents, all but two tokens received a single accent. The two non-verbal gestures with double accents were multisyllabic: [jojojojojoj] and a laugh, both of them had high accent o the initial syllable and a low(er) accent on the final syllable of the gesture. The distribution of the types of pitch accent and boundary tone in our corpus are shown in Table 2 below, and the distribution of complete intonational contours is in Table 3.

Table 2. Frequency distribution of the pitch accents and boundary tones among the non-verbal vocal gestures

Pitch accent			Boundary tone		
Type	N	%	Type	N	%
H*	54	60.7	L-L%	39	43.8
L+H*	16	18.0	H-L%	27	30.3
L*	13	14.6	!H-L%	14	15.7
H+{!H*, L*}	6	6.7	{H, !H, L}-H%	9	10.1

Table 3. Frequency distribution of the intonational contours labeled with the ToBI scheme among the non-verbal vocal gestures

Intonational contours					
Type	N	%	Type	N	%
H*L-L%	20	22.5	L+H*H-L%	9	11
H*H-L%	16	18	L+H*L-L%	5	5.6
H*!H-L%	14	15.7	H*{H, !H, L}-H%	5	5.6
L*L-L%	11	12.4	H+!H*L-L%	3	3.4
			Other	6	6.6

4 Prosody and Emotions of Non-verbal Gestures

To study the relationship between the form of the non-verbal gestures and the emotions they conveyed, we ran a pilot perception experiment. From the set of six basic emotions detectable from facial behavior [1] we selected five emotions: ANGER, JOY, SADNESS, FEAR, and SURPRISE and asked 6 subjects to judge the presence of these emotions in non-verbal gestures on the scale from 0 (no emotion) to 3 (very strong emotion). Subjects listened to the audio signal of the non-verbal gesture alone, without any surrounding context or transcription. Each rating was normalized by participant using z-scores normalization in order to account for the variation the subjects might have produced in the use of the scale. We then calculated the mean and standard deviation values for each token and emotion.

4.1 Results and Discussion

As a general measure of expressive load we took the sum of the mean z-score values for each token and emotion (the higher the value, the greater the expressive load). We also calculated a measure of agreement among the subjects, which we took as a sum of the standard deviations for each token and emotion (the higher the value, the worse the agreement). We found a highly significant positive correlation between these two general measures in our data; $r(1, 89) = 0.699$, $p < 0.01$. That is, our subjects agreed better on less expressive tokens than on the more expressive ones. Hence, the identification of the lack of emotions just from the acoustics of non-verbal gestures is easier than the identification of emotions.

Gestures with low expressive load and high annotators' agreement include backchannels [mmhm] and particles [he]/[e], and [aha]. 15 of the 20 least expressive gestures belong to this group. The primary function of backchannel [mmhm], is to acknowledge some previous event (either verbal or non-verbal). Particle [he] also seems to have rather discursive than emotive function: it was mostly used to mark the end of a speaker's turn. Particle [e] was mostly used to signal a speech error, which is similar to one of the primary functions of filled pause. Finally, [aha] may have multiple functions, one of which is to acknowledge previous information; hence, it may function as a backchannel. It is interesting that all three [aha] tokens among the group of least expressive gestures were relatively short and labeled L+H*H-L%, which is consistent with the backchannel function. Other functions of [aha] include expressing surprise and drawing attention to something, and were produced in different prosody. In sum, there are several non-verbal gestures in our corpus that seem to function primarily in managing the flow of conversation, and it is thus reasonable that these don't have high expressive load and should not be considered hot-spot items.

At the other end of the continuum are vocal gestures with high expressive load but low annotators' agreement. The most common among these gestures are clearly [joj], [jaj], and [juj], and also two inhale sounds. All [jVj] gestures are very expressive in Slovak, can contain multiple syllables within one gesture, and are able to signal a broad range of emotions. In our corpus, they were associated mostly with fear and sadness, and then with surprise. A high pitch accent (H*) was common for these emotions, followed with either a fall (L-L%) or an unfinished fall ({H, !H}-L%).

Moving now to describing the relationship between intonational contours and emotions, Fig. 1 below represents the most frequent melody contours (N > 2) in our corpus as described by SK-ToBI and how they signaled particular emotions.

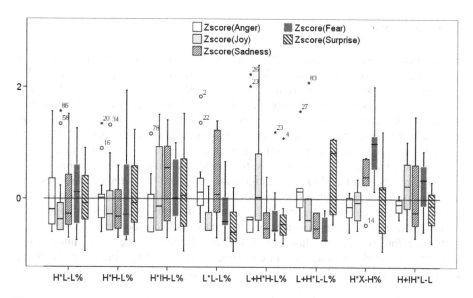

Fig. 1. Boxplots representing the intonational contours on the x-axis and mean z-score values for emotions on the y-axis. The contours are in descending ordered of frequency from the left. The bottom and the top of the box represent lower and upper quartiles of the distribution respectively, the band near the middle is the median, and the whiskers represent the minimum and the maximum values. Circles represent outlier values and asterisks extreme outlier values.

Despite the density of the data in Fig. 1, it provides two types of useful information. First, it identifies the outliers in the distributions. Outliers represent extreme emotions and are thus true hot-spot words of our corpus. The figure identifies 15 outliers, one of which is a 'negative outlier' and cues the absence rather than presence of emotion. Of the remaining 14 true hot-spot gestures, the most outliers were identified for ANGER (8), and JOY (4). Out of 8 outliers for ANGER there are 4 [he] tokens, 2 [ejha], [juj], and [a]. High anger ratings for some [he] tokens are surprising in the view of its discourse function described above. Hence, both [he] and [aha] are highly ambiguous in terms of whether they are emotionally loaded or not. Out of 4 outliers for JOY there are 2 laughs, [he] and [jaj].

The nature of an outlier in this Figure is that it has the same melody contour as other vocal gestures that don't cue a particular emotion but this outlier token cues extreme emotion. Because of this and due to the fact that there is no clear pattern in terms of the intonational contours for these outliers, we speculate that other features such as intensity, duration, pitch range or voice quality are more important in cuing these extreme emotions than the intonational contour itself.

The second information present in the Figure is that some tendencies in the relationship between the intonational contour and the other three emotions can be observed. For example, pitch accents with a clear low region (L* and L+H*) tend to signal the absence of FEAR while the presence of final rise (H%) signals its presence. However, more robust patterns are missing and further research is needed to decode the complex relationship between emotions and intonation contours.

5 Conclusion

In this paper we set to investigate the relationship between prosody and emotions in non-verbal vocal gestures extracted from a recording of a puppet play in Slovak. We reported that ToBI framework is suitable for describing Slovak intonational patterns and we discussed several issues where this framework for American English and Slovak might differ. We identified the expressive load of non-verbal vocal gestures and discovered multiple ambiguities in their emotional and discourse functions. The prosody-emotion relationship in non-verbal hot-spot words is very complex and a ToBI framework is useful but definitely not sufficient for modeling this relationship.

In future research we plan to investigate the influence of continuous features such as intensity, pitch range, duration, spectral tilt, jitter, or harmonics-to-noise ratio on the perception of emotional speech in these hot-spot words. We agree with one of the reviewers that surrounding context, namely intonation contour and other prosodic features before or after the hot-spot words, could also provide useful information. Currently we work on designing an experiment that would test the effect of lexical and prosodic context on the perceived emotions of non-verbal vocal gestures.

Acknowledgments. We would like to thank R. Kováč, R. Sabo, and the subjects in our perception experiments. This work was supported by the of the Ministry of Education of the Slovak Republic, Scientific Grant Agency project number 2/0138/08 Applied Research project number AV 4/0006/07, **by the Slovak Research and Development Agency under the contract No. APVV-0369-07,** and by the European Education, Audiovisual and Culture Executive Agency LLP project EURONOUNCE.

Education and Culture DG

This project has been funded with support from the European Commission. This publication reflects the views only of the authors, and the Commission cannot be held responsible for any use which may be made of the information contained therein.

References

1. Ekman, P., Friesen, W.V., Ellsworth, P.: What Emotion Categories or Dimensions can Observers Judge from Facial Behavior? In: Ekman, P. (ed.) Emotion in the Human Face, pp. 39–55. Cambridge University Press, Cambridge (1982)
2. Benus, S., Enos, F., Hirschberg, J., Shriberg, E.: Pauses and Deceptive Speech. In: Hoffmann, R., Mixdorff, H. (eds.) Proceedings of 3rd International Conference on Speech Prosody. TUD Press, Dresden (2006)
3. DePaulo, B.M., Lindsay, J., Malone, E., Muhlenbruck, L., Charlton, K., Cooper, H.: Cues to Deception. Psychological Bulletin 129(1), 74–118 (2003)

4. Wrede, B., Shriberg, E.: Spotting Hotspots in Meetings: Human Judgments and Prosodic Cues. In: Proceedings of European Conference on Speech Communication and Technology, pp. 2805–2808 (2003)
5. Benus, S., Gravano, A., Hirschberg, J.: Prosody, Emotions, and...'whatever'. In: Proceedings of International Conference on Speech Communication and Technology, pp. 2629–2632 (2007)
6. Rusko, M., Juhár, J.: Towards Annotation of Nonverbal Vocal Gestures in Slovak. In: Cross-Modal Analysis of Verbal and Nonverbal Communication. LNCS (in press)
7. Mozziconacci, S.: Prosody and Emotions. In: Bel, B., Marlien, I. (eds.) Proceedings of 1st International Conference on Speech Prosody, pp. 1–9 (2002)
8. Liscombe, J., Venditti, J., Hirschberg, J.: Classifying Subject Ratings of Emotional Speech Using Acoustic Features. In: Proceedings of European Conference on Speech Communication and Technology, pp. 725–728 (2003)
9. Beckman, M.E., Hirschberg, J., Shattuck-Hufnagel, S.: The Original ToBI System and the Evolution of the ToBI Framework. In: Jun, S.-A. (ed.) Prosodic Typology: The Phonology of Intonation and Phrasing, pp. 9–54. Oxford University Press, Oxford (2005)
10. Roach, P.: Techniques for the Phonetic Description of Emotional Speech. In: Proceedings of Speech Emotion 2000, pp. 53–59 (2000)
11. Rusko, M., Sabo, R., Dzúr, M.: Sk-ToBI Scheme for Phonological Prosody Annotation in Slovak. In: Matoušek, V., Mautner, P. (eds.) TSD 2007. LNCS (LNAI), vol. 4629, pp. 334–341. Springer, Heidelberg (2007)
12. Jun, S.-A.: Prosodic Typology: The Phonology of Intonation and Phrasing. Oxford University Press, Oxford (2005)
13. Rusko, M., Hamar, J.: Character Identity Expression in Vocal Performance of Traditional Puppeteers. In: Sojka, P., Kopeček, I., Pala, K. (eds.) TSD 2006. LNCS (LNAI), vol. 4188, pp. 509–516. Springer, Heidelberg (2006)
14. Boersma, P., Weenink, D.: Praat: Doing phonetics by computer,
    http://www.praat.org
15. Fleiss, J.L.: Measuring Nominal Scale Agreement among Many Raters. Psychological Bulletin 76(5), 378–382 (1971)
16. Estebas-Vilaplana, E.: Catalan Pre-Nuclear Accents: Evidence for Word-Edge Tones. In: Solé, M.J., Recasens, D., Romero, J. (eds.) Proceedings of the 16th International Congress of Phonetic Sciences, pp. 1779–1782 (2003)
17. Grice, M., Baumann, S., Benzmüller, R.: German Intonation in Autosegmental-Metrical Phonology. In: Jun, S.-A. (ed.) Prosodic Typology: The Phonology of Intonation and Phrasing, pp. 55–83. Oxford University Press, Oxford (2005)
18. Williams, C.E., Stevens, K.N.: Emotions and speech: Some acoustical factors. Journal of the Acoustical Society of America 52, 1238–1250 (1972)

Spectrum Modification for Emotional Speech Synthesis

Anna Přibilová[1] and Jiří Přibil[2]

[1] Department of Radio Electronics, Slovak University of Technology
Ilkovičova 3, SK-812 19 Bratislava, Slovakia
Anna.Pribilova@stuba.sk
[2] Institute of Photonics and Electronics, Academy of Sciences of the Czech Republic
Chaberská 57, CZ-182 51 Prague, Czech Republic
Jiri.Pribil@savba.sk

Abstract. Emotional state of a speaker is accompanied by physiological changes affecting respiration, phonation, and articulation. These changes are manifested mainly in prosodic patterns of F0, energy, and duration, but also in segmental parameters of speech spectrum. Therefore, our new emotional speech synthesis method is supplemented with spectrum modification. It comprises non-linear frequency scale transformation of speech spectral envelope, filtering for emphasizing low or high frequency range, and controlling of spectral noise by spectral flatness measure according to knowledge of psychological and phonetic research. The proposed spectral modification is combined with linear modification of F0 mean, F0 range, energy, and duration. Speech resynthesis with applied modification that should represent joy, anger and sadness is evaluated by a listening test.

Keywords: emotional speech, spectral envelope, speech synthesis, emotional voice conversion.

1 Introduction

Vocal emotion communication has been investigated by psychologists, but also psychiatrists, for a long time. Emotional arousal of a speaker is accompanied by physiological changes that affect respiration, phonation, and articulation and produce emotion-specific patterns of acoustic parameters. These acoustic changes are transmitted to the ears of the listener and perceived via the auditory perceptual system [1]. Information and communication technology development extended emotion recognition from humans to computers [2], [3], [4], [5], and emotion expression is also used to improve naturalness of synthetic speech [6].

Influence of emotions on human speech is manifested mainly in prosody [7], however, emotional state of a speaker is accompanied also by physiological changes causing shift of individual formants, different amount of low-frequency and high-frequency energy, and/or different spectral noise depending on the expressed emotion [1]. Our present work is aimed mainly at modification of these spectral parameters using known results of psychological and phonetic research. Prosody conversion is done by modification of neutral prosodic parameters according to known ratios between emotional and neutral speech.

A. Esposito et al. (Eds.): Multimodal Signals, LNAI 5398, pp. 232–241, 2009.

2 Spectral Parameters Modification

Our approach to spectral parameters modification consists of spectral envelope modification by non-linear frequency scale transformation, spectral energy distribution modification by shelving filtering, and spectral noise modification by controlling the degree of voicing in mixed excitation of the cepstral speech model.

2.1 Cepstral Speech Synthesis

The source-filter model with cepstral parametrization of the vocal tract transfer function is used for speech synthesis. For voiced speech the filter is excited by a combination of an impulse train and high-pass filtered random noise. For unvoiced speech the excitation is formed purely by a random noise source. The transfer function of the vocal tract model is approximated by Padé approximation of the continued fraction expansion of the exponential function [8].

2.2 Spectral Envelope Transformation

During pleasant emotions the larynx and the pharynx are expanded, the vocal tract walls are relaxed, and the mouth corners are retracted upward. The result is falling first formant and raised resonances. For unpleasant emotions the larynx and pharynx are constricted, the vocal tract walls are tensed, and the mouth corners are retracted downward. The result is more high-frequency energy, rising first formant, and falling second and third formants [1]. We can conclude that the first formant and the higher formants of emotional speech shift in opposite directions. For pleasant emotions the first formant shifts to the left, and the higher formants to the right. For unpleasant emotions the opposite situation occurs: the first formant shifts to the right, and the higher formants to the left.

Although the formant frequencies differ to some extent for different languages and their ranges are overlapped [9], the male voice vowel formant areas without overlap can be determined: $F1 \approx 250 \div 700$ Hz, $F2 \approx 700 \div 2000$ Hz, $F3 \approx 2000 \div 3200$ Hz, $F4 \approx 3200 \div 4000$ Hz [10]. Thus we can use the frequency of 700 Hz as a border frequency for shifting spectral envelope frequencies of male voice in the opposite directions.

For shifting the first formant and the higher formants in the opposite directions we use a smooth function of frequency $\gamma(f)$ representing formant ratio between emotional and neutral speech - see Fig. 1.

For better analytic representation of this function the frequency scale is logarithmically warped so that 700 Hz corresponds to one fourth of the sampling frequency (4 kHz for 16-kHz sampling) - see Fig. 2.

Analytic expression of the logarithmic frequency scale transformation can be derived from its inverse exponential function

$$f(f_t) = a \cdot b^{f_t} + c, \tag{1}$$

where f represents the input frequency and f_t corresponds to the transformed frequency. Three unknown variables a, b, c are determined using three points $[f_t, f] = [0$ kHz, 0 kHz], $[4$ kHz, 0.7 kHz], $[8$ kHz, 8 kHz], as zero frequency and half the sampling frequency remain unchanged. The solution of the system of the three equations is

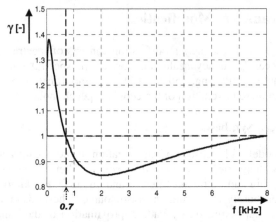

Fig. 1. Formant ratio γ between unpleasant and neutral speech with formant shift to the right for frequencies lower than 700 Hz, and formant shift to the left for frequencies higher than 700 Hz

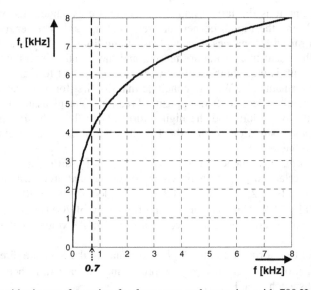

Fig. 2. Logarithmic transformation for frequency scale warping with 700 Hz corresponding to one fourth of the sampling frequency

$$a = \frac{0.49}{6.6}, \qquad b = \sqrt[4]{\frac{7.3}{0.7}}, \qquad c = -a. \qquad (2)$$

The transformed frequency is expressed by

$$f_t(f) = \log_b \frac{f+a}{a} = \frac{\ln\left(\dfrac{f}{a}+1\right)}{\ln b}. \qquad (3)$$

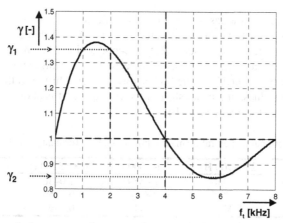

Fig. 3. Formant ratio between unpleasant and neutral speech as a function of logarithmically warped frequency

Formant ratio $\gamma(f_t)$ as a smooth function of the logarithmically warped frequency can be expressed by a fourth-order polynomial function - see Fig. 3

$$\gamma(f_t) = p \cdot f_t^4 + q \cdot f_t^3 + r \cdot f_t^2 + s \cdot f_t + t. \tag{4}$$

Coefficients of this polynomial can be computed from five equidistant points $[f_t, \gamma] =$ [0 kHz, 1], [2 kHz, γ_1], [4 kHz, 1], [6 kHz, γ_2], [8 kHz, 1]. The solution of the system of five equations is

$$p = \frac{1}{48} - \frac{1}{96}\gamma_1 - \frac{1}{96}\gamma_2, \qquad q = -\frac{1}{3} + \frac{3}{16}\gamma_1 + \frac{7}{48}\gamma_2,$$

$$r = \frac{5}{3} - \frac{13}{12}\gamma_1 - \frac{7}{12}\gamma_2, \qquad s = -\frac{8}{3} + 2\gamma_1 + \frac{2}{3}\gamma_2, \qquad t = 1. \tag{5}$$

The modified spectral envelope $E'(f)$ can be computed from the original spectral envelope $E(f)$ using similar relation as used for linear formant modification [11]

$$E'(f) = E\left(\frac{f}{\gamma(f_t(f))}\right). \tag{6}$$

Using the warping logarithmic function (3), the transformed frequency of 2 kHz corresponds to 165.5 Hz, and 6 kHz corresponds to 2426 Hz. Emotional-to-neutral formant ratios at these frequencies are chosen as shown in Table 1.

Table 1. Chosen emotional-to-neutral formant ratios γ_1 at 165.5 Hz, γ_2 at 2426 Hz

	γ_1	γ_2
joyous-to-neutral	0.70	1.05
angry-to-neutral	1.35	0.85
sad-to-neutral	1.10	0.90

In the four vowel formant areas the mean formant ratios are computed using the formant transformation function (4). Their values are shown in Table 2. For joy the first formant is shifted to the left by about 9 %, the second and third formants are shifted to the right by about 5 % and the shift gradually decreases. For anger the first formant is shifted to the right by about 12 %, the higher formants are shifted to the left by about 11 % to 14 %. For sadness the mean shift of the first formant is about 4 % to the right and the higher formants about 6 % to 10 % to the left.

Table 2. Mean emotional-to-neutral formant ratios in the four formant areas for chosen γ_1, γ_2

	250÷700 Hz	700÷2000 Hz	2000÷3200 Hz	3200÷4000 Hz
joyous-to-neutral	0.9046	1.0589	1.0436	1.0092
angry-to-neutral	1.1215	0.8884	0.8550	0.8842
sad-to-neutral	1.0410	0.9414	0.8999	0.9014

2.3 Spectral Energy Distribution

Different emotions are also characterized by different spectral energy distribution. However, the results of emotional voice analysis are sometimes contradictory. Pleasant emotional speech should have more low-frequency energy; unpleasant one should have more high-frequency energy [1]. On the other hand, increase in high frequencies was reported for joy and anger, and decrease for sadness [12]. It agrees more with our experiments, so we use high-pass filtering for joy and anger, and low-pass filtering for sadness. Both high-pass and low-pass filters are proposed by a standard procedure of second-order shelving filter design [13]. The quality factor is chosen 0.7, and the filter cut-off frequency dividing the frequency range into low and high parts is chosen 1 kHz. The filter gain for joy is chosen 2 dB, for anger and sadness it is chosen 4 dB.

2.4 Spectral Noise

Sad speech should also be accompanied by increased spectral noise [1]. We control its amount by spectral flatness measure according to which the high frequency noise is mixed in voiced frames during cepstral speech synthesis. Its value is chosen 2.5 times higher than that for neutral voice.

3 Prosodic Parameters Modification

Prosody of joyous and angry speech is marked by decreased duration, and increased F0 mean, F0 range, and energy. Opposite trend is observed for sadness where the duration is increased and F0 mean, F0 range, and energy are decreased [1]. However, some authors give different results, e.g., F0 mean and range increased more for sadness than for anger [14]; the same F0 mean for anger and sadness [15]; or too low energy for sadness [16]. We have chosen the results published by Cabral and Oliveira [17] which are in accordance with general information of Scherer [1]. According to [17] the ratio between emotional and neutral F0 mean is 1.18 for joy, 1.15 for anger, and 0.84 for sadness; F0 range ratio is 1.3 for joy and anger, 0.62 for sadness; energy ratio 1.3 for joy, 1.7 for anger, 0.5 for sadness; duration ratio 0.81 for joy, 0.84 for anger, and 1.17 for sadness.

4   Listening Test

Subjective evaluation called "Determination of emotion type" was realized by the listening test located on the web page http://www/lef.um.savba.sk/scripts/itstposl2.dll. The listening test program in the form of MS ISAPI/NSAPI DLL script runs on the server PC and communicates with the user within the framework of the HTTP protocol by means of the HTML pages. Every listening test consists of ten evaluation sets selected randomly from the testing corpus which consists of 80 short sentences with duration 0.9 to 3.6 seconds. The sentences were extracted from the Czech and Slovak stories narrated by male professional actors. For each sentence there is a choice from four possibilities: "joy", "sadness", "anger", or "other".

Twenty eight listeners (21 Czechs and Slovaks, 7 people of other nationalities, 6 women and 22 men) took part in the listening test. The partial results in dependence on sex (male / female listeners) are shown in Fig. 4, partial results in dependence on listeners' nationality (Czech and Slovak / other) are shown in Fig. 5, and the summary results are presented in the form of a confusion matrix in Table 3. Best identified is sadness, worst identified is anger. Joy is sometimes confused with anger and vice versa. Sadness and joy are very rarely confused.

It is clear from the comparison of results in the partial groups that the listeners' sex makes no difference (although, both compared groups were not of the same size) while on the other hand in the group of assessors-foreigners the percentage of successful determination is markedly lower. However, the main proportions among the individual emotions (best identified sadness) are kept in the partial groups, too.

Further, evaluation of the successful determination of the emotion type was carried out in the individual sentences from the testing corpus. Partial results for given three emotions are given in Table 4, Table 5, and Table 6 (values in the column "not classified" represent choice "other" in the listening test, "exchanged" corresponds to incorrectly chosen emotion). Table 7 shows mean values for all emotions ("not correct" comprises "not classified" together with "exchanged"). The overall results present some correlation with partial values for individual emotions, however, there exists also quite contradictory evaluation, supported e.g. by the sentence *s11* being the best for "sadness" and at the same time being the worst for "joy" and "anger".

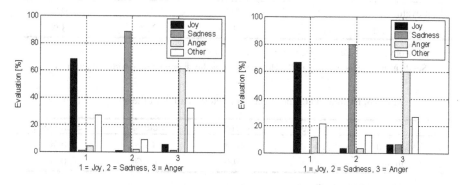

Fig. 4. Partial results of the listening test in dependence on listeners' sex: male (left), female (right)

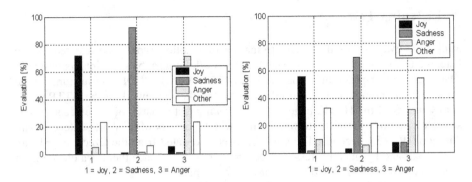

Fig. 5. Partial results of the listening test in dependence on listeners' nationality: Czech and Slovak (left), other nationalities (right)

Table 3. Confusion matrix of the listening test

	joy	anger	sadness	other
joy	**67.86 %**	6.07 %	0.36 %	25.71 %
anger	5.71 %	**61.08 %**	2.14 %	31.07 %
sadness	1.07 %	2.14 %	**86.79 %**	10.00 %

Table 4. Evaluation of the successful determination of the joyous emotion

	sentence	correct	not classified	exchanged
best evaluated	s09*	89 %	11 %	0 %
worst evaluated	s11**	39 %	50 %	11 %

* "Daroval jim kousek úhoru." ("He presented them with a small piece of barrens.")
** "Byl z obyčejného dřeva." ("He was made of a common wood.")

Table 5. Evaluation of the successful determination of the sad emotion

	sentence	correct	not classified	exchanged
best evaluated	s11*	100 %	0 %	0 %
worst evaluated	s12**	71 %	21 %	8 %

* "Byl z obyčejného dřeva." ("He was made of a common wood.")
** "Šel do učení k jednomu truhláři." ("He went to serve his apprenticeship with one joiner.")

Table 6. Evaluation of the successful determination of the angry emotion

	sentence	correct	not classified	exchanged
best evaluated	s14*	80 %	14 %	6 %
worst evaluated	s11**	39 %	61 %	0 %

* "Druhý deň sa konala svadba." ("Next day the wedding took place.")
** "Byl z obyčejného dřeva." ("He was made of a common wood.")

Table 7. Mean values for all emotions

	sentence	Correct	not correct
best evaluated	s14[*]	84.3 %	15.7 %
worst evaluated	s11[**]	59.3 %	40.7 %

[*] "Druhý deň sa konala svadba." ("Next day the wedding took place.")
[**] "Byl z obyčejného dřeva." ("He was made of a common wood.")

5 Conclusion

Results of the present work have shown that emphasis on spectral modification in emotion conversion gives best (worst) results for sad (angry) speech synthesis which was worst (best) identified in our previous work [18] where only prosodic modification had been done.[1] On the other hand, in the present work, identification of sadness is also improved by lower speech rate, energy, and F0. Joy (positive emotion) and anger (negative emotion) in our speech synthesis differ mainly in the opposite shift of the first formant and the higher formants. It seems that positive and negative emotions are distinguished well, however, instead of "joy" or "anger" many listeners have chosen possibility "other" which implies necessity of wider choice, including fear, disgust, and surprise.

Foreign assessors of the listening test have explained opinion that they did not understand meaning of the utterances and then it was rather difficult for them to decide which emotion they felt when having heard nonsense (from their point of view) sentences. It could be a reason of lower percentage of their successful determination of emotions when compared with the Czech and Slovak listeners.

Contradictory evaluation of the successful determination of the emotion type in some sentences of the testing corpus might be affected also by the fact that we have not always succeeded in selection of suitable sentences uttered in neutral speaking style without any emotion (best pronounced only by the storyteller), but the sentences used in the test were spoken also by different story characters (prince, king, tailor, etc.).

In our next research, we want to experiment with female voice emotion conversion using border frequency between the first and the second formant 840 Hz instead of 700 Hz for male voice, i.e. 20 % higher (Using the general knowledge of [9] that females have on average 20 % higher formant frequencies than males, we had been successful in voice conversion between male and female [19]).

Acknowledgments. The work has been done in the framework of the COST 2102 Action "Cross-Modal Analysis of Verbal and Non-Verbal Communication". It has also been supported by the Ministry of Education of the Slovak Republic

---

[1] However, quantitative comparison of these two approaches cannot be carried out directly considering the fact that in [18] the speech corpus for the listening test had been created by our text-to-speech system while our new developed method was tested on resynthesis of original speech of actors.

(COST2102/STU/08 – "Audio-Visual Representation of Emotional States") and the Ministry of Education, Youth, and Sports of the Czech Republic (OC08010 – "Emotional Speech Style Analysis, Modelling, and Synthesis").

The authors would also like to express thanks to all the people who participated in the listening test.

References

1. Scherer, K.R.: Vocal Communication of Emotion: A Review of Research Paradigms. Speech Communication 40, 227–256 (2003)
2. Nwe, T.L., Foo, S.W., De Silva, L.C.: Speech Emotion Recognition Using Hidden Markov Models. Speech Communication 41, 603–623 (2003)
3. Ververidis, D., Kotropoulos, C.: Emotional Speech Recognition: Resources, Features, and Methods. Speech Communication 48, 1162–1181 (2006)
4. Shami, M., Verhelst, W.: An Evaluation of the Robustness of Existing Supervised Machine Learning Approaches to the Classification of Emotions in Speech. Speech Communication 49, 201–212 (2007)
5. Tóth, S.L., Sztahó, D., Vicsi, K.: Speech Emotion Perception by Human and Machine. In: Esposito, A., Bourbakis, N.G., Avouris, N., Hatzilygeroudis, I. (eds.) Verbal and Nonverbal Features of Human-Human and Human-Machine Interaction. LNCS (LNAI), vol. 5042, pp. 213–224. Springer, Heidelberg (2008)
6. Murray, I.R., Arnott, J.L.: Applying an Analysis of Acted Vocal Emotions to Improve the Simulation of Synthetic Speech. Computer Speech and Language 22, 107–129 (2008)
7. Bänziger, T., Scherer, K.R.: The Role of Intonation in Emotional Expressions. Speech Communication 46, 252–267 (2005)
8. Vích, R.: Cepstral Speech Model, Padé Approximation, Excitation, and Gain Matching in Cepstral Speech Synthesis. In: Proceedings of Biosignal, Brno, pp. 77–82 (2000)
9. Fant, G.: Acoustical Analysis of Speech. In: Crocker, M.J. (ed.) Encyclopedia of Acoustics, pp. 1589–1598. John Wiley & Sons, Chichester (1997)
10. Fant, G.: Speech Acoustics and Phonetics. Kluwer Academic Publishers, Dordrecht (2004)
11. Laroche, J.: Time and Pitch Scale Modification of Audio Signals. In: Kahrs, M., Brandenburg, K. (eds.) Applications of Digital Signal Processing to Audio and Acoustics, pp. 279–309. Kluwer Academic Publishers, Dordrecht (2001)
12. Morrison, D., Wang, R., De Silva, L.C.: Ensemble Methods for Spoken Emotion Recognition in Call-Centres. Speech Communication 49, 98–112 (2007)
13. Dutilleux, P., Zölzer, U.: Filters. In: Zölzer, U. (ed.) DAFX – Digital Audio Effects, pp. 31–62. John Wiley & Sons, Chichester (2002)
14. Drioli, C., Tisato, G., Cosi, P., Tesser, F.: Emotions and Voice Quality: Experiments with Sinusoidal Modeling. In: Proceedings of Voice Quality, Geneva, pp. 127–132 (2003)
15. Hirose, K., Sato, K., Asano, Y., Minematsu, N.: Synthesis of F0 Contours Using Generation Process Model Parameters Predicted form Unlabeled Corpora: Application to Emotional Speech Synthesis. Speech Communication 46, 385–404 (2005)
16. Navas, E., Hernáez, I., Luengo, I.: An Objective and Subjective Study of the Role of Semantics and Prosodic Features in Building Corpora for Emotional TTS. IEEE Transactions on Audio, Speech, and Language Processing 14, 1117–1127 (2006)

17. Cabral, J.P., Oliveira, L.C.: EmoVoice: A System to Generate Emotions in Speech. In: Proceedings of Interspeech – ICSLP. pp. 1798–1801. Pittsburgh (2006)
18. Přibil, J., Přibilová, A.: Emotional Style Conversion in the TTS System with Cepstral Description. In: Esposito, A., Faundez-Zanuy, M., Keller, E., Marinaro, M. (eds.) COST Action 2102. LNCS (LNAI), vol. 4775, pp. 65–73. Springer, Heidelberg (2007)
19. Přibilová, A., Přibil, J.: Non-Linear Frequency Scale Mapping for Voice Conversion in Text-to-Speech System with Cepstral Description. Speech Communication 48, 1691–1703 (2006)

Comparison of Grapheme and Phoneme Based Acoustic Modeling in LVCSR Task in Slovak

Michal Mirilovič, Jozef Juhár, and Anton Čižmár

Department of Electronics and Multimedia Communication,
Technical University of Košice
{michal.mirilovic,jozef.juhar,anton.cizmar}@tuke.sk
http://kemt.fei.tuke.sk/

Abstract. Phonemes and allophones are the basic speech units for acoustic modeling in the majority of contemporary HMM based speech recognizers. Grapheme-based acoustic sub-word units were applied to multi-lingual and cross-lingual acoustic modeling in many tasks. Grapheme and phoneme based mono-, cross- and bilingual speech recognition of Czech and Slovak in the small and medium vocabulary task has been studied in our previous work. In this article we compare grapheme and phoneme based approach to acoustic modeling and model unit selection in large vocabulary continuous speech recognition (LVCSR) task in Slovak. The main goal of our experimental work is to investigate a possibility to select an optimal set of sub-word units for Slovak LVCSR system.

1 Introduction

In general, there are two common approaches to acoustic modeling for automatic speech recognition. The most frequent approach is based on *phonemes*, where each HMM represents different phoneme or phone. We distinguish *context dependent* and *context independent* models. Especially for LVCSR one of the most complicated tasks is phonetic transcription of lexicon words, which is hardly fully automatized because of many exceptions requiring partial expert approach.

Another approach, that occurs in the last years and issues from tight relation between orthographic and orthoepic description, is based on *graphemes*. This approach was applied for instance in hybrid phoneme-grapheme systems [1] [2] [3], multilingual speech recognition [4] [5], porting acoustic models from one language to another [6], building ASR systems for *under-resourced* languages [7] [8] [9], building ASR systems for languages with close grapheme-to-phoneme relation [10] and other [11] [12].

Experiments on different languages have shown that the quality of the resulting recognizer significantly depends on the grapheme-to-phoneme relation of the underlying language. Slovak language has a fairly close grapheme-to-phoneme relation. It should be well suited for grapheme based approach to acoustic modeling. In [13] a speech recognizer which used both phoneme and grapheme as sub-word units has been investigated. It has been shown that ASR using just

A. Esposito et al. (Eds.): Multimodal Signals, LNAI 5398, pp. 242–247, 2009.

grapheme as sub-word unit yields acceptable performance, which could be further improved by introducing phonetic knowledge in it.

We applied the phoneme and grapheme based approach to acoustic model training also in LVCSR task [14]. This preliminary comparison of phoneme and grapheme based acoustic models in LVCSR system gave us encouraging results. Grapheme based acoustic models were better in tests with higher order n-gram (bigram and trigram) language models (LM). These results were the reason for our continuing research in this area. Optimizing procedure of unit selection described in this paper is managed by pronunciation effects occurring in Slovak language (assimilation, palatalization, ...) and by their influence on word error rate and other errors of LVCSR system.

2   Basics of Slovak Orthoepy and Orthography

In basic Slovak orthoepy and orthography we have 46 graphemes and 53 phonemes. According to SAMPA phonetic alphabet Slovak phoneme set contains:

- 15 vowels and diphtongs
- 38 consonants (17 sonorants, 8 fricatives, 9 plosives, 4 affricates)

Tight relation between orthographic and orthoepic representation of speech is *typical* for Slovak language. The main differences between this two representations are in:

- *Softening*, where some Slovak consonants have a soft counterpart (c-č, d-ď, l-ĺ, n-ň, s-š, t-ť, z-ž, dz-dž) and in many cases hard consonants d,t,n,l are pronounced softly, depending on context (if they are followed by short and long form of i and e). Actually, there are rules with many exceptions.
- *Voice / unvoice assimilation*, where voiced consonants are pronounced as unvoiced if they are followed by unvoiced consonant and unvoiced consonants are pronounced as voiced if they are followed by voiced consonant. There are also rules with many exceptions.
- *Existence of two different graphemes with the same pronunciation*, where pairs: vowels i and y, liquids v and w and vowel ä (wide a) and e (in contemporary Slovak) have the same pronunciation.
- *Existence of two graphemes represent one phoneme and reversely*, where digraphemes dz, dž, ch represent single phonemes, single grapheme ô represents diphtong u o, single grapheme q represents phonemes k v and single grapheme x represents phonemes k s.

3   Experimental Setup

3.1   Levels of Phonetic Transcription

Based on these differences we made 5 levels of phonetic transcription:

1. *Zero level phonetic transcription.* At this level no phonetic transcription was applied.
2. *Basic level of phonetic transcription.* The following basic transcription rules were applied:
   - considering each digrapheme as one grapheme
   - considering y/i like one grapheme
   - considering q like two graphemes k v
3. *Middle level of phonetic transcription.* All rules from the basic level supplemented with the following softening rules were applied:
   - softening d, t, n, and l before e/i/í with exceptions
4. *Advanced level of phonetic transcription.* The assimilation rules were added to the middle level:
   - voiced (b d ď dz dž g h z ž v)/unvoiced (p t ť c č k ch s š f) assimilation
   - unvoiced (p t ť c č k ch s š f)/voiced (b d ď dz dž g h z ž v) assimilation
5. *Full phonetic transcription.* At this level all transcription rules were applied.

We started with grapheme based transcription and then we continuously added some transcription rules. Final level of transcription was full phonetic transcription (see procedure above).

3.2   Acoustic Modeling

Acoustic models were trained on SpeechDat-SK corpus. Training algorithms and procedures were implemented by the HTK tools and can be considered as standard. They come out from [15] and results to set of speaker independent crosswords triphones with 16 tied states. The training procedure consists of these steps:

1. *Embedded training* of context independent (CI) models (monophones). Result of this process were CI HMMs with increased Gaussian mixtures up to 32. Training was performed on acoustic data with word level transcription.
2. *Alignment* of phoneme borders. Result of this process were acoustic data with phone level transcription. Recognition was performed with CI HMMs with 32 Gaussian mixtures (step above).
3. *Isolated training* of CI models (monophones). Result of this process were new CI HMMs (without increase of Gaussian mixtures). Training was performed on acoustic data with new phone level transcription.
4. *Cross-word* context dependent (CD) models (triphones). Result of this process were new CD HMMs (without increase of Gaussian mixtures). These HMMs was made by the copying of previous CI HMMs and reestimation. Each CD HMM was copied from CI HMM according to its central phoneme.
5. *Decision tree* building and *tying* states. Result of this process were CD HMMs with tied states. Decision tree was build on a base of hand created phone/grapheme classes [13].
6. Increasing of *Gaussian mixtures* (16). Result of this final step were tied-state crossword CD HMMs with 16 Gaussian mixtures.

The SpeechDat family of corpora are more suitable for training and testing from small to medium vocabulary speech recognition systems. Nevertheless, each session (speaker) of the SpeechDat family also contains utterances: so-called *phonetically rich sentences*, which are usually used to initialize HMMs in the training process. Each utterance can be occurred in the whole corpus approximately from 1 to 10 times (never 2 times per same speaker). These utterances we used for LVCSR testing.

In case of LVCSR systems this option could be considered as not standard. In our case we used it because of absence of a more convenient speech corpus with sufficient amount of acoustic-phonetic data.

3.3 Language Modeling

Language model was trained on 2 corpora. The first one, Slovak National Corpus (SNC) [16] is an electronic database of Slovak linguistic resources, containing wide spectrum of language styles, genres, subject domains and additional linguistic information. The corpus version *prim-3.0* contains more than 350 millions words. It is publicly available since January 2007. It was built for linguistic purposes primarily. Despite of this, due to lack of other suitable linguistic data we used the SNC as a basic training corpus.

The second one, TUKE Text Corpus we are systematically collecting from Internet text resources in Slovak language by using a software tool developed for the purpose. The tool is written in Java and it is based on the RSS principle. It uses approximately 250 RSS channels and on average it collects 2.8 MB of text data per day. At the time of the experiments performing approximately 55 millions words were collected.

Both corpora were coupled together and used in LM training. Result of training process was bigram LM with 240k of unique words, smoothed by Knesser-Ney smoothing method. Lexicon words were selected according their occurrence in the training data.

4 Testing and Results

In the testing part of the experiment we used 1139 utterances (phonetically rich sentences) spoken by 200 speakers from the testing part of the SpeechDat-SK corpus. Speech recognition was performed by HTK tool HDecode with *maximum number of active models* set to 3072, *word end pruning* enabled and set to 50, *word insertion probability* set to -8.0, *grammar scale factor* set to 12 and *beam searching* enabled and set to 400.

Word error rate (WER) was computed between reference and hypothesis as:

$$WER = \frac{SUB + INS + DEL}{N} \tag{1}$$

where SUB is error by the substitution, INS is error by the insertion, DEL is error by the deletion and N is number of the words in the reference.

Results of the experiment are presented in the Fig. 1. The best result was reached on the HMM set with the middle level of phonetic transcription (30.786%).

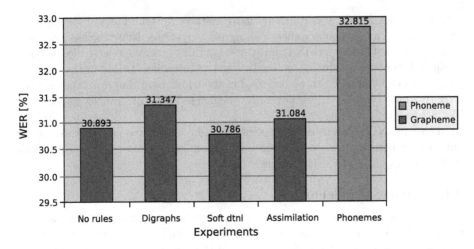

Fig. 1. Results

5   Conclusion

Experiments showed that graphemes-based LVCSR outperformed phoneme-based one. In all cases the error was *statistically spread*, so we did not see any regularity. It means, that linguistic information in language model was generally more important that acoustic one, coming from phonetic transcription. So far, we did not study this phenomenon more deeply, because our LVCSR system is *under-resourced* yet.

In the near future we need to continue in collecting acoustic and linguistic resources and working on better language model (e.g. morpheme based). Besides this we will study more deeply phenomenon of grapheme based speech recognition to use it for improving of our future ASR systems.

Acknowledgment

This work was supported by the Slovak Research and Development Agency under the contract No. APVV-0369-07 and by the Slovak Ministry of Education under contracts No. AV 4/0006/07 and AV 4/2016/08.

References

1. Schukat-Talamazzini, E.G., Niemann, H., Eckert, W., Kuhn, T., Rieck, S.: Automatic speech recognition without phonemes. In: Proceeding of the Eurospeech, Berlin, September 22-25, pp. 129–132 (1993)
2. Magimai-Doss, M., Stephenson, T.A., Bourlard, H., Bengio, S.: Phoneme-grapheme based speech recognition system. In: Proceedings of 2003 IEEE Workshop on Automatic Speech Recognition and Understanding, St. Thomas, U.S. Virgin Islands, November 30 - December 4, pp. 94–98 (2003)

3. Magimai-Doss, M., Bengio, S., Bourlard, H.: Joint decoding for phoneme-grapheme continuous speech recognition. In: Proceedings of ICASSP, Quebec, Kanada, May 17-21, pp. 177–180 (2004)
4. Kanthak, S., Ney, H.: Multilingual acoustic modeling using graphemes. In: Proceeding of the Eurospeech, Geneva, Switzerland, September 1-4, pp. 1145–1148 (2003)
5. Killer, M., Stüker, S., Schultz, T.: Grapheme based speech recognition. In: Proceeding of the Eurospeech, Geneva, Switzerland, September 1-4, pp. 3141–3144 (2003)
6. Schultz, T.: Towards rapid language portability of speech processing systems. In: Proceedings of the Conference on Speech and Language Systems for Human Communication, SPLASH 2004, Delhi, India, November 17-19 (2004)
7. Rubagotti, E.: Is it possible to train a speech recognition system on text only? In: Interspeech 2006 - ICSLP, Stellenbosch, South Africa, April 9-11 (2006)
8. Le, V.B., Besacier, L.: Comparison of acoustic modeling techniques for vietnamese and khmer asr. In: Interspeech 2006 - ICSLP, Pittsburgh, USA, September 17-21, pp. 129–132 (2006)
9. Charoenpornsawat, P., Hewavitharana, S., Schultz, T.: Thai grapheme-based speech recognition. In: Proc. of the HLT-NAACL, New York City, USA, June 5-7, pp. 17–20 (2006)
10. Stüker, S., Schultz, T.: A grapheme based speech recognition system for Russian. In: Proceedings of SPECOM 2004, Petersburgh, Russia, September 20-22 (2004)
11. Kanthak, S., Ney, H.: Context-dependent acoustic modeling using graphemes for large vocabulary speech recognition. In: Proceeding of the ICASSP, Orlando, Florida, May 13-17, pp. 845–848 (2002)
12. Schillo, C., Fink, G.A., Kummert, F.: Grapheme based speech recognition for large vocabularies. In: Proceeding of the ICSLP, Beijing, China, October 16-20, pp. 584–587 (2000)
13. Lihan, S., Juhár, J., Čižmár, A.: Comparison of Slovak and Czech speech recognition based on grapheme and phoneme acoustic models. In: Interspeech 2006 - ICSLP, Pittsburgh, USA, September 17-21, pp. 149–152 (2006)
14. Mirilovič, M., Juhár, J., Čižmár, A.: Large vocabulary continuous speech recognition in slovak. In: Proc. Int. Conf. on Applied Electrical Engineering and Informatics - AEI 2008, Greece, September 8-11 (2008)
15. Lindberg, B., Johansen, F.T., Warakagoda, N., Lehtinen, G., Kačič, Z., Žgank, A., Elenius, K., Salvi, G.: A noise robust multilingual reference recogniser based on SpeechDat(II). In: Proc. ICSLP 2000, Beijing, China, October 16-20, vol. 3, pp. 370–373 (2000)
16. Šimková, M.: Slovak national corpus history and current situation. In: Insight into the Slovak and Czech Corpus Linguistics, Veda, Bratislava, pp. 151–159 (2006)

Automatic Motherese Detection for Face-to-Face Interaction Analysis

A. Mahdhaoui[1], M. Chetouani[1], C. Zong[1], R.S. Cassel[2,3], C. Saint-Georges[2,3], M-C. Laznik[4], S. Maestro[5], F. Apicella[5], F. Muratori[5], and D. Cohen[2,3]

[1] Institut des Systèmes Intelligents et de Robotique, CNRS FRE 2507, Université Pierre et Marie Curie, Paris, France
[2] Department of Child and Adolescent Psychiatry, AP-HP, Groupe Hospitalier Pitié-Salpêtrière, Université Pierre et Marie Curie, Paris, France
[3] Laboratoire Psychologie et Neurosciences Cognitives, CNRS UMR 8189, Paris, France
[4] Department of Child and Adolescent Psychiatry, Association Santé Mentale du 13ème, Paris, France
[5] Scientific Institute Stella Maris, University of Pisa, Italy

Ammar.Mahdhaoui@robot.jussieu.fr, Mohamed.Chetouani@upmc.fr

Abstract. This paper deals with emotional speech detection in home movies. In this study, we focus on infant-directed speech also called "motherese" which is characterized by higher pitch, slower tempo, and exaggerated intonation. In this work, we show the robustness of approaches to automatic discrimination between infant-directed speech and normal directed speech. Specifically, we estimate the generalization capability of two feature extraction schemes extracted from supra-segmental and segmental information. In addition, two machine learning approaches are considered: k-nearest neighbors (k-NN) and Gaussian mixture models (GMM). Evaluations are carried out on real-life databases: home movies of the first year of an infant.

Keywords: motherese detection, feature and classifier fusion.

1 Introduction

Since more than 30 years, interest has been growing about family home movies of infants who will become autistic. Typically developing infants gaze at people, turn toward voices and express interest for communication. In contrast, infants who became autistic will be characterized by the presence of abnormalities in reciprocal social interactions and in patterns of communications [1]. In this paper, we focus on a verbal information which has been recently shown to be crucial for engaging interaction between the parent and infant. This verbal information is called "motherese" (also termed infant-directed speech) and it is a simplified language/dialect/register [2] that parents use spontaneously when speaking to their young baby. From an acoustic point of view, motherese has a clear signature (high

A. Esposito et al. (Eds.): Multimodal Signals, LNAI 5398, pp. 248–255, 2009.

pitch, exaggerated intonation contours). The phonemes, and particularly the vowels, are more clearly articulated. Motherese has been shown to be preferred by infants over adult-directed speech and might assist infants during the language acquisition process [3]. The exaggerated patterns facilitate the discrimination between the phonemes or sounds. Motherese plays also a major role during social interactions. However, even if motherese is clearly defined in terms of acoustic properties, the modeling and the detection are expected to be difficult which is the case of the majority of emotional speech. Indeed, the characterization of spontaneous and affective speech in terms of features is still an open question and several parameters have been proposed in the literature [4].

As a starting-point and following the definition of motherese [2], we characterized the verbal interactions by the extraction of supra-segmental features (prosody). However, segmental features are often used in speech segmentation. Consequently, the utterances are characterized by both segmental (short-time spectrum) and supra-segmental (statistics of fundamental frequency, energy and duration) features. These features aim at representing the verbal information for the next classification stage based on machine learning techniques.

This paper presents a framework for the study of parent-infant interaction during the first year of age focusing on the engagement produced by motherese, in normal infants or infants who will become autistic. To this purpose, we use a longitudinal case study methodology based on the analysis of home movies. We focus on a basic and crucial task namely the classification of verbal information as motherese or adult directed speech which implies the design of robust motherese detector. Section 2 presents the longitudinal corpora used. The proposed method is described in section 3 which needs specific attentions to the different stages: feature extraction, classification and decision fusion. The experiments performed are discussed in section 4. Finally, the conclusions and suggestions for further works are detailed in section 5.

2   Database

The speech corpus used in this experiment is a collection of natural and spontaneous interactions usually used for children development research (home movies). The corpus consists of recordings in Italian of mother and father as they addressed their infants. In addition, the analysis of home movies makes it possible to set up a longitudinal study (months or years) and gives information about early behaviors of autistic infants, a long time before the diagnostic would be made by the clinicians. However, this large corpus makes it inconvenient for people to review it. Also, the recordings are not done by professionals resulting in adverse conditions (noise, camera, microphones). We focus on one home video totaling 3 hours of data describing the first year of an infant. Verbal interactions of the mother have been carefully annotated by a psycholinguist on two categories: motherese and normal directed speech. From this manual annotation, we extracted 100 utterances for each class. The utterances are typically between 0.5s and 4s in length.

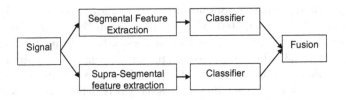

Fig. 1. Motherese classification system

3   System Description

This work aims at designing an automatic detection system for the analysis of parent-infant interaction. This system will provide an independent classification of the utterances. In order to improve the system, two different approaches have been investigated individually: segmental and supra-segmental. Figure 1 shows a schematic overview of the final system which is described in more details in the following paragraphs.

3.1   Feature Extraction

In this paper, we evaluate two approaches respectively termed as segmental and supra-segmental features. The first ones are characterized by the Mel Frequency Cepstrum Coefficients (MFCC) while the second ones are characterized by statistical measures of both the fundamental frequency (F0) and the short-time energy, these statistical measures are calculated from the voiced segments.For the computation of segmental features, a 20ms window is used, and the overlapping between adjacent frames is $1/2$. A parameterized vector of order 16 was computed. The supra-segmental features are characterized by 3 statistics (mean, variance and range) of both F0 and short-time energy resulting on a 6 dimensional vector. One should note that the duration of the acoustic events is not directly characterized as a feature but it is taken into account during the classification process by a weighting factor (eq. 5). The feature vectors are normalized (zero mean, unit standard deviation).

3.2   Classification

In this study, two different classifiers were investigated: k-NN and GMM. The k-NN classifier [6] is a distance based method while the GMM classifier [5] is a statistical model. For the fusion process, we adopted a common statistical framework for both the k-NN and the GMM by the estimation of a posteriori probabilities.

A Posteriori Probabilities Estimation. The Gaussian mixture model (GMM) [5] is adopted to represent the distribution of the features. Under the assumption that the feature vector sequence $x = \{x_1, x_2, ..., x_n\}$ is an independent identical distribution sequence, the estimated distribution of the d-dimensional feature vector x is a weighted sum of M component Gaussian densities $g_{(\mu, \Sigma)}$, each parameterized by a mean vector μ_i and covariance matrix Σ_i; the mixture density for the model C_m is defined as :

$$p(x|C_m) = \sum_{i=1}^{M} \omega_i g_{(\mu_i, \Sigma_i)}(x) \tag{1}$$

Each component density is a d-variate Gaussian function:

$$g_{(\mu, \Sigma)}(x) = \frac{1}{(2\pi)^{d/2}\sqrt{det(\Sigma)}} e^{-1/2(x-\mu)^T \Sigma^{-1}((x-\mu))} \tag{2}$$

The mixture weights ω_i satisfy the following constraint: $\sum_{i=1}^{M} \omega_i = 1$. The feature vector x is then modeled by the following posteriori probability:

$$p_{gmm}(C_m|x) = \frac{p(x|Cm)P(C_m)}{p(x)} = \frac{p(x|Cm)P(C_m)}{\sum_{j=1}^{2} p(x|C_j)P(C_j)} \tag{3}$$

where $P(Cm)$ is the prior probability for class Cm, we assume equal prior probabilities. We use the expectation maximization (EM) algorithm for the mixtures to get maximum likelihood.

The k-NN classifer [6] is a non-parametric technique which classifies the input vector with the label of the majority k-nearest neighbors (prototypes). In order to keep a common framework with the statistical classifier (GMM), we estimate the posteriori probability that a given feature vector x belongs to class C_m using k-NN estimation [6]:

$$p_{knn}(C_m|x) = \frac{k_m}{k} \tag{4}$$

where k_m denotes the number of prototypes which belong to the class C_m among the k nearest neighbors.

Segmental and Supra-Segmental Characterizations. Segmental features (i.e. MFCC) are extracted from all the frames of an utterance U_x independently of the voiced or unvoiced parts. Posteriori probabilities are then estimated by both GMM and k-NN classifiers and are respectively termed $P_{gmm,seg}(C_m|U_x)$ and $P_{knn,seg}(C_m|U_x)$.

The classification of supra-segmental features follows the segment-based approach (SBA)[7]. An utterance U_x is segmented into N voiced segments (F_{xi}) obtained by F0 extraction (cf. 3.1.). Local estimation of posteriori probabilities is carried out for each segment. The utterance classification combines the N local estimations.

$$P(C_m|U_x) = \sum_{x_i=1}^{N} P(C_m|F_{xi}) \times length(F_{xi}) \tag{5}$$

The duration of the segments is introduced as weights of the posteriori probabilities: importance of the voiced segment $(length(F_{xi}))$. The estimation is also carried out by the two classifiers resulting on supra-segmental characterizations: $P_{gmm,supra}(C_m|U_x)$ and $P_{knn,supra}(C_m|U_x)$.

3.3   Fusion

The segmental and supra-segmental characterizations provide different temporal information and a combination of them should improve the accuracy of the detector. Many decision techniques can be employed [9] but we investigated a simple weighted sum of likelihoods from the different classifiers:

$$C_l = \lambda.log(P_{seg}(C_m|U_x)) + (1 - \lambda).log(P_{supra}(C_m|U_x)) \qquad (6)$$

With $l = 1$ (motherese) or 2 (normal directed speech). λ denotes the weighting coefficient. For the GMM classifier, the likelihoods can be easily computed from the posteriori probabilities $(P_{gmm,seg}(C_m|U_x),\ P_{gmm,supra}(C_m|U_x))$ [5]. However, the k-NN estimation can produce a null posteriori probability (eq. 4) incompatible with the computation of the likelihood. We used a solution recently tested by Kim et al. [8], which consists in using the posteriori probability instead of the log probability of the k-NN:

$$C_l = \lambda.log(e^{P_{knn,seg}(C_m|U_x)}) + (1 - \lambda).log(P_{gmm,supra}(C_m|U_x)) \qquad (7)$$

Table 1. Table of combinations

$Comb_1$	$P_{knn,seg}$	$P_{knn,supra}$
$Comb_2$	$P_{gmm,seg}$	$P_{gmm,supra}$
$Comb_3$	$P_{knn,seg}$	$P_{gmm,supra}$
$Cpmb_4$	$P_{gmm,seg}$	$P_{knn,supra}$
$Comb_5$	$P_{gmm,seg}$	$P_{knn,seg}$
$Comb_6$	$P_{gmm,supra}$	$P_{knn,supra}$

Consequently, for the k-NN classifier we used equation 7 while for the GMM the likelihood is conventionally computed. We investigated cross combinations listed in table 1.

4   Experimental Results

4.1   Classifier Configuration

To find the optimal structure of our classifiers, we adjust the different parameters: the number of Gaussian (M) for GMM classifier and the number of neighbors (k) for the k-NN classifier. Table 2 shows the best configuration for both GMM and k-NN classifiers with segmental and supra-segmental features, the

Table 2. Accuracy of optimal configurations

	segmental	supra-segmental
k-nn	72.5% (k=11)	61% (k=7)
GMM	79.5% (M=15)	82% (M=16)

same table shows that GMM classifier trained with prosody features outperforms the other classifiers confirming the definition of motherese [2].

4.2 Fusion of Best Systems

To evaluate the system performance we used the receiver operating characteristic (ROC) methodology [6]. A ROC curve (Fig. 2) represents the tradeoff between the true positives (TPR = true positive rate) and false positives (FPR = false positive rate) of as the classifier output threshold value is varied. Two quantitative measures of verification performance, the equal error rate (EER) and the area under ROC curve (AUC), were calculated. It should be noted that while EER represents the performance of a classifier at only one operating threshold, the AUC represents the overall performance of the classifier over the entire range of thresholds. Hence, we employed AUC and not EER for comparing the verification performance of two classifiers and their combination. However, the result obtained in table 2 motivates an investigation on fusion of both features and classifiers following the statistical approach described in section §3.2. The combination of features and classifiers is known to be efficient [9]. However, one

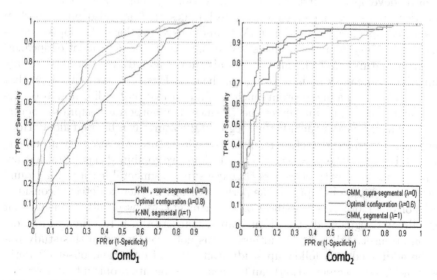

Fig. 2. ROC curves for $Comb_1$ $(k - NN_{(seg,supra)})$ and $Comb_2$ $(GMM_{(seg,supra)})$

Table 3. Optimal cross-combinations

Fusion	$Comb_1$		$Comb_2$		$Comb_3$		$Comb_4$		$Comb_5$		$Comb_6$	
	(K=1,K=11)		(M=12,M=15)		(M=12,K=11)		(K=1,M=15)		(K=11,M=12)		(K=5,M=16)	
λ	0.8	0.9	0.6	0.8	0.9	0.7	0.5	0.6	0.9	0.7	0.5	0.4
AUC	0,813	0,812	0,932	0.922	0,913	0.905	0,846	0.845	0,845	0.849	0,897	0.895
EER (%)	26	29	12	19	13	16	22	22	25	24	16	14

should be careful because the fusion of best configurations does not always give best results since the efficiency will depend on errors produced by the classifiers (independent vs dependent) [9]. Table 1 and section §3.3 show that 6 different fusion schemes can be investigated ($Comb_1$ to $Comb_6$) and for each of them we optimized classifiers (k,M) and weighting λ (eq. 6) parameters. In table 3 and figure 2 (Fig. 2) we can see that for the k-NN classifier, best scores (0,813/0,812) are obtained with an important contribution of the segmental features ($\lambda = 0.8$) which is in agreement with the results obtained without the fusion (table 2). The best GMM results (0,932/0,922) are obtained with a weighting factor equals to 0.6 revealing a balance between the two features. Despite that motherese is characterized by prosody, we showed that is interesting to combine the acoustic and prosodic features, also the fusion of two classifiers increased the performance of detection.

5   Conclusions

we have developed a first motherese detection system tested in a speaker-dependent mode. Using classification techniques that are also often used in speech and speaker recognition (GMM and k-NN) we have developed motherese detection system and we have tested them on mode dependent of speaker. Fusion of features and classifiers were also investigated. We obtained results from which we can draw interesting conclusions. Firstly, our results show that segmental features alone contain much useful information for discrimination between motherese and adult direct speech since they outperform supra segmental feature. Thus, we can conclude that segmental features can be used alone. However according to our detection results, prosodic features are also very promising features. Based on the previous two conclusions, we combined classifiers that use segmental features with classifiers that use supra-segmental features and found that this combination improves the performance of motherese detector considerably. For our motherese classification experiments, we used only segments that were already segmented (based on human transcription). In other words, detection of onset and offset of motherese was not investigated in this study but can be addressed in a follow-up study. Detection of onset and offset of motherese (motherese segmentation) can be seen as a separate problem that gives rise to other interesting questions such as how to define the beginning and end of motherese, and what kind of evaluation measures to use.

References

1. Muratori, F., Maestro, S.: Autism as a downstream effect of primary difficulties in intersubjectivity interacting with abnormal development of brain connectivity. International Journal for Dialogical Science Fall 2(1), 93–118 (2007)
2. Fernald, A., Kuhl, P.: Acoustic determinants of infant preference for Motherese speech. Infant Behavior and Development 10, 279–293 (1987)
3. Kuhl, P.K.: Early language acquisition: Cracking the speech code. Nature Reviews Neuroscience 5, 831–843 (2004)
4. Schuller, B., Batliner, A., Seppi, D., Steidl, S., Vogt, T., Wagner, J., Devillers, L., Vidrascu, L., Amir, N., Kessous, L., Aharonson, V.: The relevance of feature type for the automatic classification of emotional user states: low level descriptors and functionals. In: Proceedings of Interspeech, pp. 2253–2256 (2007)
5. Reynolds, D.: Speaker identification and verification using Gaussian mixture speaker models. Speech Communication 17, 91–108 (1995)
6. Duda, R., Hart, P., Stork, D.: Pattern Classification, 2nd edn (2000)
7. Shami, M., Verhelst, W.: An Evaluation of the Robustness of Existing Supervised Machine Learning Approaches to the Classification of Emotions. Speech. Speech Communication 49(3), 201–212 (2007)
8. Kim, S., Georgiou, P., Lee, S., Narayanan, S.: Real-time emotion detection system using speech: Multi-modal fusion of different timescale features. In: IEEE International Workshop on Multimedia Signal Processing (October 2007)
9. Kuncheva, I.: Combining pattern classifiers: Methods & algorithms. Wiley, Chichester (2004)
10. http://www.nist.gov/speech/tools/

Recognition of Emotions in German Speech Using Gaussian Mixture Models

Martin Vondra and Robert Vích

Institute of Photonics and Electronics, Academy of Sciences of the Czech Republic
Chaberská 57, CZ 18251 Prague 8, Czech Republic
{vich,vondra}@ufe.cz

Abstract. The contribution describes experiments with recognition of emotions in German speech signal based on the same principle as recognition of speakers. The most robust algorithm for speaker recognition is based on Gaussian Mixture Models (GMM). We examine three parameter sets: the first contains suprasegmental features, in the second are segmental features and the last is a combination of the two previous parameter sets. Further we want to explore the dependency of the classification accuracy on the number of GMM model components. The aim of this contribution is a recommendation for the number of GMM components and the optimal selection of speech parameters for emotion recognition in German speech.

Keywords: speech emotions, emotion recognition, Gaussian mixture models.

1 Introduction

Automatic dialogue systems with automatic speech recognition and speech synthesis suffer particularly from lack of emotional intelligence. It seems to be very important to incorporate for more natural interaction of these systems also the recognition of emotions and emotional speech synthesis.

Emotions in human speech are conveyed by complex intentional and unintentional changes of basic speech patterns given primarily by suprasegmental speech characteristics. These parameters are influenced e.g. by the individuality of the speaker, by the language etc.

At present there are no established methods for emotion recognition. In this paper we use a statistical classifier based on Gaussian Mixture Models (GMM) [1], which are commonly used for speaker recognition. Because we don't know which speech parameters characterize emotion in speech, we formulate three sets of speech parameters for the GMM classifier and evaluate the recognition score. Another issue is the optimal number of GMM components for robust emotion classification. For this reason we test also the dependency of the number of GMM components on the recognition score.

In Section 2 the configuration of the experiments is presented. The used emotional speech database, the speech parameter sets, and GMMs are described. The Section 3 describes the results of the experiments, which are represented by the percentage of correctly classified emotional sentences and by the confusion matrices. Section 4 summarizes the achieved results.

A. Esposito et al. (Eds.): Multimodal Signals, LNAI 5398, pp. 256–263, 2009.

2 Configuration of Experiment

2.1 Speech Database

For this experiment the German emotional speech database [2] was used. It contains 7 simulated emotions (anger, boredom, disgust, fear, joy, neutral, and sadness), simulated by 10 actors (5 male, 5 female) and 10 sentences (5 short, 5 longer). The complete database was evaluated in a perception test by the authors of the database. Utterances, for which the emotion with which they were spoken, were recognized better than 80% and judged as natural by more than 60% of the listeners, were used for the experiment. The speech material used for our experiment contains 535 utterances. The structure of the used speech material is summarized in Table 1.

Table 1. Structure of the German emotional speech database

Emotions	Number of utterances	Total time [min]
Anger	127	5.59
Boredom	81	3.75
Disgust	46	2.57
Fear	69	2.57
Joy	71	3.01
Neutral	79	3.11
Sadness	62	4.19

The test was performed as cross validated and speaker independent. Configuration of training and testing sets are obvious from Table 2. Speakers are marked by numbers, which mean:

03 – male speaker,
08 – female speaker,
09 – female speaker,
10 – male speaker,
11 – male speaker,
12 – male speaker,
13 – female speaker,
14 – female speaker,
15 – male speaker,
16 – female speaker.

The results for all speakers and all sentences were accomplished in three iterations by changing the speaker groups for training and testing.

Table 2. Configuration of cross validated training and testing sets

Step		Emotion	Training set	Testing set
1	Speakers		10, 11, 12, 13, 14, 15, 16	03, 08, 09
	Number of utterances and total time	Anger	88 utt., 3.91 min.	39 utt., 1.68 min.
		Boredom	62 utt., 2.84 min.	19 utt., 0.91 min.
		Disgust	37 utt., 2.06 min.	9 utt., 0.51 min.
		Fear	58 utt., 2.14 min.	11 utt., 0.43 min.
		Joy	49 utt., 2.13 min.	22 utt., 0.88 min.
		Neutral	49 utt., 1.89 min.	30 utt., 1.22 min.
		Sadness	42 utt., 2.74 min.	20 utt., 1.45 min.
2	Speakers		03, 08, 09, 10, 14, 15, 16	11, 12, 13
	Number of utterances and total time	Anger	92 utt., 4.03 min.	35 utt., 1.56 min.
		Boredom	58 utt., 2.66 min.	23 utt., 1.09 min.
		Disgust	34 utt., 1.95 min.	12 utt., 0.62 min.
		Fear	46 utt., 1.73 min.	23 utt., 0.84 min.
		Joy	51 utt., 2.10 min.	20 utt., 0.91 min.
		Neutral	57 utt., 2.23 min.	22 utt., 0.88 min.
		Sadness	46 utt., 3.10 min.	16 utt., 1.09 min.
3	Speakers		03, 08, 09, 11, 12, 13	10, 14, 15, 16
	Number of utterances and total time	Anger	74 utt., 3.24 min.	53 utt., 2.35 min.
		Boredom	42 utt., 2.00 min.	39 utt., 1.75 min.
		Disgust	21 utt., 1.14 min.	25 utt., 1.43 min.
		Fear	34 utt., 1.27 min.	35 utt., 1.30 min.
		Joy	42 utt., 1.79 min.	29 utt., 1.22 min.
		Neutral	52 utt., 2.10 min.	27 utt., 1.01 min.
		Sadness	36 utt., 2.54 min.	26 utt., 1.65 min.

2.2 Speech Parameters

For our experiment we have chosen three parameter sets. The parameters were computed for short-time speech frames similarly as in speech recognition – one feature vector for each short-time frame. Frame length was set to 25ms with frame shift 10ms. The parameter sets for training of GMMs were obtained by concatenation of feature vectors from all training sentences. This parameterization for emotion recognition is somewhat different from the experiment described e.g. in [3], where global parameters from each utterance are used, e.g. the mean, maximum and minimum values of F0, the maximum steepness and dispersion of F0, etc. We believe that these characteristics are covered in our parameter sets and can be caught by the GMM model.

Our first parameter set contains only suprasegmental features – the fundamental frequency (F0) and the intensity contours. We use the mean subtracted natural logarithm of these parameters. The second parameter set contains only segmental features – 12 mel-frequency cepstral coefficients (MFCC). We do not use mean subtraction of

MFCC. The last parameter set contains the combination of the first and second parameter sets, i.e. the F0 and intensity contours and 12 MFCCs. In each parameter set also the delta and delta-delta coefficients of basic parameters were added.

For F0 estimation the wavesurfer [5] script was used. In unvoiced parts of speech F0 was replaced by piecewise cubic Hermite interpolation (see Matlab function "pchip"). For MFCC computation the Matlab voicebox toolbox [6] was used.

2.3 Gaussian Mixture Models

For recognition of emotions we use GMMs with full covariance matrix [1]. The GMM modeling was implemented in C programming language. For training of GMMs we used the Expectation Maximization (EM) algorithm with 10 iteration steps. The iteration stop based on the difference between the previous and actual probabilities has shown to be uneffective, because the magnitude value depends on the number of training data and we have found out that relative probability in the training has a very similar behavior for different input data. For several initial iterations the probability that GMM parameters belong to training data steeply grows up, then becomes less and after 8 to 10 iterations the probability reaches the limit value. For initialization Vector Quantization (VQ) – K-means algorithm was used.

3 Results

Based on test results a proper number of GMM components is the crucial factor for good recognition score, see Fig. 1. For our tests the optimal number of GMM components has to be selected for the used parameter set. It seems to be convenient to use a smaller number of GMM components (about 4 to 8) than it is used for recognition of speakers (32 and more). In Tables 3, 4, 5 and 6 the confusion matrices are shown, which represent the dependency of classification on the number of GMM components for the third parameter set containing F0, intensity and MFCC.

The values in the confusion matrices (Table 3, 4, 5 and 6) represent the percentage of marked emotional sentences by the GMM classifier as emotions in the top line versus the number of emotional sentences for emotions in the left column. The correctly classified emotions are on the main diagonal of the matrix and the others are the confusions. From the confusion matrices for different numbers of GMM components (Table 3, 4, 5 and 6) it can be seen that if the number of GMM components is growing, the recognition of anger rises, but the recognitions of other emotions fall down (particularly fear, disgust and joy). It is clear that for a greater number of GMM components more confusion occurs.

The dependency of the classification score on parameter sets, when the number of GMM components is constant, is depicted in Fig. 2. It can be seen that a greater parameter set contributes to better recognition score, but the dependency is not as strong as for the number of GMM components (compare with Fig. 1). A more detailed view offers the confusion matrices given in Tables 7, 8 and 9.

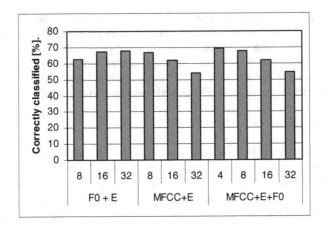

Fig. 1. Dependency of correctly classified emotions on the number of GMM components and used parameters

Table 3. Confusion matrix for 4 GMM components

	Anger	Boredom	Disgust	Fear	Joy	Neutral	Sadness
Anger	**84.25**	0.00	1.57	0.79	12.60	0.79	0.00
Boredom	1.23	**75.31**	11.11	0.00	0.00	3.70	8.64
Disgust	4.35	0.00	**71.74**	0.00	10.87	8.70	4.35
Fear	13.04	1.45	4.35	**30.43**	26.09	15.94	8.70
Joy	28.17	0.00	5.63	1.41	**60.56**	4.23	0.00
Neutral	0.00	18.99	10.13	1.27	0.00	**65.82**	3.80
Sadness	0.00	8.06	0.00	3.23	0.00	0.00	**88.71**

Table 4. Confusion matrix for 8 GMM components

	Anger	Boredom	Disgust	Fear	Joy	Neutral	Sadness
Anger	**94.49**	0.00	0.00	0.79	4.72	0.00	0.00
Boredom	2.47	**64.20**	11.11	0.00	0.00	17.28	4.94
Disgust	19.57	4.35	**56.52**	0.00	10.87	8.70	0.00
Fear	30.43	0.00	1.45	**28.99**	13.04	18.84	7.25
Joy	39.44	0.00	4.23	4.23	**49.30**	2.82	0.00
Neutral	1.27	10.13	11.39	0.00	0.00	**73.42**	3.80
Sadness	0.00	9.68	3.23	3.23	0.00	0.00	**83.87**

Table 5. Confusion matrix for 16 GMM components

	Anger	Boredom	Disgust	Fear	Joy	Neutral	Sadness
Anger	**98.43**	0.00	0.00	0.00	1.57	0.00	0.00
Boredom	4.94	**62.96**	3.70	0.00	2.47	19.75	6.17
Disgust	36.96	0.00	**28.26**	0.00	15.22	15.22	4.35
Fear	43.48	0.00	0.00	**14.49**	14.49	18.84	8.70
Joy	56.34	0.00	0.00	1.41	**42.25**	0.00	0.00
Neutral	3.80	18.99	5.06	0.00	5.06	**64.56**	2.53
Sadness	0.00	9.68	0.00	4.84	0.00	0.00	**85.48**

Table 6. Confusion matrix for 32 GMM components

	Anger	Boredom	Disgust	Fear	Joy	Neutral	Sadness
Anger	**100.00**	0.00	0.00	0.00	0.00	0.00	0.00
Boredom	12.35	**54.32**	0.00	0.00	2.47	23.46	7.41
Disgust	54.35	0.00	**17.39**	0.00	10.87	13.04	4.35
Fear	59.42	0.00	0.00	**5.80**	11.59	14.49	8.70
Joy	80.28	0.00	0.00	1.41	**18.31**	0.00	0.00
Neutral	10.13	25.32	1.27	0.00	3.80	**55.70**	3.80
Sadness	0.00	11.29	0.00	3.23	0.00	0.00	**85.48**

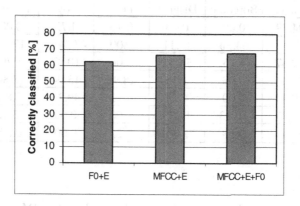

Fig. 2. Dependency of correctly classified emotions on parameter sets for 8 GMM components

Table 7. Confusion matrix for F0 and intensity parameter set and 8 GMM components

	Anger	Boredom	Disgust	Fear	Joy	Neutral	Sadness
Anger	**55.12**	0.00	6.30	3.94	33.86	0.79	0.00
Boredom	0.00	**83.95**	3.70	1.23	1.23	6.17	3.70
Disgust	0.00	6.52	**50.00**	10.87	10.87	6.52	15.22
Fear	10.14	4.35	13.04	**47.83**	11.59	10.14	2.90
Joy	19.72	0.00	4.23	8.45	**67.61**	0.00	0.00
Neutral	1.27	15.19	8.86	13.92	5.06	**51.90**	3.80
Sadness	0.00	1.61	4.84	0.00	3.23	6.45	**83.87**

Table 8. Confusion matrix for MFCC parameter set and 8 GMM componets

	Anger	Boredom	Disgust	Fear	Joy	Neutral	Sadness
Anger	**92.91**	0.00	0.00	0.00	7.09	0.00	0.00
Boredom	2.47	**66.67**	12.35	0.00	0.00	12.35	6.17
Disgust	17.39	4.35	**54.35**	2.17	10.87	8.70	2.17
Fear	27.54	2.90	1.45	**24.64**	18.84	17.39	7.25
Joy	39.44	0.00	2.82	5.63	**49.30**	2.82	0.00
Neutral	1.27	15.19	6.33	2.53	2.53	**69.62**	2.53
Sadness	0.00	9.68	0.00	4.84	0.00	0.00	**85.48**

Table 9. Confusion matrix for MFCC, F0 and intensity parameter set and 8 GMM components

	Anger	Boredom	Disgust	Fear	Joy	Neutral	Sadness
Anger	**94.49**	0.00	0.00	0.79	4.72	0.00	0.00
Boredom	2.47	**64.20**	11.11	0.00	0.00	17.28	4.94
Disgust	19.57	4.35	**56.52**	0.00	10.87	8.70	0.00
Fear	30.43	0.00	1.45	**28.99**	13.04	18.84	7.25
Joy	39.44	0.00	4.23	4.23	**49.30**	2.82	0.00
Neutral	1.27	10.13	11.39	0.00	0.00	**73.42**	3.80
Sadness	0.00	9.68	3.23	3.23	0.00	0.00	**83.87**

4 Conclusion

If we summarize the results, we can state that the number of GMM components must be optimally adjusted for the used parameter set. The parameter set is not such an important factor, but the number of used parameters has a main impact on computational requirements. It seems to be convenient to use mainly suprasegmental parameters, because the correctly classified emotions based on these parameters only are quite high compared to the classification based only on segmental parameters. The best classification score was achieved for the combination of segmental and suprasegmental parameters and for the GMM model with 4 components.

The best recognized emotions were mostly anger and sadness, followed by boredom and neutral. More difficult were disgust and joy and the most difficult seems to be fear. Joy generates most confusion and is recognized as anger, and fear is recognized as anger. This can be influenced by the used speech database which is not balanced. A similar tendency of results was also achieved in classifications accomplished in [3], where the same emotional speech database was used. In [4] the database of emotional speech of Mandarin and Burmese speakers [7] with slightly different emotions was used and their results were for a different classification technique quite similar to ours. If we compare our results with results published in [3], we have achieved a slightly better recognition score for the optimal number of GMM components and for F0, intensity and MFCC parameter set. Some differences between our results and those in [3] can be found in confusions.

If we compare our results with the perception test made in [2] (where the recognition score of human listeners is above 80%) we can say that recognition of anger, sadness and in some cases of boredom approaches that of human listeners. For other emotions the described automatic recognition is much worse than that of human listeners.

Generally it can be said that the GMM classifier has a good differentiation property between emotions with high stimulation (anger, fear, disgust, joy) and between emotions with small stimulation (boredom, neutral, sadness), but shows poor differentiation between emotions with similar stimulation, like fear and anger. This can be given by very similar distributions of selected parameters, which can cause overlapping of GMM models. Therefore our future work will focus on finding parameters which would have appropriate distributions for better separation by the classifier.

Acknowledgement. This work was supported within the framework of COST2102 by the Ministry of Education, Youth and Sport of the Czech Republic, project number OC08010.

References

1. Reynolds, D.A.: Speaker identification and verification using Gaussian mixture speaker models. Speech Communication 17, 91–108 (1995)
2. Burkhardt, F., Paeschke, A., Rolfes, M., Sendlmeier, W., Weiss, B.: A Database of German Emotional Speech. In: Proc. Interspeech 2005, Lisbon, Portugal, September 4-8 (2005)
3. Truong, K.P., Leeuwen, D.A.: An 'open-set' detection evaluation methology for automatic emotion recognition in speech. In: ParaLing 2007: Workshop on Paralinguistic Speech - between models and data, Saarbrücken, Germany (2007)
4. Morrison, D., Wang, R., De Silva, L.C.: Ensemble methods for spoken emotion recognition in call-centers. Speech Communication 49 (2007)
5. Sjölander, K., Beskow, J.: Wavesurfer,
   http://www.speech.kth.se/wavesurfer/
6. Brookes, M.: VOICEBOX: Speech Processing Toolbox for MATLAB,
   http://www.ee.ic.ac.uk/hp/staff/dmb/voicebox/voicebox.html
7. Nwe, T.L., Foo, S.W., De Silva, L.C.: Speech emotion recognition using hidden markovov models. Speech Communication 41, 603–623 (2003)

Electroglottogram Analysis of Emotionally Styled Phonation

Peter J. Murphy[1] and Anne-Maria Laukkanen[2]

[1] Department of Electronic and Computer Engineering,
University of Limerick, Limerick, Ireland
peter.murphy@ul.ie
[2] Department of Speech Communication and Voice Research,
University of Tampere, Tampere, Finland
anne-maria.laukkanen@uta.fi

Abstract. Acoustic descriptors of emotional voice quality have traditionally been provided in terms of fundamental frequency (f0), amplitude and duration. These cues have formed the basis for numerous studies of the emotional content of voice signals. The present work examines additional factors that arise as a result of the underlying production mechanism. Specifically glottal characteristics of different emotionally styled voice types are examined using the electroglottogram signal. This preliminary study, using a single speaker, investigates a number of electroglottogram measures relating to closed quotient (closed time of the glottis/cycle length) and rate of contact at closure and opening for the sustained vowel /a/, produced when simulating the emotional states sad, tender, neutral, joy and anger. The results suggest that differences exist in terms of glottal attributes for a particular emotion.

1 Introduction

The study of emotion as expressed in speech has been examined in terms of fundamental frequency (f0), syllable duration and waveform intensity in a number of studies; a review of the literature is provided in [1]. Speaker-independent automatic recognition of emotion, using four or five emotions, has been reported to be in the range of 50%-60% accuracy [2]. A more fine-grained feature extraction, such as the analysis of glottal characteristics, may allow for an improved recognition rate. Relatively few studies have focussed on glottal attributes of emotional expression [3-8]. In the present study electroglottography is used to examine emotional content in the sustained vowel /a/.

2 Electroglottography

The electroglottogram (EGG) consists of two electrodes placed external to the larynx. A high frequency current is passed between the electrodes and the output signal varies depending on the impedance of the material between the electrodes. As the vocal folds vibrate they move through high impedance (glottis open) to low impedance (glottis closed) values. As the impedance decreases with contact the electroglottogram signal provides a measure of vocal fold contact [9,10] (Fig.1 – top row). The electroglottogram provides complimentary information to the glottal flow; the maximum

A. Esposito et al. (Eds.): Multimodal Signals, LNAI 5398, pp. 264–270, 2009.

in the electroglottogram occurs when contact is maximum while the maximum in the glottal flow occurs during the open phase. An important aspect of the EGG signal is that it is essentially free of supra-glottal acoustic influences, which can produce source–filter interaction, making glottal flow determination more difficult.

2.1 Measures Taken from the EGG Waveform

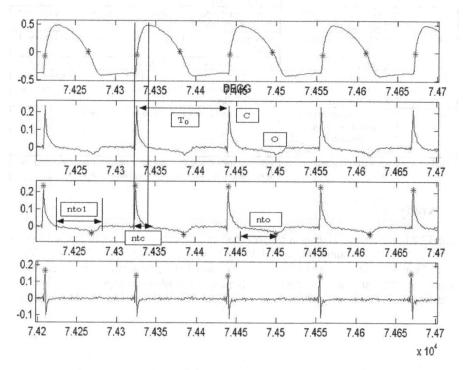

Fig. 1. EGG analysis (neutral phonation) (x-axis – sample number, y-axis amplitude - arbitrary units) top row EGG with (nearest sample to) zero crossing points indicated (negative to positive – red asterisk, positive to negative – black asterisk), 2nd row DEGG, 3rd row DEGG peaks at closure (red asterisk) and opening (black asterisk), 4th row D2EGG peak (red asterisk). Measure symbols (nto1 etc. are described in Table 1).

The following measures were extracted from the EGG signal.

Table 1. Measures estimated from the electroglottogram (EGG), first derivative of the electroglottogram (DEGG) and the second derivative of the electroglottogram (D2EGG) signals

Measure Symbol	Description	Method of Measurement
T_0	glottal cycle length	measured between points of glottal closure as determined from the positive peaks in the DEGG signal
f0	fundamental frequency	$1/T_0$
CQ	closed quotient – closed time of the glottis divided by cycle duration (T)	the closed time is measured from the positive peak to the negative peak in a glottal cycle of the DEGG signal

Table 1. (*Continued*)

CtQ	contacting quotient – contact time of the vocal folds divided by cycle duration	the contact time is measured from the beginning to end of contact
Vc	max. velocity of contact	max. positive peak amplitude occurring in a glottal cycle of the DEGG signal
Vo	max. negative velocity at opening	max. negative peak amplitude occurring in a glottal cycle of the DEGG signal
D2	acceleration of contact	max. peak in a glottal cycle cycle of the second derivative of EGG
SQ	speed quotient	Vc/Vo - velocity of closure divided by velocity of opening
ntc	normalised closing time - closing time divided by cycle length	closing time is measured from the beginning of contact – one sample point before the peak in D2EGG to the max point in the EGG signal
nto	normalised opening time – approximate opening time divided by cycle length	measured from peak in EGG to minimum in DEGG
nto1	normalised opening time one	opening time (including the final phase of opening after the minimum in the DEGG signal) divided by cycle length

3 Analysis

The EGG and speech signals were recorded in a sound treated room in the Department of Speech Communication and Voice Research, University of Tampere, Tampere, Finland. The sustained vowel /a/ was phonated while simulating the emotions angry, joy, neutral, sad and tender by a single speaker who was experienced in phonation types and emotional portrayals in voice. One hundred and thirty eight cycles of a

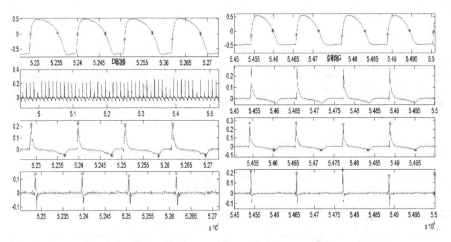

Fig. 2. EGG segment of emotions anger (left) and joy (right) (x-axis – sample number, y-axis amplitude - arbitrary units) top row EGG with zero crossing points indicated (negative to positive – red asterisk, positive to negative – black asterisk), 2nd row – first derivative of EGG (DEGG), 3rd row DEGG peaks at closure (red asterisk) and opening (black asterisk), 4th row – second derivative of EGG (D2EGG) peak (red asterisk)

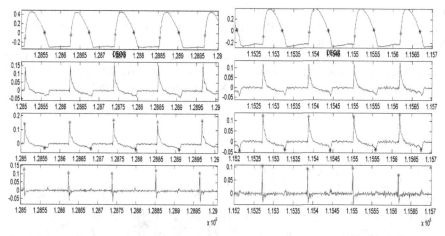

Fig. 3. EGG segment of emotions sad (left) and tender (right) (x-axis – sample number, y-axis amplitude - arbitrary units) top row EGG with zero crossing points indicated (negative to positive – red asterisk, positive to negative – black asterisk), 2nd row DEGG, 3rd row DEGG peaks at closure (red asterisk) and opening (black asterisk), 4th row D2EGG peak (red asterisk)

steady portion of the vowel were selected for analysis. The five emotions chosen have been analysed previously [3,4] and reflect positive and negative valence, and high and low psycho-physiological activity levels. Sadness and tenderness have low activity levels, while joy and anger have a high level of activity. Sadness and anger have negative valence while joy and tenderness represent positive valence. Fig.2 shows the electroglottogram and it's first and second derivatives for anger (left) and joy (right) while Fig.3 shows the same information for sad (left) and tender (right).

4   Results

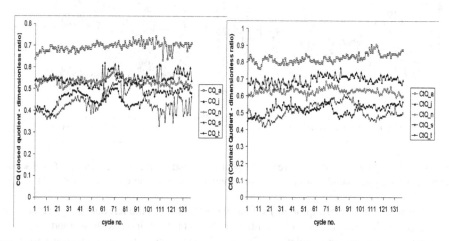

Fig. 4. (left) CQ (closed quotient) versus cycle number and right CtQ (contacting quotient) versus cycle number for the emotions anger (a), joy (j), neural (n), sad (s) and tender (t)

Fig.4 (left) shows closed quotient (CQ) and (right) contacting quotient (CtQ), versus cycle number. CtQ shows greater separability of the emotions. CQ is noticeably higher for the emotion anger.

Fig.5 (left) shows Vc (velocity of contact at closure) and (right) Vo (velocity of contact at opening) versus cycle number. Both indices show good data separability. Vc is highest for joy and lowest for tender, while Vo is highest for anger and lowest for tender.

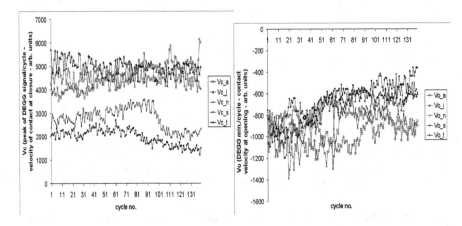

Fig. 5. (left) Vc (velocity of contact at closure) versus cycle number and right Vo (velocity of contact at opening) versus cycle number for the emotions anger (a), joy (j), neural (n), sad (s) and tender (t)

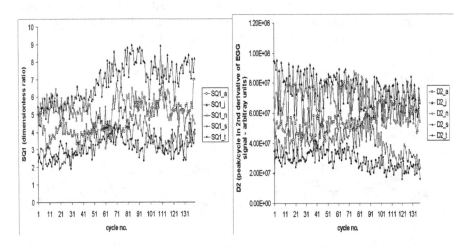

Fig. 6. (left) SQ (speed quotient-) versus cycle number and right D2 (acceleration of contact at closure) versus cycle number for the emotions anger (a), joy (j), neural (n), sad (s) and tender (t)

Fig.6 shows SQ (speed quotient) versus cycle number on the left and D2 (acceleration of contact at closure) versus cycle number on the right. Both indices show good discrimination between emotion simulations. SQ and D2 are highest for joy and lowest for tender. Each index is higher in neutral phonation than for angry phonation.

Table 2. Electroglottogram based measures averaged over 138 cycles

EGG Measure/ Emotion	f0	CQ	CtQ	Vc	Vo	SQ	D2	ntc	nto	nto1
Anger	180	**0.69**	0.82	**4547.6**	995.0	**4.68**	5.49E+07	**0.20**	0.51	**0.62**
Joy	178	**0.55**	0.70	**4940.6**	747.0	**6.84**	7.63E+07	**0.17**	0.40	**0.53**
Neutral	177	**0.53**	0.63	**4483.4**	860.0	**5.28**	6.88E+07	**0.14**	0.40	**0.48**
Sad	175	**0.44**	0.51	**2772.3**	796.0	**3.64**	4.04E+07	**0.17**	0.28	**0.34**
Tender	176	**0.46**	0.52	**1974.5**	648.0	**3.14**	2.85E+07	**0.15**	0.32	**0.37**

Table 2 summarised the average data for all measures. Normalised closing time and the normalised opening times are greatest for anger.

5 Discussion

Several electroglottogram measures show significant discriminatory ability. The results are discussed in terms of the underlying oscillatory mechanism. Contacting quotient (CtQ) is ordered as angry > joy > neutral > sad > tender. This suggests a more pressed phonatory mode for anger and a more lax configuration for sad and tender as expected. Joy is better separated from neutral using contacting quotient as opposed to contact quotient. This is because the final phase of opening (nto1-nto) is greater for joy. Speed quotient and acceleration of contact at closure are ordered as joy > neutral > angry > sad > tender. It is postulated that these values are less for anger because the more adducted glottal configuration does not allow for the vocal folds to develop to their full velocity when compared to a state of zero adduction. Normalised closing quotient did not provide clear separation of the emotions and was highest for anger. A previous study [3] examining the same emotions as those reported presently has shown that a measure of normalised glottal flow closing quotient did not provide statistically significant separation of neutral and anger simulations. It should be noted that EGG and glottal flow measures of closing quotient are not directly comparable.

6 Conclusion

Several features extracted from the EGG signal show promise for the automatic recognition of emotion e.g. contacting quotient, speed quotient and acceleration at closure distinguish between the different emotions. Future work will involve a more detailed statistical analysis with more speakers and will include a recognition task.

Acknowledgements

The recording and initial analysis development was performed during a COST 2103 (Advanced Voice Function Assessment) supported short-term scientific mission to the Department of Speech Communication and Voice Research, University of Tampere, Tampere, Finland in December, 2007.

References

1. Murray, I.R., Arnott, J.L.: Toward a simulation of emotion in synthetic speech: A review of the literature on human vocal emotion. J. Acoust. Soc. Am. 93, 1097–1108 (1993)
2. McGilloway, S., Cowie, R., Douglas-Cowie, E., Gielen, S., Westerdijk, M., Stroeve, S.: Approaching automatic recognition of emotion from voice: a rough benchmark. In: Proceedings of the ISCA workshop on Speech and Emotion (Belfast), pp. 207–212 (2000)
3. Airas, M., Alku, P.: Emotions in vowel segments of continuous speech: analysis of the glottal flow using the normalized amplitude quotient. Phonetica 63, 26–46 (2006)
4. Toivanen, J., Waaramaa, T., Alku, P., Laukkanen, A.-M., Seppänen, T., Väyrynen, E., Airas, M.: Emotions in [a]: A perceptual and acoustic study. Logopedics Phoniatrics Vocology 31, 43–48 (2006)
5. Gobl, C., Ní Chasaide, A.: The role of voice quality in communicating emotion, mood and attitude. Speech Communication 40, 189–212 (2003)
6. Johnstone, T., Scherer, K.: The effects of emotion on voice quality. In: Intl. Conf. Phonetic Sci. (1998)
7. Laukkanen, A.-M., Vilkman, E., Alku, P., Oksanen, H.: Physical variations related to stress and emotional state: a preliminary study. J. Phonetics 24, 313–335 (1996)
8. Cummings, K.E., Clements, M.A.: Analysis of the glottal excitation of emotionally styled and stressed speech. J. Acoust. Soc. Am. 98, 88–98 (1995)
9. Baken, R.J.: Electroglottography. J. Voice 6, 98–110 (1992)
10. Fourcin, A., Abberton, E., Miller, D., Howells, D.: Laryngograph: Speech pattern element tools for therapy, training and assessment. Eur. J. Disord. Commun. 30, 101–115 (1995)

Emoticonsciousness

Carl Vogel* and Jerom F. Janssen

Computational Linguistics Group, O'Reilly Institute,
Trinity College Dublin, Dublin 2, Ireland
{vogel,janssenj}@tcd.ie

Abstract. A temporal analysis of emoticon use in Swedish, Italian, German and English asynchronous electronic communication is reported. Emoticons are classified as positive, negative or neutral. Postings to newsgroups over a 66 week period are considered. The aggregate analysis of emoticon use in newsgroups for science and politics tends on the whole to be consistent over the entire time period. Where possible, events that coincide with divergences from trends in language-subject pairs are noted. Political discourse in Italian over the period shows marked use of negative emoticons, and in German and Swedish, positive emoticons.

Keywords: emoticons, intercultural analysis, extra-linguistic cues.

1   Introduction

It has been noted of conversation that in different linguistic communities, verbal and nonverbal feedback patterns vary. In a comparison of verbal interactions between Swedish and Italian interlocutors [4] it has been recorded that there is far more likely to be overlap of primary dialog contributions in Italian than in Swedish, and conversely longer pauses between turns in Swedish conversations than Italian. With respect to nonverbal communication, it is noted that Japanese and Swedish cultures exhibit less eye contact than typical Greek communications, although perhaps with different associations with eye contact between Japanese and Swedish cultures, and instead employ greater levels of verbal than visual feedback [1]. A question then arises about what communication patterns will emerge in communicative settings that lack an auditory channel, but whose visual channel is still primarily linguistic, through reading.

Other recent work uses emoticons to classify overall sentiment of documents [10,12,8] or to associate emoticons with words in texts [9]. The work reported here constitutes our initial experiments in attempting to analyze inter-cultural differences in emoticon use. One comparable study is a within-culture analysis of emoticon use which addresses the differences in emoticon use in online discussions in Greek, depending upon whether the forum [13] has access to the Greek alphabet or is confined to a Roman alphabet. Other work examines comparable

---

* This research is supported by Science Foundation Ireland RFP 05/RF/CMS002. We are grateful to anonymous reviewers for constructive critique of an earlier version of this paper, but take full responsibility for the content of this version, errors and all.

A. Esposito et al. (Eds.): Multimodal Signals, LNAI 5398, pp. 271–287, 2009.

online prose [11], and forms demographic generalizations about blog postings (e.g. teenage bloggers tend to be women; older bloggers, men, etc; more personal blogging among women, and more blogging on science and technology by men; etc.) taking into account features like inclusion of URLs (this propensity increases with age), but not emoticon use and not with an inter-cultural dimension. In contrast, other recent work has examined gender presentation in Italian and Chilean chat rooms [5], specifically identifying significant differences in emoticon use cross-culturally. While there are related studies, the analysis of inter-cultural differences in expressing sentiment using emoticons in on-line asynchronous communication is in its infancy.

In this paper, we examine informal written communication in electronic media. We focus on the forums for asynchronous exchange provided by Usenews groups. Emoticons are analyzed as a sort of non-linguistic visual feedback mechanism in written media. We want to know whether intercultural differences in verbal and non-verbal feedback from other media transfer to asynchronous electronic communication. Recently, an analysis of emoticon use in this context has been described [6]. The results presented there considered about 400,000 postings from late September 2006 to the end of December 2007 in four linguistic communities: German, Italian, Swedish and English. Two topic areas were analyzed: science and politics. With respect to politics, the Swedish discussion was more likely to include positive emoticons than negative or neutral emoticons, and the Italian postings were more likely to include negative emoticons than the others. Discussions in science newsgroups showed more positive emoticons than anything else for German, Italian and English, and more neutral emoticons for Swedish. The results presented in §2 summarize the research methods and findings from past analysis [6]. The classification of emoticons as conveying positive, negative or ambiguous sentiment was based on only our own judgments. This is expanded to address group classification of the emoticons using two different methods. The main result persists in that the Italian messages use the least proportion of positive emoticons. That study was based on an aggregation of the data over the 66 weeks sampled. The role of the present paper is to show how the data distributed over time, to demonstrate that the qualitative tendencies named above are not localized to a short time frame within the data.

2   Background

Usenews groups were sampled from a server fed by the HEANET in Ireland. Binaries were filtered by the source. Server configuration issues entail that the entirety of the remainder was not received, but messages were distributed over the monitored newsgroups without evidence of selection criteria. Spam was filtered locally using Spam-Assassin. Data on Swedish and Italian were sought as language sources for which we had *a priori* reason from other communication channels to expect differences, as mentioned above. English and German were included as baseline and contrast sources. The subdomains *.swnet, *.se, *.it, *.de and *.uk provided postings representative of the corresponding languages.

Table 1. Messages per language per topic

Language	Topic	Messages	APPI	Language	Topic	Messages	APPI
Swedish	Politics	18225	23.13	Italian	Politics	173672	32.94
Swedish	Science	814	5.73	Italian	Science	32117	5.97
Sum:		19039		*Sum:*		205789	
German	Politics	933	3.30	English	Politics	81635	10.90
German	Science	75230	12.72	English	Science	13561	10.66
Sum:		76163		*Sum:*		95196	

We did not classify or filter data further with a language guesser [3]; further, we do not presume that everyone who posts within the *.de domain is German, or correspondingly for any of the other areas. The topic areas which had coverage for all four languages during the sampled period included those in science and politics. We did not examine topics at any more fine-grained level because of data sparseness. After filtering, 396,187 postings remained, distributed across languages and topics sampled as shown in Table 1. The average number of postings per individual (APPI) provides a coarse metric of newsgroup interactivity. Analysis of emoticon use as a function of interactivity has only just begun [6].

A list of 2,161 unique emoticons with their descriptions was compiled from two web sources.[1] We added three more classes of emoticons consisting of three or more consecutive characters that are all exclamation marks, or all question marks, or a mixture, with prototypical members: "!!!", "???" and "!?!?". It is contentious to think of tokens like "???" as emoticons. Some researchers refer to this general category more specifically as containing *emodevices* with coding criteria that overlap with those of emoticons.[2] One study compares Italian and Chilean chat rooms for a number of textualized conversational moves and found significantly greater use in Italian groups of both emoticons and emodevices [5]. Instances of ALLCAPS or tokens like "!#@%$" are taken to be emodevices. Emoticons are distinguished in that work as iconic. However, emoticons like emodevices clearly also make "irregular" use of characters to form emotive tokens. The distinction between the categories is not so sharp. First of all, the use of the exclamation mark in a token like "!#@%$" is, in fact, rather regular in comic strips (e.g. *Beetle Bailey*). As words have primary and secondary senses, so also letters and punctuation marks have alternative but conventionalized uses. Secondly, if pressed to say what ALLCAPS or "!#@%$" is iconic of, one defending their iconicity might refer to the representation of a sound intensity, and then have to defend the applicability of "icon" to audible as well as visual stimuli.[3]

---

[1] One was `http://www.gte.us.es/~chavez/Ascii/smileys.txt` — last verified March 2008; the other was `http://www.windweaver.com/emoticon.htm` — last verified March 2008.

[2] The *ProjectH Codebook*: `http://www.it.murdoch.edu.au/~sudweeks/projecth/codebook.html` — last verified August 2008.

[3] It is relevant that items on computer desktops for invoking software are called "icons" even when they lack both forms of iconicity.

Fig. 1. Which is the "krikatorik" and which is the "souble"?

An argument for the appropriateness of this use of "icon" is in an old example in which image is taken to correspond to sound: reliably, presented with images like those in Figure 1, people will judge the item on the right to be the krikatorik and defend the judgement with a statement like "because 'krikatorik' *sounds* sharp". We do not argue that sound is the same as image, but that iconicity takes in both modalities. Hence, we include emodevices under the category of emoticons.

A within-Japanese qualitative study of *kaomoji*[4] used by young married women addresses the rather ornate instances used to as extra-textual bonding devices [7]. In contrast, our study focuses on the most frequently occurring emoticons in the texts sampled, which correlates directly with the least ornate. Of the 2,161 tokens considered as emoticons (including some *kaomoji*) only 121 actually occurred; the 12 most frequent are indicated with their raw frequencies in Table 2. Our parsing of the emoticons sought longest possible matches, so that, for example, the frequency of ":-)" is independent of that of ":-))".

These emoticons were classified as positive, negative or neutral/ambiguous. We analyze the distribution of positive, negative and neutral emoticons as a function of language and subject area. The initial classification of the emoticons is our own, indicated in Table 2 under the heading "Us". We evaluated our judgments by presenting the 100 most frequent of the 121 emoticons to raters who could choose one of three categories (positive, negative or neutral) with instructions that "neutral" should be selected if the emoticon is deemed either not interpretable or ambiguous between positive and negative.[5] Emoticons were presented without context and with an order randomized for each participant (who were among our friends and colleagues, and theirs). Forty-eight participants between 18 and 67 years of age (avg. 31.9) each voted for a category appropriate to each emoticon. To assess the level of agreement between our classification of the emoticons and that of the rest of the group, we began with an estimate of the group opinion on the three-way classification. For each emoticon, we assume the default group opinion of it as neutral/ambiguous; we count its classifications in each category, and if the number of positive or negative votes exceeds the number of neutral/ambiguous votes we take the group opinion accordingly.[6] We

---

[4] Consensus characterizes *kaomoji* as having an axis of orientation that is orthogonal to the majority of emoticons in other languages (e.g. (^^) vs. :)).

[5] Each item (or none at all) had to be classified: "neutral" includes "abstain".

[6] In case of a tie in votes between "positive" and "negative" votes both exceeding the number of votes for "neutral/ambiguous," the default was set to somewhat arbitrarily set to "positive", although such a situation did not actually transpire.

Table 2. Frequencies of the top 12 emoticons

Emoticon	Class Us	MK	Count	Emoticon	Class Us	MK	Count	Emoticon	Class Us	MK	Count
!!!	-	?	34313	**	?	?	14108	;)	+	+	3933
:-)	+	+	20375	:)	+	+	11478	8)	?	+	3401
???	-	?	14843	***	?	?	8698	(x)	?	?	2832
;-)	+	+	14531	*(	-	-	4611	:-))	+	+	2774

measured agreement between this construction of the group opinion and our own with Cohen's Kappa statistic ($\kappa = 0.37$).[7] However, a higher level of agreement would be desirable, since the emoticons are not evenly distributed in frequency of use. From this data we also constructed two alternative classifications.

The first alternative is provided by an individual who we dubbed "Max Kappa": this is the individual whose Kappa statistic computed with respect to the remainder of the raters (including ourselves) had the highest value (0.88). We used that individual as a coherent source of judgements across the 100 emoticons and representative of the group. The Max Kappa ratings on the 12 most frequent emoticons is also provided in Table 2 under the columns headed, "MK".

Finally, because of a separate intuition that emoticons are generally used in context to express a definite sentiment rather than ambiguous one, we constructed a third classification of the emoticons as either positive or negative based on the plebiscite, taking the neutral/ambiguous votes as abstentions on whether an emoticon was positive or negative. Emoticons where there was a tie between positive and negative votes (three) were eliminated, as were cases in which definite "quorum" (defined as at least one quarter of the votes not being regarded as abstentions). Thus, the plebiscite yielded a definite binary opinion for the remaining 79 emoticons. The top 12 of these in frequency are provided in Table 3. In can be seen that emoticons that were eliminated were not particularly high on iconicity, and were certainly low on polarized sentiment.

Table 2 shows that our own judgements differed from that of Max Kappa (the group consensus) on the most frequent and third most frequent emoticons, amounting to a disagreement between negative polarity and ambiguity that affects 28% of the tokens used. However, this is not to say that the real difference is 28% because we don't have a statement of the relative number of times the actual context fully settles the intended use of !!! or ??? as positive or negative. The consensus-driven binary classification agrees with the initial scheme for the most frequent emoticons. It is important for later observations that the equivocation between the classification schemes is between "negative" and "neutral/ambiguous" and not between "positive" and "negative".[8]

---

[7] Kappa ranges between -1 (complete disagreement) and 1 (complete agreement).

[8] For 8), the 8th most frequent on the binary scheme and 10th on the ternary scheme, we thought it neutral, while both Max Kappa and the electorate rated it positive.

Table 3. Frequencies of the top 12 emoticons with plebiscite determined polarity

Emoticon	Class	Frequency	Emoticon	Class	Frequency	Emoticon	Class	Frequency
!!!	-	34313	:)	+	11478	:-))	+	2774
:-)	+	20375	*(	-	4611	=>	+	2537
???	-	14843	;)	+	3933	:-(	-	2439
;-)	+	14531	8)	+	3401	*)	+	2294

2.1 Distributions of Emoticons by Language, Overall

Most messages posted did not contain any emoticons, and that was true for each language, even with considerable variation in the number of messages posted. The leftmost columns of Table 4 indicate this. From these frequencies, one may deduce that in comparing the type of emoticon used across the languages, in science and politics, one is comparing distributions involving small numbers with distributions involving substantially larger counts.

The language with the greatest proportion of postings with emoticons was German, and the rightmost six columns in that table indicate that of the emoticons that were used, the German postings included overwhelmingly positive emoticons. This is regardless of the classification scheme based on our own judgements or the consensus judgement provided by Max Kappa. With respect to both three-way classification schemes, we looked at the distribution of positive, negative and neutral/ambiguous emoticons each language versus each other language overall, in politics and science. Each of these two row by three column comparisons was significant using χ^2, except for German versus English political discussions on our classification (and that comparison provided the least value $\chi^2 = 15.1, p < 0.0005$ for Max Kappa's classification).

On our classification scheme, the most significant overall differences were between German and Italian ($\chi^2 = 9828.06, p < 0.0001$),[9] German and English ($\chi^2 = 2613.07$), Italian and English ($\chi^2 = 2059.75$), and Italian and Swedish ($\chi^2 = 1056.87$). On the alternative scheme provided by Max Kappa, a great frequency of the emoticon tokens shifted from the negative category to "neutral". There, German is the most distinctive, the distribution of German and Italian emoticons still providing the greatest difference ($\chi^2 = 10283.69$), followed by German and English ($\chi^2 = 5548.15$) and then German and Swedish ($\chi^2 = 2961.57$). Relative to German on either classification scheme, Italian had the least overall positive emoticons.

Table 5 shows the distribution of emoticons overall across messages when there are two categories.[10] As mentioned above, the procedure for adjudicating the categories on the basis of opinion derived from definite polarities vs. abstentions: 21 emoticons were eliminated. This entails that there are distinct counts of

---

[9] All further χ^2 values reported also have $p < 0.0001$.
[10] The values in the "Emoticon Distribution" columns of this table and the values in remaining tables are percentages.

Table 4. Postings With and Without Emoticons & Proportions of Emoticon Types

| | Message Distribution | | | Emoticon Distribution | | | | | |
| | | | | Authors | | | Max Kappa | | |
Language	Emoticons	No Emoticons	% With	% +	% -	% ?	% +	% -	% ?
Swedish	4353	14686	22.92	58.34	27.36	14.31	44.26	1.59	54.15
German	23671	52492	31.08	71.42	16.46	12.12	73.37	8.29	18.34
Italian	52179	153610	25.36	39.70	51.70	8.61	41.63	3.59	54.78
English	20099	75097	21.11	50.50	34.67	14.84	46.40	4.08	49.52

Table 5. Group Opinion: Postings With and Without Emoticons & Type Distribution

| | Message Distribution | | | Emoticon Distribution | |
Language	Emoticons	No Emoticons	% With	% Positive	% Negative
Swedish	3424	15615	17.98	62.56	37.44
German	25209	50954	33.10	82.86	17.14
Italian	54716	151073	26.59	45.50	54.50
English	18367	76829	19.29	61.23	38.77

messages containing emoticons than for the analyses described above using the three-way classification. Focusing on this binary sentiment classification of emoticons, the only overall language comparison that was not significant was between Swedish and English, and within analysis of messages in politics newsgroups, neither the German-Swedish nor the German-English comparisons were significant. The greatest overall difference was between German and Italian ($\chi^2 = 9842.00$), where German has the most positive emoticons and Italian has the greatest proportion of negative emoticons; German and English ($\chi^2 = 2566.23$), which splits in the same direction but with German positive emoticons representing a greater proportion than for English; Italian and English ($\chi^2 = 1360.34$), where the split is in the same direction as for German and Italian; German and Swedish ($\chi^2 = 788.06$), which is quite like the German and English split; and Italian and Swedish ($\chi^2 = 376.21$). On the binary classification scheme, there is an increased proportion of positive emoticons among the German messages over both the original and comparison category schemes, and a distribution of negative emoticons in Italian which is exactly like the first scheme. This relationship for Italian is to be expected since between our initial classification scheme and the second one which employed a plebiscite, negative judgements shifted to the category of "neutral/ambiguous"; however, when abstentions are disregarded in cases where quorum persists, the original positive and negative classifications are ratified. Clearly, equivocation between "negative" and "neutral/ambiguous" between the categorization schemes makes a difference in the overall distribution of negative emoticons, but in terms of positive emoticons versus non-positive emoticons, the classifications agree.

2.2   Distributions of Emoticons by Language and Topic

Initial Three-Way Classification. Table 6 shows the distribution of emoticons according to our classification scheme across topic area, by language.

Within newsgroups with a science focus, the greatest differences on our classification were between German and Italian ($\chi^2 = 715.17$), where the positive German emoticons concentrated and non-positive emoticons split closely between negative and ambiguous while Italian had fewer positive emoticons and more negative than ambiguous emoticons; Swedish and English ($\chi^2 = 547.96$), where while the English data had a pattern more like the German one, the Swedish data was closely split between positive and negative, and most emoticons ambiguous; German and Swedish ($\chi^2 = 544.37$), for which the German data concentration of positive emoticons is matched by the Swedish concentration of ambiguous ones; Italian and Swedish ($\chi^2 = 428.13$), which split along the lines of the German and Swedish comparison. On this scheme, the Germans, English and Italians have mainly positive emoticons for science discussions (Germans the most positive), and the Swedish messages have notably fewer positive emoticons.

Within newsgroups with a politics focus, the greatest differences on our classification were between Italian and English ($\chi^2 = 3200.29$), where the Italian messages have more than half negative emoticons, about half of that amount of positive emoticons and few ambiguous ones; Italian and Swedish ($\chi^2 = 1647.32$), where Italian has as great proportion of negative emoticons as Swedish messages have positive; and Swedish and English ($\chi^2 = 210.41$), where the English messages have more negative Emoticons than the Swedish ones. On this classification scheme, for the discussion of politics the use of emoticons designated as negative sharply separate the Swedish messages and the Italian ones.

Max Kappa's Categories. Table 7 shows the distributions of emoticons determined by the individual closest to the consensus opinion over the three categories, analyzed according to subject area and by language.

For science newsgroups the greatest difference is between German and Italian ($\chi^2 = 944.31$), where the pattern is in the same direction (mainly positive, some ambiguous, a small proportion of negative emoticons) but with nearly double the proportion of ambiguous emoticons in Italian than German and a greater

Table 6. Our Classification: Percentages of Emoticon Types by Language and Topic

Science				Politics			
Language	Positive	Negative	Ambiguous	Language	Positive	Negative	Ambiguous
Swedish	20.38	14.69	64.93	Swedish	60.09	27.94	11.97
German	71.60	16.29	12.11	German	45.73	40.70	13.57
Italian	59.39	26.57	14.04	Italian	33.81	59.20	6.99
English	65.48	25.27	9.25	English	48.16	36.13	15.70

Table 7. Max κ: Percentages of Emoticon Types by Language and Topic

Science				Politics			
Language	Positive	Negative	Ambiguous	Language	Positive	Negative	Ambiguous
Swedish	20.38	1.90	77.73	Swedish	45.36	1.58	53.06
German	73.55	8.30	18.15	German	48.74	7.54	43.72
Italian	61.90	6.48	31.61	Italian	35.58	2.73	61.70
English	67.89	8.66	23.46	English	43.05	3.37	53.58

proportion of positive emoticons for German than Italian; German and Swedish ($\chi^2 = 490.68$), where the proportion of ambiguous emoticons for Swedish is greater than the large proportion of positive emoticons for German; and Swedish and English ($\chi^2 = 294.91$).

In the politics newsgroups on this classification scheme, the greatest cross-linguistic difference is between Italian and English ($\chi^2 = 371.66$) and Italian and Swedish ($\chi^2 = 180.70$) where in both cases the proportion of positive emoticons in Italian is significantly lower than for the other language and the proportion of ambiguous Italian emoticons is rather higher. Again, this represents the shift of emoticons that had been classified as negative on our initial classification scheme to neutral/ambiguous on the group scheme. The low proportion of positive emoticons in messages posted to politics remains about the same for both classification schemes.

Binary Sentiment Classification. We are not ultimately satisfied with the three way classification involving the category "neutral or ambiguous" described above, partly because of its catch-all status. We have pointed out that some of the emoticons eliminated in this classification were very low on iconicity and also low on polarization of sentiment according to the plebiscite. It is true that emoticons, like any other content bearing expression, can be used ambiguously or ironically, and thus we expect that allowing the abstentions category in the plebiscite filters out those votes about emoticons where context is relatively free to determine the sentiment accented with an emoticon.

Next we describe the comparison outcome by language and subject of distributions within binary category classifications of emoticons. Within science discussions, German provided the most messages and was most distinctive. The German and Italian distributions across the two categories showed the greatest difference ($\chi^2 = 625.25$), where 83% of German emoticons were positive to 72% in Italian messages. For German and English ($\chi^2 = 127.3$) the comparison was to 74% positive. With the German and Swedish ($\chi^2 = 30.74$) comparison involving Swedish's relatively smaller 58% positive emoticons, it has to be recalled that there were only 814 messages in total posted to the Swedish science newsgroups. For politics newsgroups the greatest differences were shown by Italian and English ($\chi^2 = 1973.02$) and by Italian and Swedish ($\chi^2 = 771.74$) where only Italian had many more negative than positive.

Table 8. Binary Consensus: Percentages of Emoticon Types by Language and Topic

Science			Politics		
Language	Positive	Negative	Language	Positive	Negative
Swedish	58.11	41.89	Swedish	62.66	37.34
German	83.05	16.95	German	56.67	43.33
Italian	71.77	28.23	Italian	38.23	61.77
English	74.43	25.57	English	58.85	41.15

2.3   Observations

This section has indicated how emoticons were distributed by sentiment categorization scheme by language overall and as a function of topic. For Swedish, Italian and English, the distribution of types of emoticons used within discussions of politics closely resembles the overall distribution for the language, while for German emoticon use in science discussions corresponds to the overall use.[11] Emoticons in the Swedish discussions of politics were nearly half positive, while for Italian they were more than half negative (depending on the classification scheme) and the remainder split over the other categories. For English and German, a nearly equal distribution across the three types occurred. In discussion of science, emoticon used in Swedish were mainly ambiguous, with an equal distribution of positive and negative, while the other languages used mainly positive emoticons; however, the least number of postings was for science groups in the Swedish news groups. The dependence of the inter-cultural differences upon the classification scheme has also been discussed: the votes supplied by the raters were provided in the absence of influencing context. On one hand, context could resolve an ambiguous emoticon in either direction; on the other hand, the resolving information that was supplied through quorate non-abstentions provides an indication of how context would resolve ambiguous emoticons on average. In this evaluation of the initial classification scheme we have considered two alternatives—the classification provided by a single individual in the pool of raters who most people agreed with and the classification constructed by forcing binary classification. Other alternatives remain to be explored as well, but with the acceptable level of agreement realized between the first scheme and the judgements of the larger pool of raters some consensus among the schemes emerged. German emoticons are overwhelmingly positive with much discussion of science, and little of politics. Swedish emoticons were concentrated in politics rather more than science, and were mainly positive there. Italian messages in politics had a smaller proportion of positive emoticons than the other languages, but a comparable proportion of positive emoticons in science newsgroups. We did

---

[11] This can be explained further from Table 1; the postings for German were concentrated in science newsgroups, while for the other languages, there are more postings in the politics newsgroups.

not expect the cross-cultural analysis to work out the way that it did, expecting in some way that the Swedish discussions might actually have more emoticons proportionately than the other languages for reasons connected to those outlined in the introduction. We sought to determine if the distributions remained constant over time, thinking that politics would be more volatile than science discussion, and that it might be able to track emoticon use peaks and troughs with respect to outstanding events of the time [2].

In §3, we examine the distributions within the three categories using just the initial classification over time. We leave it to further work to analyze the divergences among the trends that would occur with the alternative classifications.

3 Chronological Analysis

The results in §2 are based on the total accumulation of postings. We noted that there was an uneven distribution of postings in each category. Particularly because one of the topic areas is politics, a source of volatile discourse sentiment, it is useful to study the distributions of emoticons over time, in case emoticon use in a particular language and topic is dominated by postings restricted to a short period. Figure 2 shows how the messages available to us over the 66 week period were distributed in each language relative to the total number of postings. The overall figures are represented in the graph on the left, politics in the middle, and science on the right. Italian and English consistently dominate the flow of postings in politics newsgroups, while German and Italian dominate science newsgroups.

In the next graphs, the lines represent the use of positive, negative and neutral emoticons, by week. The values plotted are the number of emoticons relativized to the total number of tokens over time.

Figure 3 shows on the left that emoticons in Swedish political discourse for the first 50 weeks were mostly positive, and thereafter, mostly negative. Shares in Ericsson fell by 25% on October 16, 2007 — this is exactly the week of the

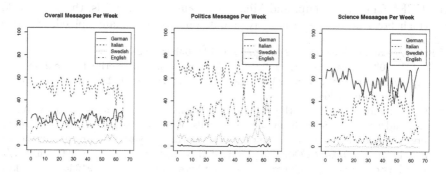

Fig. 2. Relative Message Counts per Week by Language: Overall, Politics and Science

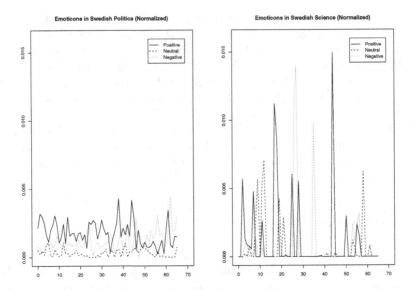

Fig. 3. Swedish Emoticons: Politics and Science

spike at 0.003 in negative emoticons.[12] Also note that the later spike in negative emoticons at the 62nd week, like the one in the 9th week, coincides with the week prior to a Nobel Week.[13] We have not examined the content of the postings to determine whether these events are mentioned, but point them out to indicate some of the facts that would be in public consciousness at the time.[14] In contrast, the figure on the right shows the relatively few postings in the Swedish science newsgroups, and no clear trends are evident. German politics (the left of Fig. 4) is similarly noisy, but the graph of emoticon use for discussions of science show a steady state of overwhelmingly more positive emoticons being used than either negative or neutral ones.

Figure 5 shows the temporal flow of emoticons in Italian discussions. On the left, with six exceptions, the use of negative emoticons exceeds the use of positive emoticons: the 27th week was the start of April and coincided with the UEFA Champions cup, and Milan advancing to semi-finals; the 47th week, in which both positive and negative emoticons nearly equally spiked, spanned

---

[12] http://www.iht.com/articles/ap/2007/10/16/business/
EU-FIN-COM-Sweden-Ericsson-Profit-Warning.php – last verified June 2008.

[13] http://nobelprize.org/nobelfoundation/press/2007/nobel-events07.html –
last verified June 2008.

[14] On September 14, 2007, the US beat Sweden in the women's football World Cup, and on September 23, in the semi-finals of the Davis cup in Tennis. Ingmar Bergman had died in July. (http://www.washingtonpost.com/wp-dyn/content/article/2007/09/14/AR2007091400783.html – last verified June 2008; http://www.firstcoastnews.com/sports/news-article.aspx?storyid=91946 – last verified June 2008; http://www.iht.com/articles/ap/2007/07/31/europe/EU-GEN-Sweden-Mourns-Bergman.php – last verified June 2008).

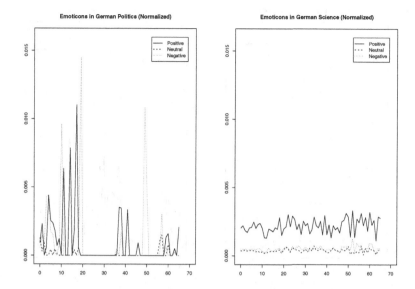

Fig. 4. German Emoticons: Politics and Science

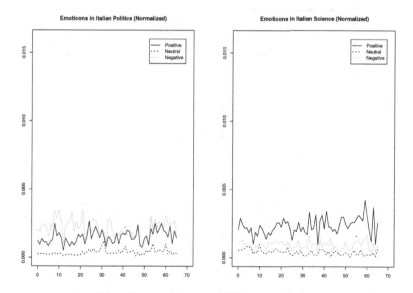

Fig. 5. Italian Emoticons: Politics and Science

August 13-20, in which six young Italians were executed in Duisburg (Germany), evidently in a mafia feud, an event that precipitated an Italian police crackdown on the mafia. The 53rd through the 55th weeks covered the first half of October 2007, and this included in the European Media Monitor summary of dominant news items an announcement of a pending sale of government shares in Alitalia (October 9), "overwhelming" worker approval of pension reform raising

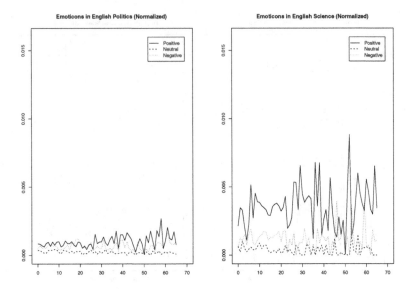

Fig. 6. English Emoticons: Politics and Science

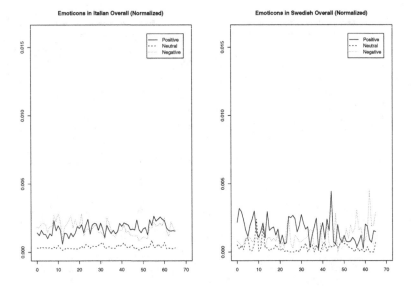

Fig. 7. Overall Emoticons: Italian and Swedish

retirement to age 60 (October 10), an announcement of the state ship building company winning the contract to build the new Queen Elizabeth (October 11), and a landslide victory for Walter Veltroni, Mayor of Rome, in a national election primary (October 14).[15] The graph on the right shows that for discussion in science newsgroups, positive emoticons dominated throughout the period.

---

[15] http://press.jrc.it/NewsExplorer/ – last verified June 2008.

Emoticon use in the *.uk newsgroups is shown in Fig. 6. Use of emoticons in politics newsgroups favored positive ones over the entire period except the week which included January 30, the same week that a controversial decision about awarding a super-casino license in Manchester rather than London or Blackpool was announced and Lord Levy, fundraiser for Tony Blair, was arrested, and Blair himself was questioned by police. Emoticons in the science newsgroups are also positive for the period, with the exception of August 19-25.

The aggregate of both subject areas over the 66 weeks (Fig. 7) shows that, coincidentally, the periods in which positive and negative emoticons dominate are in a roughly complementary distribution between Italian and Swedish. More negative than positive emoticons in Italian appear for the first half of the period, and then mainly the reverse. For Swedish, the first two-thirds are positive; the final third are mostly negative.

4 Discussion

A past study demonstrated that aggregate results differentiate Swedish and Italian emoticon use, with more positive emoticons in Swedish politics newsgroups and more negative emoticons in the same context in Italian. It is clear that certain emoticons that we have considered are in the absence of context deemed to be ambiguous by most of the participants in our rating study. The two most important of these emoticons are ! ! ! and ??? because of their rank frequency of first and third in the top ten, respectively. On none of the classification schemes that we considered are they positive. On one they are ambiguous and thus require context to disambiguate (if they can be disambiguated). It may well be that the use of these emoticons accounts for the evident preponderance of negative emoticons in messages posted to politics newsgroups. However, it remains the case that messages posted to Italian politics newsgroups had significantly fewer clearly positive emoticons than the other languages considered.

We observed the way the categorization distributions extend over time from late September 2006 to January 2008. Divergences from those trends were noted and related to contemporaneous external events with presumed impact on public sentiment, regardless of whether they were explicitly mentioned in postings.

We have reported the use of emoticons in four languages and two broad topic areas over a 66 week period. We provide a methodological starting point for interpretive cross-cultural analyses of emoticon use. Further quantitative analysis of emoticon use in terms of levels of interactivity in such discussion groups as sampled here is necessary, as is correlation of emoticon types with accompanying sentiment bearing words. The present study attempts no such content analysis, preferring instead to identify the raw patterns of emoticon use. There is a strong argument to consider use of nearly all but the most clearly negative emoticons (e.g. "!?!!?!") as actually conveying positive emotions—if a writer has bothered to use an emoticon, then this is a signal of positive affect. Certainly, negative emoticons (e.g. ":-<") can be used to indicate a sympathetic response to an adverse situation, and equally, a positive emoticon might be used to temper the content of otherwise negative companion text. These double dissociations may confound any correlations between emoticons and words or phrases. However, this potential is exactly what pragmatic analysis of emoticon use may reveal.

The next step is to conduct a follow-on study like the one we used to assess agreement with our own classification of the emoticons. We have analyzed *inter-cultural differences in the use* of emoticons with the idealizing assumption (modulo individual differences in agreement such as have been quantified here) of *universal agreement on classification* of the emoticons as positive, negative or ambiguous. The results show a dearth of positive emoticons in the Italian discussions of politics. Three possible explanations are available: this distribution might reflect a difference in underlying sentiment in Italian political discourse during the sampled period; the effect might be amplified (or eliminated) with disambiguating contextual analysis; or it might be explained by Italian differences in the classification of certain emoticons as positive that others find negative or ambiguous, such that across the four languages, the underlying sentiment was the same for each during the period, but that there are intercultural differences on the sentiment conveyed by individual emoticons. Future work should evaluate these candidate explanations.

References

1. Allwood, J.: Are there Swedish patterns of communication? In: Tamura, H. (ed.) Cultural Acceptance of CSCW in Japan & Nordic Countries, pp. 90–120. Kyoto Institute of Technology (1999)
2. Balog, K., Mishne, G., de Rijke, M.: Why are they excited? Identifying and explaining spikes in blog mood levels. In: 11th Meeting of the European Chapter of the Association for Computational Linguistics (2006)
3. Cavnar, W.B., Trenkle, J.M.: N-gram-based text categorization. In: Proceedings of Third Annual Symposium on Document Analysis and Information Retrieval. UNLV Publications/Reprographics, Las Vegas, NV, pp. 161–175 (1994)
4. Cerrato, L.: A comparative study of verbal feedback in Italian and Swedish map-task dialogues. In: Proceedings of the Nordic Symposium on the Comparison of Spoken Languages, pp. 99–126 (2003)
5. Ibarra, F.C., Galimberti, C.: Stereotypes and gender identity in Italian and Chilean chat line rooms. PsychNology Journal 4(1), 25–52 (2006)
6. Janssen, J., Vogel, C.: Politics makes the Swedish:-) and the Italians:-(. In: Ahmad, K. (ed.) Sentiment Analysis: Emotion, Metaphor, Ontology & Terminology, pp. 53–61 (2008) (EMOT 2008 Workshop at LREC 2008: Poster)
7. Katsuno, H., Yano, C.: Kaomoji and expressivity in a Japanese housewives' chatroom. In: Danet, B., Herring, S.C. (eds.) The Multilingual Internet: Language, Culture, and Communication Online, pp. 278–299. Oxford University Press, Oxford (2007)
8. Neviarouskaya, A., Prendinger, H., Ishizuka, M.: Narrowing the social gap among people involved in global dialog: Automatic emotion detection in blog posts. In: Proceedings International Conference on Weblogs and Social Media, pp. 293–294. Omnipress, Boulder (2007) (ICWSM 2007: Poster)
9. Nicolov, N., Salvetti, F., Ivanova, S.: Sentiment analysis: Does coreference matter? In: Symposium on Affective Language in Human and Machine. AISB, Aberdeen (2008)

10. Read, J.: Using emoticons to reduce dependency in machine learning techniques for sentiment classification. In: Proceedings of the ACL Student Research Workshop, pp. 43–48. Association for Computational Linguistics (2005)
11. Schler, J., Koppel, M., Argamon, S., Pennebaker, J.: Effects of age and gender on blogging. In: Nicolov, N., Salvetti, F., Liberman, M., Martin, J.H. (eds.) AAAI Spring Symposium: Computational Approaches to Analyzing Weblogs, pp. 199–205. AAAI Press, Menlo Park (2006)
12. Suzuki, Y., Takamura, H., Okumura, M.: Application of semi-supervised learning to evaluative expression classification. In: Gelbukh, A. (ed.) CICLing 2006. LNCS, vol. 3878, pp. 502–513. Springer, Heidelberg (2006)
13. Tseliga, T.: It's all Greeklish to me! Linguistic and sociocultural perspectives on Roman-alphabeted Greek in asynchronous computer-mediated communication. In: Danet, B., Herring, S.C. (eds.) The Multilingual Internet: Language, Culture, and Communication Online, pp. 116–141. Oxford University Press, Oxford (2007)

Urban Environmental Information Perception and Multimodal Communication: The Air Quality Example

Li Zhu[1], Kostas Karatzas[2], and John Lee[1]

[1] University of Edinburgh, School of Arts, Culture and Environment,
MSc progr. on Design and Digital Media, Alison House, Nicolson Square, Edinburgh, UK
[2] Aristotle University, Dept. of Mech. Eng., Informatics Applications and Systems Group,
Egnatia Str., Thessaloniki, GR
L.Zhu-4@sms.ed.ac.uk, kkara@eng.auth.gr, J.Lee@ed.ac.uk

Abstract. We address environmental information multimodal communication by making use of the air quality (AQ) paradigm. AQ information dissemination methods and tools can make use of various telecommunication channels for pull and push service provision. In addition, location based services are also emerging in the field of personalised, quality of life services. Moreover, communication per se is not based solely on written or oral language forms, but makes use of graphical, symbolical and in more general terms multimedia language communication schemes, via properly designed multimedia environmental information content, streamed via multimodal communication channels. Human perception and communication of such information is based on design schemes that may convey the message in an understandable and effective way. The present paper suggests a design approach to multimodal communication of AQ information.

Keywords: Communication, design, air pollution.

1 Introduction

Air Quality Information Services (AQIS) address environmental pressures and personalised life patterns especially in urban areas. They aim at integrating the need for improved well being, with the understanding of environmental pressures and their consequences. They also provide valuable information concerning the way that the pattern of our everyday life is associated with exposure to, and consequences of, environmental threats. For their full potential to be realised, they need to deliver information in the most immediate and effective way, anytime, anywhere, which in the contemporary context (in the developed world, but increasingly everywhere) implies the use of mobile devices. Working within the inevitable limitations of these devices is a significant aspect of good design for AQIS delivery systems. In the following sections we investigate aspects of multimodal communication of air quality information, in relation to its perception, making use of design principles for enhancing and managing the perception and presentation of such information in an effective way, recognising that the constraints of mobile devices necessitate the sharing of the information burden between the simplicity of the immediate display and a broader, more complex, contextual understanding.

A. Esposito et al. (Eds.): Multimodal Signals, LNAI 5398, pp. 288–299, 2009.

It might well be argued that some significant proportion of the population, even in the developed world, still lack mobile phones or similar devices, especially ones with highly capable displays etc. This is true, but one aspect of our response is that we are aiming towards a future in which these devices will be ever more ubiquitous and the graphical display will be as central as the telephonic function itself, and another is that when AQ alert information is of broad relevance and urgent importance it will be conveyed redundantly via similarly designed messages on large-scale public media, broadcast television, etc. It is beyond the scope of this paper to address many of the further issues that these kinds of media may raise.

2 Perception and Awareness for AQ Problems

People perceive the quality of the environment they live in on the basis of personal interests, culture and knowledge. Perception is a way to understand the relationship of the self with the world and its "constituents", in parallel with the relationship between the influences of one's personal actions on the environment that he or she lives in. Both dimensions of perception require sufficient information provision: the first part requires information on the status of the environment, the pressures it creates on living, and the consequences of such pressures, while the second part requires information concerning the influence of our actions on the environment that we live in. The issue of perception and awareness concerning AQ problems has already been discussed in some detail in previous work conducted by Karatzas and Lee [1], where a number of aspects influencing them has been recorded, making use of published research results. These findings may be summarised as follows:

- Graphical ways were found to be more effective in communicating warnings related to urban air quality episodes, in comparison to the usage of scientific terminology and numbers [2].
- AQIS that allow for the linkage between location, the incident and the individual, were of high interest for people receiving such services [3].

On this basis, it is of interest to study multimodal communication in the cases of AQIS, with the aid of proper design principles, ideas and studies for the materialisation of the proper communication scheme.

3 Multimodal Communication of AQ

Any information about AQ will be understood by people in the context of their perception of these issues. There are at least two general kinds of information that it is important to consider. On the one hand, there is material that can educate the public on the general nature and effects of air pollution, thus raising their awareness of the issues and generating a demand for further information services. On the other hand, there is the kind of information those services should provide, which is targeted, episodic data, relevant to decision making by specific individuals or classes of individuals, at a specific time. The first kind of material needs to be developed in a framework accessible in a general way to a community at large, whereas the second needs to be individually targeted and commonly delivered on a mobile platform. These kinds of information need to be communicated in an integrated way, to achieve the best effect. Unlike environmental scientists, who are educated in detail about air quality and are then able effectively to use graphs and tables of figures, the public need to be educated in simple and specific terms about particular aspects that can then be linked to bold, simple and non-technical presentations of data. This integration of general and individual information differentiates our proposal here from most typical advertising campaigns. Although AQIS are not the only context in which the approach we advocate would be desirable, they are an example that is especially important, timely and focussed, and that allows us to develop the central ideas quite clearly.

If we do not develop a strong framework for communication, there is some prospect that communities will evolve their own linguistic or symbol-like conventions to share information and concepts [4,5], but the process may be shaped and accelerated, in the best cases, by the use of good design. An effective communication system exploits "messages" that are highly noticeable, highly recognisable, and easily related to relevant background knowledge. We postulate that "branding" of air quality information, in conjunction with the use of mobile devices, can maximise these effects. In the examples discussed below, a context is created by public awareness campaigns, which is then tied by the consistent use of graphical motifs, colours and perhaps sounds, into simple messages presented via the extremely salient mobile interface. Because expectations have been created and the context for interpretation is understood, the messages can afford to be very simple – essentially, the content is just one or two numbers, but instead of these being anywhere explicit, the significance of the message is directly realised in terms of a decision, e.g. to avoid a particular area or to be prepared with some specific medication.

4   Communication Channels

In order to make AQ information services readily accessible by more citizens, we propose several media channels in order to disseminate information. Examples of these outlets are: advertising via posters, newspaper and magazines, ambient media, radio, TV and cinema, internet, mobile phone, and so on.

Posters: These should be targeted in the right place and the right location. Special buildings or public transport, for example, can be considered ideal in a city location wherever people are often passing and it will be easily noticed. The size, shape and material of the poster allow for greater flexibility to create original and eye-catching designs.

Ambient media: Human beings as mobile creatures carry certain information every day, being proper "instruments" for branding and conveying messages. For example, the logo we wear on our clothes, shoes, hats, umbrellas and the bags we carry can all serve as effective channels to disseminate AQ information. There are also several different areas of ambient media, such as life performance and street installations, etc [6]. These salient features can grab people's attention and have the ability to even unconsciously surprise audiences.

Newspapers & magazines: As the most conventional media, newspapers and magazines still have massive audiences and a strong influence. Yet, they already contain a great deal of information. This makes AQ information less likely to stand out.

TV & cinema: As more and more TV stations and digital TV channels are opening, AQ information service advertisements on TV can easily be disseminated to a broad range of audiences. Also, cinema, with its giant screen and social atmosphere is a powerful possibility for advertisers and probably the most immersive media venue. It has the possibility to entertain and at the same time spread information to a wide section of audiences.

Radio: People driving their car to the office, taxi drivers, homemakers and so on are all common listeners to a range of radio channels. Moreover, there is the chance to broadcast AQ information together with traffic or weather forecasts which are an essential part of most radio stations daily forecast. Association with listeners' favoured programs will enhance AQ awareness. This will familiarize people with the service, making them more likely to see it as daily 'required' information. Here, due to the lack of a visual impact, portraying AQ information merely by sound will be more challenging.

Internet: According to Shapiro [7] the "emergence of new, digital technologies signals a potentially radical shift of who is in control of information, experience and resources." One sixth of the world's population has access to the internet [8], and the number is still increasing, hence it's a must to develop its potential to boost AQ information services. The internet allows special effects, well-designed sound, and an impressive visual influence. But the most distinctive advantage of the internet might be the opportunity to allow users to interact with information as an instant two-way communication process. What needs to be mentioned here is both a "viral effect" [9], and "word of mouth". It is very common for internet users to take close notice of what other users are doing and often to follow their example. Furthermore, we are more likely to accept information when it is interesting, and we often save it or forward it to our friends who might do the same to their friends, and so on. We can use this persuasive power to impact our friends and this could lead to a very rapid spread of AQ information.

A **dynamic website** offers the user more opportunities to engage with information when they navigate or search for information. This process transforms them from passive information receivers to active explorers. Doing so not only tends to make using the site more enjoyable, but also helps AQ become a more meaningful part of the user's daily routine. The goal is to encourage more data input, making use of both the mouse and keyboard, thereby certainly improving the interaction. JavaScript, ActionScript, and various other technologies can allow the website to be built with a richer interface. New tools and new features (a user interface component, sophisticated video tools, and so on) give designers a much greater range of possibilities, which are increasingly easy to implement (cf. [10]).

A crucial aspect of the dynamic website is that it provides an interface for personalising the AQIS. A user can enter data about their own preferences, and more importantly their own requirements for information. For example, the asthma sufferer, or person with other specific sensitivities, can be recorded as such. Then, the most useful AQ details can be provided to their own personal mobile device just when most needed, especially if (as is increasingly possible) the device itself can relay its current location to the server.

Mobile phone: Currently there are over 3 billion mobile phone users, and this number is increasing rapidly [11]. This suggests an effective platform possibility. Having most of the advantages of the internet, the mobile phone has its own special characteristics and is easy to carry. Symbol-based design is appropriate for the mobile phone, since it is easy to understand. Also, due to the small screen size and considering the screen resolution, graphics should not have too many details and should be left simple and clean in order to disseminate enough information on a limited area. Sound can also be an effective alert for harmful AQ levels. With different gadgets and accessories, mobile phones offer a potentially very powerful resource for AQ information. The key value of the mobile world lies in its portability. Accessing AQ information from a computer is generally a static process – that is, the user sits in the office or at home and can check up on AQ information according to their planned movements throughout the day. But the mobile phone allows users to find out AQ information anywhere and anytime, giving them a much greater degree of flexibility. As noted above, phones are also more and more commonly fitted with GPS or other geolocational systems, allowing their location to be used as a further means of automatically refining the information provision they afford. The more refined this information can be, the more effectively the mobile platform can be exploited.

Additionally, it is worth mentioning here that a framework combining website and mobile phone together certainly enhances the AQIS functionality as well as its accessibility. Users are encouraged to input their own details data via the dynamic website, and therefore they can receive more personalised AQ mobile alert information wherever they are. Furthermore, they can access more detailed AQ information from the website when they have the need.

5   Communication Strategy and Design Principles

Suggested designs should make use of the multimodal communication mode and a proper communication strategy to target various groups of people. The method of conveying AQ information therefore should employ an advertising-like approach, namely, seeing AQ as an advertising program instead of simply a tool to educate and inform citizens. Accordingly, the approach adopted in this paper will not only take an advertising attitude to convey AQ information, making it easy to catch people's attention and influence them seamlessly, but will also propose a creative advertising strategy. The AQ information service interface will thus require a higher level of design, since it has to catch users' interest within a competitive field. At the same time, a well-designed platform will further contribute to more citizens using the service. Nevertheless, it is also important to consider the possibilities of visualizing AQ information, how to make invisible scientific data visible, and how to successfully convey the right information contents.

For reasons of conveying the proper message and employing multimodal communication schemes, a number of designs are developed and proposed.

Design 01: For forms of ambient media, a T-shirt design is offered. The first example is a front view of the T-shirt with a simple AQ logo and tag line 'How is the AQ today?' The logo will increase people's curiosity. The back view of the T-shirt uses a cartoon image of a gas mask, which hints at the connection with pollution, but does not give the whole story (Fig. 1).

Design 02: It is important to rapidly establish a design 'feel' for the AQIS, and this can best be done by the use of a memorable visual impact. Hence, the poster proposed on Fig. 2 (left), relies on a simple image, using a stark contrast of black and white. A silhouette of a young woman wearing a large white mask is shown, implying that she does not perceive the world with her eyes but with breathing.

Design 03: This extends the use of ambient media to a city scale (Fig. 2, right). The aim is branding AQ information services across a wider range, namely on things people can wear and carry everywhere. For instance, clothing, hats, umbrellas and so

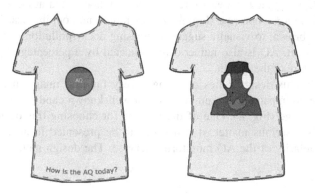

Fig. 1. Design principles for ambient media

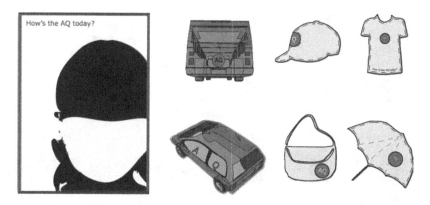

Fig. 2. A memorable visual image poster (left); city scale ambient media (right)

on are ideal to show the logo. Moreover, the image of the cap and umbrella serves to raise the idea of protection in the outdoor environment. AQ tags on cars may seem an hypocritical approach, since car exhaust is one of the major sources of air pollution. However, it is envisaged that these tags would be used on more environmentally friendly vehicles, such as public transport or low-emission/electric cars. The strategy behind this design series is to display AQ advertising everywhere, from a small scale such as clothing, bags and caps to a city scale such as public transportation. The idea is to intrigue the viewer rather than give them the full details all at once. Making the AQ tag visible and popular everywhere will, if successful, consequently trigger people's curiosity since the same logo/images will be widely observed yet not fully explained. When AQ becomes a buzz word and a topic of daily conversation, people will be much more likely to learn more about the project, discover its importance for their lives, and find out how they can use it to their advantage. This kind of technique is common in advertising campaigns, but is more art than science: all of our proposals here should be seen as generic, would of course require to be tailored for a specific target demographic and carefully piloted, and even then would be subject to all the usual uncertainties over their success.

Design 04: The pear is an easily recognisable symbol often associated with a refreshing connotation when ripe (Fig. 3). In this representation, the pear logo changes from green to brown, to visually suggest increasing decay/pollution respective to the nature of the fruit. AQ is also numerically indicated by a percentage figure that appears in the centre of the design.

Design 05: This design relies on using a very familiar image in an unfamiliar context to create impact. The 'gummy bear,' a well-known candy, is both a friendly and colorful image (Fig. 4). One of the reasons for choosing this design was that, though AQ is a serious matter, it still needs to be presented in an upbeat way to drive the popularity of the AQ monitoring service. The design method is to choose

Fig. 3. The pear as a concept of both freshness and degradation

a light-hearted approach, which is entertaining and interesting, so that users are not easily bored and meanwhile not only get the AQ information but enjoy using the services also. The idea is similar to the icon of the pear, which can be changed to a range of other icons according to different users. From the design aspect, there are multiple.icon-choosing opportunities, so users can preset icons in terms of their preferences.

Design 06: This one is a design suitable for a game portal, which people can play with. The user can chose their own favourite plant to raise. When air quality is good, the user can see the plant growing inside the jar, but when air quality is dangerous, the plant will wither. It is also possible to propose how to solve the problem, and suggestions will be given as to what the user should do in each case (Fig. 5).

Design 07: This is mainly a design for a mobile phone or any kind of similar portable device. Based on the well-known image of a speedometer/monitor gauge, this image is supplemented with visual cues to illustrate AQ. From the 'most healthy' icon of a heart to the 'most unhealthy' icon of medical contamination/radioactivity, the user sees a clear visualization of the health risks associated with AQ. The pointer can change dynamically in real time. In this portal, ideally, the second layer would offer more detailed information. When the user clicks different icons, they would receive instructive suggestions, such as what kind of actions are suitable or should be avoided according to the AQ situation (Fig. 6).

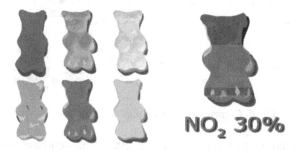

Fig. 4. A familiar image in an unfamiliar context

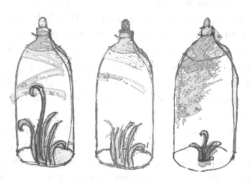

Fig. 5. Play and communicate, learn and understand

Design 08: The main idea in this mobile design [12] is to convey a more user-oriented approach to AQ data, therefore the navigation path in this design is predefined. The first layer is based on user age. The secondary content is a map, via which the user can choose where they live or the AQ in a certain location of interest. In the map layer, appealing colors and simple map shapes are provided, and the complexity of a detailed map is avoided. In terms of the location chosen, the user will see specific AQ information.

The third layer provides medical categories. In this case, the user can choose a certain group according to his/her own condition, and accordingly benefit from more accurate as well as more useful AQ information. The AQ information is represented by flash animation. Six bottles represent six main air pollutants, namely NO_2, SO_2, CO, ozone, particulates and lead. Each bottle is filled with colorful liquid, which is rising at a different speed and leads to a different percentage in the end. In this way, scientifically complicated AQ data is simplified and becomes visually appealing as well as entertaining (Fig. 7).

Fig. 6. Communicate, learn, play and understand.

Design 09: According to Karatzas and Lee (2008), location-based services, combined with mobile phone or web based information AQ services, were preferred by users over a platform without any location oriented information (cf.[1]). Hence a map application can be another appropriate approach. The following design in the web portal [13] is to demonstrate the possibility of overlapping the AQIS with a geographic map as well as forwarding more personalized AQ information, chosen by the user via the web map, to the mobile phone.. In the map, users can add their own marker to the locations for which they want to receive AQ information, while their mobile phone could automatically update itself, allowing the user to get personalized information (Fig. 8).

These designs influence each other and work together to bring the AQ idea to citizens' daily life. They aim to grab citizens' attention first and let them gradually become familiar with the topic. Only when they take AQ into consideration, as a daily basis for action, can they start to accept and look for where and how to find AQ information according to their own needs.

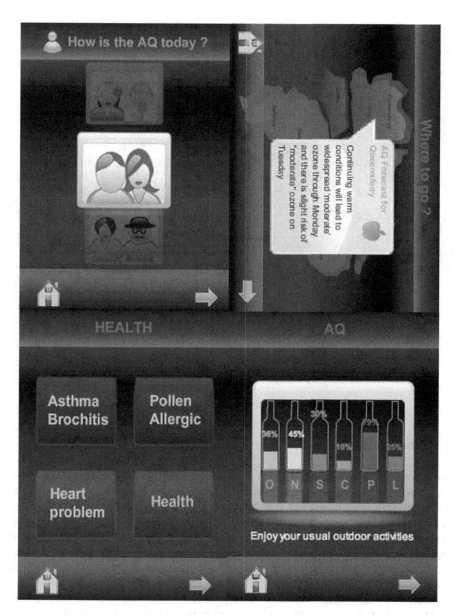

Fig. 7. Mobile portal

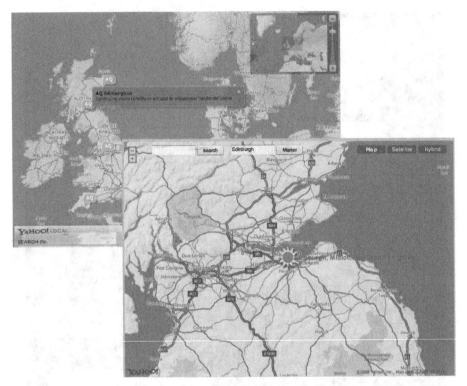

Fig. 8. City AQ information defined by user marker

6 Conclusion

In the present paper we investigated the issue of multimodal communication of air quality with the aid of proper information services, and we proposed a set of designs that apply principles of enhanced perception for a communication strategy based on public education advertisement. By exploiting simple but engaging or arresting mappings of information to various aspects of the images or other modalities used, we integrate approaches from branding and information design to develop the carefully prepared context, connecting to effective specific messages that communicate to drive decision making. The ideas presented here are based on previous research results in the area, that made suggestions in the direction of the present discussion [11], leading to development of an innovative way to exploit multimodality for guided perception and communication. AQIS are of major and increasing importance for quality of life, and may thus be considered as a good working example for the elaboration of multimodal communication services. Future work will include the development of mockups and possibly pilots of some of these designs, and a limited field trial of these services. We also intend to focus especially on the abundant opportunities presented by the present approach for the personalisation of services.

References

1. Karatzas, K., Lee, J.: Developments in urban environmental information perception and communication. In: Sànchez-Marrè, M., Béjar, J., Comas, J., Rizzoli, A., Guariso, G. (eds.) Proceedings of the iEMSs Fourth Biennial Meeting: International Congress on Environmental Modelling and Software, iEMSs 2008 (2008) (accessed September 01, 2008), http://www.iemss.org/iemss2008/index.php?n=Main.Proceedings
2. Peinel, G., Rose, T.: Dissemination of Air Quality Information: Lessons Learnt in European Field Trials. In: Proceedings of the 18th International EnviroInfo Conference, Cern, Geneva, Switzerland, pp. 118–128 (2004)
3. Karatzas, K., Endregard, G., Fløisand, I.: Citizen-oriented environmental information services: usage and impact modeling. In: Proceedings of the Informatics for Environmental Protection- Networking Environmental Information-19th International EnviroInfo Conference, Brno, Czech Rebublic, pp. 872–878 (2004)
4. Garrod, S., Doherty, G.: Conversation, co-ordination and convention: An empirical investigation of how groups establish linguistic conventions. Cognition 53, 181–215 (1994)
5. Garrod, S., Fay, N., Lee, J., Oberlander, J., McLeod, T.: Foundations of representation: Where might graphical symbol systems come from? Cognitive Science: A Multidisciplinary Journal 31/6, 961–987 (2007)
6. Burtenshaw, K., Maton, N., Barfoot, C.: The Fundamentals of Creative Advertising. AVA Publishing SA, Switzerland (2006)
7. Shapiro, A.L.: The Control Revolution. Public Affairs, New York (1999)
8. Internet World Stats: Internet Usage Statistics the Internet Big Picture (2008) (accessed July 07, 2008), http://www.internetworldstats.com/stats.htm
9. ViralManager: The Viral Effect (2008) (accessed August 16, 2008), http://employmint.wordpress.com/2006/10/23/the-viral-effect/
10. Adobe: Adobe Flash CS3 Professional (accessed July 08, 2008), http://www.adobe.com/products/flash/upgrade/
11. Thomson, A.: Google Says Android Phones Are On Schedule for 2008, (accessed July 26, 2008), http://www.bloomberg.com/apps/news?pid=20601087&sid=aR9lQgliSTas&refer=home
12. aqAlert, Mobile portal (accessed August 26, 2008), http://www.aqalert.net/mobile.php
13. aqAlert, Web portal (accessed August 26, 2008), http://www.aqalert.net

Underdetermined Blind Source Separation Using Linear Separation System

Jan Cermak[1] and Zdenek Smekal[2]

[1] Institute of Photonics and Electronics, Academy of Sciences of the Czech Republic,
Chaberska 57, 182 51 Prague, Czech Republic
cermak4@kn.vutbr.cz
[2] Brno University of Technology, Faculty of Electrical Engineering and Communication,
Purkynova 118, 612 00 Brno, Czech Republic
smekal@feec.vutbr.cz

Abstract. In automatic speech and speech emotion recognition, a good quality of input speech signal is often required. The hit rate of recognizers is lowered by degradation of speech quality due to noise. Blind source separation can be used to enhance the speech signal as a part of preprocessing techniques. This paper presents a multi channel linear blind source separation method that can be applied even in underdetermined case i.e. when the number of source signals is higher than the number of sensors. Experiments have shown that our system outperforms conventional time-frequency binary masking in both determined and underdetermined cases and significantly increases the hit rate of speech recognizers.

Keywords: array signal processing, beamforming, blind source separation, speech processing, time-frequency binary masking.

1 Introduction

Blind source separation (BSS) is a set of methods, which are dedicated to separating signals from their mixtures when the mixing process is unknown. A well-known representative of the BSS methods is independent component analysis (ICA) [1]. It is a statistical approach performing spatial filtering, which relies only on statistical independence of the source signals. However ICA cannot be used in underdetermined case (UDC).

Another separation approach is the multiple-beamformer. The beamformer [2] performs linear spatial filtering by forming a directivity pattern of an array with M sensors in order to emphasize a target signal arriving from a given direction and to suppress jammer signals arriving from other directions. A set of N different beamformers must be employed to separate N sources. The critical problem of a set of multiple-beamformers or of the beamformer itself is that the separation is not performed blindly.

Time-frequency binary masking (TFBM) [3] is a BSS method employing nonlinear spatial filtering, which can be applied even to UDC, because it relies on time-frequency sparseness of the sources. However it has musical noise problem due to zero padding in the time-frequency domain. In this paper we present a technique that

A. Esposito et al. (Eds.): Multimodal Signals, LNAI 5398, pp. 300–305, 2009.

overcomes the limitations described above. Our aim is to develop a blind audio signal separation method that can be used even in UDC and does not cause musical noise. We begin by formulating the BSS problem in section 2. Section 3 describes the proposed BSS method. Experimental results are shown in section 4.

2 BSS for Convolutive Mixtures

We consider the convolutive mixing model, which is used to describe signal observations in an reverberant environment, with M sensors and N sources

$$x_j(t) = \sum_{k=1}^{N} \sum_{l=0}^{L-1} h_{kj}(l) s_k(t-l), \quad j = 1, \ldots, M, \tag{1}$$

where $x_j(t)$ is the signal observed by the j-th sensor, t is the discrete time index, $s_k(t)$ is the k-th source signal, $h_{kj}(l)$ is the impulse response from the k-th source to the j-th sensor and L is the length of the impulse response. Except for TFBM, the separation systems usually consist of FIR filters $w_{kj}(l)$ to compute N separated signals

$$y_k(t) = \sum_{j=1}^{M} \sum_{p=0}^{P-1} w_{kj}(p) x_j(t-p), \quad k = 1, \ldots, N, \tag{2}$$

where P is the FIR filter length. The aim of BSS is to compute the separated signals $y_k(t)$ without any a priori information but the number of sources N.

By applying the short time Fourier transform (STFT) and assuming source sparseness, which holds for speech signals [3], (1) can be approximated as

$$\mathbf{X}(f, \tau) \approx \mathbf{H}_k(f) S_k(f, \tau), \tag{3}$$

where $\mathbf{X}(f, \tau) = [X_1(f, \tau), \ldots, X_M(f, \tau)]^{\mathrm{T}}$ is an observation vector, $\mathbf{H}_k(f) = [H_1(f), \ldots, H_M(f)]^{\mathrm{T}}$ is a mixing vector, T is the transpose and $S_k(f, \tau)$ is the dominant source at the time-frequency point (f, τ).

3 BSS System Based on Beamformer Array

A block diagram of the proposed two-stage system is shown in Fig. 1, where the observation vector $\mathbf{X}(f, \tau)$ is processed by multi-channel TFBM (M-TFBM) [4]. The M-TFBM accomplishes BSS over the whole observation vector $\mathbf{X}(f, \tau)$ unlike the conventional TFBM, which applies binary masking only to one observed signal $X_j(f, \tau)$. M-TFBM is a complete BSS system, which estimates the vector of pre-separated signals $\hat{\mathbf{Y}}_k(f, \tau) = [\hat{Y}_{k1}(f, \tau), \ldots, \hat{Y}_{kM}(f, \tau)]^{\mathrm{T}}$. However it introduces musical noise into the pre-separated signals $\hat{\mathbf{Y}}_k(f, \tau)$.

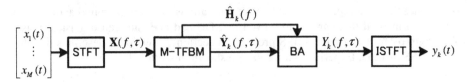

Fig. 1. Block diagram of the proposed system. ISTFT is an abbreviation for inverse STFT.

In order to remove the musical noise and improve separation performance we process the M-TFBM outputs by a beamformer array (BA), which is shown in Fig. 2. Let us assume that our goal is to extract just one signal from the signal mixture. In this case BA consists only of one column (D beamformers). D is a binomial coefficient that depends on the number of sources, sensors and jammers Z in the beamformer input mixture [4]. The main idea behind BA is to compose D different mixtures from pre-separated signals provided by M-TFBM, which are then filtered by D beamformers. All these beamformers are designed to enhance the target signal. Each input mixture includes the pre-separated target signal and different pre-separated jammers. The important point is that all jammers must be used at least once.

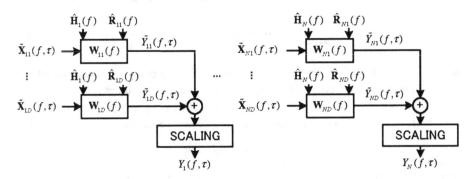

Fig. 2. Beamformer array

Let us take an example, where $N=4$, $M=3$, $Z=1$ and $k=1$. The size of the BA is $N=4$ and $D=3$. The input signals of the beamformers are $\tilde{\mathbf{X}}_{11}(f,\tau)=\hat{\mathbf{Y}}_{1}(f,\tau)+\hat{\mathbf{Y}}_{2}(f,\tau)$, $\tilde{\mathbf{X}}_{12}(f,\tau)=\hat{\mathbf{Y}}_{1}(f,\tau)+\hat{\mathbf{Y}}_{3}(f,\tau)$ and $\tilde{\mathbf{X}}_{13}(f,\tau)=\hat{\mathbf{Y}}_{1}(f,\tau)+\hat{\mathbf{Y}}_{4}(f,\tau)$.

BA utilize Frost beamformers, whose spatial filter is given as

$$\mathbf{W}_{kd}(f)=\frac{\hat{\mathbf{R}}_{kd}^{-1}(f)\hat{\mathbf{H}}_{k}(f)}{\hat{\mathbf{H}}_{k}^{H}(f)\hat{\mathbf{R}}_{kd}^{-1}(f)\hat{\mathbf{H}}_{k}(f)}, \tag{4}$$

where $\hat{\mathbf{R}}_{kd}(f)$ is the correlation matrix of jammer mixture, H is the complex conjugate transpose, d is the row index, and k is the column index. The correlation matrix $\hat{\mathbf{R}}_{kd}(f)$ and mixing vector $\hat{\mathbf{H}}_{k}(f)$ are estimated blindly in M-TFBM [4].

In one column of BA, the output signals $\tilde{Y}_{kd}(f,\tau)=\mathbf{W}_{kd}^{H}(f)\tilde{\mathbf{X}}_{kd}(f,\tau)$ of each beamformer are added up and then scaled with the number of rows D using block

SCALING in Fig. 2. Single beamformer outputs can be added up due to the constraint of the Frost beamformer $\mathbf{W}_k^H(f)\mathbf{H}_k(f)=1$.

4 Experiments

We performed experiments for both the determined case (DC) (M=3, N=3) and the UDC (M=3, N=4) in a room with a reverberation time of 120 ms, see Fig. 3. The source signals were 6-second male and female Czech utterances. The STFT frame size was B=512, the frame shift was B/4 and the sampling frequency $f_s = 8\,\text{kHz}$. Separation performance was evaluated by signal-to-interference ratio (SIR) [4], signal-to-distortion ratio (SDR) [4] and perceptual evaluation of speech quality (PESQ) [5], which is the prediction of the perceived quality that would be given by listeners in a subjective test.

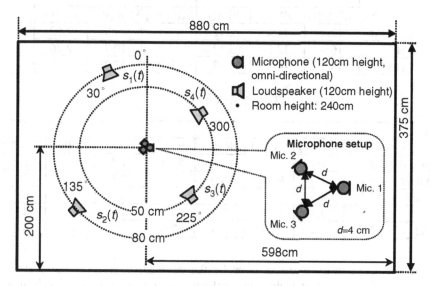

Fig. 3. Room setup

The average results over all sources for the DC, when $s_1(t),\ldots,s_3(t)$ were used, and for the UDC are summarized in Table 1. We use the notation BAZ, where Z was defined in section 3. The size of the BA was N=4, D=3 in UDC. In DC, the sizes of BA1 and BA2 were N=3, D=3 and N=3, D=1, respectively. SIR at the sensors was −3.1 dB and −4.8 dB in DC and UDC, respectively. We can see from Table 1 that the BA outperforms conventional TFBM [3] in both DC and UDC. BA1 achieves higher SIR and PESQ than BA2 because there are fewer jammers in $\tilde{\mathbf{X}}_{kd}(f,\tau)$, but on the other hand BA1 causes more distortion.

The last objective test is the evaluation by automatic speech recognizer (ASR), which has been developed by research team at the Technical University of Liberec.

The developed system [6] employs continuous ASR with a vocabulary size of about 300 thousand words. We used a testing corpus consisting of 1863 words, 14 from which were not in the vocabulary. The utterances were read by male speaker. The ASR test results are shown in Table 2, where HR is hit rate, DR is delece rate, SR is substitution rate and IR is insertion rate. The results are presented as a percentage of the testing corpus size.

The original signal achieved a HR of almost 90%. On the other hand the signal mixture observed at the arbitrary sensor has a very poor HR. More than 90% words were substituted. By applying BSS algorithms the HR rises. BA achieves about 80% in DC. The difference between BA1 and BA2 is minimal. However BA1 significantly outperforms BA2 in UDC. In both cases TFBM achieves a worse result than BA.

Table 1. Separation results

	DC			UDC		
	SIR [dB]	SDR [dB]	PESQ	SIR [dB]	SDR [dB]	PESQ
TFBM	12.0	11.4	2.92	11.4	9.9	2.52
BA1	16.9	12.1	3.12	15.7	10.7	2.76
BA2	15.2	16.2	3.03	12.9	12.2	2.62

Table 2. ASR test results

	DC				UDC			
	HR [%]	DR [%]	SR [%]	IR [%]	HR [%]	DR [%]	SR [%]	IR [%]
original	89.5	1.7	8.8	2.6	89.5	1.7	8.8	2.6
mixture	5.1	1.4	93.5	28.9	3.2	2.1	94.7	22.1
TFBM	53.2	4.5	42.2	8.6	36.6	6.3	57.1	9.2
BA1	80.5	3.4	16.1	3.3	67.6	4.5	28.0	4.8
BA2	79.6	2.7	17.7	3.9	42.6	9.1	48.3	4.2

The subjective evaluation was done by the comparison category rating (CCR) method [7]. We focused on evaluating interference (IF), musical noise, speech signal, and overall rating. The test consisted of ten pairs of 6-second utterances. The task was to compare the signals in one pair and evaluate them according to the rating scale. The rating scale range was from −3 (much worse) to 3 (much better). The reference signal in each pair was the signal separated by TFBM. The subjective test was evaluated by 15 listeners. The results are shown in Table 3.

The original signal achieved the best results. On the contrary, the mixture was evaluated with the lowest score except for the musical noise. TFBM was also compared with itself, which resulted in values close to zero over all criteria. This shows the credibility of the test. The BA systems achieved the best results. The overall rating is similar for both BA1 and BA2. The difference between DC and UDC is not significant. However, BA2 was rated with a higher interference score than BA1.

Table 3. Subjective test results

	DC				UDC			
	IF	musical noise	signal	overall	IF	musical noise	signal	overall
original	1.4	2.5	2.1	2.3	0.7	2.7	1.9	2.4
mixture	−2.9	2.0	−1.9	−2.4	−3.0	2.0	−2.1	−2.5
TFBM	0.0	0.1	0.1	0.1	0.0	0.0	0.1	0.1
BA1	0.1	1.7	1.0	1.1	−1.2	1.7	0.5	0.9
BA2	−0.1	2.2	1.0	1.3	−1.7	1.6	0.7	0.8

5 Conclusion

In this paper, we introduced a two-stage BSS approach for sparse audio signals that gives high separation performance. Furthermore, BA is a linear system that causes no musical noise and can be used even in the UDC. We compared the proposed system with conventional TFBM and evaluated it by objective and subjective methods. It was shown that the BA outperformed TFBM in all tests and could be used as an effective preprocessing technique for speech recognizers. Furthermore BA was positively evaluated by the listening tests.

Acknowledgement. This paper has been supported by the project COST 2102 of the MSMT pr. No OC08010, by the national research program "Information Society" of the ASCR pr. No 1ET301710509 and the project GACR 102/07/1303. This work was partly done during an internship of the first author at NTT Communication Science Laboratories.

References

1. Hyvarinen, A., Oja, E.: Independent Component Analysis: Algorithms and Applications. Neural Networks 13(4-5), 411–430 (2000)
2. Johnson, D., Dungeon, D.: Array Signal Processing. Prentice Hall, Englewood Cliffs (1993)
3. Yilmaz, O., Rickard, S.: Blind Separation of Speech Mixtures via Time-Frequency Masking. IEEE Transactions on Signal Processing 52(7) (2004)
4. Cermak, J., Araki, S., Sawada, H., Makino, S.: Blind Source Separation Based on a Beamformer Array and Time-Frequency Binary Masking. In: ICASSP 2007, vol. 1, pp. 145–148 (2007) ISBN 1-4244-0728-1
5. Perceptual Evaluation of Speech Quality (PESQ). ITU-T Recommendation P.862, http://www.itu.int/rec/T-REC-p
6. Nouza, J., Zdansky, J., Cerva, P., Kolorenc, J.: A System for Information Retrieval from Large Records of Broadcast Programs. In: Sojka, P., Kopeček, I., Pala, K. (eds.) TSD 2006. LNCS (LNAI), vol. 4188, pp. 485–492. Springer, Heidelberg (2006)
7. Methods for Subjective Determination of Transmission Quality. ITU-T Recommendation P.800, http://www.itu.int/rec/T-REC-p

Articulatory Synthesis of Speech and Singing: State of the Art and Suggestions for Future Research

Bernd J. Kröger and Peter Birkholz

Department of Phoniatrics, Pedaudiology, and Communication Disorders,
University Hospital Aachen and Aachen University, Aachen, Germany
bkroeger@ukaachen.de, peterbirkholz@gmx.de

Abstract. Articulatory synthesis of speech and singing aims for modeling the production process of speech and singing as human-like or natural as possible. The state of the art is described for all modules of articulatory synthesis systems, i.e. vocal tract models, acoustic models, glottis models, noise source models, and control models generating articulator movements and phonatory control information. While a lot of knowledge is available for the production and for the high quality acoustic realization of *static* spoken and sung sounds it is suggested to improve the quality of control models especially for the generation of articulatory *movements*. Thus the main problem which should be addressed for improving articulatory synthesis over the next years is the development of high quality control concepts. It is suggested to use action based control concepts and to gather control knowledge by imitating natural speech acquisition and singing acquisition scenarios. It is emphasized that teacher-learner interaction and production, perception, and comprehension of auditory as well as of visual and somatosensory information (multimodal information) should be included in the acquisition (i.e. training or learning) procedures.

Keywords: speech, singing, articulatory synthesis, articulation, vocal tract acoustics, movement control, human-human interaction, speech acquisition.

1 Introduction

Articulatory synthesis systems comprise (i) a module for the generation of vocal tract movements (control model), (ii) a module for converting this movement information into a continuous succession of vocal tract geometries (vocal tract model), and (iii) a module for the generation of acoustic signals on the basis of this articulatory information (acoustic model). It is an advantage that these systems are closely related to the natural human process of the production of speech or singing. But due to the complexity of the natural processes of speech or singing production, no current articulatory synthesis system is capable of generating high quality acoustic speech or singing signals as are generated for example by current corpus based unit selection synthesis methods.

In this paper the state of the art knowledge for articulatory synthesis of speech and singing is summarized and suggestions are made for developing a high quality system on the basis of this currently available knowledge for all levels of these systems, i.e. on the level of the control model, of the vocal tract model and of the acoustic model.

A. Esposito et al. (Eds.): Multimodal Signals, LNAI 5398, pp. 306–319, 2009.

2 Vocal Tract Model and Acoustic Model

2.1 Vocal Tract Models

The task of vocal tract models is to generate the complete geometrical information concerning the vocal tract (shape and position of all vocal tract organs, i.e. lips, tongue, palate, velum, pharynx, larynx, nasal cavity) and its variation over time. Shape, position, and motion of movable vocal tract organs are generated on the basis of the time functions of all vocal tract parameters defined by the model. A typical set of vocal tract parameters are: position of jaw, upper lips, lower lips, tongue tip, tongue body, velum, and larynx. Vocal tract models can be subdivided into statistical, biomechanical, and geometrical models.

Statistical models (e.g. Maeda 1988, Beautemps et al. 2001, Badin et al. 2002, Serrurier and Badin 2008) are based on large corpora of vocal tract movements measured by different techniques (MRI, EMA, or X-Ray). Articulatory information (local flesh point positions reflecting the position of a vocal tract organ or the whole shape of vocal tract organs) is extracted for each time instant (frame by frame) for the whole corpus and articulatory movement parameters are derived by statistical procedures (e.g. principal component analysis).

Biomechanical models aim to model the physiological basis of all vocal tract organs and their neuromuscular control (e.g. Wilhelms-Tricarico 1995, Dang 2004). These models mainly use finite element methods and are based on physiological knowledge about the muscular structure, tissue structure and cartilaginous or bone structure of vocal tract organs. The articulatory parameterization as well as the shaping and positioning of the vocal tract organs result from physiological knowledge.

For *geometrical models* (e.g. Mermelstein 1973, Kröger 1998, Engwall 2003, Birkholz et al. 2006) the positioning and shape of the vocal tract organs is calculated by using a set of a priori defined vocal tract parameters. The basis for the choice of distinct parameter sets depends mainly on assumptions about the variety of vocal tract configurations which the model aims to approximate. Due to the flexibility of this class of models the vocal tract shape can be fitted to articulatory data of different speakers, i.e. the model can be adapted to different speakers with different sex and age (e.g. Birkholz and Kröger 2006). Fitting the model to articulatroy data is basically done using static vocal configurations (e.g. vocalic and consonantal MRI-data, see Engwall 2003, Birkholz and Kröger 2006) but in addition, movement data at least of certain flesh points of articulators or of certain contact regions (e.g. EMA-data and EPG-data, see Engwall 2003) can be fitted in order do make sure that the model behaves correctly even in the case of articulatory movements.

2.2 Acoustic Models

The task of the acoustic models is to calculate the time varying air flow and air pressure distribution within the vocal tract and to calculate the acoustic speech signal radiated from the facial region of the model. The input information for acoustic models is lung pressure, subglottal air flow, and the geometric shape of the vocal tract tube (trachea, glottis, pharyngeal, oral, and nasal tract) for each time instant. A time-varying *tube model* is specified from the geometrical vocal tract model information, which represents the vocal tract cavities (trachea, pharynx, nasal, and oral cavity). The tube model consists of a succession of *tube sections* with constant cross sectional area. The aerodynamic and acoustic characteristics of these tube sections and their joints towards the neighboring tube sections are described by the acoustic models. Acoustic models can be subdivided into reflection type line analog models, transmission line circuit analog models, hybrid time-frequency domain models, and finite element wave propagation models.

In the case of *reflection type line analog models* (e.g. Kelly and Lochbaum 1962, Liljencrants 1985, Meyer et al. 1989, Kröger 1998), forward and backward traveling partial flow or pressure waves are calculated for each vocal tract tube section in the time domain on the basis of scattering equations which reflect the impedance discontinuity at tube junctions. The calculation of pressure and flow within each tube section from trachea to mouth and nostrils and the calculation of the radiated sound wave are accomplished from the forward and backward traveling flow or pressure waves. The major shortcoming of this simulation technique is that variations of vocal tract length over time – which occur in normal speech production, e.g. within an [u]-to-[i] or [a]-to-[u] transition – can not be handled.

In the case of *transmission line circuit analog models* (e.g. Flanagan 1975, Maeda 1982, Birkholz et al. 2007), pressure and flow within each vocal tract tube section is calculated by a digital simulation of electrical circuit elements, representing the acoustic and aerodynamic properties within each vocal tract tube section. Variations of vocal tract length can be handled but, as in the case of all time domain simulation techniques, frequency dependent acoustic and aerodynamic losses (from sound radiation at nostrils and mouth, from vocal tract wall vibrations, from air frication at vocal tract walls etc.) can just be approximated. But the modeling of these loss mechanisms is essential for high quality speech synthesis since loss mechanisms for example adjust the bandwidth of formants and thus also the overall signal amplitude in different frequency regions. A very detailed discussion of acoustic and aerodynamic loss mechanisms within the vocal tract and a very detailed and gainful discussion of strategies how to approximate these loss mechanisms in time domain models is given by Liljencrants (1985). On the basis of that work it is now possible to take transmission line circuit analog models as a basic approach for high-quality articulatory synthesis.

In the case of *hybrid time-frequency domain models* (e.g. Allen and Strong 1985, Sondhi and Schroeter 1987), the frequency dependence of the acoustic simulation is modeled very detailed by calculating the acoustic transfer function for each vocal tract tube section within the frequency domain. In order to calculate flow and pressure at least at the most important locations within the vocal tract tube, time-frequency domain transformations must be calculated at these locations and for each time instant. Hence the implementation of this approach is complex and the calculation of the acoustic signal is time consuming.

In the case of *finite element wave propagation models* (e.g. El-Masri et al. 1996, Mazsuzaki and Motoki 2000) the aerodynamic and acoustic behavior of air flow and air pressure within the vocal tract is calculated very precisely by directly solving basic physical equations for the aero-acoustics of wave propagation. These models are very complex and the calculation of the acoustic signal is time consuming. This kind of models is rather appropriate for addressing general problems of transmission line wave propagation (for example for addressing the problem of noise generation within the tube) than for calculating acoustic signals in real time applications.

2.3 Glottis Models

The task of glottis models is to generate the acoustic source signal for phonation and its insertion into the vocal tract tube model. The source signal is propagated through the supraglottal cavities (pharyngeal, oral and nasal cavity) as well as through the subglottal cavities (trachea, lungs) by the acoustic model. Glottis models can be subdivided into self-oscillating models, parametric glottal area models, and parametric glottal flow models.

In the case of *self-oscillating glottis models* (Ishizaka and Flanagan 1972, Cranen and Boves 1987, Story and Titze 1995, Kröger 1998, Alipour et al. 2000, Kob 2002) the oscillation behaviour of vocal folds is calculated on the basis of general physical equations of motion leading to the waveform of the glottal area over time. Subsequently the glottal flow waveform can be calculated as a function of time on the basis of the glottal area waveform. The dynamic oscillation behaviour is generated for coupled spring mass systems representing the vocal fold dynamic behaviour and is controlled by biomechanical parameters like vocal fold tension and glottal aperture. External forces acting on the spring mass system result form the pressure distribution along the glottal constriction. Note that the term "articulatory" as is used in this paper also covers "phonatory articulation", which comprises the adjustment of vocal fold tension and glottal aperture. Self-oscillating glottis models allow to control different speech sound qualities like qualities along the scales soft-normal-loud, pressed-modal-breathy, as well as for creaky voice and glottalizations (Kröger 1997a). Furthermore self-oscillating gottis models allow to approximate different registers in singing like chest and falsetto (Kröger 1997b) by an adjustment of the appropriate control parameters. In addition these models allow a wide variation of fundamental frequency by changing the control parameter vocal fold tension and by changing in addition other physiological parameters of the vocal folds (like overall length, mass distribution for the vocal folds, etc.) which has to be preset with respect to sex and age of a speaker or singer.

In the case of *parametric glottal area models* (e.g. Titze 1989, Cranen and Schroeter 1996), the time function of the glottal area waveform is predefined while glottal flow and glottal pressure results from the insertion of the glottal area model into the acoustic-aerodynamic model. An advantage of this kind of models is that fundamental frequency is a direct control parameter, while this is not the case in self-oscillating glottis models. But it should be noted that these models need a detailed description of the glottal area waveform for the control of different sound qualities like e.g. breathy, normal, pressed. In the case of self-oscillating glottis models the glottal area waveform directly results from underlying articulatory settings like more or less glottal ab-/adduction.

In the case of *parametric glottal flow models* (e.g. Fant et al. 1985) the time function of glottal flow is directly parameterized and inserted into the acoustic model. But this may prohibit the simulation of important acoustic effects like the modification of the glottal flow waveform resulting from acoustic interactions with the supralaryngeal vocal tract. Furthermore, as was mentioned in the case of parametric glottal area models, the control of voice quality in the case of these models can only be done successfully if a detailed knowledge of the flow waveform parameters is available (e.g. from inverse filtering procedures, Fant 1993).

2.4 Noise Source Models

The task of noise source models is to generate and to insert noise source signals into the acoustic transmission line model. Noise signals result from turbulent air flow, mainly occurring downstream in front of a vocal tract constriction in the case of a high value of volume flow. Noise source models can be subdivided into parametric and generic noise source models.

In the case of *parametric noise source models* (e.g. Mawass et al. 2000, Birkholz et al. 2007), turbulent noise is inserted into the vocal tract tube if a defined aerodynamic situation occurs: sufficient narrow constriction and sufficient high air flow. High quality acoustic signals can be generated in all cases of noise generation within the vocal tract (i.e. for glottal aspiration, for plosive noise bursts, and for fricative noise) by optimizing the frequency contour of the inserted noise, by optimizing the parameters controlling the noise amplitude, and by optimizing the location for insertion of the noise source within the acoustic transmission line model with respect to the location of the constriction.

In the case of *generic noise source models* (e.g. Sinder 1999) the occurrence of turbulences and its acoustic consequences are calculated by solving basic physical aero-acoustic equations. But these procedures are very time consuming and thus these kind of models are rather used for the elucidation of the basic physical aero-acoustic principles of noise source generation than for generating noise in an articulatory synthesizer for speech and singing aiming for real time applications.

3 Control Models for Speech and Singing

It is the task of control models to generate the complete vocal tract control information for each time instant of signal production. The control model specifies the whole set of vocal tract control parameters defined by the appropriate vocal tract model for each time instant during the production of an utterance or song. Thus the control model generates the complete set of movements for all vocal tract organs (articulatory movements) during the whole time course of the utterance or song. Control models can be subdivided into segmental and action based control models for speech. A first control model for singing has been established using an action based concept.

The input specification for *segmental control models* (Kröger 1992 and 1998) is a phonological description of the utterance. A succession of time intervals is specified from this input information for the production of each syllable and subsequently for the production of each sound. Time instants (labels) are specified within these sound production time intervals at which specific spatial targets (spatial goals) have to be reached by specific vocal tract organs. Coarticulation results form articulatory underspecification (Kröger 1992, 1998, and 2003) since targets are specified exclusively for those vocal tract organs which are involved in an obligatory way in the production of the intended sound; e.g. the lips in the case of a labial sound ([p], [b], [f], [v], [m], ...), the tongue tip in the case of an apical sound ([t], [d], [s], [z], [n], ...), or the tongue body in the case of a dorsal sound ([k], [g], [x], [ŋ], ...). Lips and tongue body position have to be specified in the case of all vowels since each vowel requires a specific formation of the whole vocal tract tube. The position of the velum has to be specified for all sounds with respect to the fact whether they are nasals or nasalized vowels (low position of the velum), oral sonorants (high position of the velum), or obstruents (high position of the velum and the velopharyngeal port is tightly closed). For obstruents (e.g. plosives and fricatives) it is necessary to ensure an air pressure build up within the pharyngeal and oral cavity of the vocal tract. The rest position of the vocal folds (vocal fold aperture) has to be specified for each sound with respect to the fact whether the sound is voiced (vocal folds abducted), voiceless (vocal folds adducted), or a glottal stop (vocal folds tightly adducted).

The input specification of *action based control models* for speech (Saltzman and Munhall 1989, Browman and Goldstein 1992, Kröger 1993, Saltzman and Byrd 2000, Goldstein et al. 2006, Birkholz et al. 2006, Kröger and Birkholz 2007; also called gestural control models) is the phonological description of the utterance including a prosodic annotation. This information is converted into a *discrete score of vocal tract actions*. The vocal tract actions (or gestures) are associated with each other in a specific way (Fig 1, top). Subsequently this action score is formulated in a quantitative way as *high level phonetic score of vocal tract actions* which can be interpreted from a cognitive and sensorimotor viewpoint as a *high level representation of the motor plan* of the utterance (cp. Kröger et al. 2008). Starting with the qualitative discrete description (Fig. 1 top: discrete action score) a first quantitative version of the vocal tract action score or motor plan of a syllable or word is calculated by the control model (Fig. 1 bottom). Here, the temporal duration and time course of degree of realization for each vocal tract action (including onset and offset intervals) and a specification of the vocal tract action goal in the high level somatosensory domain (not displayed in Fig. 1) is specified. Subsequently the motor plan can be executed which leads to concrete movement trajectories for all articulators (i.e. a *lower level phonetic articulatory description* which is not displayed in Fig. 1). This lower level phonetic articulatory description is obtained by using concepts of inverse dynamics, if more than one articulator is involved in the execution of a vocal tract action (e.g. lower jaw, upper and lower lips for a labial closing action, cp. Saltzman and Munhall 1989).

The advantage of action based control models in comparison to segmental control models is that the dynamics and kinematics of articulatory *movements* can be controlled explicitly. This is a very important feature since sensorimotor movement control is an essential task in all kinds of human behavior or movement generation. Furthermore coarticulation directly results from temporal overlap of actions (i.e. coproduction, Browman and Goldstein 1992) in action based models. Moreover it can be shown that the variability of segmental phonetic surface descriptions of an utterance – as occurs in many languages if speaking rate is increased – directly results from increase in overlap in time and decrease in duration and decrease in degree of realization of vocal tract actions (Kröger 1993).

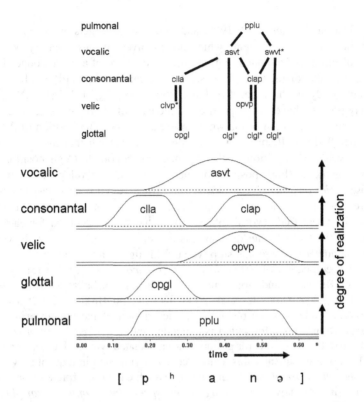

Fig. 1. Discrete score of speech actions (top) and high level phonetic speech action score (bottom) for the German word "Panne" ("glitch") using the action based control model of Birkholz et al. (2006). Top: Discrete specification of actions (4-letter-abbreviations) and their associations (lines between these abbreviations). Bottom: High level phonetic action specification, displaying (i) duration of activation time intervals for each vocal tract action and (ii) degree of realization for each vocal tract action. Action symbols (cp. Kröger and Birkholz 2007): vocal tract short /a/-shaping action (asvt), labial full closing action (clla), apical full closing action (clap), velopharyngeal opening action (opvp), glottal opening action (opgl), positive lung pressure action (pplu). In the case of full closing actions the maximum degree of realization indicates the temporal interval of full closure (see the consonantal full closing action clla and clap). Note that the activation interval for each action also includes onset and offset time intervals of the action. Default actions (default gestures) are marked by an asterisk (i.e. vocal tract schwa-shaping action swvt, velopharyngeal closing action clvp, glottal closing action clgl). Contours for degree of realization of actions are not shown for default actions within the action activation score. Note that action realization patterns not directly reflect the resulting time functions of articulator movements (i.e. lower level phonetic descriptions). These time functions are not displayed here.

A first control model for the articulation and phonation during singing has been established within an action based framework (Birkholz 2007). Here, beside the control of the articulation of speech sounds, in addition a concept is added which in parallel controls the production of notes (or tones) and which synchronizes the speech sound articulation – i.e. the *sound actions* – with respect to the musical time measure and notes – i.e. with respect to the *tone actions* (Fig 2.).

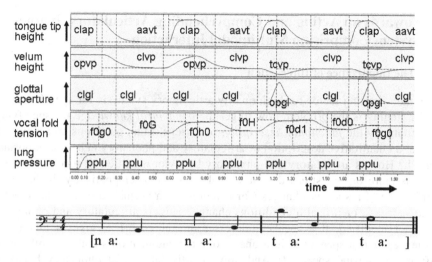

Fig. 2. Lower level phonetic action score for selected articulatory parameters (see on top: tongue tip height, velum height, glottal aperture, vocal fold tension, and lung pressure) displaying action specifications (onset time and target locations) and the resulting articulatory movement trajectories for a short singing phrase (for notes and text, see bottom). The tonal range used is that of a baritone singer. Sound action symbols (cp. Kröger and Birkholz 2007): vocal tract long /a/-shaping action (aavt), apical closing action (clap), velopharyngeal opening action (opvp), velopharyngeal closing action (clvp), velopharyngeal tight closing action (tcvp), glottal closing action (clgl), glottal opening action (opgl), positive lung pressure action (pplu). In this case of singing in addition tone actions for adjusting a specific fundamental frequency occur. These tone actions mainly adjust vocal fold tension. For example: g0 fundamental frequency action (f0g0). Occurring notes (or tones) from low to high: G, H, d0, g0, h0, d1 form different tone actions.

As is exemplified by the description of the action based control concept for speech and for singing by both examples (i.e. by the word "Panne", Fig. 1 and by the short singing phrase, Fig. 2) it is very essential to differentiate at least three levels of control: the *discrete and abstract functional (sometimes called phonological) level of action realization*, and two quantitative behavioral levels, the *quantitative higher behavioral or phonetic level of action realization*, quantitatively describing the degree of realization of a vocal tract action over time and the *quantitative lower behavioral or phonetic level of action realization*, quantitatively describing the spatiotemporal trajectories at least for the end articulators which are essential for realizing the goal of an action. Discrete tone action specification is that, what is exactly given by the notes in Fig.2 (bottom), i.e. musical tone pitch, tone length and discrete levels of tone dynamics (e.g. fortissimo, forte, mezzo forte, piano, pianissimo). High level phonetic tone action specification in addition includes further specifications like a detailed quantitative description of length, pitch, vibrato etc. and the lower level phonetic specification of a tone action includes a specification of how a tone is realized by a specific setting of articulatory (and phonatory) parameters like lung pressure and vocal fold tension.

4   Towards an Acting and Comprehending Articulatory Synthesis System Comprising Multimodal Interaction

4.1   The Importance of Interaction

The main limiting factor for high quality articulatory synthesis for speech as well as for singing is the problem how to get the *behavioral knowledge* for specifying quantitatively the *functional description* of actions. Main questions are: How can we get a quantitative description of articulatory and phonatory behavior in normal speech? How is articulatory and phonatory behavior modified in speech, if a syllable is more or less stressed, if a syllable is stressed emphatically, if the emotional state of a speaker changes (for example from normal to fear, to happiness, or to sadness), or if health conditions change? How is articulatory and phonatory behavior modified, if a speaker addresses an audience (i.e. gives a talk to an audience) or if a speaker is in a one-to-one communication situation (colloquial, informal or casual speech)?   And how is articulatory and phonatory behavior modified if a singer performs different singing styles or if a singer increases from an amateur to a professional singer?

Many of these questions are not easy to solve. But there are a lot of arguments which indicate that it is important to embed synthesis models in a broader framework including aspects of human-human interaction. Human-human interaction is essential during learning phases for speaking or singing. Thus it can be assumed that synthesis systems are able to sound more natural if behavioral or control knowledge is collected during scenarios which are similar to natural speech acquisition scenarios (e.g. Bailly 1997, Guenther 2006, Guenther et al. 2006, Kröger and Birkholz 2007, Kröger et al. 2008). Therefore it is important to integrate articulatory synthesis models into a broader communication framework. Learning or acquiring of speech and singing implies communication with partners who are capable of commenting or judging the production trials of the synthesis model.

In the case of word learning (lexical learning) as well as in the case of learning tones or short spoken or sung phrases, the synthesis model (learner) and the expert (teacher) who judges the trials or items produced by the model, provide the basis for word acquisition (Fig. 3). The synthesis model hears an item (e.g. the word "dolly") produced by the expert and has an initial hypothesis how to reproduce (to imitate) the item. The expert listens to the items produced by the model (to the imitation items) and gives feedback. The expert can ignore, reject, or question ("what do your mean?") the item if the production is not understandable or not produced in a way which allows a classification as normal or at least understandable. Thereupon the synthesis model has the chance to modify the motor plan and to produce a further or corrected realization (version) of the item. This leads to a training loop (Fig. 3). If a vesion of an item is judged as acceptable by the expert, the expert will award this version of the item (e.g. "How wonderful! Yes that is a dolly"). This commendation causes the synthesis system (learner) to store the actual motor plan of the actual item as an acceptable motor representation of this word.

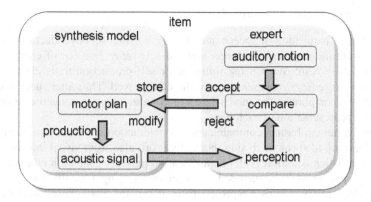

Fig. 3. The communication model for speech or singing acquisition. The model comprises a synthesis control model (or learner) and an expert (or teacher). The functioning of the communication model is described in the text.

Speech and non-specialized singing acquisition takes place during the first years of lifetime while choir singing training or solo-singing training occurs later during lifetime. But the human-human interaction scenario or learner-teacher interaction scenario described above holds for all these training situations. The term "item" introduced in Fig. 3 holds for speaking as well as for singing items.

4.2   The Importance of Action, Perception, and Comprehension

Beside this learner-teacher scenario a second scenario occurs during speech acquisition where the synthesis model by itself trains, judges, and learns acceptable realizations of spoken or sung items (e.g. words, single tones, spoken or sung phrases). This implies that the synthesis model comprises a perception and comparison component (see for example the feedback loop in models of speech production, as described by Guenther 2006). In this case the synthesis model starts by storing an auditory representation of a spoken or sung item which often has been produced by communication partners and tries actively to reproduce (to imitate) this item by himself (*action*). The model compares the perceptual representations of these self-productions with the stored auditory representation of that item (*perception*). A motor plan is stored as motor representation of this item if the auditory difference between already stored and the self-produced item falls below a certain acceptance limit. Thus in the context of Fig. 3 the synthesis model comprises (includes) the expert, since the model already includes a representation of the ideal training result and since the model comprises a perception and comparison module.

At least *comprehension*, i.e. the association between the function (concept or meaning) and the behavioral sensorimotor representation of a word, tone, or a spoken or sung phrase is a precondition for these learning (or action-perception) scenarios described above. Functional features represent the intention of a speech or singing act and thus are basic for each communication behavior.

4.3 The Importance of Multimodality

Firstly, during acquisition of speech and singing, a synthesis or production model not just stores an *auditory representation* and a *motor representation* of each speech or sung item. As a result from many imitation or self-production trials the model also stores a *somatosensory representation* of the item as well. Thus after successful training of a word or phrase, the model has stored an auditory, a somatosensory, and a motor plan representation of each item.

Secondly, human-human communication or interaction scenarios which are important for learning to speak or to sing, normally profit also from visual information, i.e. information which occurs if both communication partners gaze each other. Thus also *visual perception* should be included in speech and singing acquisition scenarios: The model or learner also stores a representation of the lips, jaw, chest and body movements for a trained spoken or sung item. It is well known for speech that even persons without hearing losses profit from visual facial information, for example if the auditory information is not fully available (e.g. in the case of disturbing noise, Schwartz et al. 2004). That is a proof for the fact that mental representations of facial speech movements (i.e. jaw and lip movements and in some cases also movements of the front part of the tongue if visible) exist.

These facts underline the need of multimodal data and an audiovisual learner-teacher scenario as an interactive framework for gathering knowledge for a control model for articulatory synthesis if high quality synthesis of speech or singing is aimed for. Beside speech production also in the case of singing production it becomes directly apparent that audiovisual learner-teacher scenarios are extremely needful. That can be audiovisual feedback from the mother or from caretakers in the case of acquisition of singing, audiovisual feedback of other chorister or of the conductor in the case of choir singing, or audiovisual feedback of the singing teacher in the case of solo-singing training.

5 Discussion

In this paper the state of the art for articulatory synthesis of speech and singing is discussed. One of the major findings is that the current vocal tract models and acoustics models including glottis and noise source models are capable of producing high quality acoustic output. This can be demonstrated at best for isolated *static* vowels and consonants (at least fricatives, laterals, nasals) in speech or singing (cp. Mawass et al. 2000, Birkholz 2007). The main problem is the generation of *control information* for the vocal tract *movements*, i.e. to generate natural *behavioral information*. In this paper it is argued for training these systems during learning to speak or to sing in a similar way as training and learning occurs during natural speech and natural singing acquisition. It is argued for developing *acting, perceiving, and comprehending virtual humans* in the context of a *multimodal learner-teacher interaction scenarios*. Therefore the development of a high quality articulatory-acoustic production or synthesis model always comprises high quality multimodal perception and comprehension tools including auditory, somatosensory, and visual perception of external as well as of feedback signals for developing high quality control modules for production. Thus it is feasible to take into account the close relationship between production and perception as is claimed in recent neurocognitive production-perception models (Hickok and Poeppel 2007).

Due to the learner-teacher scenario introduced in this paper it must be emphasized that action behavior (i.e. motor plans for speech and singing items) can be learned mainly from auditory or audiovisual information. It is not necessary to train articulatory production models for speech and singing by accessing a huge articulatory data base. If an articulatory-acoustic model and an action based control model is used, the production model comprises physiological constraints, which allow the generation of motor plans from auditory or audiovisual imitation processes without any other data (i.e. no articulatory data are needed). Motor plans can be optimized by a few trail and error loops as described above as the learner-teacher interaction scenario.

Last but not least, since the articulatory synthesis model already generates natural lip and jaw movements for speech and singing, it would be advantageous to incorporate the articulatory synthesis model within a complete facial model and moreover within a complete full length whole body model (avatar or virtual agent). And in addition the modeling of speech accompanying gesturing (eyebrow movements, head movements, hand and arm movements, whole body movements at least for the upper part of the body) could be added. Speech accompanying gestures can be described qualitatively and quantitatively in the same framework as vocal tract actions: There exist functional and behavioral levels for the description of actions, and action planning and action execution can be separated in a similar way. A further benefit from incorporating speech accompanying actions (or gestures) is that these actions facilitate the transfer of intentions and of meanings within communication and interaction scenarios. And it can easily been shown that speech accompanying gesturing increases the impression of the overall quality level of the speech or singing synthesis.

Acknowledgments. This work was supported in part by the German Research Council DFG grant Kr 1439/13-1.

References

Alipour, F., Berry, D.A., Titze, I.R.: A finite-element model of vocal-fold vibration. Journal of the Acoustical Society of America 108, 3003–3012 (2000)

Allen, D.R., Strong, W.J.: A model for synthesis of natural sounding vowels. Journal of the Acoustical Society of America 78, 58–69 (1985)

Badin, P., Bailly, G., Revéret, L., Baciu, M., Segebarth, C., Savariaux, C.: Three-dimensional articulatory modeling of tongue, lips and face, based on MRI and video images. Journal of Phonetics 30, 533–553 (2002)

Bailly, G.: Learning to speak: sensory-motor control of speech movements. Speech Communication 22, 251–267 (1997)

Beautemps, D., Badin, P., Bailly, G.: Linear degrees of freedom in speech production: Analysis of cineradio- and labio-film data and articulatory-acoustic modeling. Journal of the Acoustical Society of America 109, 2165–2180 (2001)

Birkholz, P.: Articulatory synthesis of singing. In: Bloothooft, G. (ed.) Synthesis of Singing Challenge. Antwerp, Belgium (2007),
http://www.let.uu.nl/~Gerrit.Bloothooft/personal/SSC/index.htm

Birkholz, P., Kröger, B.J.: Vocal tract model adaptation using magnetic resonance imaging. In: Proceedings of the 7th International Seminar on Speech Production, pp. 493–500. Belo Horizonte, Brazil (2006)

Birkholz, P., Jackèl, D., Kröger, B.J.: Construction and control of a three-dimensional vocal tract model. In: Proceedings of the International Conference on Acoustics, Speech, and Signal Processing (ICASSP 2006) Toulouse, France, pp. 873–876 (2006)

Birkholz, P., Jackèl, D., Kröger, B.J.: Simulation of losses due to turbulence in the time-varying vocal system. IEEE Transactions on Audio, Speech, and Language Processing 15, 1218–1225 (2007)

Browman, C.P., Goldstein, L.: Articulatory phonology: An overview. Phonetica 49, 155–180 (1992)

Cranen, B., Boves, L.: On subglottal formant analysis. Journal of the Acoustical Society of America 81, 734–746 (1987)

Cranen, B., Schroeter, J.: Physiologically motivated modeling of the voice source in articulatory analysis / synthesis. Speech Communication 19, 1–19 (1996)

Dang, J., Honda, K.: Construction and control of a physiological articulatory model. Journal of the Acoustical Society of America 115, 853–870 (2004)

El-Masri, S., Pelorson, X., Saguet, P., Badin, P.: Vocal tract acoustics using the transmission line matrix (TLM) method. In: Procedings of ICSPL, Philadelphia, pp. 953–956 (1996)

Engwall, O.: Combining MRI, EMA and EPG measurements in a three-dimensional tongue model. Speech Communication 41, 303–329 (2003)

Fant, G.: Some problems in voice source analysis. Speech Communication 13, 7–22 (1993)

Fant, G., Liljencrants, J., Lin, Q.: A four-parameter model of glottal flow. Speech Transmission Laboratory - Quarterly Progress and Status Report 4/1985. Royal Institute of Technology, Stockholm, pp. 1–13 (1985)

Flanagan, J.L., Ishizaka, K., Shipley, K.L.: Synthesis of speech from a dynamic model of the vocal cords and vocal tract. The Bell System Technical Journal 54, 485–506 (1975)

Goldstein, L., Byrd, D., Saltzman, E.: The role of vocal tract action units in understanding the evolution of phonology. In: Arbib, M.A. (ed.) Action to Language via the Mirror Neuron System, pp. 215–249. Cambridge University Press, Cambridge (2006)

Guenther, F.H.: Cortical interactions underlying the production of speech sounds. Journal of Communication Disorders 39, 350–365 (2006)

Guenther, F.H., Ghosh, S.S., Tourville, J.A.: Neural modeling and imaging of the cortical interactions underlying syllable production. Brain and Language 96, 280–301 (2006)

Hickok, G., Poeppel, D.: Towards a functional neuroanatomy of speech perception. Trends in Cognitive Sciences 4, 131–138 (2007)

Ishizaka, K., Flanagan, J.L.: Synthesis of voiced sounds from a two-mass model of the vocal cords. The Bell System Technical Journal 51, 1233–1268 (1972)

Kelly, J.L., Lochbaum, C.C.: Speech synthesis. In: Flanagan, J.L., Rabiner, L.R. (eds.) Speech Synthesis, Dowden, Hutchinson & Ross, Stoudsburg, pp. 127–130 (1962)

Kob, M.: Physical modeling of the singing voice. Unpublished doctoral thesis. RWTH Aachen University, Aachen (2002)

Kröger, B.J.: Minimal rules for articulatory speech synthesis. In: Vandewalle, J., Boite, R., Moonen, M., Oosterlinck, A. (eds.) Signal Processing VI: Theories and Applications, pp. 331–334. Elesevier, Amsterdam (1992)

Kröger, B.J.: A gestural production model and its application to reduction in German. Phonetica 50, 213–233 (1993)

Kröger, B.J.: Zur artikulatorischen Realisierung von Phonationstypen mittels eines selbstschwingenden Glottismodells. Sprache-Stimme-Gehör 21, 102–105 (1997a)

Kröger, B.J.: On the quantitative relationship between subglottal pressure, vocal cord tension, and glottal adduction in singing. Proceedings of the Institute of Acoustics 19, 479–484 (1997b) (ISMA 1997)

Kröger, B.J.: Ein phonetisches Modell der Sprachproduktion. Niemeyer Verlag, Tübingen (1998)

Kröger, B.J.: Ein visuelles Modell der Artikulation. Laryngo-Rhino-Otologie 82, 402–407 (2003)

Kröger, B.J., Birkholz, P.: A gesture-based concept for speech movement control in articulatory speech synthesis. In: Esposito, A., Faundez-Zanuy, M., Keller, E., Marinaro, M. (eds.) COST Action 2102. LNCS (LNAI), vol. 4775, pp. 174–189. Springer, Heidelberg (2007)

Kröger, B.J., Lowit, A., Schnitker, R.: The Organization of a Neurocomputational Control Model for Articulatory Speech Synthesis. In: Esposito, A., Bourbakis, N., Avouris, N., Hatzilygeroudis, I. (eds.) Verbal and Nonverbal Features of Human-Human and Human-Machine Interaction. LNCS (LNAI), vol. 5042, pp. 121–135. Springer, Berlin (2008)

Liljencrants, J.: Speech Synthesis with a Reflection-Type Line Analog. Dissertation, Royal Institute of Technology, Stockholm (1985)

Maeda, S.: A digital simulation of the vocal-tract system. Speech Communication 1, 199–229 (1982)

Maeda, S.: An articulatory model based on statistical analysis. Journal of the Acoustical Society of America 84 (supl.1), 146 (1988)

Matsuzaki, H., Motoki, K.: FEM analysis of 3D vocal tract model with asymmetrical shape. In: Proceedings of the 5th Seminar on Speech Production, pp. 329–332. Seeon, Germany (2000)

Mawass, K., Badin, P., Bailly, G.: Synthesis of French Fricatives by Audio-Video to Articulatory Inversion. Acta Acustica 86, 136–146 (2000)

Mermelstein, P.: Articulatory model for the study of speech production. Journal of the Acoustical Society of America 53, 1070–1082 (1973)

Meyer, P., Wilhelms, R., Strube, H.W.: A quasiarticulatory speech synthesizer for German language running in real time. Journal of the Acoustical Society of America 86, 523–540 (1989)

Saltzman, E.L., Munhall, K.G.: A dynamic approach to gestural patterning in speech production. Ecological Psychology 1, 333–382 (1989)

Saltzman, E., Byrd, D.: Task-dynamics of gestural timing: Phase windows and multifrequency rhythms. Human Movement Science 19, 499–526 (2000)

Schwartz, J.L., Berthommier, F., Savariaux, C.: Seeing to hear better: evidence for early audio-visual interactions in speech identification. Cognition 93 B69- 78, B69–B78 (2004)

Serrurier, A., Badin, P.: A three-dimensional articulatory model of the velum and nasopharyngeal wall based on MRI and CT data. Journal of the Acoustical Society of America 123, 2335–2355 (2008)

Sinder, D.J.: Speech synthesis using an aeroacoustic fricative model. PhD thesis, Rutgers University, New Jersey (1999)

Sondhi, M.M., Schroeter, J.: A hybrid time-frequency domain articulatory speech synthesizer. IEEE Transactions on Acoustics, Speech, and Signal Processing 35, 955–967 (1987)

Story, B.H., Titze, I.R.: Voice simulation with a body cover model of the vocal folds. Journal of the Acoustical Society of America 97, 1249–1260 (1995)

Titze, I.R.: A four-parameter model of the glottis and vocal fold contact area. Speech Communication 8, 191–201 (1989)

Wilhelms-Tricarico, R.: Physiological modelling of speech production: Methods for modelling soft-tissue articulators. Journal of the Acoustical Society of America 97, 3085–3098 (1995)

Qualitative and Quantitative Crying Analysis of New Born Babies Delivered Under High Risk Gestation

Antonio Verduzco-Mendoza[1], Emilio Arch-Tirado[1], Carlos A. Reyes García[2], Jaime Leybón Ibarra[1], and Juan Licona Bonilla[1]

[1] Instituto Nacional de Rehabilitación, Secretaría de Salud
Laboratorio de Bioacústica, Avenida México Xochimilco 289, Delegación. Tlalpan, 2do piso
Torre de Investigación, México, D.F..
cnrverduzco@hotmail.com, earch@inr.gob.mx, jaleybon@hotmail.com
[2] Instituto Nacional de Astrofísica Óptica y Electrónica. Luis Enrique Erro N° 1., Santa
María Tonantzintla, 72840, Puebla, México
kargaxxi@inaoep.mx

Abstract. High risk newborns present high irritability and poor physiological stability among other abnormalities. Two months old infants do not have phonatory control due to neurological immaturity at early age. While age increases, expiration capacity increases too, being reflected in lasting length. Crying qualitative description is complementary to quantitative analysis. The aim of this study is the qualitative and quantitative description from the spectral analysis of crying in infants considered as infants of high neonatal risk. In this paper we will present some qualitative characteristics obtained from crying analysis and how we think qualitative analysis could be considered as an early diagnostic tool by relating its results to the baby´s neurophysiologic state.

Keywords: Infant Cry Analysis, Qualitative Crying Description, Parametric Cry Representation, High Risk New Born Cry.

1 Introduction

Studies of crying in newborn infants have had a fast and growing evolution. Wasz-Hockert *et. al.* began first spectrographic studies of crying in the 60's and categorized them in anger, pain and hunger crying [1, 2]. Michelsson K. described infant crying with neonatal asphyxia [3], being his studies the first important descriptions related to spectral analysis of infant crying. Lester studied the crying of undernourished infants [4], and with the collaboration of Corwin described infant crying with post mortem diagnostic of sudden death [5].

Nowadays, many authors focus their investigations in healthy infants since birthday to one year old, and have found non important differences in the described fundamental Frequency (F0), determining also that there are not crying differences between premature infants and term infants, and neither between genders [6, 7]. Quantitative methods of crying analysis have been focused on the study of fundamental frequency, demonstrating that there is no variation of F0 related to gender and gestational age, F0 average value is 450 Hz and the range goes from 400 to 600 Hz

A. Esposito et al. (Eds.): Multimodal Signals, LNAI 5398, pp. 320–327, 2009.

[7, 21, 15], with symmetrically superimposed harmonics and crying average duration between 1 - 1.5 seconds[6, 7].

In the case of neonatal newborn children in risk of diverse pathologies, it has been demonstrated that their crying levels are high, they also present low punctuation in neonatal scales, high irritability and poor physiological stability [8]. In neonates with hyperbilirrubinemia, the cerebral shaft nuclei is affected causing hypoacousis neurosensory, an increased in; the crying frequency, F0 values and in the first formant [9]. Arch *et al.* (2002) studied quantitative and qualitative characteristics of infant crying with deep hypoacousis, finding non-significant differences in F0 values, formants and duration (inspiration and expiration) compared with healthy infants. In the qualitative analysis he mentioned that infant deafness produces alterations in the melodic control in comparison with healthy infants, due to the lack of auditory feedback. And he suggested that a detailed qualitative description is necessary to find possible differences among cries [10]. Qualitative crying description is important as a complementary part of quantitative analysis, in order to demonstrate variations or similarities between normal and pathological cries. For Wermke et al [11] the complexity in the melodic pathway is a good indicator of neuromuscular maturation, the resonance frequency variation or formant allows an estimation of the articulator activity of the pre-phoniatric vocalizations. The melodic form that prevails during the first weeks of life in healthy infants is a rising-falling [11] while in healthy infants under pain conditions it is reported only as falling [12]. Koivisto found vibratos occurrence in healthy children that diminishes as the age increases. In premature infants crying duration is short, F0 high and bi-phonic, while term gestation infants present more glides [12]. Bifurcation is reported as a normal event in phonation from newborn infant to term [13]. In this way, the importance of qualitative crying analysis is being considered for early diagnostic because the cry is an innate manifestation of behavior that reflects the recently born neurophysiologic state.

Although some studies mention statistical differences between crying of infants with pathologies and the cries of healthy infants, strong controversies and difficulties have been generated about standard crying measures on the following factors: 1) Individual phono-articulatory characteristics, 2) age (physiologic maturity), 3) laryngeal development and growth, 4) deliberated crying, 5) control in crying production, 6) registration methods, 7) crying classification (spontaneous or induced), 8)quantitative or qualitative analysis, and 9) in the case of high risk infants, it becomes complicated because of the great quantity of clinical variables present.

The aim of our study was to obtain the qualitative and quantitative description from the spectral analysis of crying in infants considered as of high neonatal risk.

2 Material and Methods

This study was carried out at the Institute National of Rehabilitation (INR), Institute National of Perinatology (INPer) and National Institute for Astrophysics Optics and Electronics (INAOE). The crying of 30 infants was registered. The selected children presented diverse birth alterations, among the most important of which are the neonatal asphyxia that was determined by the presence of metabolic acidosis (pH 7.00), *apgar* of 0 - 3 to 5 minutes and neurological manifestations as *convulsions*, *coma* or *hypotonic*, as well as evidence of multi-organic dysfunction, with cellular and bio-chemical damage and circulatory alterations. Related to the respiratory maturity, no infant presented any disorder of respiratory immaturity, since it would be a clinical variable of importance, which was discarded by the doctor.

Table 1. Definition of important variables

1.	Phonation length. - Expiration length of the audible crying after the stimulus of the following inspiration. This expiratory crying is called phonation and it can be interrupted, the parts are referred to signs, the phonation can contain one or more signs.
2.	Shift.- Is a sudden upward or downward movement in fundamental frequency. Where this change of pitch was 100Hz or more, the shift part is measured separately.
3.	Glide. – Very fast change in the fundamental frequency F0, it must be 600Hz or more and last for about 0.1 sec.
4.	Form or Melody Form. - The changes in the fundamental frequency during the phonation are in different melodic forms: Falling, Rising, Falling-Rising, Rising-Falling, Flat and unmelodic form.
5.	Biphonation.- A double series of fundamental frequencies with different types in melodic form and fundamental tone (Hz). E.g. A series falls while the other one rises. The biphonation is noticed when the duration is of 0.1 sec or more.
6.	Noise concentration. - Audible high energy peak, usually between 2000-2500 Hz. during each phonatory expression.
7.	Double break harmonics. - Presence of other simultaneous series of harmonics with the same melodic form as F0 or the harmonic of low intensity. These are perceptible if their lasting exceeds 0.1 sec.
8.	Glottal plosives. - All the blows or explosions like sounds of cough are classified as glottal blows.
9.	Vibrato. - Series of waves with remarkable variations of frequency.
10.	Glottal Roll or vocal fry. - Phonation of weak and low intensity, F0 below the normal average. It often happens at the end of the phonation. Glottal Roll is considered if its lasting exceeds 0.1 Sec.

Another important alteration is lung immaturity. The breathing dysfunctions include illness of the *hialina* membrane, newborn transitory *taquipnea* and bronchi-pulmonary dysplasia. There could be other factors associated to these alterations; among the more frequent are *neurological disorders* as *inter-ventricular hemorrhage, hydrocephaly* and *spasticity*. The study group is represented by 8 infants with neurological dysfunctions, 5 with asphyxia and 17 with lung immaturity. Three neonatal groups were formed, the first one constituted by 9 two months old infants, the second for 12 three months old infants and the third group, for 9 four months old infants. All the infants were audio-recorded in crying sessions during clinic exploration at the

INPer. The registration took place when an infant was carried for a clinic auscultation session, placed in supine position.

2.1 Acoustic Analysis

Audio recordings were analyzed with the Cool Edit 2000 software which digitize crying signal in WAV format at 16 kilo-Hertz with 16 bits resolution in monaural format. An acoustic signal from the original recording was selected with a 10 seconds duration, and a high pass filter applied with 5 Hertz. For each cry unit, defined as the cry expiratory phase, the Fast Fourier Transform was applied to compute the spectrum magnitude for every 25 milliseconds segment. The spectrograms were analyzed by measuring the fundamental frequency length and by extracting the harmonics, and the qualitative and quantitative characteristics.

2.2 Statistical Analysis

For the F0 analysis, by month of age and times of inspiration and expiration, parametric statistics like average and standard deviation were used. The test ANOVA was applied to compare the F0's behavior with respect to age, as well as the pathology associated to high risk birth. The total probability analysis was applied to determine the occurrence of qualitative characteristics of cry. Finally, relationship between expiration times was established by Pearson correlation and the frequency formants were visualized by spectrograms.

3 Results

Cries of the 30 infants were analyzed and classified by ages of 2, 3 and 4 months. 175 spectrograms were examined to obtain qualitative and quantitative results. F0 average values were obtained from the three age groups. F0 average for 2 months old infants was: 452.28 ± 73.47 Hz, for 3 months old infants: 466.90 ± 95.85 Hz and for 4 months old infants: 427.52 ± 49.48 Hz, see Figure 1.

We performed ANOVA variance analysis to carry on the analysis of F0 by age (2, 3, and 4 months old) and by pathology associated to neonatal high risk characteristics (neurological damage, asphyxia, and respiratory immaturity). When applying ANOVA to age groups we got a value of 0.367, and for the comparison among groups related to the pathology associated to high risk we got a value of 0.567. In both cases we did not find significant differences among the studied groups.

For expiration and inspiration times, results show age and expiration capacity increase, being reflected in the lasting length. The average expiration and inspiration times for the two, three and four months old groups were: Expiration 2 months: 1.2269 ± 1.4475; expiration 3 months: $1.1228 \pm .9646$; expiration 4 months: 1.5989 ± 1.1486 and inspiration times: Inspiration 2 months: $.5782 \pm .8462$; inspiration 3 months: $.5405 \pm .7773$; inspiration 4 months: $.4945 \pm .3235$. In these results we could not find information showing statistical variability with respect to standard deviation.

3.1 Qualitative Analysis of Cry Files

According to literature, the qualitative features in infant cry are common in healthy infant cries. However, an increase on events presents uncertain neurophysiologic indicative due to immaturity in their development. As it can be observed, the children of 3 months are those who present a major score of qualitative variables (see Table1) with a total of 72 observations. On the other hand, the more frequently repeated variables were vibratos and glottal rolls as well as double break harmonics with a frequency of 54, 40 and 23 respectively. biphonation was registered only in one occasion. After making the analysis of total probability to determine the occurrence of qualitative characteristics of the infants crying at 2, 3 and 4 months of age, it was found that: with regard to the glide, the probability of finding it in a sample studied at the age of 2 months is 33.444 %, at the age of 3 months 44.606 % and at 4 months 22.303 %. With regard to biphonation, since it was found in only one subject at age of 2 months of age, we can say that it is the most atypical qualitative characteristic in the studied sample.

Related to noise concentration, the probability of finding this feature at 2 months is 31.03 %, at the 3 months 27.57 % and at the 4 months 41.38 %. With respect to double harmonics break, it was determined a probability of 13.04% for the 2 months, 52.18 % for 3 months and 34.77 % for 4 months. In vibrato we found 37.03%, 44.44% and 18.51% for 2, 3 and 4 months respectively. Glottal explosion presented: 33.44%, 16.72% and 50.16% for 2, 3 and 4 months correspondingly. For glottal roll it was 37.50% in 2 months old, 42.49% in 3 months old and 19.99% in 4 months old infants. Finally, for shift it was 16.66% for 2 months, 33.33% for 3 months and 50.01 % for the 4 months old.

3.2 Expiration and Formants Correlation

Due to the fact that harmonics are produced by the vocal tract articulatory movements, which function as a resonance camera, we consider that the older infants in this study (4 months old) should have a larger amount of harmonics in their vocalizations which could indicate certain neurological maturity. Since longer duration crying waves allow to observe clearer some spectrographic characteristics, we thought that correlation could exist between the duration of crying and the amount of harmonics present in the spectrogram.

The Pearson Correlation study was carried out to determine if there is a relationship between expiration times and the harmonics quantities per cry unit.

All with a positive value, at 2 months of $r = 0.548$ with 7 degrees free, and confidence interval of 0.05, at 3 months an $r = 0.496$ with 10 degrees free, confidence interval 0.05, and at 4 months of $r = 0.326$ with 7 degrees free, and confidence interval of 0.05

It could be concluded that correlation does not exist between the mentioned variables at different ages.

A table of frequencies of crying characteristics per pathology was done (see Table 2), in this table we can observe that vibratos and glottal rolls are present more frequently in infants that have had pathologies like: Breathing dysfunctions and neurological disorders, while in infants with neonatal asphyxia predominate double harmonic breaks. In 1980 Koivisto mentioned that biphonation, gliding and bifurcation do not occur or are extremely rare in the cries of healthy infants. Double harmonic breaks and glottal rolls are fairly common in all cases.

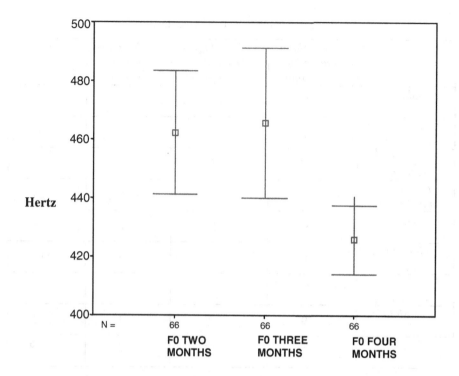

Fig. 1. There is a decrease of F0 in infants of 4 months old compared with those of two and three months old, possible due to neurological maturation

4 Conclusions

Cry was described from the quantitative and qualitative point of view. In current literature, this kind of analysis has not been described, however, findings after the analysis in Mexican infant population provide interesting results that encourage us to continue the studies. After the spectrographic analysis of cries from 2 to 4 months old infants, it was determined that results obtained when analyzing F0 in a quantitative way (400 - 600Hz) as well as length times (1-1.5 sec) were inside the ranges of healthy infants. Results are similar to those reported by Baeck [14] who mentioned that in hunger cry F0 diminishes during the first 15 days of life.

In our study, certain variability of F0 at ages of 2, 3 and 4 months (452.28Hz, 466.90Hz and 427.52 Hz) was observed. Our discoveries coincide with those mentioned by Roob M.P [13] and Michelsson K [21] who observed irregular spectral characteristics like: biphonations, double break harmonics and changes in F0 among others. These characteristics can also be found in the crying of healthy babies or in those who went through neonatal complications.

Table 2. Contingency of observed frequencies by type of pathology

	Breathing Dysfunctions (17 infants)	Neurological Disorders (8 infants)	Neonatal Asphyxia (5 infants)	Total
Glide	9			9
Biphonation	1			1
Noise Concentration	11	5	3	19
Double Harmonic Break	8	6	9	23
Vibrato	34	12	8	54
Glottal Plosives	8	3	7	18
Glotal Roll	22	16	2	40
Shift	9	2	1	12
	102	44	30	**176**

Related to the qualitative aspects analysis, Koivisto (1987) [12] mentions that in healthy infants, as the age increases presentation frequency of some qualitative characteristics of crying diminishes, vibratos in particular. Nonetheless, in our study there is no evidence of this trend, because even in the glottal plosives we can notice an increment.

We can notice that between the 2 and 3 months there is an increase in the observed frequencies, which does not agree with the reported by Koivisto. We think that this event can be due to the fact that there is an integral process of maturation of the phonoarticulatory apparatus in infants around 3 and 4 months of ages. In this process there is the intervention of the motor and sensitive control given by the intrinsic and extrinsic innervations of the larynx, the adjustment of the phonorespiratory mechanics and the modification in the anatomy given by the laryngeal descent. In this way, it is explainable the unorganized crying during the 2-4 months period, which makes difficult the systematic study and complicates the standardization and homogenization of the qualitative and quantitative values during these ages. Another valid explanation is related with the neurophysiologic sequels produced by diverse pathologies (prematurity, asphyxia, respiratory immaturity, etc.) suffered by infants during their neonatal period.

This kind of studies are important, since they describe in certain way the high risk newborn acoustic-vocal behavior, that can bear to the identification of cry patterns that support diagnosis of pathologies at early ages. Still, analysis on sound power should be carried out to relate lung and neurological maturity with the emitted sound. We propose to apply both qualitative and quantitative analysis to each patient. It is possible to consider cry analysis as a helpful tool to identify those infants who could present a pathology and as an aid for clinical diagnostics in perinatology..

References

1. Wasz-Hockert, O., Vuorenkoski, V., Valanne, E., Michelsson, K.: Sound spectrographic studies of the cry of newborn infants. Experientia 15(18), 583–584 (1962)
2. Wasz-Hockert, O., Valanne, E., Vuorenkoski, V., Michelsson, K., Sovijarvi, A.: Analysis of some types of vocalization in the newborn and in early infancy. Ann Paediatr Fenn. 9, 1–10 (1963)
3. Michelsson, K., Sirvio, P., Wasz-Hockert, O.: Pain cry in full-term asphyxiated newborn infants correlated with late findings. Acta Paediatr Scand. 66(5), 611–616 (1977)
4. Lester, B.M.: Spectrum analysis of the cry sounds of well-nourished and malnourished infants. Child Dev. 47(1), 237–241 (1976)
5. Corwin, M.J., Lester, B.M., Sepkoski, C., Peucker, M., Kayne, H., Golub, H.L.: Newborn acoustic cry characteristics of infants subsequently dying of sudden infant death syndrome. Pediatrics 96(1 Pt 1), 73–77 (1995)
6. Michelsson, K., Eklund, K., Leppanen, P., Lyytinen, H.: Cry characteristics of 172 healthy 1-to 7-day-old infants. Folia Phoniatr Logop 54(4), 190–200 (2002)
7. Lind, K., Wermke, K.: Development of the vocal fundamental frequency of spontaneous cries during the first 3 months. Int. J. Pediatr Otorhinolaryngol. 64(2), 97–104 (2002)
8. Ohgi, S., Gima, H., Akiyama, T.: Neonatal behavioural profile and crying in premature infants at term age. Acta Paediatr. 95(11), 1375–1380 (2006)
9. Rapisardi, G., Vohr, B., Cashore, W., Peucker, M., Lester, B.: Assessment of infant cry variability in high-risk infants. Int. J. Pediatr. Otorhinolaryngol. 17(1), 19–29 (1989)
10. Arch-Tirado, E., Mandujano, M., García-Torices, L., Martínez-Cruz, C.F., Reyes-García, C.A., Taboada-Picazo, V.: Cry analysis of hypoacoustic children and normal hearing children. Cir. Cir. 72(4), 271–276 (2004)
11. Wermke, K., Mende, W., Manfredi, C., Bruscaglioni, P.: Developmental aspects of infant's cry melody and formants. Med. Eng. Phys. 24(7-8), 501–514 (2002)
12. Koivisto, M.: Cry analysis in infants with Rh haemolytic disease. Acta Paediatr Scand. Suppl. 335, 1–73 (1987)
13. Robb, M.P.: Bifurcations and chaos in the cries of full-term and preterm infants. Folia Phoniatr Logop. 55(5), 233–240 (2003)
14. Baeck, H.E., de Souza, M.N.: Longitudinal Study of the Fundamental Frequency of Hunger Cries Along the First 6 Months of Healthy Babies. J. Voice (May 25, 2006) (Epub ahead of print)
15. Gilbert, H.R., Robb, M.P.: Vocal fundamental frequency characteristics of infant hunger cries: birth to 12 months. International Journal of Pediatric Otorhinolaryngol. 34, 237–243 (1996)
16. Grau, S.M., Robb, M.P., Cacace, A.T.: Acoustic correlates of inspiratory phonation during infant cry. J. Speech Hear Res. 38(2), 373–381 (1995)
17. St James-Roberts, I., Halil, T.: Infant crying patterns in the first year: normal community and clinical findings. J. Child Psychol. Psychiatry 32(6), 951–968 (1991)
18. Laufer, M.Z., Horii, Y.: Fundamental frecuency characteristics on infant non-distress vocalization during the firts 24 weeks. J. child Lang. 4, 171–184 (1997)
19. Sheppard, W.C., Lane, H.L.: Development of the prosodic features of infant vocalizing. J. Speech Hear Res. 11(1), 94–108 (1968)
20. Prechtl, H.F., Theorell, K., Gramsbergen, A., Lind, J.: A statistical analysis of cry patterns in normal and abnormal newborn infants. Dev. Med. Child Neurol. 11(2), 142–152 (1969)
21. Michelsson, K., Michelsson, O.: Phonation in the newborn, infant cry. Int. J. Pediatr Otorhinolaryngol. 49 (suppl. 1), S297–S301 (1999)

Recognizing Facial Expressions
Using Model-Based Image Interpretation

Matthias Wimmer, Christoph Mayer, and Bernd Radig

Image Understanding and Knowledge-Based Systems Chair,
Technische Universität München, Germany
http://www9.cs.tum.edu

Abstract. Even if electronic devices widely occupy our daily lives, human-machine interaction still lacks intuition. Therefore, researchers intend to resolve these shortcomings by augmenting traditional systems with aspects of human-human interaction and consider human emotion, behavior, and intention.

This publication focusses on one aspect of this challenge: recognizing facial expressions. Our approach achieves real-time performance and provides robustness for real-world applicability. This computer vision task comprises of various phases for which it exploits model-based techniques that accurately localize facial features, seamlessly track them through image sequences, and finally infer facial expressions visible. We specifically adapt state-of-the-art techniques to each of these challenging phases. Our system has been successfully presented to industrial, political, and scientific audience in various events.

1 Introduction

Nowadays, computers are capable of efficiently solving mathematical problems and of memorizing an enormous amount of information, but interacting with electronic machines in general still lacks intuition. This aspect is even more important to human-robot interaction. Since some robots look like humans, people expect humanoid robots to behave similar to humans. A non-humanoid behavior of robots generates confusions to the interacting person. Therefore, researchers augment traditional systems with human-like interaction capabilities. Widespread applicability and the comprehensive benefit motivate research on this topic. Natural language recognition has already been successfully deployed in commercial systems since a few years. However, to construct convenient interaction mechanisms further knowledge is necessary, e.g. about human behavior, intention, and emotion. For example in computer-assisted learning, a computer acts as the teacher by explaining the contents of the lesson and questioning the user afterwards. Being aware of human emotions, the quality and success rate of these lessons will significantly rise. For a comprehensive overview on applications in emotion recognition, we refer to [16].

Today, dedicated hardware often facilitates this challenge [14,26,24]. These systems derive the emotional state from blood pressure, perspiration, brain

A. Esposito et al. (Eds.): Multimodal Signals, LNAI 5398, pp. 328–339, 2009.

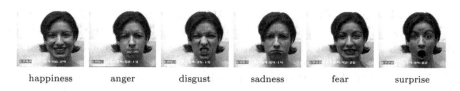

| happiness | anger | disgust | sadness | fear | surprise |

Fig. 1. The six universal facial expressions as they occur in [15]

waves, heart rate, skin temperature, etc. In contrast, humans interpret emotion via visual and auditory information only. As an advantage, this information is acquired without interfering with people and computers are able to easily acquire this information with general purpose hardware. However, precisely deriving human emotion from this vast amount of sensor data poses great challenges.

This publication focuses on one of the aspects of natural human-computer interfaces. Our goal is to build a real-time system for facial expressions recognition that robustly runs in real-world environments. It bases on model-based image interpretation techniques, which have proven its great potential to fulfill current and future requests on real-world image understanding [28]. Our approach comprises methods that robustly localize facial features, seamlessly track them through image sequences, and finally infer the facial expression. As explained in Section 3, some components require to be improved over the state-of-the-art, others are specifically adapted to the face interpretation scenario. Our experimental evaluation is conducted on a publicly available image database and is therefore well comparable to related approaches. Our demonstrator has been successfully applied to various real-world scenarios and it has been presented to the public and to industrial and political audience on various trade fairs.

This paper continues as follows. Section 2 explains the state-of-the-art of facial expression recognition covering both psychological theory and current algorithms. Section 3 describes the various components of our model-based approach. Section 4 experimentally evaluates our approach on a publicly available image database and draws a comparison to related approaches. Section 5 summarizes our achievement and points out future work.

2 Facial Expression Recognition: State-of-the-Art

This section elaborates on psychological aspects of facial expression recognition and indicates the state-of-the-art of current techniques.

2.1 Universal Facial Expressions and the Facial Action Coding System (FACS)

Ekman and Friesen [7] find six universal facial expressions that are expressed and interpreted in the same way by humans of any origin all over the world. They do not depend on the cultural background or the country of origin. Figure 1 shows one example of each facial expression.

The Facial Action Coding System (FACS) [8] precisely describes the muscle activities within a human face. Action Units (AUs) denote the motion of particular facial parts and state the facial muscles involved. Facial expressions are generated by combinations of AUs. Extended systems like the *Emotional FACS* [12] specify the relation between facial expressions and emotions.

2.2   Benchmark DB

The Cohn-Kanade-Facial-Expression database (CKFE-DB) contains 488 short image sequences of 97 different persons performing the six universal facial expressions [15]. It provides researchers with a large dataset for experimenting and benchmarking purpose. Each sequence shows a neutral face at the beginning and then develops into the peak expression. Furthermore, a set of AUs has been manually specified by licensed FACS-experts for each sequence. Note that this database does not contain natural facial expressions, but volunteers were asked to act. Furthermore, the image sequences are taken in a laboratory environment with predefined illumination conditions, solid background and frontal face views. Algorithms that perform well with these image sequences are not immediately appropriate for real-world scenes.

2.3   The Common Three-Phase Procedure

According the survey of Pantic et al. [19], the computational task of facial expression recognition is usually subdivided into three subordinate challenges, face detection, feature extraction, and facial expression classification as shown in Figure 2. Chibelushi et al. [1] added a pre- and a post-processing step. This section presents several state-of-the-art approaches, which accomplish the involved steps in different ways. For a more detailed overview we refer to Chibelushi et al.

Phase 1, the human face and the facial components have to be accurately located within the image. This is often accomplished using a bounding box that roughly specifies the location and the extent of the entire face. More elaborate approaches make use of a fine grain face model, which has to be fitted precisely to the contours of the visible face. As an advantage, the model-based approach provides information about the relative location of the different facial components and their deformation, which turns out to be useful for the subsequent phases.

On the one hand, this task is executed automatically, as in [18,10,4]. On the other hand, researchers specify the necessary information by hand, because they rather focus on the interpretation task itself, as in [23,2,22,25].

Fig. 2. The common three-phase procedure for recognizing facial expressions, see [19]

Phase 2, knowing the exact position of the face, features that are descriptive for facial expressions are now extracted from the image data. Facial expressions consist of two important aspects: the muscle activity while the expression is performed and the shape of the peak expression. Algorithms that are intended to solve the challenge of this phase preferably extract features that represent one or both of these aspects.

Michel et al. [18] extract the location of 22 feature points within the face and determine their motion between an image that shows the neutral state of the face and an image that represents a facial expression. They use feature points that are mostly located around the eyes and around the mouth. The very similar approach of Cohn et al. [3] uses hierarchical optical flow in order to determine the motion of 30 feature points. They call their approach *feature point tracking*. Littlewort et al. [17] utilize a bank of 40 Gabor wavelet filters at different scales and orientations to extract features directly from the image. They perform convolution and obtain a vector of magnitudes of complex valued responses.

Phase 3, the facial expression is derived from the previously extracted features. Mostly, a classifier is learned from a comprehensive training set of annotated examples. Some approaches first compute the visible AUs and then infer the facial expression by rules stated by Ekman and Friesen [9]. Michel et al. [18] train a Support Vector Machine (SVM) that determines the visible facial expression within the video sequences of the CKFE-DB by comparing the first frame with the neutral expression to the last frame with the peak expression. Schweiger and Bayerl [22] compute the optical flow within 6 predefined regions of a human face in order to extract the facial features. Their classification is based on supervised neural network learning.

3   Facial Expression Recognition via Model-Based Techniques

Our approach makes use of model-based techniques, which exploit a priori knowledge about objects, such as their shape or texture, see Figure 3. Reducing the large amount of image data to a small set of model parameters facilitates and accelerates the subsequent facial expression interpretation. Our approach sticks

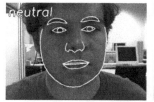

Fig. 3. Interpreting facial expressions with a deformable face model

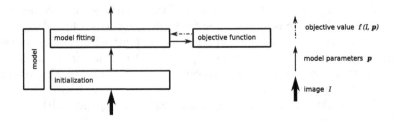

Fig. 4. Model-based techniques split the challenge of image interpretation into computationally independent modules. The upper right corners refer to the sections with detailed explanation.

to the three phases stated by Pantic et al. [19], see Section 2.3. Phase 1 is executed by fitting a face model to the camera image, see Section 3.1. Section 3.2 describes the extraction of meaningful features and Section 3.3 shows how we derive the facial expression visible from these features.

3.1   Model-Based Image Interpretation

Model-based techniques consist of four components: the model, the initialization algorithm, the objective function, and the fitting algorithm, [28], see Figure 4.

The model contains a parameter vector **p** that represents its possible configurations, such as position, orientation, scaling, and deformation. Models are mapped onto the surface of an image via a set of feature points, a contour, a textured region, etc. Referring to [6], deformable models are highly suitable for analyzing human faces with all their individual variations. Our approach makes

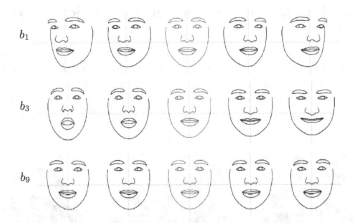

Fig. 5. Deformation by change of just one parameter in each row. Top row: b_1 rotates the head. Center row: b_3 opens the mouth. Bottom row: b_9 moves pupils in parallel.

Fig. 6. Our localization algorithm yields a region of interest for the face and also determines the positions of the eyes within a second application of the Viola and Jones approach as indicated by these two exemplary images. This information is now used to roughly parameterize the face model.

use of a statistics-based deformable model, as introduced by Cootes et al. [5]. Its parameters $\mathbf{p} = (t_x, t_y, s, \theta, \mathbf{b})^T$ comprise the translation, scaling factor, rotation, and a vector of deformation parameters $\mathbf{b} = (b_1, \ldots, b_m)^T$. The latter component describes the configuration of the face, such as the opening of the mouth, roundness of the eyes, raising of the eye brows, see Figure 5.

The initialization algorithm roughly localizes the object to interpret, which is often represented by a *region of interest*. It computes an initial estimate of the model parameters that needs to be further refined by the subsequent model fitting step. Our system integrates the approach of Viola and Jones [27], which is able to detect the affine transformation parameters $(t_x, t_y, s, \text{and } \theta)$ of frontal faces.

In order to obtain higher accuracy, we apply a second iteration of the Viola and Jones object detector to the previously determined image region of the face. This extension allows to roughly estimate the deformation parameters $\mathbf{b}$ as well, because we learn the algorithm to localize facial components, such as eyes and mouth. In the case of the eyes, our positive training examples contain the images of eyes, whereas the negative examples consist of image patches in the vicinity of the eyes, such as the cheek, the nose, or the brows. Note that the resulting eye detector is not able to robustly localize the eyes in a complex image, because it usually contains a lot of information that was not part of the training data. However, it is highly appropriate to determine the location of the eyes within a pure face image or within the face region of a complex image, see Figure 6 for some examples. [1]

The objective function $f(I, \mathbf{p})$ yields a comparable value that specifies how accurately a parameterized model $\mathbf{p}$ describes an image I. It is also known as the likelihood, similarity, energy, cost, goodness, or quality function. Without losing generality, we consider lower values to denote a better model fit. Traditionally, objective functions are manually specified by first selecting a small number of

---

[1] Our object detectors are published at this page:
   http://www9.in.tum.de/people/wimmerm/se/project.eyefinder/

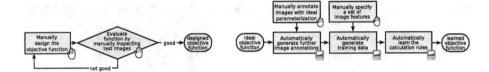

Fig. 7. The traditional procedure for designing objective functions (left), and the proposed method for learning objective functions from annotated training images (right)

simple image features, such as edges or corners, and then formulating mathematical calculation rules. Afterwards, the appropriateness is subjectively determined by inspecting the result on example images and example model parameterizations. If the result is not satisfactory the function is tuned or redesigned from scratch. This heuristic approach relies on the designer's intuition about a good measure of fitness. Our earlier works [29,30] show that this methodology is erroneous and tedious. This traditional approach is depicted to the left in Figure 7.

To avoid these drawbacks, we recently proposed an approach that learns the objective function from annotated example images [29]. It splits up the generation of the objective function into several independent pieces partly automated. This provides several benefits: firstly, automated steps replace the labor-intensive design of the objective function. Secondly, this approach is less error-prone, because giving examples of good fit is much easier than explicitly specifying rules that need to cover all examples. Thirdly, this approach does not rely on expert knowledge and therefore it is generally applicable and not domain-dependent. The bottom line is that this approach yields more robust and accurate objective functions, which greatly facilitate the task of the fitting algorithm. For a detailed description of our approach, we refer to [29]

The fitting algorithm searches for the model that best describes the face visible in the image. Therefore, it aims at finding the model parameters that minimize the objective function. Fitting algorithms have been the subject of intensive research and evaluation, e.g. *Simulated Annealing, Genetic Algorithms, Particle Filtering, RANSAC, CONDENSATION*, and *CCD*, see [13] for a recent overview and categorization. We propose to adapt the objective function rather than the fitting algorithm to the specifics of our application. Therefore, we are able to use any of these standard fitting algorithms, the characteristics of which are well-known, such as termination criteria, runtime, and accuracy. Due to real-time requirements, our experiments in Section 4 have been conducted with a quick *hill climbing* algorithm. Note that the reasonable specification of the objective function makes this local optimization strategy nearly as accurate as a global optimization strategy, such as *Genetic Algorithms*.

3.2 Extraction of Structural and Temporal Features

Two aspects generally characterize facial expressions i.e. structural and temporal features: first, they turn the face into a distinctive state [17] and second, the involved muscles show a distinctive motion [22,18]. Our approach considers both aspects by extracting structural and temporal features. This large amount of feature data provides a profound basis for the subsequent classification step, which therefore achieves great accuracy.

Structural features. The deformation parameters **b** describe the constitution of the visible face. The examples in Figure 5 illustrates the relation between the facial expression and the value of **b**. Therefore, we consider **b** to provide high-level information to the interpretation process. In contrast, the transformation parameters t_x, t_y, s, and θ are not related to the facial expression and therefore, we do not consider them as features.

Temporal features. Since facial expressions emerge from muscle activity, the motion of particular feature points within the face gives evidence about the facial expression. Real-time capability is important, and therefore, a small number of feature points are considered only. The relative location of these points is connected to the structure of the face model. Note that we do not specify these locations manually, because this assumes a good experience of the designer in analyzing facial expressions. In contrast, we automatically generate G feature points that are uniformly distributed, see Figure 8. We expect these points to

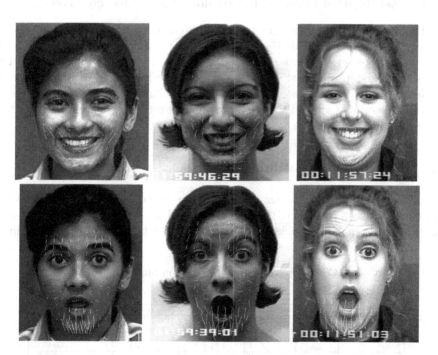

Fig. 8. Model-based image interpretation for facial expression recognition: Fitting a deformable face model to images and inferring different facial expressions by taking structural and temporal image features into account

move descriptively and predictably in the case of a particular facial expression. We sum up the motion $g_{x,i}$ and $g_{y,i}$ of each point $1 \leq i \leq G$ during a short time period. We set this period to 2 seconds to cover slowly expressed emotions as well. The motion of the feature points is normalized by the affine transformation of the entire face (t_x, t_y, s, and θ) in order to separate the facial motion from the rigid head motion.

In order to determine robust descriptors, Principal Component Analysis (PCA) determines the H most relevant motion patterns (principal components) visible within the set of training sequences. A linear combination of these motion patterns describes each observation approximately correct. This reduces the number of descriptors ($H \ll 2G$) by enforcing robustness towards outliers as well. As a compromise between accuracy and runtime performance, we set the number of feature points to $G = 140$ and the number of motion patterns to $H = 14$. Figure 8 visualizes the obtained motion of the feature points for some example facial expressions.

The feature vector $\mathbf{u}$ is assembled from the m structural and the H temporal features mentioned, see Equation 1. This vector represents the basis for facial expression classification.

$$\mathbf{u} = (b_1, ..., b_m, h_1, ..., h_H)^T \qquad (1)$$

3.3   Classification of Facial Expressions Using Decision Trees

With the knowledge of feature vector $\mathbf{u}$, a classifier infers the correct facial expression. We learn a Binary Decision Tree [20], which is a robust and quick classifier. However, any other multi-class classifier that is able to derive the class membership from real valued features can be integrated as well, such as a k-Nearest-Neighbor classifier. We take 67% of the image sequences of the CKFE-DB as the training set and the remainder as test set, the evaluation on which is shown in the next section.

4   Experimental Evaluation

In order to evaluate the accuracy of our proof-of-concept, we apply it to the previously unseen fraction of the CKFE-DB. Table 1 shows the recognition rate and confusion matrix of each facial expression. The facial expressions happiness

Table 1. Confusion matrix and recognition rates of our approach.

ground truth	classified as						recognition rate
	surprise	happiness	anger	disgust	sadness	fear	
surprise	28	1	1	0	0	0	93.33%
happiness	1	26	1	2	3	4	70.27%
anger	1	1	14	2	2	1	66.67%
disgust	0	2	1	10	3	1	58.82%
sadness	1	2	2	2	22	1	73.33%
fear	1	5	1	0	2	13	59.09%
mean recognition rate							70.25%

Table 2. Recognition rate of our approach compared to the results of different algorithms

facial expression	Our results	Result of the algorithm of Michel et al. [18]	Result of the algorithm of Schweiger et al. [22]
Anger	66.7%	66.7%	75.6%
Disgust	64.1%	58.8%	30.0%
Fear	59.1%	66.7%	0.0%
Happiness	70.3%	91.7%	79.2%
Sadness	73.3%	62.5%	60.5%
Surprise	93.3%	83.3%	89.8%
Average	71.1%	71.8%	55.9%

and fear are confused most often. The reason for this confusion is the similar muscle activity around the mouth. This coincidence is also reflected by FACS.

The accuracy of our approach is comparable to the one of Schweiger et al. [22] who also conducted their evaluation on the CKFE-DB, see Table 2. For classification, they also favor motion from different facial parts and determine principal components from these features. However, Schweiger et al. manually specify the region of the visible face whereas our approach performs an automatic localization via model-based image interpretation. Michel et al. [18] also focus on facial motion by manually specifying 22 feature points that are predominantly located around the mouth and around the eyes. They utilize a support vector machine (SVM) for determining one of the six facial expressions.

5   Summary and Outlook

Automatic recognition of human facial gestures has recently attained a significant place in multi-modal human-machine interfaces and further applications. This paper presents our proof-of-concept for Facial Expression Interpretation, which is real-time capable and robust enough to be deployed to real-world scenarios. We exploit model-based techniques and adapt them specifically to facial expression recognition. As the main point, we learn the objective function for model fitting from example images as opposed to constructing it manually. The obtained system shows promising referring to its recognition results and we have successfully conducted live demontrastions that were attended by industrial and political audience, such as in [11].

In future work, we aim at integrating multi-modal feature sets, for which we have already preliminary results [21]. We will apply Early Sensor Fusion in order to keep all knowledge for the final decision process and to exploit the ability of a combined feature-space optimization.

References

1. Chibelushi, C.C., Bourel, F.: Facial expression recognition: A brief tutorial overview. In: Fisher, R. (ed.) CVonline: On-Line Compendium of Computer Vision (January 2003)

2. Cohen, I., Sebe, N., Chen, L., Garg, A., Huang, T.: Facial expression recognition from video sequences: Temporal and static modeling. Computer Vision and Image Understanding (CVIU) special issue on face recognition 91(1-2), 160–187 (2003)
3. Cohn, J., Zlochower, A., Lien, J.J.-J., Kanade, T.: Featurepoint tracking by optical flow discriminates subtle differences in facial expression. In: Proceedings of the 3rd IEEE International Conference on Automatic Face and Gesture Recognition, April 1998, pp. 396–401 (1998)
4. Cohn, J., Zlochower, A., Lien, J.J.-J., Kanade, T.: Automated face analysis by feature point tracking has high concurrent validity with manual facs coding. Psychophysiology 36, 35–43 (1999)
5. Cootes, T.F., Taylor, C.J.: Active shape models – smart snakes. In: Proceedings of the 3rd British Machine Vision Conference, pp. 266–275. Springer, Heidelberg (1992)
6. Edwards, G.J., Cootes, T.F., Taylor, C.J.: Face recognition using active appearance models. In: Burkhardt, H., Neumann, B. (eds.) ECCV 1998. LNCS, vol. 1407, pp. 581–595. Springer, Heidelberg (1998)
7. Ekman, P.: Universals and cultural differences in facial expressions of emotion. In: Cole, J. (ed.) Nebraska Symposium on Motivation 1971, Lincoln, NE, vol. 19, pp. 207–283. University of Nebraska Press (1972)
8. Ekman, P.: Facial expressions. In: Dalgleish, T., Power, M. (eds.) Handbook of Cognition and Emotion. John Wiley & Sons Ltd, New York (1999)
9. Ekman, P., Friesen, W.: The Facial Action Coding System: A Technique for The Measurement of Facial Movement. Consulting Psychologists Press, San Francisco (1978)
10. Essa, I.A., Pentland, A.P.: Coding, analysis, interpretation, and recognition of facial expressions. IEEE Transactions on Pattern Analysis and Machine Intelligence 19(7), 757–763 (1997)
11. Fischer, S., Döring, S., Wimmer, M., Krummheuer, A.: Experiences with an emotional sales agent. In: André, E., Dybkjær, L., Minker, W., Heisterkamp, P. (eds.) ADS 2004. LNCS, vol. 3068, pp. 309–312. Springer, Heidelberg (2004)
12. Friesen, W.V., Ekman, P.: Emotional Facial Action Coding System. Unpublished manuscript. University of California at San Francisco (1983)
13. Hanek, R.: Fitting Parametric Curve Models to Images Using Local Selfadapting Seperation Criteria. PhD thesis, Department of Informatics, Technische Universität München (2004)
14. Ikehara, C.S., Chin, D.N., Crosby, M.E.: A model for integrating an adaptive information filter utilizing biosensor data to assess cognitive load. In: Brusilovsky, P., Corbett, A.T., de Rosis, F. (eds.) UM 2003. LNCS, vol. 2702, pp. 208–212. Springer, Heidelberg (2003)
15. Kanade, T., Cohn, J.F., Tian, Y.: Comprehensive database for facial expression analysis. In: International Conference on Automatic Face and Gesture Recognition, pp. 46–53, France (March 2000)
16. Lisetti, C.L., Schiano, D.J.: Automatic facial expression interpretation: Where human interaction, articial intelligence and cognitive science intersect. Pragmatics and Cognition, Special Issue on Facial Information Processing and Multidisciplinary Perspective (1999)
17. Littlewort, G., Fasel, I., Bartlett, M.S., Movellan, J.R.: Fully automatic coding of basic expressions from video. Technical report, University of California, San Diego, INC MPLab (March 2002)

18. Michel, P., El Kaliouby, R.: Real time facial expression recognition in video using support vector machines. In: Fifth International Conference on Multimodal Interfaces, Vancouver, pp. 258–264 (2003)
19. Pantic, M., Rothkrantz, L.J.M.: Automatic analysis of facial expressions: The state of the art. IEEE Transactions on Pattern Analysis and Machine Intelligence 22(12), 1424–1445 (2000)
20. Quinlan, R.: C4.5: Programs for Machine Learning. Morgan Kaufmann, San Mateo (1993)
21. Schuller, B., Wimmer, M., Arsic, D., Rigoll, G., Radig, B.: Audiovisual behavior modeling by combined feature spaces. In: IEEE International Conference on Acoustics, Speech, and Signal Processing (ICASSP), Honolulu, Hawaii, USA, April 2007, vol. 2, pp. 733–736 (2007)
22. Schweiger, R., Bayerl, P., Neumann, H.: Neural architecture for temporal emotion classification. In: André, E., Dybkjær, L., Minker, W., Heisterkamp, P. (eds.) ADS 2004. LNCS (LNAI), vol. 3068, pp. 49–52. Springer, Heidelberg (2004)
23. Sebe, N., Lew, M.S., Cohen, I., Garg, A., Huang, T.S.: Emotion recognition using a cauchy naive bayes classifier. In: Proceedings of the 16th International Conference on Pattern Recognition, vol. 1, pp. 17–20. IEEE Computer Society, Washington (2002)
24. Sheldon, E.M.: Virtual agent interactions. PhD thesis, Elizabeth Sheldon, Major Professor-Linda Malone (2001)
25. Tian, Y.-L., Kanade, T., Cohn, J.F.: Recognizing action units for facial expression analysis. IEEE Transactions on Pattern Analysis and Machine Intelligence 23(2), 97–115 (2001)
26. Vick, R.M., Ikehara, C.S.: Methodological issues of real time data acquisition from multiple sources of physiological data. In: Proceedings of the 36th Annual Hawaii International Conference on System Sciences, p. 129. IEEE Computer Society, Washington (2003)
27. Viola, P., Jones, M.: Rapid object detection using a boosted cascade of simple features. In: Computer Vision and Pattern Recognition, Kauai, Hawaii, vol. 1, pp. 511–518 (2001)
28. Wimmer, M.: Model-based Image Interpretation with Application to Facial Expression Recognition. PhD thesis, Technische Universitat München, Institute for Informatics (December 2007)
29. Wimmer, M., Stulp, F., Pietzsch, S., Radig, B.: Learning local objective functions for robust face model fitting. IEEE Transactions on Pattern Analysis and Machine Intelligence (PAMI) 30(8), 1357–1370 (2008)
30. Wimmer, M., Stulp, F., Tschechne, S., Radig, B.: Learning robust objective functions for model fitting in image understanding applications. In: Michael, J. (ed.) Proceedings of the 17th British Machine Vision Conference (BMVC), Edinburgh, UK, vol. 3, pp. 1159–1168. BMVA (September 2006)

Face Localization in 2D Frontal Face Images Using Luminosity Profiles Analysis

Marco Grassi[1], Marcos Faundez-Zanuy[2], and Francesco Piazza[3]

[1, 3] Department of Electronics, Artificial Inteligence and Telecomunication
Università Politecnica delle Marche, Ancona, Italy
margra75@hotmail.com, fpiazza@univpm.it
[2] Departimento de Telecomunicaciones y Arquitectura de Computadores
Escola Universitaria Politecnica de Mataró, Adscrita a la UPC, Mataró (BC), Spain
faundez@eupmt.es

Abstract. Face detection from a single image represents a challenging task because of variability in scale, location, orientation and pose. Facial expression, occlusion, and lighting conditions also change the overall appearance of faces. In this work we propose a fast face localization method in 2D frontal face images, through eyes detection, based on the analysis of the horizontal and vertical profiles of image's average luminosity and the definition of rules describing the relations between these profiles and the positions of characteristic face elements. Experimental results over the AR face database show high rates of successful detection together with reduced computational times that make this method particularly suitable for real time applications.

Keywords: Face detection, biometrics, image segmentation, face recognition.

1 Introduction

In the last years, face processing techniques have been used for a spread and growing number of applications. Face recognition has become a very active research field due to the increasing security demand and its potential commercial application [1]. Automatic facial expression analysis has drag a growing interest too, making possible more engaging human-computer interfaces, talking heads, image retrieval and human emotion analysis [2]. Furthermore, the constant decrease in the price/performance ratio of images and videos acquisition devices has made possible their integration in every day use devices like pda and mobile phone, extending incredibly the possible applicative scenarios for computer vision applications.

Whatever the application, detecting the position in images where faces are located represents a first and crucial step of any automatic face processing system, affecting inexorably the performances of the entire system. Notwithstanding the great progresses of the last years, face detection from a single image represents till now a challenging task because of the variability of face due to many factors like the pose in front of the camera, the presence or absence of structural components (such as beards, mustaches and glasses) or of occlusion (e.g. scarf, sunglasses), changes in the facial expression. Also the conditions in which the image is formed such as lighting

A. Esposito et al. (Eds.): Multimodal Signals, LNAI 5398, pp. 340–346, 2009.

(spectra, source distribution and intensity) and camera characteristics (sensor response, lenses) strongly affect the appearance of a face [3]. A great research effort has been done in this field to overcome all these problems and many different techniques have been developed. The choice of the used approach and method depends not only from the absolute performances in terms of correct detection rate but also from the kind of the application. Dealing with real time conditions, in particular, the computational time becomes often the critical parameter.

2   Face Detection Using Intensity Profiles and Image Segmentation

We are actually working to implement a system for access control based on face recognition using a simple device we are in possession [4]. In our system a 2D frontal, still, grey scale images acquisition is performed by a low cost webcam. In fact, a common 20€ webcam allows the acquisition of images with a resolution more than sufficient for face recognition operation. It's worth to remember that in the most of the cases the extraction of the characteristics used for the biometric recognition is made at low resolution in order to limit the dimensional weight of the model and the computational time. Furthermore, a webcam represents the ideal device for many web applications based on face recognition or face detection. The webcam is hidden behind a special glass. This glass performs as a transparent glass in one direction and as a mirror on the other, helping the user in the correct positioning of the face in front of the camera. The face has to be extracted from the image before to proceed to face verification or identification process [5].

In our proposed method we use the intensity profile of the image, as defined by Kotropopoulos and Pitas [6] and a particular image segmentation process (in less steps) to locate the position of the eyes and nose in the image. Once in possession of such information is possible to proceed to image normalization (correcting vertical rotation of the image, zoom and pans) and finally to image cropping.

From Fig. 1 results evident that there is a strong relationship between the position of face characteristics like eyebrows, eyes, nose, mouth and the maximum and minimum in the intensity profile. These horizontal (HP) and vertical (VP) profiles are obtained by averaging the pixels luminosity for respectively each row and column of the image, as

$$HP(x) = \frac{1}{N} \sum_{i=1}^{N} I(i,x) \tag{1}$$

$$VP(y) = \frac{1}{M} \sum_{j=1}^{M} I(y,j) \tag{2}$$

So the method deal with the identification of rules that connect the face components with significant minima and maxima in the luminosity profiles, analyzing VP and OP and their associated difference vector VPdiff and OPdiff, that are representative of the difference of average luminosity between adjacent pixels.

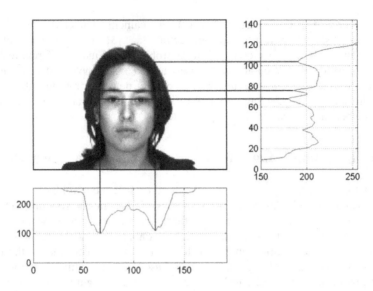

Fig. 1. Horizontal and vertical intensity profiles and their correlation with face characteristics

From the horizontal profile it's easy to determinate the face edges, that in all the images are clearly identified by two local minima characterized by an abrupt transition in the intensity profile. In not all the images the vertical profile's local maxima and minima are so univocally related to face characteristics, in particular due to the effect of the hair and of glasses that originate misleading minima and maxima in the profiles. For this reason we introduce an image segmentation process in order to eliminate or reduce insignificant maxima and minima and to focus the detection process in the most significant area. Such process consists in the following steps, as shown in Fig. 3:

1) *Identification of the horizontal face edges*, as described above, and first image crop.

2) *Identification of the forehead coordinate*, which is identified by a strong minima in the VP, and second image crop (Fig. 2.1). At this point the effect of the hair has been almost completely eliminated and the cropped image contains only the face and it is possible to extract three vertical bands, two containing the eyes and one containing the nose and subsequently focus the detection process. To such purpose, next step deals with the identification of the face center.

3) *Identification of the face center* which also coincide with the nose center. It has to be remarked that the center of the nose not always coincide with the medium position between the face edges, as a result of an horizontal face rotation or of a not perfect positioning of the subject in front of the camera. A more precise information can be achieved by considering the intrinsic symmetry of the human face. To such purpose, we introduce the *Autocorrelation Matrix C* (nxn) associated to the M(mxn) matrix,

$$C = \begin{pmatrix} c_{11} & \cdots & c_{1n} \\ \vdots & \ddots & \vdots \\ c_{n1} & \cdots & c_{nn} \end{pmatrix} \qquad (3)$$

that contains the Pearson correlation coefficients for each couple of columns in the image matrix M, whose value ranging between 0 and 1, defined by:

$$c_{ij} = \frac{\overrightarrow{x_{oi}} \bullet \overrightarrow{x_{oj}}}{\left\| \overrightarrow{x_{oi}} \right\| \left\| \overrightarrow{x_{oj}} \right\|} \qquad (4)$$

where $\overrightarrow{x_{oi}}, \overrightarrow{x_{oj}}$ are the column vector of the image matrix $\overrightarrow{x_i}, \overrightarrow{x_j}$ shifted by their means as to have an average of 0, according to:

$$\overrightarrow{x_{oi}} = \overrightarrow{x_i} - mean(\overrightarrow{x_i})$$
$$\overrightarrow{x_{oj}} = \overrightarrow{x_j} - mean(\overrightarrow{x_j}) \qquad (5)$$

Detecting the image centre means to detect the column, respect to which the correlation coefficients relative to symmetric columns assume their maxima. At this point it's possible to proceed to

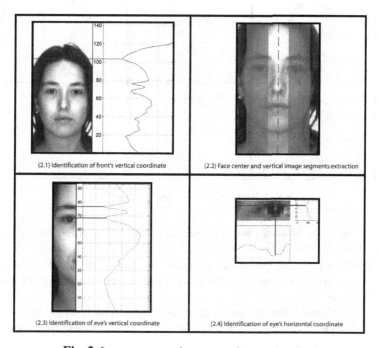

(2.1) Identification of front's vertical coordinate   (2.2) Face center and vertical image segments extraction

(2.3) Identification of eye's vertical coordinate   (2.4) Identification of eye's horizontal coordinate

Fig. 2. Image segmentation process for eyes localization

4) *Vertical face image segments extraction.* Considering that the eyes are located around in the middle between the face centre and the face edges we will extract two vertical segments of the image and we will use the other central part of the image for the nose (Fig. 2.2).

5) *Identification of the eyes' vertical positions.* Using the extracted segments it becomes easier and more accurate to estimate the position of the eyes and the eventual presence of the glasses that originate a new local minimum between eyebrows and eyes, which are characterized by two local minima with the steepest slope (Fig. 2.3).

6) *Identification of the eyes' horizontal position.* Known the vertical coordinate of the eyes we can proceed to the last horizontal cropping centred in the eye coordinate to localize also the horizontal coordinate (Fig. 2.4).

7) *Identification of the vertical nose position,* which is associated to a strong maxima in the vertical profile.

3   Experimental Results

Before of the practical implementation of the system, the method has been tested over the AR Database (http://cobweb.ecn.purdue.edu/RVL/ARdatabase/ARdatabase.html), a publicly available database of 126 individuals, with 26 images for each, taken in two different sessions at a time distance of two weeks, varying the lighting and the facial expression [7].

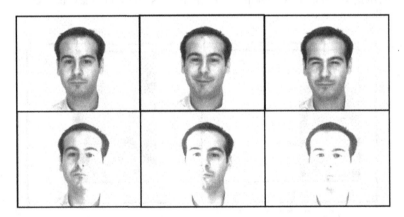

Fig. 3. First set of images from AR database

We have used 12 of the 26 images, excluding the ones in which the face was partially occluded by sunglasses or scarves, of 117 of the 126 individuals, those of the rest being either not complete or not available. In order to reduce the computational weight the images have been scaled to 192x144 pixels, being the original dimension of 678x576 pixels.

It's worth to remark that the presence in the images of an homogeneous and white background doesn't represent a limitation for the generality of the tests. Dealing with

Table 1. Experimental results of the correct detection rate for the first 3 images of each set, considering each image singularly and evaluating the average value

	First Image	Second Image	Third Image	Average
Left eye	92,73%	91,45%	90,17%	91.45%
Right eye	93,16%	92,37%	91,02%	92.19%
Nose	97,43%	97,86%	96,58%	97.29%
Eyes+Nose	89,31%	88,46%	87,17%	88.31%

a webcam it is in fact easy to extract the face from the images through background cancellation, using previously and periodically taken images in order to distinguish what in a image is a face and what the background.

Table 1 shows the results for the first 3 image of both images' set for each person in the AR database. We have manually detected the position of eyes and nose and we have considered the automatic detection correct if there is a discrepancy between automatic and manually detection smaller than 3 pixels. The method reaches a successful detection rate of both eyes and nose superior to the 88%, showing that face expression variations doesn't affect remarkably the performances. On the contrary drastic variation of the luminosity, as those in the last 3 image of the set, cannot be handled with the method and the correct detection rate falls below of the 30%, evidencing the necessity in these cases of the introduction of an image preprocessing in order to limit the effect of the illumination. In condition of strong luminosity variations, in fact, face loses its symmetry and the use of correlation for face centre detection does not work properly.

It is not possible to make a perfect comparison with the results of the Kotropoulos and Pitas which reach a successful detection rate of 86,5%, considering that they have used a different database with only 36 people but look also for the mouth position.

The results appears particularly interesting from a computational point of view. The application has been developed in Matlab, which is not a language optimized for computational speed (as for example c++), anyway computational times are limited to less then 0.2 second for each image.

4 Conclusions

In conclusion a fast and efficient method for face localization has been developed, which appears particularly suitable for practical applications requiring a very limited computational weight. Future efforts will be the improvement of the actual results using different resolutions and different luminosity levels in the images, in order to emphasize the most significant maxima and minima, the introduction of a image preprocessing algorithm in order to deal with luminosity variations and the practical implementation of the face detection system.

References

1. Abate, A.F., Nappi, M., Riccio, D., Sabatino, G.: 2D and 3D Face Recognition: A Survey. Pattern Recognition Letters (December 2006)
2. Fasel, B., Luettin, J.: Automatic Facial Expression Analysis: A Survey. Pattern Recognition 36(1), 259–275 (2003)
3. Faundez-Zanuy, M., Espinosa-Duro, V., Ortega-Redondo, J.A.: A low-cost webcam & personal computer opens doors. IEEE Aerospace and Electronic Systems Magazine 20, 23–26 (2005)
4. Yang, M.-H., Kriegman, D.J., Ahuja, N.: Detection Faces in Images: A Survey. IEEE Transaction On Pattern Analysis and Machine Inteligence 24(1), 34–58 (2002)
5. Grassi, M., Faundez-Zanuy, M.: Face recognition with facial mask application and neural networks. In: Sandoval, F., Prieto, A.G., Cabestany, J., Graña, M. (eds.) IWANN 2007. LNCS, vol. 4507, pp. 709–716. Springer, Heidelberg (2007)
6. Kotropoulos, C., Pitas, I.: Rule-based face detection in frontal views. In: Proc. Int. Conf. Acustics, Speech and Signal Processing, vol. 4, pp. 2537–2540 (1997)
7. Martinez, A.M.: Recognizing Imprecisely Localized, Partially Occluded, and Expression Variant Faces from a Single Sample per Class. IEEE Transaction On Pattern Analysis and Machine Intelligence 24(6), 748–763 (2002)

Author Index